The European Union and National Industrial Po

G000153787

Although the implications of European Union membership have been the subject of intense political and academic enquiry in all fifteen member states, the actual impact of EU action on the member states remains curiously under-researched. This book, the first in a new series, **The State and the European Union**, will look at how the EU has affected traditional policy making in the member states through a study of a range of industrial, financial and service sectors.

The authors investigate the impact of EU initiatives on the policies traditionally pursued by the four larger member states in these areas. In doing so they shed light on how national actors have responded to the growing importance of the EU and how relationships between actors – especially governments and state-owned companies – have been affected. The contributors use their findings to assess the impact of the EU on state autonomy and to evaluate claims that have been made about the consequences of European integration for the member states.

In a domain where much of the literature concentrates on the functioning of EU institutions, offers summaries of what the EU has done or abstractly speculates on its nature, *The European and National Industrial Policy* offers a unique empirical and theoretically reflective investigation of the relationship between the Union and the member states.

Hussein Kassim is Lecturer in Politics at Birkbeck College, University of London.
Anand Menon is Lecturer in the Politics of European Integration at the Oxford University Centre for European Politics, Economics and Society.

The State and the European Union series
Edited by Anand Menon, *Oxford University, Centre for European Politics, Economics and Society*, Hussein Kassim, *Birkbeck College, London* and David Hine, *Christ Church, Oxford*

This new series presents books based on an ESRC-funded interdisciplinary seminar series on the theme of state autonomy in the European Union. The series considers the impact of the EU's institutions, policy processes and laws on the policies of member states. The series will consider issues related to the nature of policy formation in order to assess the impact of the EU on the member states in this sphere. The primary focus is on France, Germany, Italy and the United Kingdom.

Beyond the Market
The European Union and National Social, Environmental and Consumer Protection Policy
Edited by Hussein Kassim, Anand Menon and David Hine

The European Union and National Macroeconomic Policy
Edited by Anand Menon and James Forder

The European Union and National Industrial Policy

Edited by Hussein Kassim and Anand Menon

London and New York

First published 1996
by Routledge
11 New Fetter Lane, London EC4P 4EE

Simultaneously published in the USA and Canada
by Routledge
29 West 35th Street, New York, NY 10001

Routledge is an International Thomson Publishing company

Typeset in Times by Datix International Limited, Bungay, Suffolk
Printed and bound in Great Britain by Redwood Books, Trowbridge, Wiltshire

British Library Cataloguing in Publication Data
A catalogue record for this book is available from the British Library

Library of Congress Cataloguing in Publication Data
The European Union and national industrial policy / edited by Hussein Kassim
and Anand Menon
    p. cm. — (The state and the European Union)
   Includes bibliographical references and index.
   1. Industrial policy—European Union countries. 2. Industrial policy—
European Union countries—Case studies. I. Kassim, Hussein, 1965– .
II. Menon, Anand, 1965– . III. Series.
HD3616.E8E874 1996
338.94—   dc2096–11345

ISBN 0–415–14177–X (hbk)
ISBN 0–415–14178–8 (pbk)

Contents

Tables

Contributors

Matthew William Fraser is an experienced broadcasting consultant based in Canada. He wrote his doctoral thesis at the Institut d'Etudes Politiques de Paris.

Stephen George is the Jean Monnet Professor in the Department of Politics at the University of Sheffield.

Leigh Hancher is Professor of Public Economic Law at Erasmus University, Rotterdam.

Professor Jack Hayward is Director of Oxford University Centre for Politics, Economics and Society, and a Fellow of St Anthony's College, Oxford.

Christopher Jones is a consultant with KPMG Consulting in Canada. He wrote his doctoral thesis at Nuffield College, Oxford.

Hussein Kassim is Lecturer in Politics in the Department of Politics and Sociology, Birkbeck College, University of London.

Antony Masi is Professor in the Department of Sociology, McGill University, Canada.

Francis McGowan is Lecturer in Politics at the School of European Studies, University of Sussex.

Anand Menon is Lecturer at the Oxford University Centre for Politics, Economics and Society.

Phil Molyneux is Senior Lecturer in the School of Accountancy, Banking and Economics and Director of the Institute of European Finance at the University of Wales, Bangor.

John Peterson is Jean Monnet Senior Lecturer in European Integration in the Department of Politics, University of Glasgow.

Jeremy J. Richardson is Professor of European Public Policy at the University of Essex.

Mark Thatcher is ESRC Research Fellow and Lecturer in Public Administration and Public Policy, Department of Government, London School of Economics.

Preface

This volume is based on a series of ESRC-funded research seminars entitled 'State Autonomy in the European Community', held in Oxford in the academic year 1993–4. The seminars examined the impact of EC action on the content of national policy and on the relationship between policy actors at the national level, with the aim of assessing the implications of EC policy for the member states and extent to which their autonomy has been circumscribed or enhanced. The seminars, which were interdisciplinary, addressed developments in the following areas: industrial, financial and service sectors; social policy, environmental protection and consumer policy; macroeconomic policy, and defence policy. The impact of EU membership on national administrative systems was also the topic of a seminar.

Neither the Research Seminar Series nor this book would have been possible without the support of ESRC Award No. A 451 264 400 248.

Acknowledgements

We should like to acknowledge the efforts of David Hine and William Wallace, who made the project possible, and to express our thanks to David for inviting us to be his co-conveners. Jack Hayward and Vincent Wright have offered advice and assistance throughout, and we should like to express our gratitude to them.

We are grateful to the Warden and Fellows of Nuffield College, Oxford, who very kindly allowed us to hold the seminar on which this volume is based at the college in December 1993, and who offered us generous financial support. Thanks are due to Christopher Jones for his part in arranging the seminar, to Kate Hill for her assistance in its organisation, and to Simon Kenyon for helping out on the day.

Jane Tinkler's secretarial assistance has been invaluable in the later stages, and we would also like to thank Sara Connolly for her practical help and general forbearance.

Finally, we should like to thank all participants of the seminar on industrial, finance and service sectors for making it a stimulating and successful event. Our greatest debt of gratitude is owed to the contributors to this book for their efforts in producing this volume and their patience in dealing with two young editors.

1   The European Union
and state autonomy

Hussein Kassim and Anand Menon[1]

This book examines the impact of European Union (EU) action on the industrial policies of the member states. It considers how developments at the European level have affected both the substance of national policy and the strategies and behaviour of national actors. In addressing the interaction between the EU and the member states it tackles an issue which is central not only to understanding the process of integration and the nature of the EU, but also in assessing the power and capacity for independent action of the state in western Europe. Its importance is reflected in the intense political debate in the Fifteen about 'Europe', the costs and benefits of membership, as well as in the tremendous volume of academic output on the EU and European integration.

However, despite the claims made about the extent to which power has migrated from national capitals to Brussels, about the freedom of the governments to make policy, and about the 'Europeanisation', supranationalisation, communitarianisation and 'Europeification' (Andersen and Eliassen 1993: 3) of policy making, the precise impact of EU action on the member states has been curiously under-researched. The focus in the academic literature has usually been directed either towards what the EU has done and how, or towards the politics of membership of individual countries. The actual consequences of Euro-level action have not been a matter of empirical investigation.

This book goes some way towards remedying this deficiency. It offers an examination of the extent to which action by the EU has affected the substance of national policy in the member states and the behaviour of, and relationships between, national policy actors in a range of industrial, finance and service sectors.[2] The impact of the EU has been the subject of many claims. For example, the claims that the Community has actually served to preserve states by in effect regenerating them and adapting them to the world of today (Hoffmann 1982), that member states have not lost their autonomy as a consequence of EC action (Moravcsik 1991, 1993, 1994), and that the EC is 'largely toothless' (Mann 1994: 128). Many studies have emphasised how the EC/EU has reduced ability for independent action on part of the member states. Thus the editorial of a new journal on European policy asserts that:

'[a]t least for the Twelve, the notion of state autonomy in the field of public policy is largely outdated' (Richardson and Lindley 1994:1). The author of a recent chapter in a book on economic policy making and the European Union contended that: 'there is no doubt that EU states no longer have the autonomy to depart radically from the policies of the Union as a whole' (Blouwer 1994: 7). However, these contentions share a general characteristic in that they are not grounded in detailed empirical research. It is only when this empirical work has been completed that it will be possible to evaluate the contentions made in the literature about the consequences of EU member-ship and the extent to which national policy has been 'Europeanised'.

Detailed empirical work will, moreover, provide an informed perspective from which it is possible to begin to answer a number of key questions. What freedom is still enjoyed by the member states? In what ways have national governments, individually and collectively, sought to use the EU? Has EU action been equally effective in all sectors and across all countries? What sort of creature is the EU – a state-in-the-making, a federation of states, an inter-national regime or something else again? (for discussions of this question, see Hoffmann 1982, Schmitter 1992, Wallace 1982.) Is the development and functioning of the EU best approached from an international relations or a political science perspective? (See George and Richardson, chapters 2 and 3, this volume, Hix 1994, Hurrell and Menon, 1996.)

Most treatments of issues relating to the state – and the relationship between the EU and the member states is no exception to this – make use of the notion of sovereignty. However, this book uses state autonomy as a con-ceptual tool to investigate the impact of the EU on the member states. The following section argues that this constitutes a more flexible and subtle instrument.

AUTONOMY, NOT SOVEREIGNTY

Discussions about the state, its freedom to determine its destiny, its capacities and its power, has traditionally been conducted in terms of sovereignty (Howe 1990, Lord 1992). This remains the case in both political debate and academic discussion, not only about the relationship between the EU and the member states, and the implications of further European integration, but also concerning the development of the state as a particular form of political organisation, the nature of the international order, the implications of inter-dependence, and more recently, of globalisation (see for example, Hirst and Thompson 1995).

Sovereignty, according to Hinsley's authoritative treatment, can be con-ceived as the idea that there exists within a political community a final and absolute authority, and that no final and absolute authority exists elsewhere (Hinsley 1986, Held 1989). When the first states, recognisable today as such and thus marking a departure from medieval conceptions of allegiance, came into being after the Treaty of Westphalia was signed in 1648, they laid claim to this authority and within western Europe, principalities mutually recognised the authority of each to the exercise of sovereignty within its territory (See Held 1989, Hirst and Thompson 1995).

Sovereignty, then, is a particular form of political and legal authority, which emerged at the same time as the first modern states came into being. However, *authority* is not the same as *power*. In the centuries when markets and forms of production were nation-centred, and when cross-border transactions were few, this distinction was not so important, since the state, by virtue of its authority, was able to regulate inward movements of goods and products. However, in an interdependent world, the economic fortunes of one country are influenced by the policies adopted by governments in other states, domestic policy cannot be made without regard to political or economic developments elsewhere, and so *de jure* authority and *de facto* power no longer coincide (Keohane and Nye 1974, Hanrieder 1978, Hoffmann 1987). In such a world, national governments may retain ultimate and final decision-making authority in a formal sense, but they do not have the power to guarantee that particular policy objectives are attained or even to make certain policy choices. Famously, for example, the Socialist government in France was compelled to abandon its reflationary policies in 1983, since the international economy and the policies pursued in neighbouring countries made it impossible (or inhibitively costly) to attempt 'socialism in one country'. Thus, although sovereignty identifies one attribute of the state, it does not capture all aspects of its power.

The notion of autonomy seems better suited to capture the capacities of the state than sovereignty, despite some conceptual confusion which has led some writers to conflate the notion referred to here as autonomy with that of sovereignty (Lintner and Newman 1994: 9). Nordlinger (1981) defines autonomy as the ability of the state to transform its policy preferences into authoritative actions. However, his use of the concept is limited to a discussion of state autonomy from societal forces. He therefore addresses only half the problem. Focusing only on internal constraints on state autonomy ignores the fact that the state faces challenges not only from society, but also from external sources, as illustrated by the case studies which follow. Moreover, such an approach perpetuates the division between international relations and political science at a time when many are claiming that the lines and divisions between the two need to be overcome. As James A.Caporaso has asked, 'Why does the gap between scholars of comparative and international politics persist when boundaries between domestic and international politics have crumbled?' (Caporaso 1989: 8).

Autonomy is a far more precise analytical instrument than sovereignty. First, sovereignty is concerned only with formal authority and its transfer. Autonomy, on the other hand, is a more flexible conception, able to capture the freedom of the state in relation to, for example, domestic social forces, developments in the economy and international pressures. Second, sovereignty is both too wide and too narrow. It is too narrow, for instance, for understanding the extent to which EU membership has circumscribed the power of the member states, because a change in the *de facto* power of a state may be unaccompanied by a formal transfer of authority. In such cases, although the autonomy of the state has been diminished, its sovereignty remains constant. It is too wide, because, although the formal authority of the state to act in a particular sector may be transferred or pooled in collective decision making at the European level, the Community may not have acted on its competence. In this case, a state's sovereignty may have been diluted, but its autonomy is undiminished.

Not only is autonomy a more subtle instrument than sovereignty, but thinking about the state exclusively in terms of the latter concept carries with it at least two dangers. The first is that it tends to perpetuate the anachronistic idea that states can stand alone and determine their own economic and social destinies, even though in an interdependent world states no longer have the power of economic self-determination. As James Rosenau puts it, 'the state is in chains, but virtually everywhere it is thought to be free' (Rosenau 1989: 21). Second, sovereignty seems to be inextricably associated with a conception which sees interaction in zero-sum terms, and therefore precludes the possibility of positive sum games, for instance. This is particularly problematic as far as the EU is concerned, since one common argument is that the EU has enabled the member states to achieve collectively what was not possible to attain individually. It also imposes an artificial construction on EU-member state relations; rather than seeing the EU as an institutional ensemble in which the member states in the Council of Ministers play a leading part and collectively contribute to the determination of policy, it regards the EU as a separate organ which imposes its decisions on the member states.

Having argued that it is more profitable to use autonomy rather than sovereignty in analysing the relationship between the EU and the member states, three points need to be made. First, the distinction drawn here is not original. Other writers, notably Stanley Hoffmann and David Held, have made it either explicitly or implicitly (Hoffmann 1982, Held 1989). Others have been sensitive to the need to distinguish between different elements of state freedom, but they have made the distinction between different types of sovereignty (Howe 1990, Lord 1992, Taylor 1991). However, making this distinction internally does not significantly contribute to analytical clarity. Moreover, despite the recommendations of some authors, autonomy has not yet gained the wider use it warrants, and sovereignty remains well entrenched as the organising concept by means of which the state is approached. Second, it is not claimed here that the concept of sovereignty should become redundant. Indeed, it has important uses in many fields. However, its utility for the purpose of measuring the impact of EU action on national policy and policy making is limited. Third, sovereignty and autonomy may not exhaust the conceptual armoury necessary for thinking about the freedom of the state to determine its own fate. For example, Hoffmann distinguishes between *strength* – understood as both the capacity to be autonomous and the internal capacity to act – and *effectiveness* – the ability to achieve results (Hoffmann 1982: 27).

THE IMPACT OF EU ACTION ON STATE AUTONOMY IN INDUSTRIAL, FINANCIAL AND SERVICE SECTORS

The concept of autonomy is used to examine two issues in the policy sectors that follow. The first is the impact of the EU on the substance of national policy; and the second, its impact on national actors. By looking at policy change in the member states since the mid-1980s, the extent to which action by the EU has affected the ability of national governments to translate their policy preferences into authoritative decisions will be ascertained. However, not only can EU action influence national policy in different ways, but policy change at the national and European levels may be the result of a complex interaction of different factors. It is worth dwelling on these points.

With respect to the first element of autonomy, that is the impact of the EU on the substance of national policy, EU action can exert an influence in a number of ways. First, the development of sectorally specific policies at the EU level may have had an impact on the policies traditionally pursued by the member states. National governments may be compelled to abandon or dilute existing policy objectives, deprived of policy instruments which they have traditionally deployed, or forced to comply with new policy orientations. Second, national policy may be affected by the application of general Community rules, such as the competition rules. The implementation in particular of those rules which apply to relations between public authorities and firms, notably state aid and public procurement, may lead to the reduction or even the abandonment of state support for national champions and make it increasingly difficult to pursue policies of industrial patriotism (see Thatcher and Peterson, chapters 10 and 12, this volume; see also Hayward 1995). Third, the European Court of Justice may limit the set of policy options available to the member states by means of its jurisprudence, as can the Commission in certain areas, such as competition policy, where it has a quasi-judicial function (see Molyneux, Chapter 13, this volume). Fourth, the development of an industrial policy by the EC at the supranational level may have implications for the pursuit of existing national policies.

State autonomy in the industrial domain may also be constrained by EU commitments and policies in other areas. For example, the development of a common fiscal policy may have significant consequences for national policy, since governments have typically adapted their taxation regimes to benefit home companies, and to offer targeted support to particular economic sectors or companies. Moreover, EU social, environmental and consumer policy may well impose constraints on, or attach costs to, particular policy choices at the national level. Also, the conclusion of external trade agreements by the Community on behalf of the member states can have policy consequences at the national level.[3] Finally, the mobilisation of transnational or national interests in coalition with EU institutions, most usually the Commission and the European Parliament, may constrain state autonomy.

The way in which EU action can affect the autonomy of the member states thus takes a variety of forms. However, it is by no means the only source of national policy change, since the Fifteen, both individually and collectively, have responded to the influence of a number of external and internal factors. External factors have been emphasised, in recent years, by a burgeoning literature on international pressures which are alleged to undermine the capacities of the state for independent action (Camilleri and Falk 1992, Ohmae 1990). Technological innovation, developments in the international economy, trends towards globalisation, increased competitiveness on the part of trading rivals, transnational linkages between commercial or non-commercial interests, and action taken by and within international organisations all constitute possible external influences prompting national policy change.

Internally, the action of ideologically motivated governments, the mobilisation of domestic private interests ranging from organisations representing producers or consumers to trade unions and individual firms, demands expressed by the electorate or pressure on public spending may lead to the modification or abandonment of existing policies. Moreover, it is rarely the case that only one of these factors is at work or that activity is restricted to a single level of analysis; rather, policy change is often brought about as a consequence of the complex interaction between a multiplicity of actors at the international, the European, the national and the sub-national level. Distinguishing clearly between these influences is a challenge met by the empirical studies which follow.

The picture becomes even more complicated in view of the fact that the member states have different policy traditions, interests and policy preferences. This means that EU action which constitutes a constraint on one member state may extend opportunities for another. A number of the case studies which follow indicate that member states use the machinery of the Community to multilateralise their own policy preferences, using the EU as a mechanism for exporting their own policy preferences. This was the case with the Netherlands and the UK in the air transport sector, for example. In some instances, the action taken at the EU level has little impact at all, since some member states will have introduced more radical policies than are acceptable to the majority of members or will have acted in advance of the EU (see Thatcher's discussion of high technology and Matthew Fraser's analysis of developments in the audiovisual field, chapters 10 and 11, this volume). Sometimes this can lead to the penalising by the EU of member states that have begun to innovate, even though their new policies appear to be in line with the neo-liberal philosophy of the Single European Market (see Richardson, Chapter 9, this volume). There are some member states who have been able successfully to use the EU as an alibi for overcoming domestic opposition to policy change (see Thatcher's discussion of France in the area of telecommunications). This, of course, does not work in all cases. Witness the difficulties that the management of Air France has had in attempting to restructure the company to compete effectively in the single market.

Another complexity derives from the fact that it is not sufficient to regard the development of Community competence in a particular area as constituting communitarianisation. John Peterson's discussion of research and development demonstrates the need to inspect very closely the institutional arrangements in any area before reaching such a conclusion. His examination of research and development policy indicates that it is quite possible for EU policy or collective action at the EU level to take the form of intergovernmental bargaining, with little evidence of the so-called 'Community method'. Moreover, even though the EU may enjoy competence and the formal power to act in a particular area, whether it does so may depend upon how the relevant Treaty provisions distribute power between EU institutions, and whether the Commission has the institutional resources or political will to initiate action.

The second element of the investigation into the impact of the EU on the member states relates to the impact of EU action on national policy making, that is on the behaviour of, and the relationships between, the actors traditionally involved in making policy. This represents an important aspect of the consequences of EU activity for state autonomy, since action at the European level may profoundly affect relations between the state and other actors, while the way in which it may privilege one set of interests as opposed to another may constrain a government's autonomy. EU action can affect policy making at the national level in a number of ways. It may influence the distribution of power between actors and thereby transform existing policy-making dynamics. Notably, Community action may deprive governments of the powers which enabled them to offer support to certain firms or sectors designated as strategically important, or to sustain clientelistic relationships with particular interests. Typically, it may no longer be possible for states to protect public enterprises and such firms may be exposed to commercial pressures for the first time. Privately owned firms might find their own position enhanced. Thus EU action may limit the capacity of the state to intervene, thereby loosening the ties between governments and national champions, and transforming the market-place. As well as strengthening the private as against the public sector, EU action may underpin the interests of consumers *vis-à-vis* producers. Moreover, new interests can be constituted as a result of activity at the European level. Conversely, entrenched interests at the national level can undermine the impact of the EU (see Jones, Chapter 6, this volume). Closed policy networks may enable policy continuity in the face of EU attempts to initiate Euro-level policy development. In new policy areas, however, interest groups may not have had the opportunity to mobilise or consolidate. Consequently, it may be easier for the EU to act in these areas.

In the second place, EU action has had a significant impact on interest intermediation. Many writers have discussed the proliferation of lobbying and the dramatic increase in the number and range of interests represented in Brussels (Greenwood *et al.* 1992, Mazey and Richardson 1993, Pedlar and Van Schendelen 1994). Not only have interest groups which previously concentrated their attentions on national policy makers extended their lobbying activities to EU institutions, but new Euro-level federations have come into being and new constituencies mobilised. The extent to which interest groups have redirected their efforts towards Brussels and, in particular, the degree to which governments have lost their role as 'gatekeepers' between domestic interests and the EU, serves as an important indicator of the extent to which the locus of power has moved from national capitals to the supranational tier. Caution must be exercised, however, that the increase in the number of interest groups in Brussels is not conflated with an increase in their influence.

These are all ways in which action taken by the EU can affect national policy and policy making, but there are others too. The fact of EU intervention may, for instance, influence politics and the policy process in a member state by making an issue more or less salient. This will depend on the capacity of interest groups to mobilise relevant constituencies. It will also be influenced by the decision of governments or political parties to draw attention to European action. In some cases, EU intervention may facilitate policy change; in others, it may make it more difficult.

THE PLAN OF THE BOOK

The sectoral studies in this volume consider the multiplicity of ways in which EU action impacts upon the member states. A range of industrial, financial and service sectors are examined. These deal with declining sectors, such as steel, increasingly important areas of industrial policy, such as high technology, and traditional services, such as water. Each case study considers traditional policy orientations and the respective roles of influential actors and interests, looks at EU initiatives and action, and examines policy change and its sources, external and internal, at the national level. Although some authors concentrate their attention on a single country (Masi on steel and Richardson on water), most look to the experience of the four larger member states – France, Germany, Italy and the United Kingdom.

The sectoral organisation of the book does not signal an indifference or insensitivity to differences between member states. Indeed, one of the tasks of the contributors has been to identify whether sectoral or national differences have emerged. National differences, deriving from different historical experiences, constitutional traditions, economic and social dynamics, political cultures, institutional arrangements, and attitudes towards Europe, may well become apparent when developments across the various sectors are compared.

This volume is concerned with examining the impact of EU action on state autonomy, but also how the relationship between the EU and the member states is best conceptualised. This second theme is treated first in chapters by

Jeremy Richardson and Stephen George who consider the utility of approaches drawn from political science and international relations. The case studies are introduced by Leigh Hancher's discussion of the regulatory role of the EU and issues raised by the implementation of the single market programme. The sectoral chapters then follow. In the concluding chapter, Anand Menon and Jack Hayward examine the implications of the sectoral findings and consider what the impact of EU action has been on state autonomy relative to other factors accounting for policy change, whether national policy has been Europeanised, what sectoral or national differences emerge, and what conclusions should be drawn for existing and future theorising.

NOTES

1 The authors would like to thank Paul Hirst for his useful comments on this chapter.
2 For the most part, these areas have been influenced by action taken within the EC.
3 Although the Commission conducts negotiations with third countries under terms set out by the Council and the latter's approval is required for any agreement, member states will inevitably be forced into intergovernmental bargaining in order to reach a common position. This may mean that some governments are forced to make policy decisions that they otherwise would not have done, which, for example, might displease important domestic constituencies.

REFERENCES

Anderson, S.S. and Eliassen, K.A. (1993) *Making Policy in Europe. The Europeification of National Policy-making*, London: Sage.
Blouwer, F. (1994) 'Conclusion', in Lintner, V. and Newman, M. (eds) *Economic Policy Making and the European Union*, London: The Federal Trust.
Camilleri, J.A. and Falk, J. (1992) *The End of Sovereignty? The Politics of a Shrinking and Fragmenting World*, Aldershot: Edward Elgar.
Caporaso, James A. (1989) 'Introduction: The State in Comparative and International Perspective', in *idem* (ed.) *The Elusive State: International and Comparative Perspectives*, California: Sage.
Greenwood, Justin, Grote, Jurgen R. and Ronit, Karsten (eds) (1992) *Organized Interests and the European Community*, London: Sage.
Hanrieder, Wolfran F. (1978) 'Dissolving International Politics: reflections on the nation-state', *The American Political Science Review*, 72,4, 1276–87.
Hayward, K. (1995) *Industrial Enterprise and European Integration: From National to International Champions in Western Europe*, Oxford: Oxford University Press.
Held, David (1989) 'Sovereignty, National Politics and the Global System', in *idem Political Theory and the Modern State*, Oxford: Polity.
Hinsley, F.H. (1986) *Sovereignty*, 2nd edn, Cambridge: Cambridge University Press.
Hirst, Paul and Thompson, Graham (1995) 'Globalisation and the Future of the Nation State', *Economy and Society*, 4,24, 408–42, August.
Hix, Simon (1994) 'Approaches to the Study of the EC: The Challenge to Comparative Politics', *West European Politics*, 17,1, 1–30.
Hoffmann, Stanley (1982) 'Reflections on the Nation-State in Western Europe Today', *Journal of Common Market Studies*, 21, 21–37.
—— (1987) 'Domestic Politics and Interdependence' in *idem* (ed.) *Janus and Minerva: Essays in the Theory and Practice of International Politics*, Oxford: Westview Press.

Howe, Geoffrey (1990) 'Sovereignty and interdependence: Britain's place in the world', *International Affairs*, 66,4, 675–95.

Hurrell, Andrew and Menon Anand (1996) 'Politics Like any Other? Comparative Politics, International Relations and the Study of the EC', *West European Politics*, 19(2) April.

Keohane, Robert O. and Nye, Joseph S. (1974) 'Transgovernmental Relations and International Organizations', *World Politics*, 27,1, 39–62.

Lintner, V. and Newman, M. (eds) (1994) *Economic Policy Making and the European Union*, London: The Federal Trust.

Lord, C. (1992) 'Sovereign or confused? The "Great Debate" about British entry to the European Community Twenty Years on', *Journal of Common Market Studies*, 30,4.

Mann, Michael (1994), 'Nation-states in Europe and Other Continents: Diversifying, Developing, Not Dying', *Daedalus*, 13, 115–140.

Mazey, Sonia and Richardson Jeremy J. (eds) (1993) *Lobbying in the European Community*, Oxford: Oxford University Press.

Moravcsik, Andrew (1991) 'Negotiating the Single European Act: National Interest and Conventional Statecraft in the European Community', *International Organization*, 45, 651–688.

—— (1993) 'Preferences and Power in the European Community: A Liberal Intergovernmental Approach', *Journal of Common Market Studies*, 31, 473–524.

—— (1994) 'Why the European Community strengthens the State: Domestic Politics and International Cooperation', presented at the Annual Meeting of the American Political Science Association, New York, 1–4 September.

Nordlinger, Eric A. (1981) *On the Autonomy of the Democratic State*, Cambridge, Massachusetts: Harvard University Press.

Ohmae, K. (1990) *The Borderless World: Power and Strategy in the Interlinked Economy*, London: Collins.

Pedlar, R.H. and Van Schendelen, M.P.C.M. (eds) (1994), *Lobbying the European Union: Companies, Trade Associations and Issue Groups*, Aldershot: Dartmouth.

Richardson, J.J. and Lindley, R.M. (1994) 'Editorial', *Journal of European Public Policy*, 1,1, 1–7.

Rosenau, James A. (1989) 'The State in an Era of Cascading Politics: Wavering Concept, Widening Competence, Withering Colossus, or Weathering Change?', in James A.Caporaso (ed.) *The Elusive State: International and Comparative Perspectives*, California: Sage.

Schmitter, Philippe (1992) 'Representation and the Future Euro-Polity', *Staatwissenschaften and Staatpraxis*, 3,2, 379–405.

Taylor, Paul (1991) 'British Sovereignty and the European Community: What is at Risk?', *Millennium: Journal of International Studies*, 20,1, 73–80.

Wallace, William (1982) 'Europe as a Confederation: The Community and the Nation-State', *Journal of Common Market Studies*, 21, 57–68.

2 The European Union

Approaches from international relations

Stephen George

From its inception as the European Coal and Steel Community (ECSC) to the creation of the European Union (EU), the European Community (EC) in its various guises has attracted attention from scholars whose intellectual origins lie in the discipline of international relations (IR). European integration seemed a natural subject for a discipline that concerned itself with relations between states, since what was taking place in western Europe was an experiment in putting interstate relations on a new footing.

In the 1960s particularly, there developed a considerable body of IR literature on how to explain and predict the development of European integration, which made certain assumptions about the autonomy of the state in this process, and this sparked off a fierce debate within IR that still rumbles on today. More recently scholars from other disciplines, notably political science, comparative politics and public policy, have become much more interested in the study of the EU, and there has been a tendency for them to play down the value of IR approaches (Hix 1994). It is the contention of this chapter that such approaches should not be dismissed; they have an important contribution to make alongside other approaches. In passing it might be noted in support of this contention that one of the range of concepts favoured by Jeremy Richardson in his contribution to this volume, the idea of 'epistemic communities', is itself derived from the IR literature.

Indeed, it is the contention of this chapter that in order to understand the EU a model which combines attention to international, EU-level and domestic processes is needed, and that some of the approaches derived from IR have moved a long way towards developing such a model, while scholars within the other disciplines still have not woken up to the importance of the phenomenon of the EU.

REALISM AND PLURALISM

The debate in the 1960s about how to understand the EC formed part of a more general debate on the nature of the international system. Neofunctionalism, the approach that dominated the study of the EC in the early 1960s, was just one part of a wider pluralist critique of realist assumptions in the discipline. Although pluralism dominated political science in the United States in the 1960s, realism dominated the study of IR. The main text on most courses in the 1950s and early 1960s, and a seminal work in realism, was Hans Morgenthau's *Politics Among Nations* (1948, 1954, 1960), which emphasised the central role of states as actors pursuing clearly defined national interests in conflict with other states. On this view the primary constraint on the autonomy of states was the international system. They always had to calculate the effect of their actions on the reactions of other states.

Pluralism, as an analysis of policy making within states, emphasised the political process that influenced decision makers, particularly the role of interest groups (Dunleavy and O'Leary 1987: 32–7). It also disaggregated the concept of the government itself to distinguish bureaucratic actors from the political elite who formed the elected government of the state.

When applied to IR, pluralism initially produced a criticism of the assumption by realists that states could be treated as homogeneous actors, and that there was such a thing as a national interest that was somehow independent of the political process. The state was disaggregated to reveal the role of interest groups and bureaucratic actors in the process of formulating what constituted the national interest (Little and Smith 1991: 182–211). On this view it was not meaningful even to talk of the autonomy of 'the state' in IR: what was in question was the autonomy of the political elite which formed the government at any particular time. This elite was simply one group of actors existing alongside other internal actors, and the primary restriction on its autonomy came from the constraints imposed by the presence of these other actors within the state.

The pluralist critique of realism went on from there to argue that these other internal actors – interest groups and bureaucratic actors – also extended their activities beyond the boundaries of the state. Not all contacts between states were mediated through the offices of the heads of government or through the foreign offices. Interest groups in different states interacted in transnational networks that had a separate existence from official state-to-state contacts; and bureaucrats in the functional departments of each national government had routine contact with their counterparts in the functional ministries of other governments through participation in international bodies such as the various United Nations agencies, economic organisations like the International Monetary Fund, and regional organisations such as the Council of Europe and, of course, the European Community (Keohane and Nye 1974: 39–62; 1977: 23–37). These transnational and transgovernmental networks acted as further constraints on the autonomy of the politicians in office. In the technical, functional policy sectors the networks would develop co-ordinated policy positions that it would be very difficult for the political elites to unravel or block. Although these ideas were only fully developed in the 1970s, neofunctionalism was squarely in this tradition, and indeed in the vanguard of the developing critique of realism.

NEOFUNCTIONALISM

Neofunctionalism was a strong explanatory theory that aspired to prediction. As developed by Haas (1958, 1968) and Lindberg (1963), it asserted that once the first steps had been taken in the integrative process, others would follow as a result of processes of spillover. Functional spillover would occur as a result of the interdependence of different sectors of the modern industrial economy: any attempt to integrate across national boundaries in one sector would be frustrated unless other, cognate sectors were also integrated; this would create a dynamic in which the further integration would require still further integration, and so on. As Haas put it: 'Sector integration . . . begets its own impetus toward extension to the entire economy even in the absence of specific group demands' (Haas 1968: 297).

However, group demands would be present as part of the process of political spillover, in which interest groups were seen as crucial actors in the process. Once the initial integrative steps had been taken, key sectoral interest groups would switch a part of their political activity to the supranational level. As a result of contact with similar interest groups from other participating states, and through interaction with the European Commission, they would come to appreciate the benefits of the degree of integration already achieved, and the risks of it being frustrated if further integration did not take place. They would therefore become lobbyists in their national political arenas for further integration.

The Commission would play an important role in this process as the central bureaucratic actor, manipulating the pressures that arose from sectoral integration. It would foster integrative solutions to the problems that partial integration would pose; it would encourage supranational links between groups; and it would prompt the groups to interpret their interests in ways that furthered integration. In this process, the governments of states were seen as having very little autonomy. Standing at the junction of supranational and domestic pressures, they would be obliged to go along with a greater degree of integration than they had originally envisaged.

INTERGOVERNMENTALISM

In response to the neofunctionalist analysis of European integration, a counter-argument was put forward by Stanley Hoffmann (1964, 1966) which drew heavily upon realist assumptions. In essence, there were three main elements in Hoffmann's critique of neofunctionalism: the first was that regional integration had to be viewed in the wider context of international relations on a global scale; the second was that national governments were uniquely powerful actors in the process of European integration, and remained committed to the defence of the national interest; and the third argument was that, although for reasons of mutual national benefit, states might be prepared to go along with closer integration in the technical functional sectors, the process would never cross the threshold into the areas of high politics, of national security and defence.

It is the second of these arguments – that states are uniquely powerful actors in the process – which is the most obviously relevant to this discussion. It was a direct denial of the assumption in neofunctionalism that the whole process of European integration was one of bargaining between elites over the extent to which functional competences would shift from the national level to the supranational level, a process in which the national political elites would not be in a particularly strong position. According to this neofunctionalist view, the national political elites would find that the logic of sectoral integration in an interdependent Europe pushed them to consider further steps to full unification, and they would rapidly find that the other elite groups – national and supranational administrative elites, and industrial, financial, and commercial interest groups – were united in pushing them down this road.

The realist response was that the apparent weakness of national governments was based on a false arithmetic, which assumed the power of each elite-group to be approximately equal, so that if the governments were outnumbered they would lose. The counter argument was that the governments of the states were uniquely powerful because they possessed legal sovereignty and political legitimacy. As Hoffmann put it:

> even in the economic and social sphere, where the various interest groups and the technocrats have undoubtedly played a major role in the process of integration, it is a mistake to forget that some of the actors are neither of the same kind nor the same level as the others; I refer to states or, if one prefers, the governments: for their decisions during the process are not explainable only in terms of pressures and counter-pressures from interests; often political calculations lead governments to take positions to which powerful groups are hostile.
>
> (Hoffmann 1964: 93).

In this passage, two aspects of the second point in Hoffmann's critique are touched upon. First, there is the substantive point of the passage that actors are not all of the same weight. This is the classic realist point, and Hoffmann goes on to argue that governments will only agree to increase the power of central institutions where they believe it to be in their national interest to do so, and that 'the bigger the functional scope of integration, the more interests [member states] tend to see as vital are likely to be at stake – and the less smooth the process may become' (Hoffmann 1964: 89). These words appeared prophetic soon afterwards, when de Gaulle precipitated the biggest crisis to date in the development of the EC by withdrawing from the work of the Community for six months in protest at plans to extend the powers of the European Parliament and, as it turned out, to block the planned movement to majority voting in the Council of Ministers (Lambert 1966: 195–228).

The second part of the passage quoted makes the point that governments do not just respond to pressures from organised interests. According to classical realism, states were generally treated as unified rational actors, and little attention was paid to internal political processes. Hoffmann's intergovernmentalist position was somewhat more sophisticated in this respect, and his political awareness was also greater than that of the neofunctionalist writers who tended to adopt a rather simplified pluralist view of political processes (George 1991: 29–32).

It was recognised by Hoffmann that in areas of 'low politics', interest groups did influence the actions of states: but as he pointed out, they were not the only influence. Other considerations were what government officials considered to be in the long-term interests of the national economy, and the impact on the electorate (Hoffmann 1964: 89). However, this aspect was not fully developed by Hoffmann in his writings in the 1960s. Although the influence of domestic politics was acknowledged, it was not very adequately factored into the explanation of developments.

In this respect, the picture that Hoffmann painted of the process of integration was one in which the governments of states had much more autonomy than in the neofunctionalist view. The process remained essentially intergovernmental: it would only go as far as the governments were prepared to allow it to go. However, he also pointed to the fact that regional integration was only one aspect of the development of the global international system, and the implication of that insight was a more restrictive view of the autonomy of the state. In this respect Hoffmann, like the realists, stressed the external limitations on autonomy: states are seen as independent actors, but their governments are constrained by the position of the state in the world system.

POST-NEOFUNCTIONALISM

In the course of the late 1960s neofunctionalism seemed to be knocked out of contention as an explanatory theory by developments in the Community itself. The 1965 crisis led to serious reappraisals of the central theorems (Haas 1968, Lindberg 1966). Interestingly, one of the key aspects of these reappraisals was the acknowledgement that the initial neofunctionalist analyses had paid too little attention to the wider international system. This appeared to open the way to a model that would combine the pluralist emphasis on domestic and regional constraints on the autonomy of the governments of states with the realist emphasis on the international constraints. However, the line of analysis was not followed very far. Lindberg, in collaboration with Stuart Scheingold, did develop a revised version of neofunctionalism (Lindberg and Scheingold 1970) stripped of much of its predictive intent, and drawing heavily on the systems theory of David Easton; but it was not immediately followed up, largely because the attention of scholars within the tradition that produced it turned to wider concerns.

INTERDEPENDENCE

Scholars working within the pluralist tradition soon moved away from a special concern with the EC and processes of European integration, and turned instead to develop their framework into a broader theory of interdependence. Within this theory the idea was developed of international regimes as ways in which states dealt with the problems of interdependence, and the EC was treated as just a special example of this general structure of regimes (Haas 1975). In moving from the particular to the general, the theories within the interdependence perspective lost some of the specificity of the EC; in particular they lost sight of the special institutional characteristics of the EC. From being celebrated as the motor of integration, the Commission came to be treated as just another international secretariat, and the roles of both the European Parliament and the Court of Justice were overlooked in favour of a concentration on the one intergovernmental institution within the original structure, the Council of Ministers (Nau 1979).

This brought thinking within the interdependence tradition, which had grown out of pluralism, close to the intergovernmental position that Hoffmann had developed out of realism: both treated the EC as essentially an intergovernmental organisation. How far the member states retained autonomy remained an open question in this context, to be answered only with reference to specific case studies. In practice, though, there were very few North American studies of the EC at all during what have recently been categorised as 'the doldrum years' (Caporaso and Keeler 1993). Such new work as did take place on the EC was on the European side of the Atlantic, and it received only limited attention in North America.

BRITISH APPROACHES

In the late 1970s there appeared a prime example of a British text to which lip-service is always paid, but which has received less serious attention as a theoretical contribution than it deserves (Wallace *et al.* 1977). Generally this book is classified as an example of intergovernmentalism. Although historians of the development of thinking on integration sometimes recognise that in places it went beyond strict intergovernmentalism (Caporaso and Keeler 1993), it is not generally recognised how far the book took forward the intergovernmental framework of analysis. It advocated an approach that started with the analysis of domestic politics before turning to look at the process of intergovernmental bargaining, an approach that was carried through in most of the case study chapters (Nau 1979). As such it was a precursor of the 'liberal intergovernmentalist approach' that is examined later in this chapter.

A similar problem in securing recognition for a theoretically coherent approach has plagued what is known as 'the domestic politics approach', which bears some resemblances to that adopted in the Wallace *et al.* volume.

This approach was first elaborated by Simon Bulmer (1983). He identified the dominant approaches to the study of the EC at the time as supranationalism and intergovernmentalism, and argued that this dichotomy obscured the role of national non-state actors in the process of formulating national positions on European policy.

Bulmer's analysis made five assumptions. First, it assumed that the national polity was the basic unit: it was the level at which governments, interest groups, parliamentary bodies and political parties derived their legitimacy and their power, and the level at which they could be called to account. Second, it assumed that each state was different in certain important respects: each had a different set of social and economic conditions; each had different ideological cleavages and each had a different relationship to the outside world. Third, it held that EC policy was dealing with essentially the same topics as much domestic policy making, and the two should therefore be analysed in tandem. Fourth, it assumed that governments occupied a key strategic position at the junction of national and EC politics, but that their autonomy varied greatly. Finally, it considered that the concept of policy style could be used to analyse governments' relationships with other domestic actors. It was with this last assumption that Bulmer provided the basis for empirical analysis. Policy style referred to 'the interaction between (a) the government's approach to policy-making and (b) the relationship between government and other actors in the policy process' (Richardson *et al.* 1982: 13). In introducing this concept to the analysis, Bulmer provided a bridge between studies of the EC based on IR and some of the literature on the analysis of domestic policy making.

Although sophisticated and illuminating, Bulmer's approach was largely ignored in the United States, where the general lack of interest in the EC continued until the successful launch in 1985 of the 1992 programme to create the internal market. This produced a new wave of interest in the subject, and a renewal of the dispute between neofunctionalism and intergovernmentalism.

THE REVIVAL OF NEOFUNCTIONALISM

The success of the 1992 programme and the signing of the Single European Act (SEA), led some writers to suggest that perhaps neofunctionalism had not been so wrong after all (Taylor 1989: 23–4, George 1990: 210). Two features of the new developments in particular suggested that there might still be explanatory force in neofunctionalism: first, the role of the Commission as a central bureaucratic actor manipulating circumstances to further integration; and second, the role played by multinational business interests in pressuring governments to complete the internal market.

There was widespread agreement that the role of the Commission was of central importance in the launching of the programme. As one influential article put it: 'The renewed drive for market unification can be explained only if theory takes into account the policy leadership of the Commission'

(Sandholtz and Zysman 1989: 96). The same authors also recognised the role played by leading industrialists in launching and sustaining the single market project, a role emphasised even more strongly by one of those very industrialists, Giovanni Agnelli. He contrasted the situation in the 1950s, when the European Economic Community (EEC) was launched, with the position in the 1980s when the 1992 project was launched:

> Ironically, it was politicians who in 1957 first conceived the idea of a common market – often over objections from the business community. Now the situation has been reversed; it is the entrepreneurs and corporations who are keeping the pressure on politicians to transcend considerations of local and national interest
>
> (Agnelli 1989: 62).

However, the revived perspective also took account of some of the criticisms levelled at the original neofunctionalist theory. In particular, Sandholtz and Zysman accepted the criticism that neofunctionalism had focused on the regional level to the neglect of the wider international system. They set their explanation of the success of the 1992 programme within the framework of changes in the structure of the international system, particularly the ascent of Japan.

They argued that this shift in global power resources was the trigger for the 1992 process, but it was not the whole of the explanation. Whereas an extreme structural realist position would lead to the argument that the state lacked all autonomy, and that governments had no choice but to respond to these challenges in the way they did, Sandholtz and Zysman argued

> that structural situations create the context of choice and cast up problems to be resolved, but they do not dictate the decisions and strategies ... the global setting can be understood in neo-realist terms, but the political processes triggered by changes in the system must be analyzed in other than structural terms.
>
> (Sandholtz and Zysman 1989: 127)

At this point, having set the context, the authors introduced the analytical factors identified above, which allowed them to construct an explanation of the 1992 programme that was compatible with neofunctionalist assumptions while recognising the specific international circumstances within which such an initiative would be acceptable to the governments of states.

THE REASSERTION OF INTERGOVERNMENTALISM

It did seem as though the debate of the 1960s had been superseded when even Hoffmann, perhaps influenced by his profound respect for Jacques Delors, acknowledged the role of the Commission (Hoffmann 1989). But that impression was proved false by the appearance of Andrew Moravcsik's analysis of the factors that accounted for the agreement on the SEA (Moravcsik

1991). It constituted a blistering intergovernmentalist counter-attack against the echoes of neofunctionalism. He considered two broad explanations for developments that furthered European integration: supranational institutionalism and intergovernmental institutionalism. His first category, supranational institutionalism, covered explanatory factors such as pressure from the EC institutions (primarily the European Parliament and the European Court of Justice), lobbying by transnational business interests, and political entrepreneurship by the Commission; it was therefore a model consistent with neofunctionalist theory. Moravcsik tested it against the empirical evidence relating to the SEA and found it wanting. He argued that the European Parliament was largely ignored in the negotiation of the SEA; the transnational business groups came late to the single market, when the process was already well under way as a result of a consensus between governments on the need for reform; the Commission's White Paper on the single market was 'a response to a mandate from the member states' rather than an independent initiative from a policy entrepreneur (Moravcsik 1991: 45–8).

His second category, intergovernmental institutionalism, stressed bargains between states, marked by lowest-common-denominator bargaining and the protection of sovereignty. It was an example of what Keohane (1984) had described as the 'modified structural realist' explanation of the formation and maintenance of international regimes, but it took more account of domestic politics. Indeed, in his application of the model to the SEA, Moravcsik put a good deal of emphasis on domestic politics, and he ended his article with a plea for more work on this aspect of EC bargaining. In doing so he brought the intergovernmentalist perspective round to a similar position to that already marked out by Wallace *et al.* and by Bulmer, and again suggested an interface between theories of the EC derived from IR and those derived from domestic approaches to the study of public policy.

Liberal intergovernmentalism

Moravcsik subsequently developed the theoretical underpinnings of his approach, and labelled it 'liberal intergovernmentalism' (Moravcsik 1993). In doing this he clearly demonstrated the roots of the approach in the work of Hoffmann from the 1960s. Like Hoffmann, Moravcsik started out from a critique of neofunctionalism. He restated the argument that neofunctionalism failed to explain developments in the EC itself, but he put more weight on a theoretical critique. In particular, he argued that the self-criticisms of the neofunctionalists themselves had to be taken seriously.

He identified three such self-criticisms: that theories of regional integration had to be supplemented (or even be supplanted) by more general theories of national responses to international interdependence; that the development of common policy responses needed to be looked at as much as did institutional transfers of competence; and that unicausal theories were inadequate to deal with the phenomenon under consideration. Instead of reviving neofunctionalism, Moravcsik argued that these criticisms should be taken seriously, and a theory constructed that took account of them. He believed that all of the points could be accounted for if the analysis of the EC was rolled into what he called 'current theories of international political economy' (Moravcsik 1993: 480).

Moravcsik's liberal intergovernmental approach assumed that states were rational actors, but departed from traditional realism in not treating states as black boxes or billiard balls. Instead it was assumed that the governments of states were playing what Putnam called 'two-level games' (Putnam 1988). That is, their definition of the national interest was determined by a domestic political process. This constituted the first part of the analysis and determined the position that governments took with them into the international negotiation. The second part of the analysis was to see how conflicting national interests were reconciled in the negotiating forum of the Council of Ministers. This was exactly the approach that had been adopted in the Wallace *et al.* volume.

Moravcsik's basic assumption was that the EC could be explained with reference to general theories of IR, as an example of a successful international regime. In such a regime, the behaviour of states reflected the rational actions of governments constrained at home by societal pressures and abroad by their strategic environment. Essentially, Moravcsik was reasserting the claims of realism while accepting the validity of some of the criticisms that had been made of it. His position accepted some of the ideas raised by neofunctionalism, and by the wider pluralist approach of which it was a part, while continuing to assert that states remained in charge of the process, and giving little credence to the claims that supranational actors were at least as significant as state actors in explaining what was going on in the EC.

A critique of Moravcsik

Moravcsik's writings attracted a considerable amount of attention in the early 1990s. In the extent to which he drew upon the writings of Hoffmann, he was clearly the heir to one important tradition in the debate within IR about European integration. In his 1993 article he deliberately laid claim also to be heir to the ideas of Haas and Lindberg by asserting that his starting point was to take seriously the autocritiques that the neofunctionalists made after the 1965 crisis.

For these reasons, although it is worth asking how far his position represented an advance over those reached in the British writings of the 1970s and 1980s which are discussed above, it is perhaps worth mounting a critique of Moravcsik's approach so far as it touches on the key issue of the autonomy of the state. A convenient way of approaching the critique is through a closer examination of Moravcsik's arguments concerning the SEA. In his 1991 article, Moravcsik insisted that the role of supranational pressure group activity was unimportant in the promotion of the SEA because, he claimed, the timing was wrong. On the other hand, he did give a certain amount of credit to what he called 'firm-level business pressure at the domestic level' (Moravcsik 1991: 54).

Here there seems to be a certain failure in the conceptualisation of supranational pressures as against domestic pressures. As Moravcsik admitted, the pressure for market liberalisation would come most strongly from those businesses that were most Europeanised or globalised in their operations. These were precisely the corporations that formed the basis of the European Round Table of Industrialists, the influence of which Moravcsik dismissed.

The explanation for this apparent contradiction is presumably that the test is whether supranational or national institutional processes were used to put pressure on governments. However, this seems a particularly unhelpful distinction. The key element is that governments were under pressure to agree to market liberalisation, that the pressure came from businesses that were European or global in their operations, and that many of those businesses were in contact with one another through forums such as the Round Table.

The idea of transnational links between states, which was developed within the interdependence tradition, is thus brought back into the analysis. As explained above, these are links between non-governmental actors that cross national boundaries, but are not mediated through the central institutions of the state. The Round Table constitutes a transnational network through which such links can be forged and strengthened. The consequence of the existence of the network is that when the governments of the member states come to tackle problems of public policy and turn for advice to national interest groups, they are all likely to be met by the same advice from the largest and most influential commercial enterprises, because a common view of the problem has already been developed through the transnational network. So in the case of the single market programme, when the governments in the early 1980s turned to tackle the serious problems of persistent recession and lack of investment, they all met with the same advice from their largest businesses; those that were the most Europeanised or globalised in their operations – whether British, Dutch, French, or German – advised their governments that the prerequisite for their success was the removal of the non-tariff barriers that had grown up during the 1970s, and the creation of a genuine single market in the EC.

This co-ordination of pressure from national actors, who had developed their thinking through transnational links, more satisfyingly explains the reorientation of the definition of national interests that took place in the major states than does Moravcsik's analysis, which treats each state as a closed political system, and therefore has to rely on coincidence to a large extent.

At this point it may be asked why the transnational networks should be thought to support integrative solutions. The answer is that they may not, but that in some important cases they do appear to have had this characteristic. One important example would be the single market programme; another would be the formulation of a European technology policy (Peterson 1991,

Sharp and Shearman 1987, Sharp 1989, 1990). In both cases, the European Commission seems to have played a key role in bringing transnational networks into existence and in fostering the idea of integrative solutions to common problems. So the original neofunctionalist stress on the role of the Commission as the motor of integration perhaps needs to be re-examined.

The argument about the linking of national systems can be taken further if the idea of transgovernmental links is also brought in from the interdependence perspective. These are links between civil servants in different states who occupy positions in the same functional ministries as one another, e.g. environment ministries, transport ministries. The theory posits that through regular meetings these officials will develop a commonality of outlook on the problems that they face, and will co-ordinate their positions within their separate national capitals in trying to get support from their governments for the consensus solutions to these problems. Again, the links between these officials from functional ministries and the Commission deserve further empirical investigation.

CONCLUSIONS

When considering the autonomy of the state it is important first to be clear about the definition of the state. Realism treated states as unified rational actors; but the pluralist critique of realism stressed the need to disaggregate the concept of the state; and both Hoffmann and Moravcsik, although deriving more of their analysis from realist than from pluralist insights, accepted that what was really under discussion were the actions of the governments of states, and that those governments had to operate in a pluralistic domestic political arena which in itself constrained their autonomy.

With the concept of transgovernmental links, pluralist analyses went even further in the disaggregation of the state, distinguishing the central departments of state (the Prime Minister's Office, the Foreign Office) from the functional ministries. The latter were expected to develop their own links across national boundaries, which also came to act as a constraint on the autonomy of the central departments of state.

Both these approaches suggest an interface with theories of domestic policy making, such as those outlined by Jeremy Richardson in Chapter 3, this volume. This raises the whole question of the relationship between approaches drawn from IR and those drawn from political science or comparative politics.

Hix (1994) has argued that approaches from IR lack the concepts to analyse what he calls European Community 'politics'. He argues that approaches from IR were concerned with how far and under what conditions states would integrate their economies and policies, whereas if we want to understand the output of the policy process once the decision to integrate has been taken, we need to turn to approaches derived from comparative politics. However, Hix seems to draw a line between the analysis of European integration and the analysis of EC politics that is too hard and fast. Neofunctional-ism in particular put a good deal of emphasis on the integrative effects of incremental common policy making in mundane functional sectors. Indeed, there is a distinct meeting of concerns between writers in the tradition identi-fied by Richardson and neofunctionalists on the question of policy networks. Neofunctionalists argued that a powerful agent of further integration once the initial integrative steps had been taken would be the emergence of what later came to be called transnational and transgovernmental networks. Writers on domestic policy making who have adopted the concept of policy networks have increasingly had to address the question of how far domestic policy networks have become Europeanised. Essentially both are addressing the same question.

While it seems likely that both neofunctionalist approaches and the inter-governmental approach of writers like Moravcsik would benefit greatly by cross-fertilisation from the literature on domestic policy making, which oper-ates with a more sophisticated understanding of internal policy processes, it is also interesting to note that Hix makes one exception to his generalisation about the problems of applying theoretical discourses derived from IR to the discussion of EC politics. This is for the domestic politics approach, which he quotes Bulmer as admitting is of 'somewhat mixed intellectual parentage' (Hix 1994: 26). Indeed, in adopting the concept of 'policy style' Bulmer draws on the same tradition of analysis of domestic politics as Richardson reviews in this volume.

Bulmer was also clear that national governments stood at the intersec-tion of domestic and international pressures, a point that has subsequently informed the writings of theorists from within both the main IR traditions. Drawing attention to the wider international context of the actions of states is one way in which approaches derived from IR can supplement the analyses based on political science. Wallace (1990: 81–91) has summarised much of the thinking on this subject, identifying the role in the revival of European integration both of the changing relationship between the United States and Europe and of the rise of Japan to technological leader-ship. In an interdependent capitalist world economy, governments may have the formal power to follow any line of policy they wish; in practice, they are constrained by the damaging economic effects of not responding successfully to the challenges posed by the dynamics of the capitalist system.

Although scarcely contested ground so far as general developments in the EU are concerned, the extent to which changes in the international system have played a distinct role in particular policy sectors remains a question for empirical analysis, as does the much more contested question of how far policy networks have become Europeanised. Both issues directly affect judgements about the limits on the autonomy of the state, and both receive attention in the case studies that follow in the remainder of this volume.

REFERENCES

Agnelli, Giovanni (1989) 'The Europe of 1992', *Foreign Affairs*, 68, 61–70.

Bulmer, Simon (1983) 'Domestic Politics and European Community Policy-Making', *Journal of Common Market Studies*, 21, 349–63.

Caporaso, James A. and Keeler, John T.S. (1993) 'The European Community and Regional Integration Theory'. Paper prepared for delivery as a plenary address at the Third Biennial Conference of the European Community Studies Association, 27–29 May.

Dunleavy, Patrick and O'Leary, Brendan (1987) *Theories of the State: The Politics of Liberal Democracy*, London: Macmillan.

George, Stephen (1990) *An Awkward Partner: Britain in the European Community*, Oxford: Oxford University Press.

—— (1991) *Politics and Policy in the European Community*, Oxford: Oxford University Press.

Haas, Ernst B. (1958, 1968) *The Uniting of Europe: Political, Social and Economic Forces, 1950–1957*, Stanford, California: Stanford University Press.

—— (1975) 'The Obsolescence of Regional Integration Theory', Research Series no. 25, Berkeley: Institute of International Studies, University of California.

Hix, Simon (1994) 'Approaches to the Study of the EC: The Challenge to Comparative Politics', *West European Politics*, 17, 1–30.

Hoffmann, Stanley (1964) 'The European Process at Atlantic Crosspurposes', *Journal of Common Market Studies*, 3, 85–101.

—— (1966) 'Obstinate or Obsolete? The Fate of the Nation-State and the Case of Western Europe', *Daedelus*, 95, 862–915.

—— (1989) 'The European Community and 1992', *Foreign Affairs* 68, 27–47.

Keohane, Robert (1984) *After Hegemony: Co-operation and Discord in the World Political Economy*, Princeton, NJ: Princeton University Press.

Keohane, Robert O. and Nye, Joseph S. (1974) 'Transgovernmental Relations and International Organizations', *World Politics*, xxvii, 39–62.

—— (1977) *Power and Interdependence: World Politics in Transition*, Boston: Little Brown.

Lambert, John (1966) 'The Constitutional Crisis 1965-66', *Journal of Common Market Studies*, 4, 195–228.

Lindberg, Leon N. (1963) *The Political Dynamics of European Economic Integration*, London: Oxford University Press.

—— (1966) 'Integration as a Source of Stress on the European Community System', *International Organization*, 20, 233–65.

Lindberg, Leon and Scheingold, Stuart (1970) *Europe's Would-Be Polity*, New Jersey: Prentice Hall.

Little, Richard and Smith, Michael (eds) (1991) *Perspectives on World Politics*, London: Routledge.

Moravcsik, Andrew (1991) 'Negotiating the Single European Act: National Interests and Conventional Statecraft in the European Community', *International Organization*, 45, 19–56.

—— (1993) 'Preferences and Power in the European Community: A Liberal Intergovernmentalist Approach', *Journal of Common Market Studies*, 31, 473–524.

Morgenthau, Hans J. (1948, 1954, 1960) *Politics Among Nations: The Struggle for Power and Peace*, New York: Knopf.

Nau, Henry (1979) 'From Integration to Interdependence: Gains, Losses and Continuing Gaps', *International Organization*, 33, 119–47.

Peterson, John (1991) 'Technology Policy in Europe: Explaining the Framework Programme and EUREKA in Theory and Practice', *Journal of Common Market Studies*, 29, 269–90.

Putnam, Robert (1988) 'Diplomacy and Domestic Politics', *International Organization*, 42, 427–61.

Richardson, Jeremy, Gustafsson, Gunnel and Jordan, Grant (1982) 'The Concept of Policy Style' in Jeremy Richardson (ed.) *Policy Styles in Western Europe*, London: George Allen & Unwin, pp. 1–16.

Sandholtz, Wayne and Zysman, John (1989) '1992: Recasting the European Bargain', *World Politics*, 42, 95–128.

Sharp, Margaret (1989) 'The Community and the New Technologies', in Juliet Lodge (ed.) *The European Community and the Challenge of the Future*, London: Pinter Publishers, pp. 202–20.

—— (1990) 'The Single Market and European Policies for Advanced Technologies', in Colin Crouch and David Marquand (eds) *The Politics of 1992: Beyond the Single European Market*, London: Political Quarterly Publishing Co., pp. 100–20.

Sharp, Margaret and Shearman, Claire (1987) *European Technological Collaboration*, London: Routledge & Kegan Paul.

Taylor, Paul (1989) 'The New Dynamics of EC Integration in the 1980s', in Juliet Lodge (ed.) *The European Community and the Challenge of the Future*, London: Pinter Publishers, pp. 3–25.

Wallace, Helen, Wallace, William and Webb, Carole (eds) (1977) *Policy-Making in the European Communities*, London: John Wiley & Sons.

Wallace, William (1990) *The Transformation of Western Europe*, London: Royal Institute of International Affairs.

3 Actor-based models of national and EU policy making

Jeremy Richardson

MULTIPLE POLICY STAKEHOLDERS IN THE EXERCISE OF 'LOOSE-JOINTED' POWER

One of the main attributes of the nation state is the ability to make 'authoritative allocations' for society in the Eastonian fashion. In practice this means an ability to formulate and implement public policy programmes governing the operation of society. Whether the European Union (EU) can be considered a fully fledged state is not the concern of this chapter. However, it is beyond dispute that the EU has acquired for itself at least the policy-making attributes of a modern state, across an increasingly wide range of policy sectors. Indeed, much of the criticism of the EC during the Maastricht debates was centred upon the alleged excessive policy making role of the EC in general and of the Commission in particular. The anti-Maastricht argument was that the EC had become a 'nanny' state, over-regulating the economic and social life of member states. In practice, the erosion of national autonomy means the erosion of the power of the member states to decide much of their public policy via domestic policy-making processes.

The debate about competing theories of European integration and European policy making is, in fact, centrally concerned with the focus of this volume – state autonomy. All the theories outlined in this chapter and in Chapter 2 by Stephen George address the nature of the European (and sometimes global) policy process and the role of the traditional nation state within that process. The intellectual challenge is to identify or formulate a theory (or more likely a range of theories) which can help explain the complex and varying balance between the nation state as an autonomous policy-making system, and the nation state as a totally interdependent participant in transnational policy processes. The central argument here is that the EU has developed as a policy-making system and that this has implications for the autonomy of the nation state. Empirically, it is beyond dispute that the EU level is now the level at which a high proportion (possibly 60 per cent) of what used to be regarded as purely domestic policy making takes place. The locus of decision, and therefore possibly of power, has shifted. A much more complex structure of policy making has developed, encompassing a wider range of actors. All these actors, especially national governments, are having to adjust to the reality of this situation. In a very real sense, therefore, they have all 'lost' some power in a common pooling of sovereignty. For those European nations who are members of the EU, and for many who are not, at least two policy-making systems now co-exist: the domestic political system and the EU (Richardson 1996).

Though state-like in at least this key attribute, the EU is, of course, a complex and unique policy-making system. Its multinational, neo-federal nature, the extreme openness of decision making to lobbyists and the considerable weight of national politico-administrative elites within the process, create an unstable and multi-dimensional policy-making environment. Even the relationships between key institutions – the Commission, the European Parliament (EP), the Council of Ministers (CM) and the European Court of Justice (ECJ) – are still in a considerable state of flux. Indeed, no one quite understands how the new post-Maastricht decision rules will operate and there will be much jockeying for policy space between the different institutions. We know that the EP will further increase its influence (Judge and Earnshaw 1995) and that the extended use of qualified majority voting (QMV) will further erode the powers of the individual nation states. At best the EU policy process might exhibit some stable patterns of cross-national coalition building; at worst it may exhibit some of the extreme aspects of a garbage can model of decision making. At this relatively early stage in the development of the EU policy process it is difficult to formulate reliable descriptions, let alone theoretical models, which will capture more than a few aspects of the policy process as a whole. The objective of this chapter is, therefore, limited. It is to analyse the possible utility of the policy community/policy network model (originally developed to analyse national policy making) at the level of the EU.

Fortuitously, approaching EU policy making via this perspective also enables us to utilise a related approach which is regarded as increasingly important by international relations scholars interested in the EU; namely, the concept of epistemic communities. It will be argued that there are inherent similarities in these two actor-based approaches, even though they originate from quite different academic perspectives. Essentially, they both focus on sets of actors as *stakeholders* in the policy process. The advantage of combining these two approaches is that they also enable us to focus on a phenomenon now recognised as central to any understanding of the policy process; the role of knowledge and ideas in bringing about policy change at both the national and international levels. Over thirty years ago, E. E. Schattschneider reminded us that the supreme instrument of political power was the ability to determine what politics was about (Schattschneider 1960). The epistemic communities concept is especially useful as it enables us to focus on the agenda-setting stage in the EU. Although this is a neglected aspect of the workings of the EU (Peters 1994), evidence does suggest that the EU agenda-setting process is especially problematic because of its transnational nature and because of the wide range of state and non-state actors involved in the EU policy process (Mazey and Richardson 1993). Moreover, as with nation states, the EU's policy agenda is susceptible to extra-territorial influences, from non-EU states such as the USA and Japan, but also from international standard setting bodies and organisations such as the World Health Organisation (WHO). As epistemic communities are usually *transnational*, focusing on their nature and role should prove especially fruitful in shedding more light on this key aspect of political power. The policy community/policy network approach, in contrast, appears to have some utility in assisting our understanding of the ways in which agenda issues are translated or 'processed' into technical and workable EU legislative proposals, especially in areas of 'low politics'. Other related concepts from public policy, such as Sabatier's 'advocacy coalitions' and Kingdon's 'policy streams', may also prove useful in assisting our understanding of the policy dynamics of the EU.

The 'level of analysis' question is, of course, important. Thus it may be mistaken to look for *one* model of the EU policy process. Within the EU, policy can be determined at a number of levels and, as at the national level, the policy process goes through a number of stages. Different models of analysis may be useful at different levels within the EU and at different stages of the policy process. For example, if we were to conceptualise the EU policy process into four stages – agenda setting, policy formulation, policy decision and policy implementation – we might need to utilise rather different conceptual tools in order to understand fully the nature of the processes in each stage. For example, the epistemic communities approach might be particularly useful in understanding stage 1, the policy community/network model for stage 2, institutional analysis for stage 3, and inter-organisational/behaviour implementation analysis for stage 4. Even then, reality is likely to be much more messy, suggesting that a fairly eclectic use of concepts and models is necessary. 'Grand theory' must await a much stronger empirical base!

In searching for useful theories and concepts, the notion of the EU as a policy-making state is important. As Hix has argued, traditional international relations approaches to analysing the EU have tended to focus on the question of degrees of integration. As he suggests, 'since its birth in the 1950s . . . the EC has mainly been studied as an example of supranational integration of, or intergovernmental co-operation between, (previously) sovereign nation-states' (Hix 1994: 1). His main contention is that now that the EU is more than an 'international organisation', theories of international politics are of limited use for studying the internal politics of the Community. The solution he proposes – the use of comparative politics approaches – is not inconsistent with the thrust of this chapter, except that the emphasis here is more on the use of concepts used in the analysis of public policy and decision making. Our central argument here is that the 'stuff' of European integration is as much about detailed, often technical, Euro-legislation, and especially Euro-regulation, as it is about high politics issues such as monetary union or the creation of a European super-state. While these issues are, of course, absolutely crucial, and certainly absorb the interest of national governments, the 'European game' continues to be played at the policy level and to attract the attention and efforts of a plethora of interest groups in the manner predicted by the neofunctionalists. 'Low politics' this may be, to use Hoffmann's well-known phrase (Hoffmann 1966), but it is probably the nine-tenths of the 'policy iceberg' that is below the water line. There is an increasing amount of political activity at this level within the EU and some means has to be found of analysing it. Moreover, this policy-making activity is not simply a question of intergovernmental relations, if only because such a wide range of non-governmental actors is so obviously involved at the national and EU levels, and beyond. EU policies are not simply the outcome of inter-state bargaining, but of a complex process involving different types of actors, institutional and non-institutional, governmental and non-governmental.

Thus, as Stephen George's chapter suggests, a purely intergovernmentalist approach to even a 'high politics' issue such as the passage of the Single European Act (SEA) is very misleading. National governments were fully aware of the interests of those industries and firms likely to benefit from greater national integration and were subject to all the pressures for change that those interests who benefit from greater globalisation mobilise. Stephen George's critique of pure intergovernmental and realist approaches is entirely consistent with the line of argument pursued in this chapter, namely that a complex array of actors and institutions is involved. Moreover, the concern here is also to point out the role of ideas in the policy making process. For example, the SEA project can be seen as part of a more general shift in intellectual fashion which affected policy makers at all levels: local, regional, national, supranational. In a sense, they were all 'victims' of a fashion created by a category of actor usually neglected in studies of policy making – those 'experts' who shape the way in which problems are recognised and defined. The rapid internationalisation of agenda-setting, and the internationalisation of policy solutions, has been an enormously powerful dynamic which has shown no more respect for nation states than it has for other policy actors. If power is shared between such a range of actors, it seems sensible to explore the utility of the approach currently dominant in western Europe for analysing the policy process, the so-called 'network' model.

POLICY COMMUNITIES AND POLICY NETWORKS: THE ORIGINS AND LIMITATIONS OF THE CONCEPT

It is worth remembering that the term 'policy community' was originally used, at least in Britain, with a quite deliberate emphasis on *community,* at a time when policy stability rather than policy change seemed more common. Moreover, it was developed as a counterweight to more traditional analyses of the British policy process. For example, the subtitle of *Governing Under*

Pressure, first published in 1979, was provocative in claiming that Britain was a *post-parliamentary* democracy. The focus of the analysis was on the informal relationships between policy actors rather than on the roles of formal institutions. The concept was in part developed to conteract the then dominance of institutionalism and to take account of the growing body of empirical research on the day-to-day processes of policy making. Thus:

> In describing the tendency for boundaries between government and groups to become less distinct through a whole range of pragmatic developments, we see policies being made (and administered) between a myriad of interconnecting, interpenetrating organisations. It is the relationship involved in committees, the policy community of departments and groups, the practices of co-option and the consensual style, that perhaps better account for policy outcomes than do examinations of party stances, of manifestos or of parliamentary influence.
>
> (Richardson and Jordan 1979: 73–4)

The term 'policy community' was meant to convey a very close and stable relationship between policy actors. This is quite close to the dictionary definition of 'community', as meaning 'joint ownership of goods, identity of character, fellowship [. . . or interest]'. This formulation was in fact prompted by Heclo and Wildavsky's study of the spending community in Whitehall, which they likened to village life (Heclo and Wildavsky 1974). Use of the word community also implied some notions regarding *level of analysis*. If policy actors could be brought together in a long-term and stable relationship which presented the prospect of an *exchange relationship,* then this was most likely at the sub-sectoral or even micro level. There was also an implication of stable policies as well as stable relationships and a stable membership. Thus it was argued that:

> The logic of negotiation also suggests that policy-makers in both government and groups will share an interest in the avoidance of sudden policy change. Working together they will learn what kind of change is feasible and what would so embarrass other members of the 'system' as to be unproductive. Members of the system will begin to debate in the same language (if not with the same values), and arguments will be treated seriously only if discussed in these common criteria. There is a role diffusion in that all members – government officials, academic experts and group officials – become policy professionals.
>
> (Jordan and Richardson 1982: 93–4).

In practical terms, this sectorisation, and indeed *secularisation,* of policy making was seen as being operationalised at a middle management level in policy formulation, 'at the level of detail covered by a civil service assistant or under-secretary – rather than at departmental level' (Jordan and Richardson 1982: 88). Thus, there was a considerable note of caution in these early formulations of the concept. *The implication was that the concept had its greatest utility when analysing a particular level of decision* – almost exactly the thrust of the argument in this chapter.

Jordan has more recently further emphasised both the *stability* of policy communities and the existence of *shared views*. Thus he sees policy communities as:

A special type of *stable* network, which has advantages in encouraging bargaining in policy resolution. In this language the policy network is a statement of shared interests in a policy problem: a policy community exists where there are effective shared 'community' views on the problem. *Where there are no such shared views no community exists.*

(Jordan 1990: 327, original emphasis)

The explicit assumption of stability of relations and stability of actor participation, verging on exclusiveness, is also evident in more recent attempts to refine the policy community concept. Thus, as Judge points out, Rhodes repeatedly states (Rhodes 1985: 15, 1988: 78, 1990: 204, Rhodes and Marsh 1992a: 182, 1992b:13) that:

policy communities are networks characterised by stability of relationships, continuity of a highly restrictive membership, vertical interdependence based upon shared delivery responsibilities and insulation from other networks and invariably from the general public (including Parliament).

(Cited in Judge 1993: 122)

The difficulty of using policy community in this apparently more refined, but quite restrictive sense, is that it appears to reject the notion that new 'members' might be admitted and absorbed relatively easily. Moreover, the Jordan formulation places emphasis on a shared *community of views,* suggesting that policy communities do not exhibit very much conflict. However, in many cases (rather like families!) the community holds together, in the sense of *exchange relationships*, despite quite serious disputes and in spite of the fact that new members may be admitted. If 'policy community' is to be used in the very restrictive way that both Jordan and Marsh and Rhodes appear to be using it, it is unlikely to be of much utility as a concept in analysing EU policy making, if only because the differences between national systems in, for instance, banking, air transport, pollution control, are often so wide as to preclude a shared '*community of views*' (Jordan 1990: 122) between the wide range of actors claiming stakeholder status. Moreover, even at the national level, it might be argued that the emphasis on stability and consensus is one of the causes of the intellectual fatigue which the concept now exhibits. Politics in the 1980s and 1990s has been very different to the politics of the 1960s and 1970s, not least because of radical policy change and the steady extension of the Europeanisation of the policy process.

There is also a danger that these definitions significantly underestimate the linkages between different policy communities, which is now a very common feature of the policy process at the national and especially at the EU level.

Indeed, Jordan and Richardson had themselves begun, as early as 1982, to emphasise the *linkages* between policy communities, both within and between policy sectors. They argued that

> 'there will be many linkages between various policy communities in each sector (for example, between branches of medicine, social services and social policy) . . . but there will also be some linkages between sectors . . . what evidence we have suggests that consultation of various types is more extensive than formerly.
>
> (Jordan and Richardson 1982: 89–90)

The gradual shift in emphasis from a world of policy making characterised by tightly knit policy communities to a more loosely organised and therefore less predictable policy process was also reflected, somewhat earlier, in the USA. The seminal work on either side of the Atlantic is still Heclo's analysis, which began to redirect us towards policy *dynamics* rather than policy stability (Heclo 1978). Just as many authors were identifying *stable* policy communities, Heclo observed a trend which appears to be still running strongly at both the national and international levels, namely that policy decisions often escaped the confined and exclusive 'worlds' of professionals and are resolved in a much looser configuration, if indeed such a structured term can be used, of participants in the policy process. Heclo argued that the nature of power in Washington had begun to change; that exercising power was not as much fun as it had been in the 'clubby' days of Washington politics (Heclo 1978: 94). Politics was less 'clubbable' because more and more groups had entered the policy process. Thus 'as proliferating groups have claimed a stake and clamoured for a place in the policy process, they have helped diffuse the focus of political and administrative leadership' (Heclo 1978: 94–5). This image was quite different to the USA version of 'policy community'. For example, Jordan *et al.* noted that Jack Walker first used the term in the USA in 1974 (Jordan *et al.* 1993: 2). Indeed, Campbell is quoted as suggesting that the concept is one which 'so far has mainly been developed in the rather exceptional context of American politics' (Campbell 1989, cited in Jordan *et al.* 1993: 2). Campbell's formulation is heavily directed towards the recognition of the role of *professionals* in the policy process and the considerable power that they wield (Campbell 1989: 5). Heclo's formulation suggested a much less structured policy process. The process had gone so far, he argued, that:

> With more public policies, more groups are being mobilized and there are more complex relationships among them. Since very few policies ever seem to drop off the public agenda as more are added, congestion among those interested in various issues grows, the chances for accidental collisions increase, and the interaction tends to take on a distinctive group-life of its own in the Washington community. One scene in a recent Jacques Tati film pictures a Paris traffic circle so dense with traffic that no one can get in or

out; instead, drivers spend their time socializing with each other as they drive in endless circles. Group politics in Washington may be becoming such a merry-go-round.

(Heclo 1978: 97)

In the context of the EU, all we need do is to substitute for Washington the traffic circle in front of the Berlaymont building, or the professional and social networks in Kitty O'Shea's bar just off it. Heclo argued quite rightly that existing notions of political power had to be reconsidered, since they were not well suited to the 'loose-jointed' power play of influence that was emerging. In a now classic formulation, he argued that:

Obviously questions of power are still important. But for a host of policy initiatives undertaken in the last twenty years it is all but impossible to identify clearly who the dominant actors are. Who is controlling those actions that go to make up our national policy on abortions, or on income redistribution, or consumer protection, or energy? Looking for the few who are powerful, we tend to overlook the many whose webs of influence provoke and guide the exercise of power. These webs, or what I will call 'issue networks', are particularly relevant to the highly intricate and confusing welfare policies that have been undertaken in recent years.

(Heclo 1978: 102)

Again one is reminded of the EU policy process, where interest groups and national governments often feel that policies come from 'nowhere' (Mazey and Richardson 1993). Even Heclo was reluctant to accept a total disorder thesis, however. He made at least two important qualifications to the new model of confusion, of diffuse power, and of lack of accountability. He pointed out a paradox of disorder *and* order when he argued that there was a second tendency, cutting in the opposite direction to the widening group participation in public policy. In the midst of the emergence of the loose issue networks cited above we could also see what he called 'policy as intramural activity'. Thus:

Expanding welfare policies and Washington's reliance on indirect administration have encouraged the development of specialized subcultures composed of highly knowledgeable policy-watchers. Some of these people have advanced professional degrees, some do not. What they all have in common is the detailed understanding of specialized issues that comes from sustained attention to a given policy debate.

(Heclo 1978: 49)

In a passage that is quoted less often, he deftly links the two apparently contradictory trends as follows:

Whatever the participants' motivation, it is the issue network that ties together what would otherwise be the contradictory tendencies of, on the one hand, more widespread organizational participation in public policy and, on the other, more narrow technocratic specialization in complex modern policies. Such networks need to be distinguished from three other more familiar terms used in connection with political administration. An issue network is a shared-knowledge group having to do with some aspect (or, as defined by the network, some problem) of public policy. It is therefore more well-defined than, first, a shared-attention group or 'public', those in the networks are likely to have a common base of information and understanding of how one knows about policy and identifies its problems. But knowledge does not necessarily produce agreement. Issue networks may or may not, therefore, be mobilized into, second, a shared-action group (creating a coalition) or, third, a shared-belief group (becoming a conventional interest organization). Increasingly, it is through networks of people who regard each other as knowledgeable, or at least as needing to be answered, that public policy issues tend to be refined, evidence debated, and alternative options worked out – though rarely in any controlled, well-organized way.

(Heclo 1978: 103–4)

So, how can sense be made of these contrasting images of the policy process? On the one hand we have the policy community concept as originally formulated by Richardson and Jordan in Britain and by Walker in the USA, and more recently refined by Jordan, and by Marsh and Rhodes. On the other hand there is the rather 'disorderly' issue network concept formulated by Heclo. The suggestion by Rhodes and Marsh that policy communities and issue networks are part of a continuum, and that policy networks should be used as a *generic* term, is a sensible reminder that there is not *one* model of policy making. They draw on Benson's 1982 definition of a network as 'a cluster or complex of organisations connected to each other by resource dependencies and distinguished from other clusters or complexes by breaks in the structure of resource dependencies' (Benson 1982:148). However, they go on to distinguish five types of networks 'ranging along a continuum from highly integrated policy communities to loosely integrated issue networks' (Marsh and Rhodes 1992: 13).

Recognising the network concept as a continuum does enable us to focus on the possibility of *changes* in the nature of the policy process. Thus it may be that at any given time *several* types of policy networks are in operation. If so, we need to analyse the interrelationships, if any, between these and the conditions under which they emerge. Also, over time, the policy process might change its characteristics quite significantly along the continuum. And, of course, it may often be unhelpful to use the network analogy at all, the danger being that it may always be possible to find some kind of 'network' if one looks carefully enough.

Critics of the approach have rightly argued that to claim, or indeed to demonstrate, that networks exist may not mean very much by way of *explan-*

ation. For example, Dowding, though sometimes attacking a straw man which he has created in order to make his point, argues that

> the policy community literature is an interesting way of organising pluralist thought but it cannot be expected to give *explanations* of policy outcomes. Rather it is a descriptive theory which leads us to ask the questions pertinent to policy outcomes. Describing some policy communities as 'open' and others as 'closed' tells us about the nature of the network of group and state actors; but this description does not explain why these different sorts of policy community exist.
>
> (Dowding 1991: 123)

As he notes, a theory of power is needed. (Unfortunately, his solution, the rational choice model, is equally limited, since it does not explain how preferences are formed, particularly in situations of high uncertainty.)

Judge, too, has observed that the concept of policy community was derived 'from relatively simple origins, where the notion of "community" was descriptive rather than definitional, and where it was used to contrast established models of parliamentary government with a new reality' (Judge 1993: 121). He has rightly identified the original purpose of the formulation of the concept as both an 'antidote' to existing models and an attempt to achieve in Britain what Stein Rokkan had achieved in Norway, that is to point out that there were many different *arenas* of politics (Rokkan 1966). From these humble beginnings, the concept has taken on a life of its own and has, without doubt, been taken much too far as a 'model' for the analysis of the policy process. There is no need to repeat this mistake at the European level. As Judge's wry comment suggests, British academics have created as much heat as illumination in their attempts to build upon and reform a simple idea. He points out that 'the distinction between "policy communities" and the associated terms of "policy networks", "issue networks" and "policy universe" have led to an overly desiccated academic exchange between commentators (see, for example, Atkinson and Coleman 1989, Jordan 1990, Marsh and Rhodes 1992 cited in Judge 1993: 12,1, Wilks and Wright 1987)'. Perhaps the greatest difficulty with the concept is that it may always be possible to find *some* type of policy network as it is difficult to imagine a policy process which at some stage did not involve some kind of network of actors who need to be involved before anything can happen. Thus care is needed, even at the national level, in seeing policy communities or generic policy networks as *the* model of analysis.

Describing certain stages of the policy process in network terms can be useful and illuminating, but as Judge argues in the case of Parliament in the UK, we must not neglect the role of *institutions*. For example, in the EU, the role of the Council of Ministers is obviously crucial, yet it is difficult to see network analysis as being central to an analysis of the Council. No doubt ministers will to some degree reflect the power of national networks in the manner suggested by Putman (Putman 1988), but clearly, they do not follow their national interest group systems slavishly. Similarly, the Commission, as an institutional actor in its own right, is enormously powerful in the EU policy process. Again it can be seen as a broker of interests, or a *bourse* of ideas and interests (Mazey and Richardson 1994), but it is much more than that and has its own institutional interests to protect and expand (Edwards and Spence 1994). Moreover, the role of ideas, of ideology, or the special powers of state actors in setting the agenda for policy change at both the national and international levels must not be neglected. For example, British politics post-1979 cannot be explained simply in terms of policy networks and certainly not in terms of policy communities. Quite clearly, the power of policy communities to either prevent or control policy change was subject to severe and often successful challenges from governments and from other exogenous forces (Richardson 1993). In many instances policy networks were responding to rather than creating policy change.

What then *is* the utility of the policy network approach and what is its potential for EU level analysis? Two *modest* but sensible claims might be made. First, by trying to identify networks of policy actors we at least focus on what might be called the *stakeholders* in the EU policy processes. If EU politics is about who gets what, how and when, then identifying the networks of actors involved and trying to describe those networks is at least the starting point for understanding how the system of making EU policies works. Sensible research questions are: who has an *interest* in this policy problem? How are they mobilised and organised? What is the timing and nature of their involvement in the policy process? We also need to ask who is likely to gain and who is likely to lose from different policy outcomes. In addressing these questions within the EU, we need to be cautious in transposing some of the alleged characteristics of various types of policy network in Britain. For example, many groups involved in the EU policy process have little or no formal involvement in policy delivery, nor are they necessarily involved in any direct resource dependencies except in a most general sense. Similarly, they may have quite different value systems and often exhibit very contrasting and conflicting views of the policy problem and of possible solutions. The basis of the relationship between these different actors is twofold: first, recognition of each other as legitimate stakeholders in the policy area/problem; and second, appreciation that collaboration may be the best means of extending the pareto boundary to mutual advantage. In other words, co-operation within various types of policy network is sensible for pareto maximisers. There are mutual gains to be had. This is rather different from direct resource *dependency* or a shared direct involvement in *service delivery*, or from *shared values. Focusing on networks of stakeholders may therefore help us to analyse the detailed process by which policy ideas* are translated into specific policy proposals via the involvement of the wide variety and large number of stakeholders which can be identified.

Here, the *institutional* context of the EU is crucial. Thus the Commission is both an adolescent and a promiscuous bureaucracy (Mazey and Richardson 1995). At the stage of translating ideas into detailed and workable public policies in fifteen member states, the resource dependencies identified by Marsh and Rhodes at the national level may begin to emerge. At the detailed and technical stage, Commission officials in particular need the expertise of other policy actors. If the devil is in the detail, then policy networks, and indeed policy communities, may come into their own as concepts for advancing our understanding of the EU as a policy making state.

POLICY MAKING UNDER UNCERTAINTY: KNOWLEDGE AND MUTUAL GAINS

If one were to take an uncharitable perspective, work on policy networks, and especially on policy communities, may look like the 'politics of the piddling', that is the *processing* of issues at the lowest level. Again, the British case post-1979 is illustrative. The Thatcherite revolution was not so much about *excluding* pressure groups in an attempt to govern without consensus; it was more about determining the new agenda for each policy sector and *then* consulting the affected interests about how best to implement the new policies for health, education, the legal profession, etc. (Richardson 1994). The new policy style was to introduce radical new ideas into the system, such as market principles into the NHS, causing disturbance and conflict, after which negotiation could take place. The benefit, to the government, was that it could create a new kind of 'consensus' once the interest groups had come to realise that policy change would be imposed if necessary. Most of the radical policy change which took place did not emanate from policy communities or policy networks – they reacted to it. Policy making within the EU may bear some similarities to this policy style. The EU is faced with fifteen different policy systems, each reflecting national power structures (and national policy networks) and national compromises in determining the 'national interest'. If European integration is to take place, these national policy arrangements must be challenged in some way and new policy settlements agreed. Aspects of an impositional policy style (Richardson 1982) can be seen, ultimately, in the way European Court of Justice decisions affect the nation states, in the pressure for more effective national implementation of EU laws, and of course, in the increased use of qualified majority voting within the Council of Ministers post-Maastricht. In the end, both national policy making styles and national policy frameworks are challenged by EU legislation. It is not surprising therefore that the range of potential actors in this process is enormous and the patterns of interaction are sometimes unpredictable.

How, then, does policy change take place within the EU in the absence of a government and of a stable governing coalition? In a key passage, Adler and Haas argue that it is useful to turn the study of the political process into a question about *who learns what, when, to whose benefit and why?* (Adler and Haas 1992: 370). Perceiving the policy process as centrally concerned with knowledge and its use is both helpful and consistent with our concern with actor-based models of the policy process (Radaelli 1995). Moreover, the work of Peter Haas and his colleagues is of special relevance to the workings of the EU. Although concerned with international co-operation, and therefore approaching the EU from an international relations perspective, Haas' comment that 'a related question/debate is the extent to which state actors fully recognise and appreciate the anarchic nature of the system and, consequently, *whether rational choice, deductive-type approaches or interpretative approaches are most appropriate*' (Haas 1992: 1–2 emphasis added) is most relevant in thinking about EU processes. Virtually all interest group respondents, and most national officials, for example, who were interviewed in our study of the role of interest groups in the EU policy process, emphasised the fluidity and unpredictability of the process (Mazey and Richardson 1993). Adopting the rational actor model was difficult for them in situations of high uncertainty and in the absence of crucial information about the policy positions and behaviour of other key actors. Indeed, they may be totally unaware of other key actors in the process, let alone of their policy preferences and strategies. In such situations, the team network should be used with great caution. Literally, 'network' should mean that the various actors do interconnect in some way. Empirically, this is sometimes difficult to determine and policy actors are often puzzled as to the identity of other actors elsewhere in the 'system'. Again, this is as true for national governments as for, say, firms or associations. The total 'system' is large and amorphous, with many part-time participants and a range of ideas floating around in some etherial fashion. In these situations, the policy process may resemble the Cohen, Marsh and Olsen garbage-can model, in which problems are chasing solutions and solutions are chasing problems (cited in Mazey and Richardson 1993).

The Haas argument is, centrally, that the politics of uncertainty leads to a certain mode of behaviour, namely that policy makers, when faced with 'the uncertainties associated with many modern responsibilities of international governance [will] turn to new and different channels of advice, often with the result that international co-ordination is advanced' (Haas 1992: 12). As he argues, the concept of uncertainty is important for two reasons:

> First, in the face of uncertainty . . . many of the conditions facilitating a focus on power are absent. It is difficult for leaders to identify their potential political allies and to be sure of what strategies are most likely to help them retain favour. And, second, poorly understood conditions may create enough turbulence that established operating procedures may break down, making institutions unworkable. Neither power nor institutional cues to behaviour would be available, and new patterns of action may ensue.
>
> (Haas 1992:14)

Thus, one important characteristic of the EU policy process is that a given policy issue can meander in a rather circuitous way, hence the lobbying advice that the game is not over until the final whistle. Decisions that appear to be agreed are subsequently unstitched as new actors catch up with events and persuade Euro policy makers to change direction. In that sense, the Euro 'policy game' is more like ice hockey than football!

However, as Sebenius points out, uncertainty and power go hand in hand. Uncertainty presents opportunities for power to be exercised if individuals or institutions are sufficiently alert to the opportunities. He argues that it is important to emphasise the interplay of power and knowledge in influencing outcomes (Sebenius 1992: 325). Alongside uncertainty in the policy process there are opportunities for mutual learning and joint problem solving, especially when technical uncertainties are involved as, for example, in scientific, environmental, economic and security matters. By combining the politics of uncertainty and the politics of learning, Sebenius in fact captures the core meaning of 'policy community' as a concept. Thus he states that 'beyond understanding technical uncertainties, finding joint gains also requires that each party learn about the other's priorities in order to craft mutually beneficial trades' (Sebenius 1992: 329). Co-operation, therefore, can produce what Walton and McKersie term 'integrated bargaining' as opposed to 'distributive bargaining'. In the former, the effort is directed towards expanding the pie, whereas in the latter it is a more adversarial process of dividing the pie (Walton and McKersie 1965). Sebenius goes on to quote Howard Raiffa as follows:

> In complicated negotiations where uncertainties loom large, there may be contracts that are far better for each negotiating party than the non-contract alternative, but it may take considerable skill and joint problem solving to discover these possibilities. *Without the right atmosphere and without some reasonably trustful communication of values, such jointly acceptable contracts might never be discerned.*
>
> (Raiffa quoted in Sebenius 1992: 329, emphasis added by this author)

This is not too dissimilar to our original formulation of the policy communities concept suggested in *Governing Under Pressure*. This emphasised the development of a common understanding of each other's problems and a recognition that mutually beneficial bargains could be struck over time. Logically, this does not imply consensus on values or on outcomes, but it does imply a consensus that collaboration will produce efficiency gains all round. There may be considerable and bitter disputation, but the game continues to be played in order to secure mutual gains or to avoid individual losses. Lax and Sebenius have emphasised that the bargaining process indeed exhibits both conflict and consensus. Thus:

> the competitive and co-operative elements are inextricably entwined. In practice they cannot be separated. This bonding is fundamentally important to the analysis, structuring and conduct of negotiation. There is a central, inescapable tension between co-operative moves to create value jointly and competitive moves to gain individual advantage. This tension

affects virtually all tactical and strategic choice. Analysts must come to grips with it; negotiators must manage it.

(Lax and Sebinius 1986: 30).

Participating in joint policy-making activity therefore has the potential to maximise benefits to the parties involved. Using concepts from negotiation analysis, Sebenius points out that outcomes can be influenced by favourably affecting the zone of possible agreement between the parties. The 'zone of possible agreement' means 'a set of possible agreements that are better for each potential party than the non-cooperative-operative alternatives to an agreement' (Sebenius 1992: 333).

The value of these approaches is that it reminds us that policy actors are often operating under considerable degrees of uncertainty and are prepared to engage in a negotiative process even when there is considerable disagreement. The key role of epistemic communities in this process relates directly to the principle that policy makers are operating under conditions of uncertainty. Thus:

> Given the technical uncertainties regarding an issue and the legitimacy of claims to expertise of members of an epistemic community, especially those placed close to the decision-making process, their influence may cause the perceived interests of key players in different countries to grow closer together, along with their understanding of underlying causal relationships. In this situation, the epistemic community members may come to act as a coordinated set of common interpretative filters.

(Sebenius 1992: 354)

It is the knowledge-based, or at least apparently knowledge-based, nature of epistemic communities that provides these networks of actors with the potential to influence the policy process. Authoritativeness, and therefore legitimacy, are the key currencies of these types of networks and these are central to the definition of epistemic communities formulated by Peter Haas:

> An epistemic community is a network of professionals with recognised expertise and competence in a particular domain and an authoritative claim to policy-relevant knowledge within that domain or issue-area. Although an epistemic community may consist of professionals from a variety of disciplines and backgrounds, they have (1) a shared set of normative and principled beliefs, which provide a value-based rationale for the social action of community members; (2) shared causal beliefs, which are derived from their analysis of practices leading or contributing to a central set of problems in their domain and which then serve as the basis for elucidating the multiple linkages between possible policy actions and desired outcomes; (3) shared notions of validity – that is, intersubjective, internally defined criteria for weighing and validating knowledge in the domain of their expertise; and (4) a common policy enterprise – that is, a set of common practices associated with a set of problems to which their profes-

sional competence is directed, presumably out of the conviction that human welfare will be enhanced as a consequence.

(Haas 1992: 3)

As with the policy network, the concept of epistemic communities is also subject to refinement and redefinition. In a useful footnote, Haas reveals that other characterisations of epistemic communities were discussed during the preparation of the special issue of *International Organization* in which his seminal paper appears. Some of the additional notions used were as follows:

> members of an epistemic community share intersubjective understand-
> ings; have a shared way of knowing; have shared patterns of reasoning;
> have a policy project drawing on shared values, share causal beliefs, and
> the use of shared discursive practices; and have a shared commitment to
> the application and production of knowledge.

(Haas 1992: 3)

Interestingly, Haas sees some kind of logic in this process of policy co-ordination via epistemic communities. The situation in which policy makers find themselves leads almost naturally to the use of experts of various kinds. Just as it has been argued in Britain that there is a 'logic of negotiation' (Jordan and Richardson 1982), so do the dynamics of uncertainty, interpret-ation and institutionalisation at the international level drive policy makers towards the use of epistemic communities. Haas argues that 'in international policy co-ordination, the forms of uncertainty that tend to stimulate demands for information are those which arise from the strong dependence of states on each other's policy choices for success in obtaining goals and those which involve multiple and only partly estimable consequences of action' (Haas 1992: 3–4). Uncertainty gives rise to demands for information, particularly about social or physical processes, their interrelationship with other processes, 'and the likely consequences of actions that require consider-able scientific or technical expertise' (Haas 1992: 4).

Haas goes on to suggest that state actors are 'uncertainty reducers' as well as power and wealth pursuers. In conditions of high uncertainty, it becomes difficult for national governments to define clearly just what the national interest is. They are not only engaged on a two-level game as suggested by Putnam; rather they are involved in a multi-dimensional international game where strategies consistent with the national interest in one sector may be inconsistent with the national interest being pursued in another sector. It is not surprising that state actors look for ways of reducing uncertainty. They recognise that changing the world is going to be very difficult and may have to settle, therefore, for minimising surprises. Again, this is consistent with what we know about national policy making. Many policy makers are risk averse and one way of reducing risk to them is to share it. For example, Henderson's now classic study of a series of British policies describes risk-sharing behaviour via consultation, as follows:

making sure that, at every stage of the policy process, the right chairs have been warmed at the right committee tables by the appropriate institutions, everything possible has been done and no one could possibly be blamed if things go wrong.

(Henderson 1977: 189)

Bearing in mind just how small the EC Commission is, it would be surprising if Commission officials did not engage in similar behaviour. Indeed, our interviews suggest that they do this to the nth degree, reflecting the dual problem of relative lack of expertise and the extra complexity of trying to formulate policies which can be applied in fifteen very different member states (Mazey and Richardson 1993, 1994). Moreover, by drawing other policy actors into the policy process, the Commission may be able to build coalitions in favour of its own notions of desirable policy change. By assisting the formation of networks of 'relevant' state and non-state actors, or by 'massaging' the way that these networks operate, the Commission can maintain its position as an 'independent' policy-making institution and can increase its leverage with the Council of Ministers and the European Parliament.

In a key passage, Haas argues that epistemic communities play a key role in providing much needed information and ideas.

Epistemic communities are one possible provider of this sort of information and advice. As demands for such information arise, networks or communities of specialists capable of producing and providing the information emerge and proliferate. The members of a prevailing community become strong actors at the national and transnational level as decision makers solicit their information and delegate responsibility to them. A community's advice, though, is informed by its own broader world view. To the extent to which an epistemic community consolidates bureaucratic power within national administrations and international secretariats, it stands to institutionalise its influence and insinuate its view into broader international politics.

Members of transnational epistemic communities can influence state interests either by directly identifying them for decision makers or by illuminating the salient dimensions of an issue from which the decision makers may then deduce their interests. The decision makers in one state may, in turn, influence the interests and behaviour of other states, thereby increasing the likelihood of convergent state behavior and international policy coordination, informed by the causal beliefs and policy preferences of the epistemic community. Similarly, epistemic communities may contribute to the creation and maintenance of social institutions that guide international behaviour. As a consequence of the continued influence of these institutions, established patterns of cooperation in a given issue-area may persist even though systematic power concentrations may no longer be sufficient to compel countries to coordinate their behavior.

(Haas 1992: 4)

His suggestion that 'systemic power concentrations' can also prevent policy co-ordination is an important qualification of the epistemic communities concept. Thus no one is arguing that epistemic communities explain everything about the policy process. The advocates of the concept have been notably more cautious than current 'network' supporters in making claims for its explanatory power. Haas cites Ikenberry's analysis of post-war economic management as illustrating the limitations on the effects of the consensual views of specialists. The influence of epistemic communities is over the form of policy choices, 'the extent to which state behavior reflects the preferences of these networks remains strongly conditioned by the distribution of power internationally' (Haas 1992: 7).

We should add that not only is the power of epistemic communities constrained by the realities of the distribution of power internationally, it is also constrained by the need for policy makers, at both EU and national levels, to involve other forms of actors, particularly conventional interest groups. Not only are there rival epistemic communities, but they get caught up in conventional interest group politics. For example, telecoms is often cited as a classic example of epistemic communities at work (Cowhey 1990). The argument that much of the deregulatory trend can be traced to epistemic communities in the telecoms field looks convincing, yet national interests are directly affected, as are the interests of individual firms in the telecoms sector. Policy has to be mediated in some way via these powerful actors. It is here, perhaps, that the policy community, policy network concept comes back into its own. Thus, a Commission official may place considerable weight on the knowledge-based influence of an epistemic community, concerning the threat posed by CFCs for example, but practical action has to involve the close co-operation of the industries involved, such as refrigeration or foam manufacturers. In practice, the Commission did indeed set up various working parties to 'process' the CFC problem and it is at this stage that familiar policy networks, indeed policy *communities* in the sense defined earlier, emerged to process the CFC issue (Mazey and Richardson 1993). Similarly, environmental groups are effective at the European level in acting as a megaphone for epistemic communities, but are less effective in influencing the detailed processing of environmental issues once those issues have been 'accepted' on the political agenda.

This later 'processing' stage in the EU policy process is possibly less problematic in terms of finding useful models. It is reasonable to suggest that some combination of network, institutions and intergovernmental bargaining seems effective. It is the *emergence* of problems, issues and policy proposals which seems much more problematic in terms of available models of analysis, hence the attractiveness of the epistemic communities approach. As Kingdon suggests, the phrase 'an idea whose time has come, captures a fundamental reality about an irresistible movement that sweeps over our politics and our society pushing aside everything that might stand in its path' (Kingdon 1984: 1). He identifies a number of possible actors in the agenda-setting process, including the mobilisation of relevant publics by leaders, the diffusion of ideas in professional circles among policy elites, particularly bureaucrats, changes in party control or in intra-party ideological balances brought about by elections. The *processes* involved in agenda-setting are identified as of three kinds: problems, policies, politics (Kingdon 1984: 17). His objective is to move the analysis from the usual political science preoccupation with pressure and influence – possibly a criticism of network analysis – and instead to explore the world of ideas. Using a revised version of the Cohen, March and Olsen garbage can model, he analyses three 'process streams' flowing through the system – streams of problems, policies and politics – largely independent of each other. He likens the generation of policy proposals to a process of biological natural selection. Thus:

> many ideas are possible in principle and float around in a 'primeval soup' in which specialists try out their ideas in a variety of ways ... proposals are floated, come into contact with one another are revised and combined with one another, and floated again ... the proposals that survive to the status of serious consideration meet several criteria, including their technical feasibility, their fit with dominant values and the current national mood, their budgetary workability, and the political support or opposition they might experience. Thus the selection system narrows the set of conceivable proposals and selects from that large set a short list of proposals that is actually available for serious consideration.
>
> (Kingdon 1984: 21)

The separate streams of problems, policies and politics come together at certain critical times, he argues. Solutions are joined to problems, and both are joined to favourable political forces. The timing of this coupling is influenced by the appearance of 'policy windows'. These windows are opened either by the appearance of compelling problems or by happenings in the political stream (Kingdon 1984: 21).

For example, he cites one of his (US) respondents as saying that it is almost impossible to trace the origin of a proposal. 'This is not like a river. There is no point of origin' (Kingdon 1984: 77). Again he draws upon the garbage can model and the concept of 'organised anarchies'. These have three general properties: problematic preferences, unclear technology and fluid participation (Kingdon 1984: 89). He cites the Cohen, Marsh and Olsen core description of organised anarchies as 'a collection of choices looking for problems, issues and feelings looking for decision situations in which they might be aired, solutions looking for issues to which they might answer, and decision makers looking for work' (Cohen *et al.* cited in Kingdon 1984: 90). Although Kingdon's 'streams' differ from the Cohen *et al.* formulation, the broad characterisation of the process is very similar. It is a characterisation which is very different to that produced in the policy communities model and indeed also from the generic network model. The relationship between these two opposing models of policy making is that even the garbage can model, which does indeed seem to capture much of what we know empirically about the EU agenda-setting process, can eventually result in a more structured network of policy actors concerned with policy decisions. In this sense, there is, of course, some kind of 'resource dependency' as suggested by Rhodes. Even Kingdon is at pains to point out that the processes he describes are not entirely random. Thus, 'some degree of pattern is evident in these fundamental sources: processes within each stream, processes that structure couplings, and general constraints on the system' (Kingdon 1984: 216).

One reason why the process is not random is, of course, that policy problems and policy ideas attract coalitions of actors. Thus Sabatier argues that, within the subsystem

> actors can be aggregated into a number of advocacy coalitions composed of people from various organisations who share a set of normative and causal beliefs and who often act in concert. At any particular point in time, each coalition adopts a strategy(s) envisaging one or more institutional innovations which it feels will further its objectives.
>
> (Sabatier 1988: 133)

An advocacy coalition can include actors from a variety of positions – elected and agency officials, interest group leaders, researchers – who share a particular belief system, including, for example, a set of basic values, causal assumptions and problem perceptions, and who show a non-trivial degree of co-ordinated activity over time. Sabatier developed the model partly in response to the complexity of policy subsystems. Using the air pollution control subsystem in the USA as an example, he found a large and diverse set of actors. Normally, he argues, the number of advocacy coalitions would be quite small. In a 'quiescent sub-system', there might be only a single coalition, in others between two and four (Sabatier 1988: 140). To Sabatier, it is shared beliefs which provide the principal 'glue' of politics. Indeed, he emphasises stability of belief systems as an important characteristic of policy subsystems. Policy change within a subsystem can be understood as the product of two processes: first, the efforts of advocacy coalitions within the subsystem to translate the policy cores and the secondary aspects of their belief systems into governmental programmes; and second, *systemic* events, such as, for instance, changes in socio-economic coalitions, outputs from other subsystems, and changes in the system-wide governing coalition, which affect the resources and the constraints on the subsystem actors, so that policy change may take place when there are significant 'perturbations' external to the subsystem (Sabatier 1988: 148).

One of his hypotheses, hypothesis 7, which holds that '[p]olicy-orientated learning across belief systems is most likely when there exists a forum which is a) prestigious enough to force professionals from different coalitions to participate and b) dominated by professional norms' seems particularly relevant to more recent developments in the EU (Sabatier 1988: 156). There is some evidence that Commission officials are moving towards institutionalised structures which do just this namely they bring together groups of policy actors in a forum, be they epistemic communities, advocacy coalitions or different policy communities, such as the Environmental Forum within DG X1. As Sabatier suggests, the purpose of these structures:

> is to force debate among professionals from different belief systems in which their points of view must be aired before peers. Under such conditions, a desire for professional credibility and the norms of scientific debate will lead to a serious analysis of methodological assumptions, to the gradual elimination of the more improbable causal assertions and invalid data, and thus probably to a greater convergence of views over time concerning the nature of the problem and the consequences of various policy alternatives.
>
> (Sabatier 1988: 156)

Again, we see a suggestion that policy makers are intent on securing agreement and stability, and recognise that this process must involve the participation of the various types of 'stakeholders' in the policy area or policy subsystem. The stakeholders can be members of epistemic communities, conventional interest groups such as trade associations or environmental groups, firms, members of national administrations, and other institutional actors such as MEPs.

The very fact that EU policy making is a collective exercise involving large numbers of participants, often in intermittent and unpredictable 'relationships', is likely to re-inforce the processes by which national autonomy is being eroded. The chances of any one government or any one national system of policy actors, for example, governments and interest groups together, imposing their will on the rest is rather small. National governments know this. Therefore, two apparently contradictory trends may be expected to emerge. First, the need to construct complex transnational coalitions of actors will force all actors to become less focused on the nation state. Just as large firms have long since abandoned the notion of the nation state, so will other policy actors. They will seek to create and participate in a multi-layered system of transnational coalitions. Second, the 'politics of uncertainty' will lead national governments and national interest groups to try to co-ordinate their Euro-strategies. In that sense, Euro policy making may bring them closer together. For example, in Britain, the Department of Trade and Industry has concluded that a more effective effort is needed to co-ordinate British lobbying in Brussels. As part of this process it has proposed the setting up of 'consultative colleges' of key business interests as soon as there are signs that the Commission is developing an interest in and possible proposals on a subject (DTI 1993: 5). However, as the intergovernmentalists always point out, the national interest as defined by governments will not always coincide with the interests of national interest groups – the position of British trade unions being a classic example.

Thus, retaining unity of purpose between national governments and national interest group systems is going to be exceedingly difficult. In the end neither national governments nor national interest groups are likely to turn out to be very reliable partners in the scramble for Euro-level influence in the policy process. Thus, the DTI has recognised that QMV presents problems and has suggested that 'Ministers and officials should therefore have the confidence to be open about the difficulties they sometimes face in Brussels, and should be prepared to make use of business contacts and networks in reinforcing the UK negotiation position' (DTI 1993: 7). Ultimately, it noted, 'the requirement to reach agreement by recognising the needs and fears of others, by trading concessions and identifying common interests, is as pressing in the board room as it is in the Council of Ministers' (DTI 1993). One reason for the difficulty in maintaining stable coalitions is that membership of the EU presents policy actors with a choice of venue for the resolution of policy conflicts. As Baumgartner and Jones argue, political actors are capable of strategic action by employing a dual strategy of controlling the prevailing image of the policy problem and also seeking out the most favourable venue for the consideration of issues (Baumgartner and Jones 1991: 1046). The tendency of the EU policy process to pass through periods of stability and periods of dramatic change, in the episodic fashion suggested earlier, will also lead to instability in actor relationships. Thus, as Baumgartner and Jones suggest, changes in institutional structures – as noted above, a feature of the EU – can also often lead to dramatic and long-lasting changes in policy outcomes (Baumgartner and Jones 1993: 12).

CONCLUSION: A GARBAGE CAN FOR ANALYSING GARBAGE CANS?

Fundamentally, all these models and concepts, whether directed at the emergence of policy problems, policy ideas or the processing of these into workable policies and programmes, are concerned with the policy process as a collective enterprise. Policy making and policy implementation are *collective* activities, and models which help characterise the process of problem solving in a collective setting are required.

Earlier, we suggested caution in adopting any *one* model for analysing the EU policy process. Clearly there is an ongoing and very 'productive' policy process with now an enormous amount of EU public 'policy'. Equally clearly, there is a vast range of actors, institutions, problems and ideas from which EU policy finally emerges. It often seems like Kingdon's 'primeval soup' or the Cohen *et al.* 'garbage can'. Certainly, identifying the broad characteristics of this process is proving difficult. In part, this is due to the disaggregated nature of much EU policy making. The common problems of secularisation and segmentation, and hence of policy co-ordination, are writ larger in the EU. Thus, EU policy making is often sectoral or sub-sectoral policy making. Partly this is due to the fact that the process is changing; the politics of the EU seems constantly to be about modifying and revising the decision rules of the system. And in part it is because analysing the EU is being approached from two rather different academic perspectives: models of national policy making on the one hand and models of international policy making on the other. The thrust of this chapter has been to suggest that progress can best be made if attention is paid to the behaviour of policy actors, as well as to institutions and institutional relationships, so that the search for a better understanding of the EU as a policy system or series of policy subsystems can begin.

If the focus is on actors as 'stakeholders' in the governance of the EU, it becomes possible to survey a range of actor types and a range of relationships. Different types of actors and different types of relationship may emerge at different times. In this sense the policy process may be episodic, and it may take place in several arenas at any one time. Thus, analysing the behaviour of each actor might need to recognise that actors may be involved in a series of 'nested games' (Tsebelis 1990). This might explain the fact that actors may settle for sub-optimal choices. Actors are involved in a whole series of games. Hence, Tsebelis argues that it is vital for observers to take into account contextual factors (i.e. the situation in other arenas, as these may lead actors to choose different strategies (Tsebelis 1990: 9)). The multiplicity of games in which national governments are involved inevitably affects their autonomy as policy actors. Moreover, the relationship between the EU and its member states is directly affected by the extremely complex nature of the EU policy process itself, hence the advocacy of multiple models. Clearly, intergovernmentalism is important. Nation states still exist, national governments try to act in either the national interest or in their own interests, and these governments are accorded a strong institutional presence via the Council of Ministers. Yet two phenomena, largely the focus of this chapter, place significant limits on intergovernmentalism as a model of analysis. First, there is the proliferation of various types of policy network, more usually the loose, dynamic networks suggested by Heclo than the policy community model suggested in Britain by Richardson and Jordan. Put simply, the traditional 'clients' of national governments have become transnationally promiscuous in their relationships. Second, the 'politics of expertise' has become especially important in situations where there are loose networks and a high level of uncertainty. This weakens national sovereignty because of the increasingly cross-national nature of expertise and the ability of other EU policy actors, particularly the Commission, to choose which body of expertise to mobilise at any one time. For these reasons, the concept of epistemic communities seems especially useful at the EU level.

The complexity of the EU policy process means that we must learn to live with multiple models and to utilise concepts from a range of models in order to at least describe the policy process accurately. In the event, the EU policy process may be closer to a garbage can model than to any 'rational' policy process. Similarly, attempts to conceptualise the process may need to be somewhat like the garbage can in these early years, before it is possible to explain the 'why' as well as the 'how'. The conclusion is that so far the traditional 'policy network' concept does provide some help in understanding both the nature of the EU policy process and the relationship between the EU and member states. However, as at the national level, it has some major limitations. Thus more sophisticated approaches which combine a number of features are likely to be more useful. Of particular note are the concepts of epistemic communities and advocacy coalitions. They appear to facilitate our understanding of a policy process which has to balance national and transnational interests and which no one set of players can dominate.

REFERENCES

Adler, Emanuel and Haas, Peter (1992) 'Conclusion: Epistemic Communities, World Order and the Creation of a Reflective Research Program', *International Organisation*, 46, 1, 367–90.

Atkinson, M. and Coleman, W. (1989), 'Strong States and Weak States: Sectoral Policy Networks in Advanced Capitalist Economies', *British Journal of Political Science*, 19, 1, 47–67.

Baumgartner, F. R. and Jones, B. D. (1991) 'Agenda Dynamics and Policy Subsystems', *Journal of Politics*, 53, 4, 1044–74.

—— (1993) *Agendas and Instability in American Politics*, Chicago: Chicago University Press.

Benson, J. K. (1982) 'A Framework for Policy Analysis', in Rogers, D. and Whitten, D. *Interorganizational Coordination,* Ames: Iowa State University Press, pp. 137–76.

Campbell, J. C. (1989) 'A Note from the Guest Editor', *Governance*, 2, 1, iii–iv.

Cohen, Michael, March, James and Olsen, Johan P. (1972) 'A Garbage Can Model of Organizational Choice', *Administrative Science Quarterly*, 17, 1–25.

Cowhey, Peter F. (1990) 'The International Telecommunications Regime: The Political Roots of Regimes for High Technology', *International Organization*, 44, 2, 169–99.

Department of Trade and Industry (DTI) (1993) *Review of the Implementations and Enforcement of EC Law in the UK*, London: DTI.

Dowding, Keith (1991) *Rational Choice and Political Power*, Aldershot: Edward Elgar.

Edwards, Geoffrey and Spence, David (eds) (1994) *The European Commission*, London: Longman.

Haas, Peter (1992) 'Introduction: Epistemic Communities and International Policy Co-ordination', *International Organization*, 49, 1, 1–35.

Heclo, H. (1978) 'Issue Networks and the Executive Establishment', in King, Anthony (ed.) *The New American Political System*, Washington DC: American Enterprise Institute.

Heclo, H. and Wildavsky, A. (1974) *The Private Government of Public Money*, London: Macmillan.

Henderson, P. D. (1977) 'Two British Errors: Their Probable Size and Some Possible Lessons', *Economic Papers*, 29, 2, 159–205.

Hix, Simon (1994) 'The Study of the European Community: The Challenge to Comparative Politics', *West European Politics*, 17,1, 1–30.

Hoffmann, Stanley (1966) 'Obstinate or Obsolete: The Fate of the Nation State and the Case of Western Europe', *Daedalus*, 95, 3, 862–915.

Jordan, Grant (1990) 'Sub-Governments, Policy Communities and Networks: Refilling the Old Bottles?' *Journal of Theoretical Politics*, 2, 3, 319–38.

Jordan, Grant and Richardson, Jeremy (1982) 'The British Policy Style or the Logic of Negotiation?', in Richardson, Jeremy (ed.) *Policy Styles in Western Europe*, London: Allen & Unwin, pp. 80–110.

Jordan, Grant, Maloney, William and McLaughlin, Andrew (1993) *Assumptions About the Role of Groups in the Policy Process. The British Policy Community Approach*, Aberdeen: British Interest Group Project.

Judge, David (1993) *The Parliamentary State*, London: Sage.

Judge, David and Earnshaw, David (1995) 'From Co-operation to Codecision: The European Parliament's Path to Legislative Power', in Richardson, Jeremy (ed.) *Policy-Making in the European Union*, London: Routledge.

Kingdon, John W. (1984) *Agendas, Alternatives and Public Policies* (NY: HarperCollins).

Lax, David and Sebenius, James K. (1986) *The Manager as Negotiator*, New York: Free Press.

Marsh, D. and Rhodes, R. A. W. (1992) *Policy Networks in British Government*, Oxford: Clarendon Press.

Mazey, Sonia and Richardson, Jeremy (1992) 'Environmental Groups and the EC', *Environmental Politics*, 1,4, 109–28.

—— (eds) (1993) *Lobbying in the European Community*, Oxford: Oxford University Press.

—— (1994) 'The Commission and the Lobby', in Edwards, Geoffrey and Spence, David (eds) *The European Commission*, London: Longman, pp. 169–201.

—— (1995) 'Promiscuous Policy-Making: The European Policy Style?', in Mazey, Sonia and Rhodes, Carolyn (eds) *The State of the European Union*, Boulder: Lynn Reinner Longman.

Peters, Guy (1994) 'Agenda Setting in the European Community', *Journal of European Public Policy*, 1,1: 9–26.

Putnam, Robert, D. (1988) 'Diplomacy and Domestic Politics', *International Organization*, 42, 3, 427–60.

Radaelli, Claudio (1995) 'The Role of Knowledge in the Policy Process', *Journal of European Public Policy*, 2,2: 159–83.

Rhodes, R. A. W. (1985) 'Power Dependence, Policy Communities and Inter-Governmental Networks', *Public Administration Bulletin*, 49, 4–29.

—— (1988) *Beyond Westminster and Whitehall*, London: Unwin Hyman.

—— (1990) 'Policy Networks: A British Perspective', *Journal of Theoretical Politics*, 2, 3, 292–316.

Rhodes, R. A. W. and Marsh, D. (1992a) 'New Direction in the Study of Policy Networks', *European Journal of Political Research*, 21, 1, 181–205.

—— (1992b) 'Policy Networks in British Politics', in Marsh, D. and Rhodes, R. A. W. (eds) *Policy Networks in British Government*, Oxford: Clarendon Press.

Richardson, Jeremy (ed.) (1982) *Policy Styles in Western Europe*, London: Allen & Unwin.

—— (1993) 'Doing Less by Doing More', EPPI Occasional Paper no. 2, Warwick, England.

—— (1994) 'Doing Less by Doing More. British Government 1979–1994', *West European Politics*, 17(3): 178–97.

—— (1996) 'Policy-Making in the EU. Interests, Ideas and Garbage Cans of Primeval Soup', in Richardson, Jeremy (ed.) *European Union: Power and Policy-Making*, London: Routledge.

Richardson, Jeremy and Jordan, Grant (1979) *Governing Under Pressure: The Policy Process in a Post-Parliamentary Democracy*, Oxford: Martin Robertson.

Rokkan, Stein (1966), 'Numerical Democracy and Corporate Pluralism', in Dahl, R. A. *Political Opposition in Western Democracies*, New Haven: Yale University Press.

Sabatier, Paul (1988) 'An Advocacy Coalition Framework of Policy Change and the Role of Policy-orientated Learning Therein', *Policy Sciences*, 21, 128–68.

Schattschneider, E. E. (1960) *The Semi-Sovereign People. A Realist's View of Democracy in America*, New York: Holt.

Sebenius, James K. (1992) 'Challenging Conventional Explanations of International Cooperation: Negotiation Analysis and the Case of Epistemic Communities', *International Organization*, 46, 1, 323–65.

Smith, Martin (1993) *Pressure Power and Policy*, London: Harvester Wheatsheaf.

Tsebelis, George (1990) *Nested Games: Rational Choice in Comparative Politics*, Berkeley: University of California Press.

Walton, Richard and McKersie, Robert (1965) *A Behavioral Theory of Labour Negotiations*, New York: McGraw Hill.

Wilks, S. and Wright, M. (1987) 'Conclusion: Comparing Government–Industry Relations: States, Sectors and Networks', in Wilks, S. and Wright, M. (eds) *Comparing Government–Industry Relations*, Oxford: Clarendon Press.

4 The regulatory role of the European Union

Leigh Hancher

The point of departure for this chapter is a marketing campaign: the marketing of the single market programme, with its sell-by date of 31 December 1992, proved a resounding success. It captured the attention of the public at large and placed 'Europe' at the centre of the political agenda. In addition, it has proved to be a hard act to follow. However, in selling the single market idea, the authors of the exercise can legitimately lay claim to an even greater achievement. By persuading the member states to embrace so wholeheartedly the single market idea, the European Commission succeeded in convincing them to embark upon a radical exercise, while giving very little thought as to what kind of European Community was likely to emerge on its successful completion.

Two issues subsequently need to be addressed: first, and most obvious, what type of community has emerged from the internal market exercise? and second, what have been the consequences of that exercise for the process of European integration, and in particular for the regulatory role of the European institutions? For example, would it be fair to conclude that the European Community is progressing towards becoming a state and is no longer simply a market?

The first of these questions raises an alarmingly wide range of problems. The European integration process was likened to an elephant long ago. Those whose sorry task it is to research that process have been compared to blind people who, by touching various parts of the animal, try to draw some conclusions about its overall shape (Puchala 1972). Researchers into this still relatively novel and frustratingly complex process run up against the constraints imposed by their chosen discipline.

Certainly, devising suitable analytical tools to make sense of the abundance of policy developments at EU level is a major challenge for all engaged in research in this area. Hopefully, in the meantime the researcher can be forgiven if, in applying only those analytical tools with which they have some familiarity, the assessment of the European integration process which emerges is a partial or incomplete one. The analysis presented in this chapter is launched from the perspective of public economic law. The content of this particular branch of legal study is, rather like the integration process itself, somewhat fluid and often difficult to pin down. Views as to what the main directions and preoccupations of this discipline are, or ought to be, vary considerably depending on which side of the Channel one happens to be. What might loosely be described as the continental tradition in economic law takes as its starting point government policies rather than constitutional principles. It seeks to establish the aims of these policies and the means chosen to achieve them (Joerges 1994). Its focus is principally on the relationship between these means and the legal form of instruments chosen to realise them. In this context a fundamental, if rudimentary, distinction is often drawn between the means chosen and legal instruments adopted in furtherance of *Ordnungspolitik* (or market-ordering policy) and those adopted in the pursuit of a *prozesspolitik* (or economic planning policy).

The scope of this chapter is confined to what are often referred to as meso- as opposed to macro-economic issues. In other words, to the impact of the integration process on EU industrial policy, and the role of the EU institutions in its formulation and implementation. Broader matters of monetary and fiscal integration are not considered; neither are equally important but, in political and legal terms, quite distinct issues of social policy. After considering the broad objectives of recent European industrial policy, the means chosen to achieve these aims will be described. In this way it will be possible to demonstrate that, although a near complete European market is in place, a European state has not as yet been constructed.

INDUSTRIAL POLICY AND THE INTERNAL MARKET EXERCISE

A convenient and logical starting point is the very cornerstone of Community industrial policy, the internal market programme itself and the programme which launched it – the Commission's 1985 White Paper, '*Completing the Internal Market*' (CEC 1985). The aims of that document and the means proposed to realise them will first be discussed, and then the outcome of this process, in terms of the respective roles assigned to national governments and the EC institutions by the institutional arrangements subsequently adopted in the Treaty on European Union (TEU), will be examined.

As indicated above, the internal market initiative was an outstanding marketing success. It was convincingly sold to, and subsequently supported by, political leaders of diametrically opposed ideological persuasions. On the one hand, a former British Conservative Prime Minister in a now famous speech delivered at Bruges in 1988 hailed it as a charter of economic liberty for European industry, a massive exercise in deregulation which would remove constraints on trade and open up the Community market. Two years later the then President of the European Commission, Jacques Delors, could point to exactly the same document as the blueprint for the creation of a single economic and social area, and refer to its long list of proposed measures to defend the Commission against accusations of deregulating the economy

(CEC 1990: 14). Delors further suggested that by the mid-1990s, perhaps 80 per cent of economic legislation would derive from Brussels.

Looking back, it seems that the secret of the internal market's success owes much to the fact that the 1985 White Paper itself concentrated primarily on *aims*, while at the same time being carefully evasive about the means by which these aims were to be achieved. Four of that White Paper's salient features may be briefly recalled. In the first place the internal market was about rules not money: it was presented as a programme for the *elimination of barriers*, with no apparent financial burdens to be borne by the member states. In the second place, the language of the White Paper was mainly technical and low key in nature. It acknowledged that a number of what are now referred to as 'flanking policies', such as regional, social, environmental, consumer, transport, research, competition, economic and monetary policies are all closely linked to the internal market and the integration of national economies. However, looking back we see that these matters are only touched upon by the White Paper where they have a direct bearing on the abolition of physical and technical barriers to trade. Thus, although progress on these policies would inevitably become more important because of the completion of the internal market, they were not to constitute a precondition of its completion.

Arguably, the real success of the internal market programme is to be found in its two last features. First, any fears of creeping interventionism on the part of the Commission, and in particular of any transfer of powers to the Community, were allayed by the White Paper's apparent commitment to the then newly fashionable economic concepts of supply-side policies and positive adjustment. This commitment implied at least a partial rejection of established notions concerning the mixed economy in Western Europe and a shift towards the market and more competition. It also implied an acceptance of another prevailing fashion: economic deregulation. On the question of rule-making, the White Paper introduced a new strategy on harmonisation of national rules and regulations; the emphasis was to be on mutual recognition of divergent national technical regulations and standards. Recourse to legislative harmonisation at Community level would be limited to essential cases only. The task of setting detailed technical specifications was transferred to specialised private European standard organisations. This emphasis on minimum harmonisation and self-regulation confirmed the Community's apparent commitment to economic deregulation.

Last but not least, institutional reforms were not explicitly called for in the White Paper. The apparent commitment to the institutional *status quo* can be attributed to one of the White Paper's most enduring merits: it did not attempt to present detailed solutions, but only to identify the problems (CEC 1985). In summary, the internal market exercise did not appear to be a real threat to national sovereignty. Paradoxically, this helped to tip the balance in favour of the institutional reforms which were introduced in the subsequent year with the adoption of the Single European Act in 1986. It also served to persuade the most sceptical of political leaders to believe that in signing this

Act they were doing little more than providing the necessary legal framework to realise the internal market initiative. In the words of one of the most trenchant opponents of European federalism, Margaret Thatcher: 'The Single European Act does not change anything; if it had we would not have signed it.' One can only regret that the author of this remark failed to read the preamble of the Single Act, which spoke in unequivocal terms of the will to move towards a European Union.

These four features of the internal market exercise – its goal-oriented approach, its emphasis on negative integration,[1] its commitment to minimal regulation and the supposed absence of any threat to the institutional *status quo* – seem in retrospect to explain the lack of any immediate concern over the crucial question of what kind of Community would result at the end of that process. The pro-market and competition-oriented aims of the exercise suited the political and economic climate of the times, while the means proposed to achieve it were couched in innocuous terms.

Thus, it is not difficult to understand in retrospect why political attention was so effectively deflected from the fact that, by agreeing to the internal market exercise in general, and to the liberalisation of capital movements by 1990 in particular, the member states were effectively committing themselves to further economic and monetary integration. The subsequent speed at which the Commission embarked upon its follow-up 'one market, one money' campaign in 1988 would only confirm the speed and direction in which economic integration was moving.

Yet a careful reading of the 1985 White Paper confirms that it concealed much more than it revealed. Despite its emphasis on technical and physical barriers to trade, the White Paper obviously aimed to eliminate the very causes of those obstacles at source, namely the distortions and barriers created by government intervention in the market in all its infinite variety. Further, the focus of the internal market exercise was less on goods and more on services and factors of production, areas in which very little progress in terms of integration had been accomplished in the past thirty years. In other words, the successful completion of the internal market would signal a qualitatively new phase in the process of economic integration (Tsoukalis 1993).

DEREGULATION

The Community measures subsequently adopted to complete the internal market exercise, (for example, the opening up of public procurement, the liberalisation of financial, insurance and transport services, and renewed attempts at tax harmonisation) threatened to lead to serious depletions in the stock of traditional instruments used to steer the mixed economy at national level. Even in politically sensitive areas not touched upon by the 1985 White Paper, such as the role of public or state-owned enterprises in the mixed economy, Commission policy on, for example, transport, post, telecommunications, energy and more recently, media, and the recent jurisprudence of the

Court of Justice, has been directed at the steady erosion of the traditional monopoly power enjoyed by such firms. This case law clearly illustrates the potential of the basic principles of Community law to strike at the heart of that most traditional instrument of the mixed economy (Hancher 1994a).

By undermining the traditional policy instruments of the mixed economy, the internal market exercise appeared to leave decreasing scope for national governments to influence the allocation of resources between and within countries. Yet if there is to be a more European market in this brave new economic order, does this necessarily imply that there must also be a more European state? In this new phase of economic integration we are confronted with fundamental questions about what has been termed the political economy of liberalisation and regulation (Tsoukalis 1993). Major issues such as the distribution of power between different levels of political authority, as well as the distribution of economic power between public and private agents, are increasingly being raised if not always resolved in the European, and not in a purely national context (Sandholtz and Zysman 1989). Sensitive questions about the allocation and redistribution of resources, about choices between efficiency and stability, and between production and protection of the environment are fast becoming European, and not merely national, matters. One need only look to air transport and the Commission's intervention with regard to future subsidies for national airlines, or its role in mediating disputes over access to essential airport services for confirmation of this trend (Balfour 1994, Kassim, Chapter 7, this volume).

THE TREATY OF UNION

Clearly, this new phase of European integration, if taken to its logical conclusion, would lead to a steady erosion of national autonomy and a concomitant transfer of competence to the Community institutions across all sectors of the economy. Such a process imposes quite different demands on the Community's political and constitutional system. The Treaty on European Union was intended, among other things, to create the foundations for the new political and constitutional context in which the grand issues of liberalisation and regulation were supposed to be tackled. Commitment to a federally organised Community survived in the various texts of the draft Treaty until, at the eleventh hour, all references to the 'f word' were expunged at British insistence.[2]

Critics have been quick to point out that the new compromise arrangements and resulting institutional schema were unlikely to live up to either of the two claims made of it: efficiency of action and democratisation of the decision-making process at Community level (Piris 1994, Rowarth 1994).[3] Title II of the TEU introduced a radical amendment to the EEC Treaty, now known as the EC Treaty, and has increased Community competencies in a number of fields. Its Article 2 has recast the Community's tasks to ensure the creation of an economic and monetary union as well as the common market. Articles 3 and 3(a) list the common policies or activities necessary to meet these tasks. Industrial policy is not explicitly included in this list, but Article 3(l) refers to the 'strengthening of competitiveness of Community industry', and mention is also made, albeit in the same indirect manner, of some of the other 'flanking policies', including research and development and consumer protection, as well as the establishment of trans-European networks. These activities are further developed in titles XIII, XV and XII, respectively.

Article 3(a) enshrines, if not entrenches, the commitment to deregulation and liberalisation referred to above: the activities of both member states and the Community must include the adoption of an economic policy which is to be conducted 'in accordance with the principle of an open market economy with free competition'. Although this article is intended to provide a framework within which the alignment of policies leading to EMU is to be pursued, it is a general principle which can be applied to limit the freedom of the Community institutions in formulating other policies under the Treaty. Article 130, the article which addresses industry and the Community's industrial competitiveness, repeats the commitment articulated in Article 3(a), that Community action in this field must be 'in accordance with a system of open and competitive markets' and that it 'shall not provide a basis for the introduction by the Community of any measure which could lead to the distortion of competition'.

From the perspective of the issue of state autonomy, the wording of the industry title is complex: it is clear that both the Community *and* the member states must ensure achievement of the objectives listed in Article 130(1). Article 130(2) requires that they consult with one another and co-ordinate their actions, but gives the Commission a 'right of initiative to promote such co-ordination'. Finally, in its third paragraph, the new Article recognises the need for the Community to co-ordinate action in other sectors pursued under other provisions of the Treaty. The Council is empowered to adopt specific measures, but in support of the action of member states to achieve the objectives set out in para.1. The related titles on R&D (Articles 130 (f-p)) and Trans-European Networks (Article 129 (b-d)) also stress co-ordination between the Community and member states.

The issue of state autonomy is further clouded when one recalls that the pursuit of these objectives must not conflict with basic Treaty principles. It will of course be recalled that the Commission retains primary competence for applying the EC competition rules: Article 85 (cartels); Article 86 (the abuse of dominant position), and Articles 92–3 (state aids). The use to which all three of the new titles is put will require a considerable balancing act with the general rules of the Treaty. What can either the Community or the member states do in order 'to encourage an environment favourable to co-operation between undertakings', in terms of Article 130(1), if a primary principle of the Treaty, for instance Article 85, is to maintain competition between them? Is it legitimate for member states continually to bail out ailing companies if this is aimed at 'speeding the adjustment of industry to structural changes'? Once again, this objective is explicitly accepted by Article

130(1)EC, but Article 92 EC prohibits the granting of aid which distorts competition.

Finally, when examining the strange brew that is the TEU, mention must be made of Maastricht's most well-known stalking horse, the principle of subsidiarity. The latter is now encapsulated in Article 3(b) as follows:

> The Community shall act within the limits of the powers conferred upon it by this Treaty and of the objectives assigned to it therein.
>
> In areas which do not fall within its exclusive jurisdiction the Community shall only act if certain objectives cannot be sufficiently achieved at national level, because of the scale and effects of the proposed action.
>
> Community action should go no further than what is necessary to achieve the Treaty aims.

It is generally acknowledged that the idea of subsidiarity is easier to state than to apply, and in practice may turn out to be a double-edged sword, justifying the transfer of competencies to the Community (Dehousse 1994). Essentially, the concept raises two questions about the policy powers of the EC. First, it raises questions about the divisions of powers and competences between the Community and the member states. Second, it raises questions about how power and responsibility can best be shared between the Community and the national level when competence as such is not the issue, but the choice of the most appropriate level at which to implement and enforce policy is.

Unfortunately, there is little consensus among lawyers on how far EC competence is in fact exclusive (Dehousse 1994, Steiner 1994, Toth 1994). The TEU itself is silent on this matter, but it is generally agreed that the member states agreed to transfer power to the Community in matters relating to the establishment and functioning of the common or internal market many years ago. Moreover, while member states will formally retain their general responsibility for economic policy, 'they will however, be required to formulate such policies in the face of independent monetary policy, the soft Community regulation of fiscal policy through non-legal means and the mandate of the Council to defend general economic policy in Europe' (Joerges 1994: 56).[4]

Maastricht is also resoundingly silent on the second issue: who is going to ensure the operation of the internal market, and by what means? The completion of the original 1992 programme, as set out in the 1985 White Paper, still requires an immense amount of detailed implementation and enforcement.[5] To guarantee and facilitate the competitiveness of European industry requires active intervention to ensure that markets operate efficiently. As the Commission's various communications on Community industry policy make eminently clear, there is limited scope for *laisser-faire* policies in the political economy of liberalisation and regulation (Nicolaides 1993). The incorporation of the industry title has generated something of a neo-liberal backlash from critics, who claim that it implies a weakening of the Community's commitment to a competition-based economic system (Siebert 1990, Streit 1994) and a mandate for Community interventionism which will erode national autonomy on industrial policy matters. This is a debate which has already assumed almost theological dimensions.

In the following sections, the way in which the Commission has responded to the first of the issues mentioned here, the implementation problem, will be considered. Subsequently, the way in which the Commission has come to view the use of the Treaty competition provisions as instruments of active intervention is examined.

REALISING THE INTERNAL MARKET

It is already evident that the process of realising the internal market has imposed an enormous strain on the Community institutions, particularly upon the Commission. This is not only because of the limited manpower and financial resources available at Community level; it is also the inevitable result of legal and institutional constraints within which the Commission must operate. Four major institutional constraints should be singled out.

First and foremost, the Commission as the executive branch of the Community structure of government is of course atypical in comparison to national executives. Although the Commission proposes legislation it rarely implements, applies or enforces that legislation. This task has traditionally been delegated to the administrations of the member states (Lenaerts 1993).

Second, even where the Commission has departed from its supposed commitment to minimalist regulatory strategies, and is prepared to propose more detailed legislation, this invariably takes the form of a Directive. The problems caused by diversity between the member states and the difficulties of monitoring implementation and checking enforcement at national level are rarely eliminated by the adoption of a Directive: arguably, they become even more acute (Macrory 1992). The Community-wide implementation deficit has become almost as well known as the democratic deficit (Majone 1990). The related issue of full and faithful enforcement of Community legislation presents slightly more novel, but no less serious problems.

Third, inherent limitations of integration strategies based on mutual recognition and minimal harmonisation are now becoming evident (Joerges 1990, Woolcock 1994). This is particularly true where certain types of highly regulated product, ranging from pharmaceuticals and foodstuffs to fertilisers are concerned. Member states clearly do not trust each others' systems of supervision, and prefer to rely on their own tried and true tests and controls (Hancher 1990). In legal terms, they can justify their reticence on grounds of consumer protection and health policy – sensitive areas where the Court of Justice understandably has proved reluctant to tread.

A fourth and final constraint is to be found in the type of 'regulatory instruments' which the Commission has at its disposal. As 'guardian of the Treaties', the Commission enforces the basic principles of Community law. The EC Treaty rules on the freedom of movement of goods, persons, services and capital and the rules on competition have certainly withstood the test of time, and more. But their inherent limitations in tackling certain types of non-tariff barriers to trade or structural barriers to competition cannot be overlooked. Although the Treaty competition rules can be used to prohibit conduct, or even, as the Court of Justice has recently confirmed, to remove a structural distortion which is inconsistent with the EC Treaty, their usefulness is limited when it comes to putting a different regime in its place (Hancher 1994b). In some sectors of the economy structural distortions are unavoidable, such as transport, telecommunications and energy, where natural monopolies are the rule. Yet these very sectors represent the basic infrastructure on which the internal market will increasingly depend. This is clearly recognised by Title XII TEU and recent Commission initiatives on trans-European networks. At the same time, since natural monopolies cannot be eliminated, their activities need to be supervised. Once again it would appear that the Community's regulatory hand will inevitably be forced. Indeed, it has already been so in the telecommunications and transport sectors, and draft proposals on both post and energy are now before the Council. In the meantime, issues of effective implementation and enforcement of Community regulatory measures ostensibly designed to secure market liberalisation have surfaced, in particular in the field of telecommunications (Sauter 1994).

If regulatory trends continue to develop in this way at Community level, it is evident that it is at the implementation stage that the most immediate and greatest pressure will be put on the growing body of common Community rules. Can the effectiveness of these rules only be guaranteed if the Commission assumes a more active or direct operational role, as opposed to the traditional approach of delegating implementation and monitoring to the member states? This is surely a central question in this new political economy of liberalisation and regulation. Yet it is one which the Commission has only belatedly chosen to address (CEC 1993, Sutherland 1992).

Towards European regulatory agencies

Recent developments suggest that the response to the implementation challenge appears at first sight contradictory: on the one hand new regulatory agencies have been created at Community level. A 1992 Regulation establishing a European Agency for the Evaluation of Medicinal Products opts for a centralised system of Community licences for biotechnology and so-called 'high-tech' products.[6] In some respects the proposed agency comes close to its American equivalent, the Food and Drug Administration. On the other hand, there has been a new emphasis placed on better Community co-ordination of national implementation practices. The draft directive on assistance and co-operation in the scientific examination of questions relating to food is a good illustration of the latter approach. The Commission proposed a system for the pooling of national scientific resources on additives. Instead of creating a centralised regulatory agency to approve new products on a Community wide basis, the Commission proposes to set up a small administrative secretariat to process and distribute work to the existing national agencies. This type of Community agency will assume a mainly organisational or directive role. Similar advisory committees have been created to oversee implementation at national level in the field of taxation and to ensure the mutual recognition of diplomas (CEC 1993).

The creation of a vast range of European regulatory agencies and accompanying squads of Euro-inspectorates would undoubtedly signal a major transfer of power to the Community, with a resulting loss in political and regulatory autonomy for the member states. Political as much as legal constraints combine for the present, however, to prevent a large-scale delegation of powers to independent Euro-regulatory agencies in most of the fields which currently fall within the Community's competence (Lenaerts 1993). Calls for the establishment of an independent European Cartel Office have similarly been resisted, primarily for constitutional reasons (Ehlermann 1992).

This situation may of course only be temporary. It seems highly likely that precisely these sort of issues will appear on the agenda for the next round of institutional reforms at the intergovernmental conference in 1996.

Interactive networks

In the meantime, the Commission is acutely aware of both the implementation gap, the growing practical pressures on it to assume a greater regulatory role, as well as the political pitfalls inherent in doing so. In late 1992, the Director-General responsible for the Internal Market summed up the Commission's general orientation on industrial policy matters as follows: 'we are on our way to creating an effective, decentralised but inter-active, common approach to economic regulation across the Community' (Perrisch 1991).

Now what exactly, one might justifiably ask, are decentralised but inter-active regulatory systems? A cursory survey of recent Community initiatives suggests that they come in a variety of shapes and sizes and, depending on the policy field, seem to exhibit varying degrees of interactivity and decentralisation.

A unifying theme emerging from some of the most recent Commission initiatives is the creation of Community networks which are to co-ordinate the various activities of existing bodies and institutions within the member states, with the aim of moulding some sort of uniformity out of national diversity. These networks also take a variety of forms, and will operate at a number of levels. In some of these networks the participants operate as equal partners. In other cases, co-ordination will be directed by one of the central or Community agencies referred to in the previous section. But the size, powers and functions of these agencies vary quite substantially from one policy area to the next. The different gradations in the hierarchy of centralised powers embraced by the Community network strategy can best be pictured as a pyramid structure.

At the base of the pyramid, networks of a largely informal nature have been developed, which will entail little more than enhanced co-operation between national administrations. Thus there exist programmes to swap officials from national administrations to give them experience of administrating Community policies either at Commission level or in another country.[7] The Council has recently adopted a general action plan for exchange of national officials engaged in the enforcement of single market legislation.[8]

In some cases co-operation within networks is underwritten by informal guarantees of rights of access for one set of national officials to records or facilities located in another member state (Dehousse *et al.* 1992). In other policy fields such as health and safety, or the environment, the networks are also expected to function as systems for exchange of information and expertise. However in this instance, the networks will be co-ordinated by new Community agencies – albeit agencies whose powers are limited to collecting and collating data. The Agency for Safety and Health at Work and the European Environmental Agency are two examples of this type of body.

At the apex of the pyramid, centralised Community agencies exercise considerable regulatory powers. At this time, the European Agency for the Evaluation of Medicinal Products (see p. 60) is the only example of this type, and it should be noted that it is concerned with highly technical matters. Nevertheless, the new Community agency will be kept small and will rely heavily on decentralised scientific experts operating at national level to test and evaluate new drug products.

It will be readily apparent from this brief overview that as well as restricting the evolution of an overt or explicit operational role in the implementation process, the various initiatives just outlined are also designed to reaffirm the Commission's continuing commitment to minimal regulation and indeed minimal intervention into national policy spheres. The exponents of these interactive, decentralised but common, co-ordinated policies also have a political advantage working in their favour; they can call upon the principle of subsidiarity in support of these assorted policies.

Competition and mergers

A new emphasis on co-ordination and decentralisation is even creeping into areas where it might have been safely assumed that the forces of integration were working in quite the opposite direction. Competition policy enforcement is a case in point. The adoption of the Merger Control Regulation in 1989, creating a 'one-stop' shop for large cross-border mergers exemplifies a centralising trend, enhancing the regulatory power and status of the Commission at the expense of member states.[9] Nevertheless, as a result of the reluctance of some member states to transfer too much power to the Commission to intervene in highly sensitive issues of industrial policy, the thresholds for Community jurisdiction were set at a level which would only catch the largest transactions: 5 billion ECUs world-wide turnover and 250 million ECUs European turnover. In its first two years the Commission took some 180 decisions under the Merger Regulation; in 1993 it approved 188 mergers, that is 90 per cent of the operations notified to it. When the original thresholds were reviewed in 1993 it was decided not to lower them further, so that national authorities continue to have an important role to play in approving mergers which still can have a significant European dimension.

At the same time, and faced with an ever increasing work-load, the Competition Directorate has been compelled to set priorities and to tackle only those cases which it deems to have wider significance for the maintenance of competition in the single market. A Commission Communication of 1993 outlines the principles on which effective co-operation between the Commission and national courts and cartel authorities should be based.[10] The Court of First Instance has endorsed the Commission's approach to selecting only priority cases for further investigation.[11] In a system based on priorities, the further decentralization of the implementation of competition law, including the power to grant exemption from the competition provisions on the basis of Article 85(3), may in the long run be unavoidable. This means that some of the tasks previously performed exclusively by the Commission will be delegated to national cartel authorities and courts.

Delegation of control to national governments over such crucial matters as the granting of state aids, however, would seem a quite unrealistic option. Indeed, state aids is one of the areas of economic regulation where we might expect an expansion of centralized Community powers in these recessionary times (Hancher *et al.* 1993). The Commission's Twenty-Third Report on Competition suggests that:

> the control of state aid at Community level is vital, first of all, for the success of the single market programme. . . . Opening markets and keeping them open has always been one of the main functions of state aid control. . . . In a more integrated market, the distortive effect of certain types of aid is magnified and so control of aid is even more important.
>
> (CEC 1994)

Nevertheless, the Commission has announced that it is prepared to temper its intervention in the relations between national governments and publicly controlled enterprises through the application of the 'market investor principle'. In 1991 the Commission issued a Communication on financial transfers to major public undertakings.[12] The 1991 Communication recognises that within private groups certain practices, such as cross-subsidisation, are often prevalent when a long-term strategy is pursued to restore the profitability of a loss-making sector, or when there will be a net benefit to the group as a whole. The Commission will take account of similar strategic goals in the public sector and will consider cross-subsidisation as aid only when there is no reasonable explanation other than that they constitute an aid. This approach not only confers considerable discretion on the Commission but also indicates that in the majority of suspected aid cases, the companies and governments involved will be given the benefit of the doubt. The recent, controversial approval of massive subsidies, for example, to Air France and to the computer group, Bull, have been in part justified on the basis of this principle.

ASSESSMENT

The developments reviewed in the previous section suggest that at least insofar as the implementation of competition and industrial policy matters is concerned, it cannot be readily concluded that the internal market exercise or the inclusion of new competencies in the TEU have led, or are likely to lead automatically, to a transfer of regulatory power to Community institutions at the expense of member states.

With the aim of securing the implementation of the internal market rules, the Commission has been engaged in setting up a multitude of mini 'joint executives' or even agencies, comprising Community and national officials. While it might be argued that the primary task of these 'joint executives' is administrative, i.e. to implement policy or to monitor implementation, but not to make it (Commission of the European Communities 1993), the leap from policy taker to policy maker is not necessarily always a large one.

In attempting to assess this process it would be perilous to ignore a basic, persistent feature of Community regulation: that is that 'the regulatory dilemma of a Community which has to resolve federal questions but which is not a Federal state has repeatedly led – in theory and in practice – to attempts to get around the difficulties of substantive decision-making at European level' (Joerges 1988).

It should not be forgotten, therefore, that these regulatory developments reflect a pragmatic attempt to live with the constraints imposed by the Community's present institutional structure, and, in particular, the inherent limitations in the Commission's executive powers. They do not necessarily result from any clear blueprint about a rational or efficient allocation of tasks. Pragmatic solutions should be recognised for what they are, even if vague but fashionable concepts such as subsidiarity offer enormous potential for elegant *post hoc* rationalisation. Certainly, better co-ordination between the Community and national administrations is urgently needed in the name of improved efficiency. The annual reports of the European Court of Auditors provide ample evidence for this. One might even venture to add that the Commission could usefully apply its ideas on interactive administration to put its own house in order.

We should not, however, allow ourselves to be seduced a second time round by Community strategies which focus on ends, and gloss over the means to be used to achieve them. If the new emphasis on networks, partnerships and interactive decentralised systems is to be elevated from a mere pragmatic response to the Community's present institutional shortcomings, to a future strategy, blessed in the name of subsidiarity, that will span the new European Union, it also deserves serious scrutiny on that basis.

Even if it can be assumed that these networks will lead to more efficient policy implementation or, ultimately, regulation, the question must be asked as to whether they will pass the equally important test of democratic accountability. The wider political and constitutional implications of the Commission's new strategy must be carefully thought through. If proposals for Community-wide interactive regulatory networks are to be democratically acceptable, these networks must at the very least be required to exercise their powers within acceptable margins of transparency and accountability, and to provide certain basic guarantees to those whose activities they seek to regulate. At present, neither at Community nor at national level does there exist a constitutional system which is capable of controlling joint executive decision making or of even subjecting it to the most minimal degree of scrutiny. Lack of procedural transparency exposes Community organs to accusations of regulatory capture. The Commission's Merger Task Force has been alleged to be overly responsive to the interests of the firms seeking approval for proposed ventures (Nevens *et al.* 1993: 163). While competition between regulatory authorities is viewed by some commentators as a cure for the purported evils of regulatory capture (Woolcock 1994), the Community's present strategy is based on co-ordination and partnership between institutions, and not competition.

Taking one of the most basic forms of control over the executive, parliamentary supervision, it remains the case that, despite the reforms introduced by the TEU, it features only marginally in the Community's constitutional system (Lodge 1994). At present, for example, there is no requirement for national officials to appear before the committees of inquiry established by the European Parliament, nor can Commission officials be summoned to appear before national parliamentary institutions. The new Article 138C of the TEU merely provides that the detailed provisions governing the exercise of the right of inquiry shall be determined by common accord of the Parliament, Council and Commission.

Much more thought needs to be given to the type of information which can legitimately be exchanged between the component parts of these interactive systems, the conditions which should be attached to that exchange and the terms under which individuals should have access to that information. One cannot safely assume that the domestic regulatory functions of the national administrations will coincide neatly with those which they assume within these Euro-networks (Ferry 1994).

These basic concerns about the legal implications of the implementation of economic regulation through new types of co-ordinating networks obviously reflect the narrow concerns of the lawyer. But the wider political issues which the decentralised network strategy raises should not be ignored. After all, economic regulation is in the final event about the distribution of power and resources (Hancher and Moran 1989).

Policy science studies confirm what common sense suggests. All too frequently, important political choices are made at the implementation stage of the policy process as well as during the initial formulation of that policy. The literature on policy studies also testifies to the enduring nature of networks and their ability to control the policy agenda (Wilks and Wright 1987). Before embarking on the network route, it is therefore necessary to consider their wider distributional effects. To what extent will they favour those economic interests which can command better organisation and knowledge, and the financial resources which can usually buy both?

This leads to a final observation. As a strategy, networks and decentralised interactive systems should not be viewed as offering either a permanent or a comprehensive solution to the complex matter of regulating a Community-wide market. There can be no guarantee that these systems will retain their decentralised qualities on a permanent basis. Indeed, the application of the subsidiarity test – with its emphasis on better or more effective attainment of policies – might, paradoxically, produce centralising trends. There can be no guarantee that, once established, the so-called co-ordinating Community agencies will not seek to assume wider tasks. The Commission's latest proposal to expand the powers of the European Environmental Agency from a data collection body to an agency with responsibility for monitoring and enforcement is a case in point. The European Medicines Agency began life as an advisory committee whose task was to co-ordinate the work of national officials. In the field of telecommunications the Commission has now put forward proposals to subsume national committees which began life as equal partners with the task of monitoring implementation, into a more structured hierarchy, with the Commission perched firmly at its apex (Sauter 1994).

CONCLUSION

The process of integration has undoubtedly been greatly speeded up by the internal market exercise and in turn consolidated by the TEU. That this process has led to an erosion of national autonomy cannot be denied, but the tensions between national sovereignty and economic interdependence remain: as experience in the area of industrial policy at least tends to show, one cannot conclude that regulatory competencies have been straightforwardly transferred to the Community level. The process of 'Europeanisation' of regulatory policies has led to the emergence of subject-related policy networks which for the large part exist outside the institutional framework of both the EC Treaties and national constitutional controls. This suggests that academics from all disciplines need to embark upon new ways of thinking about concepts of state autonomy, as well as the values which are attached to it.

In conclusion, critical attention should be directed at the means and instruments which are needed to make the internal market work. Greater centralisation of regulatory power at Community level is neither the best nor the inevitable solution to the problems outlined here (Majone 1993). Serious attention must be paid to designing regulatory frameworks which not only meet criteria of efficiency but which can also be subject to full and effective democratic control at both national and Community level. Indeed, the basic task of devising relevant criteria and standards of democratic control and accountability, capable of meeting the constitutional, legal and political demands of liberalisation and regulation in the new European Union, where political and legal responsibility for the operation of the internal market is likely to remain a competence which is shared, but shared in a variety of ways, is one which requires urgent consideration.

NOTES

1 This term is used to refer to the obligations on member states to withdraw existing legislation or policy which hinders free movement.
2 See Article A(3) of the draft Treaty on the Union, the working Document prepared by the Netherlands Presidency for the Conclave of Foreign Ministers on 12 November 1991: the Treaty marks a new stage in the process leading gradually to a Union with a federal goal.
3 See the preamble to the TEU.
4 The Council and Commission recommendations on broad economic guidelines adopted in respectively, July and June 1994, are reprinted in *European Economy*, 1994, vol 56.
5 Article 5 of the Luxemburg Presidency Draft of June 1991 would have required the member states and the Community to commit themselves to close co-operation between their administrative agencies.
6 Regulation 2309/93, OJ L 214, 1993, 1. See also Council Regulation 2062/94 establishing a European Agency for Safety and Health at Work, OJ L216, 1994, 1.
7 For example, the Matthaeus exchange programme for customs officials, Council Decision 91/3412, OJ L 187, 1991; The Interfisc programme will lead to the exchange of 'national indirect taxation officials' while other programmes are envisaged for officials competent in veterinary matters: Council Decision 91/280, OJ L142, 1991.
8 Commission, COM (91) 408 final, Luxemburg, Office for the Official Publications of the European Communities.
9 Council Regulation 4064/89 OJ L 257, 1990, 14.
10 OJ C 39, 1993, 6.
11 Case T-24/90 *Automec II* [1992] 5 CMLR 431.
12 OJ C 257, 1991, 2.

REFERENCES

Balfour, J. (1994) 'Air Transport: A Community Success Story', *Common Market Law Review*, 31: 1025–54.
Commission of the European Communities (CEC) (1985) *Completing the Internal Market*, COM (85) 310 final, Luxemburg: Office for Official Publications of the European Communities.
——(1989) *Committee on the Study of Economic and Monetary Union, Report on Economic and Monetary Union in the EC* ('Delors I'), Luxemburg: Office for Official Publications of the European Communities.

—— (1990) *Bulletin of the European Communities, Supplementary 1990*, Luxemburg: Office for Official Publications of the European Communities.

—— (1993) *Communication on Reinforcing the Effectiveness of the Internal Market*, COM (93) 256, Luxemburg: Office for Official Publications of the European Communities.

Dehousse, R. (1994) *Europe After Maastricht – An Ever Closer Union?* Law Books in Europe, Munchen.

Dehousse, R., Snyder, F. and Majone, G. (1992) 'Europe after 1992: New Regulatory Strategies', EUI Working Paper, Law, 92/31.

Ehlermann, C-D. (1992) 'The Contribution of EC Competition Policy to the Single Market', *Common Market Law Review*, 29: 257–82.

Ferry, J. (1994) Annotation on SEP v Commission, *Utilities Law Review*, 5, 3: 84–9.

Hancher, L. (1990) *Regulating for Competition*, Oxford: Clarendon.

—— (1992) 'Competition and the European Pharmaceutical Market', *Anti-Trust Bulletin*, XXVII: 387–428.

—— (1994a) 'Competition and the Regulated Sector', in Lombay, J. (eds) *New Frontiers in Competition Law and Policy*, Chichester, Sussex: Chancery/John Wiley.

—— (1994b) Case C320/91 *Corbeau*, judgment of May 1993, annotation in *Common Market Law Review* 31: 105–122.

Hancher, L. and Moran, M. (1989) *Capitalism, Culture and Economic Regulation*, Oxford: Clarendon.

Joerges, C. (1988) in Beiber, R. (ed.) *1992, One European Market?*, Baden-Baden: Nomos.

—— (1990) 'Paradoxes of Deregulatory Strategies at Community Level' in Majone, G. (ed.) *Deregulation or Reregulation*.

—— (1994) 'European Economic Law, the Nation State and the Maastricht Treaty' in Dehousse, R. (ed.) *Europe After Maastricht*.

Lenaerts, K. (1993) 'Regulating the Regulatory Process', *European Law Review* 18: 23–49.

Lodge, J. (1994) 'Transparency and Democratic Legitimacy', *Journal of Common Market Studies* 32, 3: 343–368.

Macrory, R. (1992) 'The Enforcement of Community Environmental Laws: Some Critical Issues', *Common Market Law Review* 29: 346–369.

Majone, G. (1990) *Deregulation or Reregulation? Regulatory Reform in Europe*, London: Pinter.

—— (1993) 'The European Community between Social Policy and Social Regulation', *Journal of Common Market Studies* 31: 153–170.

Nevens, D., Nuttall, R. and Seabright, P. (1993) *Merger in Daylight*, London: CEPR.

Nicolaides, P. (ed.) (1993) *Industrial Policy in the EC: A Necessary Response to Economic Integration*, Dordrecht: M. Nijhoff.

Pelkmans, J. (1988) In Bieber, R. (ed.) *1992: One European Market?*, Baden-Baden: Nomos.

—— (1989) 'The New Approach to Harmonization', *Journal of Common Market Studies*, 25: 249–63.

Perrisch, R. (1991) Regulatory Strategies Conference, London, December 1991.

Piris, J-P. (1994) 'After Maastricht – are the Community Institutions more Efficacious', *European Law Review*, 19, 5: 447–87.

Puchala, D. (1972) 'Of Blind Men, Elephants and International Integration', *Journal of Common Market Studies*, 10, 3: 267–84.

Rowarth, P. (1994) 'A Timid Step Forward: Maastricht and Democratization of the EC', *European Law Review*, 19, 1: 16–33.

Sandholtz, W. and Zysman, J. (1989) 'Recasting the European Bargain', *World Politics*, 42: 95–128.

Sauter, W. (1994) 'EC Telecommunications Policy', *Utilities Law Review*, 5, 3: 91–102.

Siebert, H. (1990) 'The Harmonization Issue in Europe, Prior Agreement or a Competitive process', in H. Siebert (ed.) *The Completion of the Internal Market*, Tubingen: Mohr.

Steiner, J. (1994) 'Subsidiarity under the Maastricht Treaty', in O'Keefe, D. and Twomey, P. *Legal Issues of the Maastricht Treaty*, London: Chancery.

Streit, M. (1995) 'The Economic Constitution of the European Community: From 'Rome' to 'Maastricht', *European Law Journal*, 1, in press.

Sutherland, P. (1992) Report to the Commission by the High Level Group on the Operation of the Internal Market, *The Internal Market After 1992, Meeting the Challenge*, Brussels.

Swann, D. (1992) 'The Single European Market in Context', *Anti-Trust Bulletin*, XXXVII, 2: 283–306.

Toth, A. (1994) 'A Legal Analysis of Subsidiarity', in O'Keefe, D. and Twomey, P. *Legal Issues of the Maastricht Treaty*, London: Chancery.

Tsoukalis, L. (1993) *The New European Economy: The Politics and Economics of Integration*, 2nd edn, Oxford: Oxford University Press.

Van Miert, K. Foreword to Hancher, Ottervanger, Slot *EC State Aids*, London: Chancery/Wiley.

Wilks, S. R. M. and Wright, M. (1987) *Comparative Government–Industry Relations, Western Europe, the United States and Japan*, Oxford: Clarendon.

Woolcock, S. (1994) 'Competition Among Rules in the Single European Market', London: RIIA.

5 Steel

Anthony C. Masi[1]

For more than twenty years the European steel industry has been in a state of crisis. Over this period, the European Community has adopted a series of policies designed to ameliorate the situation. Despite this however, the steel industries in all member states still suffer from excess productive capacity, the very problem that initially defined the 'manifest crisis' and Community-wide measures in the first place. In the design and implementation of these policies, the member states ceded a considerable amount of decision-making authority to supranational institutions. However, narrower national interests have informed, if not dominated, the content, procedures and outcomes of measures adopted at the European level.

This chapter addresses four issues. First, it provides a brief outline of the prevalent policy choices and policy-making processes of the Italian steel sector. Second, it sketches significant EC actions dealing with the sector during the period under consideration. In particular, it outlines these EC actions in relation to other attempts to deal with the steel crisis. Third, it analyses the organisational, procedural and strategic responses of the Italian state to the various Community initiatives, noting the effects of EC measures on Italian public policies and policy objectives for the sector and its component sub-sectors. This section also outlines the power relations and responses of the various actors involved in and affected by the EC's policies. Finally, it considers the impact of the Community on Italian steel policy, and offers a critique of the Community approach to the specific features of the Italian steel industry and crisis.

It should be noted at this stage that despite often being labelled as a 'sunset' sector, steel is still in the mid-1990s a significant component of the EC's industrial apparatus with production at over 140 million tonnes, sales invoices at over $US 90 billion and employment at 350,000. In addition, steel feeds into a multitude of downstream production facilities. Italy is a significant player in the European and world markets. Even after repeated restructuring, the Italian state steel firm remained the country's second largest manufacturing concern and was the country's fourth largest industrial firm.

ITALIAN POLICIES FOR THE STEEL INDUSTRY: RESTRUCTURING AND PRIVATISATION

From Italsider to ILVA Laminati Piani

Italy's state-controlled steel firms used to be part of the Institute for Industrial Reconstruction (IRI), and specifically the Finsider which was the financial holding for the state's steel interests until 1989. The Finsider was reorganised by the creation of Italsider as the basic steel producer in 1959, and its evolution into Nuova Italsider in the early 1980s, followed by the establishment of ILVA in 1987, and finally its rebirth in a form ready for privatisation as ILVA Laminati Piani (flat rolled products) in 1994. Even after considerable down-sizing, ILVA Laminati Piani remains Italy's largest steel company, whether measured by production or sales, and it is one of the ten largest steel companies in the world today. Because the policies of particular interest to this chapter deal with the transitions between Nuova Italsider and ILVA and then between ILVA and ILVA Laminati Piani, the chapter deals with the structure of the Italian state's steel interests in the period 1987 to 1994.

Operating rates for the state steel sector in Italy reached their lowest point in 1982. In 1980, six years after the steel crisis was 'officially' declared in Europe, employment in the Italian steel industry actually rose slightly (Masi 1987). However, between 1980 and 1987, employment in the Italian state steel sector fell by more than 40 per cent. The economic impact of this second phase of the industry's crisis was tremendous, and Italian steel companies, both public and private, suffered huge financial and employment losses for a decade. Only in 1987, as a result of major restructuring efforts, were aggregate profits again seen in the Italian state steel industry. However, cumulative net income was still deeply in the red for the state-sponsored steel sector in Italy and further labour shedding was still necessary.

In 1960, Finsider produced about half of Italy's total steel output. However, huge investments, almost totally debt financed, had a heavy impact on net profitability through disproportionate depreciation and financial charges. Indeed, the Finsider reported an unbroken string of negative financial performances since 1975. By 1987, the cumulative net losses had reached $US 9.7 milliard (current). Perhaps more worrying was the fact that performance ratios were far below the average of the Finsider's principal competitors: operating margins just covered operating costs, equity covered only one-fifth of invested capital, and the capital turnover ratio was extremely low.

In an attempt to correct this situation, Italian politicians and bureaucrats took several steps. In mid-1987 a new management team was appointed and several studies were commissioned to analyse the company's problems, perspectives and prospects. In addition to some streamlining, a radical restructuring was needed to make the company viable; a strategic plan was defined and submitted to IRI (the sole shareholder). The Finsider and Nuova

Italsider were to be liquidated and ILVA, a new operating company, was to take its place.The IRI approved the Finsider Three Year Plan 1988–1990 in February 1988. By June, the Italian government granted formal approval to the plan. ILVA was incorporated and the liquidation of Finsider began.

The plan was predicated on the assumption that industrial restructuring alone would not be sufficient to turn the Italian national steel company around. Financial restructuring was also required. The plan called for production to be concentrated in the most profitable works. By the end of 1990, 2.7 million tonnes of steel-making capacity were scheduled to close together with another 700,000 tonnes of rolling mill capacity.[2] A number of self-sufficient units, not essential to ILVA's business portfolio, were sold to independent entrepreneurs, but ILVA kept minority stakes and established special agreements with the buyers for the larger units involved.

Cost reduction was to be the essential element for improving ILVA's weak competitive position. Employment levels in the Italian state sector fell dramatically over the twenty-year period under consideration: in 1974 there were 109,200 jobs at Finsider plants; by 1980 that number had risen to 121,800, but in 1987 it was only 76,100 (of which 64,600 were in the direct steel sector); by 1989, ILVA reported only 48,500 employees to be reduced to 42,000 by 1990, and projected for the end of 1994 to become less than 30,000 employees.

In December 1989, the EC approved the restructuring plan and financial requirements. It authorised the provision of state aids of up to $US 3.9 billion, subject to certain conditions. First, the achievement of productivity and efficiency targets as defined in the approved plan. Second, a ratio of financial charges to sales not lower than 5.5 per cent in 1989 and 1990. Finally, a pre-defined schedule for plant closures and the sale of assets.

Thus a new state-sector steel company was created by a plan, developed by the IRI, the Finsider, and steel managers and technical experts from the operating companies of Nuova Italsider that established the principles of operation for this new Italian state sector steel company. These principles, approved by the Italian government and subsequently by the EC, were as follows. First, the new company was to concentrate on the production of steel only at plants that were determined to be profitable on the basis of previous industrial or commercial criteria. ILVA was given all the profitable or potentially profitable activities of the Finsider. Second, every effort would have to be made to increase productivity by reducing operating costs and maximising 'synergy' within the new group. The Finsider, which had supported the entire weight of all previous financial losses, was to be liquidated. Third, a simplification of decision-making processes was to be introduced by delegating business management to operating divisions and centralising planning and control functions. Along these lines, negotiations with the trade unions for the restructuring plan had to obtain the latter's approval for a plant that would require considerable reductions in personnel. Fourth, a serious attempt would be made to minimise the social and economic impact of the restructuring process through a parallel programme of re-industrialisation of the affected areas. Fifth, there was to be an extensive programme of rationalisation and a significant reduction in productive capacity for the operating plants themselves.

McKinsey and Co reported to the European Commission that first quarter results were 47 per cent ahead of targets (ILVA, documents). During its first year of activity, ILVA sales were $US7.7 milliard with a before tax income of $US478 million. Moreover, gross operating margins (GOM) improved substantially between 1987 and 1989. By 1990, then, although IVLA's results remained inferior to those of its major competitors (which had begun restructuring earlier), it appeared to have reversed a difficult position and begun the process of bridging the gap with its competitors. It was still among the world's ten leading steel producers and it was operating profitably in Europe's second largest domestic steel market. At the operative level, the distance between ILVA and its most direct competition was reduced considerably with respect to the past. For example, ILVA's value-added per employee in 1989 was among the highest in Europe. This type of result is potentially very important because it underscores the difficulty in making judgements about individual steel undertakings based on profit alone. In 1989, the year of its founding, ILVA produced more than 11 million tonnes of steel, had sales of 10,800 billion lire, and employed 49,000 individuals (including some from the former state participation firm, Italsider, which was being 'liquidated'.)

Further reorganisation, 1990 to 1994

The reorganisation and restructuring of production at ILVA appeared to be successful, especially given the fact that its budgetary performance during the first year of its existence was encouraging as compared to those of Finsider. Having absolved itself of the commitments underwritten by the Three Year Plan for 1988–1990, particularly those imposed by the EC, top management at ILVA proposed a new Four Year Plan for 1990–1993 to the Italian government.

The new plan had three principal objectives. First, to continue to reduce costs and improve quality and service. Second, to strengthen the firm's 'patrimonial situation,' that is, its assets and operating facilities. Finally, to increase its presence on domestic and foreign markets, purchasing new companies downstream from the productive process, and improving its distribution networks.

Obviously, in order to realise this strategic plan, an important new investment programme had to be defined. The Four Year Plan for 1990–1993 included investments of 4240 billion lire, divided into two principal categories: 3440 billion for new industrial plant and equipment and 800 billion for the strengthening of commercial activities and the acquisition of downstream companies. In addition to the objectives explicitly defined by the strategic plan for 1990–1993, ILVA was to strengthen its financial situation by means of an increase in its capital by selling a part of its shares to a diversified base of investors, including foreigners. A firming up of profitability was to permit the company to remunerate its shareholders with planned distributions of dividends.

The 1988–1990 Plan anticipated a liquidation package of 7600 billion lire, to be financed by the Italian state treasury. However, the EC limited that amount to 5170 billion and tied this to an imposed debt payment structure of 5.5 per cent of invoiced sales for the two-year period 1989–1990 (compared to 3.7 per cent envisaged in the Plan). ILVA found itself caught between the need to restructure and that of acceding to the wishes of the Italian government since (in part on the request of the Italian government), it temporarily maintained in operation the Bagnoli (Napoli) integrated steel plant that was destined for closure. Thus the company was asked to carry a debt that was far above those of its principal European competitors.

With the completion of the 1988–1990 Plan and a continuation of 'efficiency recovery measures' in 1991, ILVA seemed to have moved to a position in line with its average European competitors. Its operating results were superior to the sector's average and showed promise of improvement; its 'core business' had good market share and had benefited from recent investments in technology; and efforts had been made to retrain and provide professional development for personnel. Yet ILVA was not able to complete its financial restructuring, in part because the EC denied access to some 2500 billion lire for debt restructuring. This weakened the company, prejudiced its capacity for further development and threatened the stability of its income.

The EC refusal to go along with a second transformation of ILVA into a new steel company meant that another iteration of the planning process was required in spring 1994. The second plan envisaged a somewhat smaller core business for the redesigned ILVA Laminati Piani. The company would be limited to four operating facilities (Taranto, Novi Ligure, Torino and Genova). Further reductions of its verticalised operations were demanded, and the state aids package called for the successful privatisation of the company by December 1994 (subsequently extended to 1 March 1995). The potential purchasers were narrowed to two, both consortia led by Italian industrialists. One, the Riva group, included a leading Italian industrialist from the steel sector, who had purchased other parts of the state's holdings in prior privatisations, together with local entrepreneurs from the areas in which the operating facilities are located. The second, the Lucchini group, was also lead by an Italian 'steel-man', but contained French and Brazilian capital. It was the presence of the French that made the second consortium less attractive to Italian national interests, in both the government and private sectors. The French steel plant at Fos is a competitor to the Taranto works, both specialising in coils, principally for the automotive industry. If that French group owned a part of ILVA, so the Italians reasoned, then future cuts in European production for that sub-sector would take place on Italian, and not French, soil.

Ironically, however, the delays in approving the Italian plan may have made the steel company more difficult to privatise (insofar as it allowed the company to improve its operations and thus become more costly). The mix of public and private ownership was initially not a real issue as the two occupied very different market niches. However, given the privatisations already achieved, some convergence between public and private steel producers in Italy has already taken place.

While I have described the restructuring of Italian public sector steel almost entirely in terms of national efforts, mention has been made of the role of the EC. Indeed, the EC has exerted an impact on these Italian developments since the onset of the manifest crisis in the steel sector, most notably through imposing conditions on, and therefore actually slowing, the restructuring process. The following section examines EC policies in more detail, particularly the role they have played in altering state relations with public enterprises.

EUROPEAN COMMISSION POLICIES FOR THE STEEL SECTOR

An outline of the parameters of EC attempts to deal with the world steel crisis

European Union policy for the steel industry has most recently been managed by the Competitions Directorate-General of the Commission and has centred on the elimination of excess capacity by tying reductions in production (*capacity*, not just output) to permission to give state aids to facilitate the restructuring of individual plants and whole companies. In addition to Competition, the Directorates-General for Social Affairs and Employment, Economic and Monetary Affairs, External Economic Relations and Development and Co-operation have all played some role in formulating and implementing EC steel policy. This does not mean, however, that the individual member states themselves have not also attempted to deal with the continuing crisis in the steel sector. Rather, precisely this interplay between the Community and national strategies has contributed to making the crisis of this sector a quasi-permanent feature of European economic policy making.

The crisis in steel is a continuing one for Europe and has been especially difficult for Italy in the most recent period. Along with the rest of the European and indeed world steel industries, Italian state participation steel companies suffered considerable losses and accumulated massive debt during the first steel crisis of 1974 to 1984. In earlier research I (among others) indicated, however, that the Italian producers, private as well as public, entered the crisis somewhat later and were particularly hard hit by the fact that they had just begun a major investment cycle, from which, for a variety of reasons, they could not retreat (Balconi 1991, Eisenhammer and Rhodes 1987, Masi 1987, 1988, 1990, Picchierri 1990; for comparison see the other chapters in Mény and Wright 1987). Indeed, as real prices fell and capacity utilisation in already existing facilities reached dramatic and historic lows, Italy completed construction on Europe's (then and still) largest integrated steel plant at Taranto, Puglia.

Earlier efforts by the European Coal and Steel Community (ECSC) to deal with the crisis, from Simonet's voluntary deliveries programme to Davignon's more draconian price controls (on secondary re-sellers as well as on producers) fell apart in the early 1980s. By declaring a 'manifest crisis', output and sales quotas were imposed. However, a potentially more serious, and pervasive, problem emerged as member states contrived to provide state aids to their national champions (whether state-controlled or not). In 1981, the EC took responsibility for administering a special code on state aids to be applied to the iron and steel industry. The new aid code specified that '[u]ndertakings benefiting from aids had to be engaged in implementing a systematic and specific restructuring program. Such programs should lead to an overall reduction in production capacity and should not add to capacity in areas for which there was no growth market' (Swann 1992: 326). In 1985, an even stricter set of competition rules were put into place. No company was to receive any aids with regard to its operating budget, and more importantly, no state aids could be given to finance investments, unless the latter were directed to environmental protection (which most people in the industry initially considered as non-productive investments), or to strictly controlled and defined expenditures for research and technology developments, or to facilitate plant closures.

No agreement, however, was reached between the EC and European operating firms with regard to a liberalisation plan. Consequently, quotas that were to have been removed by 1985 were, in some form or other, still in place by 1990. Voluntary cuts were insufficient to deal with the emerging chronic over-capacity in the European steel industry, and so in June 1987 the Commission undertook to find the cuts: excess capacity would be closed as the only condition that would allow state aids. A move to a truly free market in steel for Europe finally seemed to be under way. However, state aid provision continued, mostly in the form of debt restructuring, and cuts in productive capacity mostly took the form of closing plants or lines of production for which orders were non-existent in any case.

The driving force for EC steel policies has been a desire to make the European steel industry internationally competitive, to be achieved through a massive restructuring of the sector. However, such attempts have affected other policy areas. In the short run, all the social dislocations associated with de-industrialisation had to be confronted, especially worker benefits and retraining (and often relocation, a less politically acceptable alternative). More importantly, alternative employment opportunities had to be created in the local economies affected by the lay-offs, closures and down-sized mills and plants.

While the goal of the policies was to achieve global competitiveness, the most important criterion used in designing recent EC steel policy initiatives has been a focus on the profitability of firms. However, this yardstick alone can introduce serious distortions in competition among individual undertakings. For example, if a national steel industry underwent a radical restructuring early in the crisis years, it may now have amortised most of its capital debt and be able to show a profit on its product line, even if some of its output-per-head productivity measures are relatively low. On the other hand, a steel plant with modern, recently installed technology and large debt may not be able to show a profit under present market conditions, even with good output per worker. In other words, it can be difficult to combine profitability and competitiveness, and European Community policy has proved unable to accomplish the task.

Another problem facing the EC is that of who makes the investments and how they are made. No official distinction is made between private and public undertakings, provided the latter are not the beneficiaries of special treatment by their national governments (CEC 1991b). The test usually applied in these cases is the extent to which private investors would have made decisions similar to those made by the state for nationalised companies or by the state-holding company in countries that have a nominally arm's length relationship with these productive enterprises. However, if an industry is in crisis, even private entrepreneurs and the directors of companies whose stocks are held widely might decide to invest in anticipation of better market conditions at some time in the future. Alternatively, such institutions may be viewed as permanently failing (Meyer and Zucker 1989), in which case all investments, public or private, over a long period are destined to be money-losing. The difficulty is how to decide what investments by whom are in the interests of competition, and which ones are not.

EC efforts to deal with the steel crisis in Italy

Member states have tended to try to co-ordinate restructuring policies in order to stabilise the crisis. In practice this has meant a conscious drive to render national policies compatible with the overall aims of the Community, although the member states must respond to domestic political pressures as well as to Community discipline (although, in the case of steel in Italy, the two pressures have often been used to neutralise each other, cf. Masi 1990).

The cornerstone of national efforts in the second half of this two-decade long crisis has been to backslide on digressive state aids. Rather than ban them completely, the EC has allowed 'state aids' as a transitional measure if designed to further restructuring in order to restore competitiveness to the industry. In practice, the price that the EC has extracted from member states that have given such subsidies to their ailing public or private steel plants has been high – state aids can be given only if 'commensurate' cuts in productive capacity accompany them. The notion of commensurate, however, is problematic, allowing decision makers considerable latitude. For example, the cuts do not have to fall on the same plant that receives the subsidies; however, they must often come from recently modernised plants. Hence the indebted, but modern, plants have to close down capacity to repay debts, but with less capacity they lose orders and are forced to resort to temporary lay-offs. They thus accumulate deficits and struggle to pay off their debts. If the enterprise is owned or controlled by the state, then its privatisation would be made more problematic.

Consider the deliberations concerning the privatisation plans for Italy's state-participation operating company in the steel sector, ILVA.[3] A technical examination of the industrial restructuring plan proposed by and for the company itself was concluded in 1993–1994 in Brussels by DGIV. The plan was a costly one for the IRI, Italy's once state-owned holding and, since December 1992, nominally private joint stock company, as the latter was asked, and agreed, to absorb some 4 billion ECU (7200 billion current lire) in debt previously acquired by various state sector steel plants and commercial activities. A new operating company was to be formed, tentatively named La Nuova Siderurgica, and it was to carry a debt of only 900 billion lire. The plan was also to see the privatisation through both public offerings of shares on the Milan Stock Exchange of one of ILVA's subsidiaries that was already quoted on the bourse (Dalmine, near Bergamo in Northern Italy) and the direct sale of certain assets (Terni Special Steel works, which is Italy's largest stainless steel producer) to interested individuals or groups of investors.

Italian decision makers felt the approval and implementation of the plan would have guaranteed a return to profitability of the Italian public sector steel industry, as it would have allowed it to operate on the same conditions as its principal European competitors. The plan also called for the company to float a full privatisation offering on the Milan bourse within five years. In short, it appeared to be a preparatory step in finally seeing the Italian state exit from steel production, without, however, having the whole economy suffer the shock of a drastic and immediate failure of one of the country's largest industrial enterprises.

However, the plan increased tension between the Italians and the Commission. From the Commission's perspective, the Italian public sector steel producers had just finished doing exactly what they were proposing to do. In 1988–1989 they were allowed to consolidate debt, liquidate holdings, privatise assets and move to profitability. In Italy, on the other hand, there was a growing feeling that in many Directorates-General, but particularly DGIV, decisions that seemed on the surface to be ideologically pure and based soundly on the provisions of the relevant treaty, are in fact highly politicised and tend to favour sectoral interests in Germany or France. Moreover, the fact that the principal operating facility of the company was in the *Mezzogiorno*, Italy's less developed southern region, made cutting its employment and production potentially delicate with regard to relations between DGIV and DGXVI (cf. Leonardi 1993; Yule *et al.* 1992).

The comparative performance of Italy's state participation steel sector showed that its position is really less anomalous than the EC admits. Although its overall financial performance was less attractive, the post-restructuring industrial indicators for the Italian state participation company compared favourably with its principal European rivals. However, relative

Commission insensitivity to such factors rendered this distinction irrelevant. The profit-based (as opposed to performance-based) market-orientated logic of the Commission eventually triumphed over other considerations. The Commission rejected the restructuring plan, forcing the Italians to produce another restructuring scheme. The 'final' plan called for a further reduction in the size of the new steel company, which will be called ILVA Laminati Piani (meaning flat rolled steel products), and, most importantly, its privatisation through a sale of assets no later than December 1994 (a deadline which could not be met and which was extended into the first quarter of 1995).

RESPONSES OF THE ITALIAN STATE AND NATIONAL INTERESTS TO EC STEEL POLICIES

External constraints: the steel market, state participation, the EC

Although the Commission and most member states view subsidisation of industry as generally unacceptable and a potential distortion to competition, the EC has been willing to accept the trade-off of state aids to national producers (public or private) in exchange for significant reductions in productive capacity. It faces pressure to treat government-controlled enterprises in the same manner as it does private firms.

Most significantly, however, the Commission has appeared unable to act as an independent, technocratic regulator in this sector. Individual member states seem to have the 'ear' of DGIV on the steel issue. This applies particularly to the French and Germans who, despite not adhering to strict free market principles themselves, have a vested interest in using Community mechanisms to handicap the Italian steel industry. For example, German producers see Italian efforts as blocking the entire EC restructuring process for the steel sector. Yet German steel producers have continued a set of market sharing practices for products that appear very cartel-like. In addition, the French decision to attempt the privatisation of Usinor-Sacilor, Europe's biggest steel company, is predicated on finding new markets for the hot rolled coils from the Fos plant. Northern Italy looks like a good outlet for them, particularly if capacity is cut from Taranto. Thus the Italian fear of the second international consortium (see above) interested in purchasing these assets that contains French capital.

However, neither the EC, nor Italy, nor even the Germans and French would like to see what remains of Italian state sector steel go bankrupt, as that would lead to two additional problems. Assets would become under-valued and therefore available to extra-Community buyers, including but not limited to the Japanese. Further, accumulated debt and previous state aids would, under bankruptcy procedures, be wiped clean, so that these credits would be in the system as yet another distortion of European trade and there would be no way to recover them.[4]

Italian governments have for some time expressed an interest in privatising most government-controlled enterprises (Tedeschi 1993). Admittedly, much of the pressure to do so comes from technical experts within these firms, but it is also obvious that the continued subsidisation of some of these enterprises is a drain on the state's resources. As budget deficits and accumulated debt increase, they create real pressure to sell assets, particularly if operating them costs yet more money. In order to accomplish a privatisation plan, the Italian state has had to reorganise its holding apparatus. The Ministry of State Participations has been abolished and responsibility has shifted to Industry and the Treasury. The IRI has become a joint stock company, nominally private.

Privatisation raises a number of issues. On the one hand, given the explicit interest of the state in privatisation, EC pressure in this direction acts as a welcome constraint. On the other hand, there is good reason to doubt the genuine nature of this state commitment to privatisation (given past experience), especially given the tight patron–client relations that, especially under the Christian Democrats, have always characterised state–industry relations in this sector. Questions should also be asked concerning whether, without political patronage, the companies can be made at best profitable, or at least attractive to potential private purchasers.

Privatisation also involves a welter of other actors apart from the state itself. In the first place, there is the issue of how private sector producers will react. Some private producers are already looking abroad for their supplies of raw steel – notably to the cheap producers of eastern Germany and Poland. Second, the three large metal workers' unions must be taken into account. They have already made concessions to facilitate the restructuring of state steel production, and have seemed to accept privatisation as preferable to closure. Yet it is not clear what price they will be willing to pay for such an outcome. Moreover, there is always the danger that they will be unwilling to believe claims that privatisation reflects simply EC pressure on an Italian state that has battled hard to protect their interests.

Finally, the fate of the state steel industry has crucial implications for local communities. Taranto is one of the ten poorest provinces in Italy. Its economic history over the last thirty-five years has been tied to the integrated steel complex that was conceived, built and operated as a government-controlled enterprise. Its socio-economic future is at best uncertain without state steel. One possible strategy for Taranto, Puglia or Italy itself is to attempt to exert influence on the EC (and DGIV in particular), via DGXVI. Whatever the strategy chosen and the eventual outcome, what is clear is that, especially where declining sectors such as steel are concerned, wider socio-economic factors are every bit as important as questions of industrial competitiveness. Such issues will be important in the debates over privatisation: thus the presence of local entrepreneurs in the Riva consortium must be considered a positive feature for Italian regional and local interests no matter how nominal their actual participation.

NEW STRATEGIES

The EC and the 1993 Plan

The 1993 restructuring plan for the Italian state sector was based on the provision of 'digressive' state aids amounting to 4 billion ECU (current). Around it there crystallised often heated disagreement between Italian officials and the EC. According to the EC Commissioner responsible for competition policy, 'in order to justify this massive public subsidy, commensurate reductions in productive capacity, estimated at some 3 million tonnes will be required' (ILVA, documents). In the Italian press, the Commissioner was quoted as having said, in a bitter tone, that Italian state-sector steel has 'always been heavily subsidised, and has always been in the red'. Italy's Minister of Industry and Privatisation retorted that such arguments represented 'a prejudice rather than a judgement' and that the Commissioner merely 'shot out figures on congruent cuts in production that were summary and based on preconceived notions'. Since the EC Commission had hoped to close all the various negotiations on the final restructuring of the European steel industry by the end of July 1994, the ILVA situation led to a delay of half a year or more.

The EC did not really contest the 'validity' of the plan proposed by the Italians. While they offered some adjustments and asked for more precise guarantees, no practical objections were raised. The plan was alarmingly simple: transfer to a new operating company the vital, productive and profitable parts of the old firm, and liquidate through closure or sale the rest. However, the Italians completed such a manoeuvre between 1988 and 1990. Finsider was liquidated, along with several operating companies, to create ILVA, which was to have been made up of the state holding's best facilities. According to the new plan, ILVA was to be liquidated to make way for a company called 'La Nuova Siderurgica', consisting of what was, presumably, the best of the best of what was already supposed to be good. The EC forced the Italians to come up with another plan, a smaller core business, less state aids, faster liquidation of peripheral assets (so-called ILVA 'in liquidation') and the total privatisation of the new company, now to be called 'ILVA Laminati Piani', by December 1994.

While the 31 December deadline was not met, the privatisation package received the approval of IRI in March 1995. The purchaser (much to the relief of those who feared the possible nefarious influence of the French in reducing Italian production should French capital own a stake in the Italian steel industry) is to be the Riva group, the one without French capital. ILVA Laminati Piani, as a private company, will remain a serious European competitor in its narrower market of flat products. Indeed, when added to Riva's other holdings, it forms part of a grouping of almost the same size as British Steel, and just behind Usinor-Sacilor.

At the same time, the EC has continued programmes for the financing of what Italians refer to as 'social shock-absorbers' for those workers who will be made redundant by the restructuring and thus expelled from the productive cycle. Indeed, across Europe the EC anticipates that by the end of the restructuring of the steel industry, which the Commission hopes to complete in 1995 to 1996, there will be a further 60,000 redundancies with which to deal. Italy has allocated 450 billion lire to confront the problem for the period 1993 to 1995. In addition, Italian industrialists have created a 'Special Fund' financed by those who remain in the steel business, to aid the costs of this restructuring exercise. Finally, the social fund of the EEC will undoubtedly have to play a role in these processes.

The new Italian plan called for a transfer of ownership and assets of some parts of the old ILVA (it only existed for five years) to the new ILVA Laminati Piani, and left the IRI (and the Italian taxpayers), its only real shareholder, to pay off the debts. The new steel company is thus to be cleansed of its excessive debts and of those activities that are not 'strategic' to its 'core business'. The company was to concentrate on what it does best: flat rolled products, principally at Taranto and at Novi Ligure. The plan as finally approved did not call for turning the company around or making it profitable in three years at which time it was to have been quoted on the Milan Stock Exchange. It called for its privatisation by the end of 1994 or early 1995 at the latest. It accomplished this, albeit a little late (April 1995). But, as noted above, this was almost exactly what the Italians had proposed in 1988. The rather minor modifications imposed by the EC and the consequent long delays at arriving at an agreement demonstrate a preference towards privatisation, notwithstanding official dogma of non-discrimination concerning public undertakings.

EC industrial policy and competition

In 1970 the Commissioner for industrial affairs at the EC issued a daring report calling for the creation of a single European market and industrial base, for companies with truly European-scale organisational structures, for *dirigiste* research and technology development policies, and for mechanisms to foster the economic adaptation of Europe as existing industries encountered structural difficulties and began to decline and as new ones emerged to take their place (Swann 1992: 308). It is interesting to note that a recent survey of state aids to industry has indicated that national governments, and indeed the Commission itself, are more likely to help declining sectors than promote new ones (CEC 1992), since the original intention of the 1970 report focused more on labour mobility and programmes for applying new technologies and improving managerial efficiency. In short, structural difficulties have come to be the principal preoccupation of DGIV, and decision making on industrial policy, competition and state aids has come to be dominated by declining rather than emerging sectors of the economy.

In gearing up to a single Europe market, the Treaty of Rome and the Treaty of Paris provided substantial powers for regulating markets (for example, by preventing imports of certain products to protect European firms in a process of restructuring) and controlling state aids (which are to be used to help companies or sectors to restructure, not to keep inefficient producers with no prospects for success on the market as national champions). However, crucially, it 'should be emphasised that while industries may be in difficulty, and while chronic excess capacity may exist and a need to slim down and modernise may be apparent, the *EC Commission is not empowered to step in and carry out the rationalisation process*' (Swann 1992: 320, emphasis added).

With regard to the steel industry, it must be remembered that the Treaty of Paris provides for much stronger intervention in the operations of the market for ECSC-defined steel products (CEC 1990, 1991a). In fact, the EC has the power to set prices and impose limits on internal competition as well (by means of production and sales quotas on individual establishments), and it has done so with vigour. Swann (1992: 323) notes that the specific rules and procedures of the Paris document 'call for competition, but impose conditions in respect to price, output and investment decision making'. This is a crucial point, and may indeed help to account for the continuing failures of efforts to pull, at least the Italian, but probably the entire European steel market, out of its crisis.

IMPLICATIONS OF EC ACTION

The 1985 code for state subsidies to the steel industry, in addition to prohibiting all operating aids, also forbade direct financial assistance for investments (with the three above noted exceptions: environmental protection, research and development and plant closures). In the case of the Italian producer in the steel sector, first Nuova Italsider, then ILVA, this meant a rather cautious approach to technological developments. There has been a lot of shoring up of existing production techniques, but not much in terms of what might be called innovative investments, although technological possibilities exist in even a declining sector like steel.

Restrictions on the use of state aids for investment strategies actually prolonged the crisis in the sector, and the agony for the producers and workers. In particular the latter, in the Italian case, have made important concessions on work rules and pay schemes in order to help the company meet the crisis. Yet, as demonstrated above, these efforts have so far not been rewarded with adequate returns and the steel sector in Italy is still in a structural crisis, but one that may be masked by a favourable cyclical climate for the sector which started in the last quarter of 1993 and the first of 1994.

The imposition of further cuts to a facility like Taranto will probably prove detrimental, and without sufficient means to invest in innovative production techniques the situation in Italy will likely worsen. The cuts seem ill-judged for several reasons. First, while technical analyses now indicate that 90 per cent of the economies of scale obtainable from a plant such as Taranto might be achieved from a plant with only one-fifth of its 10 million-tonne per annum capacity, there seems little logic in arguments for cutting back on its production if markets are available. Moreover, Italian figures indicate that closing one of the hot rolling mills at Taranto (as the EC demanded before provisionally accepting the April 1993 Restructuring Plan) would entail losses of 2500 billion lire a year and, given internal demand, the shortfall which would need to be made up by imports. Second, the Taranto works would be uneconomical to run at half capacity, hence full-scale closure would be preferable. Yet, third, even ignoring the socio-economic implications of closure, liquidation of the entire ILVA group would cost around 11,600 billion lire.

The rationale for Italian resistance to EC pressure to further cut production at Taranto is thus clear. Further, forcing the closure of the plant would have made Italy reliant on imports from sources that themselves are potentially in crisis so that downstream utilisers, in particular in the automotive sector, but also in domestic appliances ('white goods'), will suffer. EC pressure for a reduction in capacity, coming as it did at a time when Fiat was increasing its presence in the southern regions (hence, if Taranto had reduced capacity, necessitating the search for new – probably French or German – imports from the North) increased Italian suspicions concerning the influence of Paris and Bonn in Brussels.

CONCLUSIONS

In this discussion of Italian state-sector steel restructuring and European Commission policies and actions for the sector, I have emphasised two fundamental points. First, the criteria used by the EC to determine the 'best' competitive structure for the European steel industry were and are, in my opinion, inadequate to the task. The EC should not be using short-term profitability, but rather long-term operating results, to judge individual plants and operations. Companies can turn profits with fully paid up capital, but may not be in a position to compete in the future because of a lack of new investment in technologies. Companies that have invested heavily in new plant and equipment, and that have maintained existing operations well, may not show profits immediately, but their superior output numbers will probably aid future competitiveness. European policy makers should beware of the dangers of abandoning strategies that strengthened Europe *vis-à-vis* the United States – namely a concern for a longer-term market presence rather than an obsession with short-term return on investment.

Second, at least in the perceptions of Italian steel managers and trade unionists, European policy often appears to be captured by the interests of Germany or France, rather than serving the needs of the Union as a whole. Despite this, however, national leaders can play the European card to do things that they want to do but which would be difficult or impossible in the national context without claiming that 'Brussels insists'. However, the opposite tactic can also be employed: namely, avoiding doing things that the EC wants done but which national political leaders do not want to do, by arguing that such actions appear to be an infringement of national sovereignty. Both types of arguments have appeared in the Italian context in relation to EC policies for the steel industry – claiming the EC wanted Bagnoli shut (when Italy's own plans actually called for it first) so they had to do it, and complaining that the EC was going too far in asking for reductions at Taranto (which Italian plans did not call for, but EC logic insisted upon).

The proximate causes of the current restructuring of the European steel industry are many and varied. Certainly, the actions of the European Commission have played a role in attempting to ameliorate the situation. However, a potentially unanticipated consequence was to weaken the sector in the context of global competition. However, there are others factors to consider; hence it is not easy to understand if EC policies have been the decisive influence in the shape of national restructuring efforts for the steel sector. Globalisation, domestic political change and domestic pressures on public finance are a few of the other candidates for the distinction. The possible 'capture' of Commission Directorates-General by French and German interests may have lengthened the crisis, especially, but arguably not exclusively, for Italy. None the less, it is possible that the Italian government (and state) welcomed EC intervention as a way of being able to impose a solution on the industry, while at the same time deflecting responsibility for plant closures and redundancies – especially in the South. Further, especially for the case of Italian steel, the privatisation of enterprises that have traditionally been state-owned cannot be unambiguously called a result of an EC bias against public ownership, insofar as technological change, globalisation, political dogma or pressure on public finances have also been key factors in favouring the exit of the state, especially the Italian state, from manufacturing enterprises.

NOTES

1 I would like to acknowledge the support of the SSHRC-Canada, the FCAR-Quebec and especially the Centre for European Studies, Nuffield College, University of Oxford for support which made this research possible. Particular thanks are owed to Dr V. Wright, who encouraged me to think about European policy issues as related to my own area of industrial sociology, to Dr Petrosino and Dr F.S. Nisio, who helped in the collection of relevant documents. Fieldwork could not have been conducted without the co-operation of the managers and trade unionists of the Italian steel sector companies, who are too numerous to be named individually. A special debt of gratitude is owed, however, to Dr S. Morando, Dr G. Insolera and Dr A. Iavarone, all of ILVA. Finally, I would like to thank Hussein Kassim and especially Anand Menon for imposing some order on my thoughts and for their editing suggestions that gave this chapter its present form. I remain, of course, solely responsible for errors of fact and interpretation.
2 There were numerous closures of Italian state sector steel operating plants during the restructuring of Finsider-Nuova Italsider holdings: at Campi, a steel plant

(350,000 tonnes capacity) and a plate mill (500,000 tonnes); at Torino, a steel plant (365,000 tonnes) and a sections mill (250,000 tonnes); at Terni, a 300,000 tonne rebar mill; at Sesto San Giovanni, a bar and wire rod mill with 230,000 tonnes capacity; at Massa, a finishing facility (400,000 tonnes); and at Vittuone, an unspecified amount of finishing activities (ILVA, internal documents).

3 In reconstructing the events and various proposals reported in this chapter I have drawn on three principal sources. First, I have read the documentation made available from the Commission of the European Communities and from IRI, Finsider, Nuova Italsider, and, of course, ILVA. Second, I had research assistants comb through the Italian press (and explore the ANSA on-line service) for articles on steel, privatisation and the EC. Third, I interviewed managers and trade unionists in Italy at six of the operating plants of ILVA. Many of the figures cited come from compilations of various internal documents and reports; many did not carry any archive number or file reference. More precise citations, if available, can be provided upon request.

4 These opinions were expressed to me in a series of interviews with plant managers and trade unionists that I conducted at various operating facilities of ILVA in 1993 and 1994.

REFERENCES

Balconi, Margherita (1991) *La Siderurgia Italiana (1945–1990): Tra controllo pubblico e incentivi del mercato*, Bologna: Il Mulino.

Commission of the European Communities (CEC) (1980) 'Commission Directive 80/723/EEC of 25 June 1980 on the Transparency of Financial Relations Between Member States and Public Undertakings'.

—— (1990) *Competition law in the European Communities*, Volume I: 'Rules Applicable to Undertakings', and Volume II: 'Rules Applicable to State Aids', Brussels and Luxemburg: Commission of the European Communities.

—— (1991a) 'European Industrial Policy for the 1990s', Bulletin of the European Communities, Supplement 3/91, Luxemburg: Office for Official Publications of the European Communities.

—— (1991b) 'Commission Communication to the Member States – Application of Articles 92 and 93 of the EEC Treaty and of Article 5 of Commission Directive 80/723/EEC to public undertakings in the manufacturing sector' (OJ C 273, 18.10.1991).

—— (1992) *Third Survey on State Aids*, Luxemburg: Office for Official Publications of the European Communities.

Eisenhammer, John and Rhodes, Martin (1987) 'The Politics of Public Sector Steel in Italy: From the "Economic Miracle" to the Crisis of the Eighties', in Yves Mény and Vincent Wright (eds) *The Politics of Steel: Western Europe and the Steel Industry in the Crisis Years (1974–1984)*, New York and Berlin: de Gruyter.

ILVA (n.d.) various internal documents, reports and publications.

Leonardi, Robert (ed.) (1993) *The Regions and the European Community: The Regional Response to the Single Market in the Underdeveloped Areas*, London: Frank Cass.

Masi, Anthony C. (1987) 'Nuova Italsider-Taranto and the Steel Crisis: Problems, Innovations and Prospects', in Yves Mény and Vincent Wright (eds) *The Politics of Steel: Western Europe and the Steel Industry in the Crisis Years (1974–1984)*, New York and Berlin: de Gruyter.

—— (1988) 'Industrial Strategy and Regional Economic Policy: The Case of Nuova Italsider-Taranto', *Journal of Regional Policy*, 8,1, January–March.

—— (1990) 'The Bagnoli Steel Complex: Too Little Too Late or Too Much Too

Soon', in Raffaella Nanetti and Raimondo Catanzaro (eds) *Italian Politics: A Review, Volume 4*, London and New York: Pinter.

Mény, Yves and Wright, Vincent (eds) (1987) *The Politics of Steel: Western Europe and the Steel Industry in the Crisis Years (1974–1984)*, New York and Berlin: de Gruyter.

Meyer, Marshall W. and Zucker, Lynne G. (1989) *Permanently Failing Organizations*, London: Sage Publications.

Pichierri, Angelo (1990) 'Crisis and Restructuring in the Steel Industry' in Nanetti, Raffaella and Catanzaro, Raimondo (eds) *Italian Politics: A Review, Volume 4*, London and New York: Pinter.

Swann, Dennis (1992) *The Economics of the Common Market*, Middlesex: Penguin.

Tedeschi, Michele (1993) 'Privatizations in Italy: The IRI Case', paper presented at the Il Sole 24 Ore Seminar on 'Privatisation in Italy', 12 January 1993, Merchant Taylor's Hall, London.

United Nations (1987) *Structural Changes in International Steel Trade*, New York: Economic Commission for Europe.

Yule, D. *et al.* (eds) (1992) *European Regional Incentives*, University of Strathclyde, European Research Centre.

6   Aerospace

Christopher Jones

The European Union's (EU) role in aerospace has traditionally been characterised by the modesty of both its ambitions and impact. Aerospace serves as
a stark contrast to a sector such as steel where the authority of the EU is well
established and where member governments have conceded significant
powers to Brussels.[1] However, despite the retention of national prerogatives
in this domain by member states, the EU's role in aerospace has recently
assumed greater significance.

This chapter has three aims. First, it seeks to explain how national governments were able to maintain exclusive control over aerospace policy, and why
they were particularly concerned to preserve their prerogatives in this area.
Second, it considers the efforts of the Commission to develop a role for the
Community in this area, looking both at its early, unsuccessful initiatives and
at more recent actions directed towards aspects of competition, technology
and procurement. Third, it assesses the relative influence of wider international developments on national aerospace policy, including the negotiations in the GATT, the end of the cold war and globalisation. Discussion is
confined to the aircraft branch of the sector, and does not consider the
spatial component of the industry.[2]

AEROSPACE AND THE SOVEREIGNTY OF THE STATE

Until very recently, aerospace has been regarded as an area of exclusive
national jurisidiction, inextricably linked to the sovereign authority of the
state. Following the Second World War, the recognition of the importance of
the aerospace sector for military security obliged the architects of the Treaty
of Rome to exempt the aerospace and other defence industries from the pro-
market requirements upon which the European Economic Community
(EEC) was founded. Thus, Article 223 of the EEC Treaty permits a member
state to 'take such measures as it considers necessary for the protection of the
essential interests of its security which are connected with the production of
or trade in arms, munitions and war material' (Nelson 1993: 41). A year later,
a list was drawn up by the member states of those products that would be
eligible for exemption from the internal market provisions of the Treaty.

Attached as an appendix to Article 223, it included the following: aircraft, warships, tanks, artillery, missiles, electronic equipment, explosives and fire-arms (Brzoska and Lock 1992: 219).

Since many of the technological innovations pioneered in the military sector have a 'dual use' – that is, they often have civilian applications – critics have argued that Article 223 causes significant economic distortions within commercial aerospace markets. This has led the Commission periodically to attempt to repeal this provision and to subject the sector to the same rules regarding state aids, competition and subsidies that apply to other sectors. However, efforts to abolish Article 223 or to give the Community some competence with respect to aerospace were opposed by the member states. National governments were determined to resist any instrusion on their powers for four main reasons: first, governments feared the loss of control over an industry deemed vital to the national defence effort; second, they de-sired to protect military aircraft manufacture since it has traditionally been an important source of highly skilled employment and a useful instrument of regional policy; third, sensitivity to the export potential of defence products, especially of combat aircraft, has led them to oppose measures which might ultimately threaten their revenues from this trade; and finally, a desire to maintain the prestige which derives from possessing a state-of-the-art aircraft industry acts as an important constraint on the development of policies which could, in the future, emasculate national efforts in this regard.

During the cold war era, a system of cosy national policy communities characterised west European aerospace and defence sectors. The French military-industrial complex (MIC) was perhaps the most conspicuous. At its core, the public Délégation Générale pour l'Armement (DGA) acts as sponsor and guardian to a range of public and private armaments firms, state arsenals and research laboratories. Less prominent but equally potent is the British MIC which revolves around a number of private, high technology aerospace and electronics firms based in the south, west and north-west regions of the country. Protected, for the most part, from foreign competition, MICs are constituencies of scientists, engineers, technicians, skilled craftsmen, poli-ticians, bureaucrats, serving military officers and retired generals and admirals. Their traditional influence on the defence posture and procurement practices of their respective states has been well documented in the literature.[3]

AEROSPACE AND THE EUROPEAN UNION

In 1975, the European Commission published its *Action Programme for the European Aeronautical Sector*, the 'Spinelli Report',[4] urging member states to:

> set up for the aircraft industry a true common policy and provide the Euro-pean Community with the means to implement it, both at an industrial and commercial level and in terms of air transport.

> (WEU 1975: 9)

Greeted with relative indifference by European manufacturers intent either on securing funding from their own governments for national programmes, or tempted by the possibilities of one-off collaboration with the American industry, the Spinelli Report failed to generate political momentum in support of consolidating the different national regimes into a single EC-controlled system. The ability of national 'flagship' airframe and aero-engine firms to block changes that threatened existing arrangements suggested that 'divergent national policies' and insulated national policy communities would remain in place (WEU 1975: 5). A 1977 proposal by the Commission that the EU should research, develop, build and market a large civil transport aircraft to compete with Boeing's '747' aircraft met a similar fate. Member states remained committed to the variable-geometry – and much less transparent – method of the Airbus consortium.[5] (Curzon Price 1990: 177).

The Commission has continued to argue that the organisation of the aerospace industry along national lines puts western Europe at a disadvantage in relation to its USA competitors. In 1990, for example, it asserted that 'the long term viability of Europe's aircraft industry will . . . depend more and more on the ability of the member states and their aerospace companies to give precedence to a Community rather than a national approach' (CEC 1990: 5).[6] None the less, conscious of the legal limits on its own capacity for action in this sector, given Article 223, and sensitive to prevailing neo-liberal orthodoxies about the wisdom of intervening in markets, the Commission's policy prescriptions for the industry, termed 'horizontal measures', bear little resemblance to conventional notions of industrial policy and are decidedly 'non-*dirigiste*'.[7] The primacy attached by the Commission to the role of companies and markets, and the reluctance to intervene in matters other than those with a transnational dimension, are recurring themes of recent EU policy in the aerospace sector. In a sense, having implicitly identified the need for a vigorous and well-funded policy to support aerospace, the Commission, paradoxically, then failed to develop the kind of industrial policy necessary to achieve that end.[8] Illustrating this rather ambiguous approach, an official from the Commission's Industry Directorate (DG III) remarked, 'the Commission does what the others cannot do themselves and tries to complement the action taken on a national basis' (Interview, Aerospace Unit, DG III, Brussels: 1992).

Although the Commission has not been able to convince the member states of the benefits of developing a Euro-level strategy, this does not mean to say that the EU has been prevented from exercising any influence on aerospace policy in recent years. Indeed, EU action in recent years with respect to competition, technology and public procurement has had an important impact on national policy.

Competition policy

It is in the area of competition and merger policy that the European Union has perhaps had its greatest impact on national aerospace policy making. In May 1991, in conformity with the requirements of the Merger Control Regulation (MCR), the ATR (Avions des Transports Régional) consortium, which comprises Aérospatiale of France and Alenia of Italy, informed the European Commission of its intention to acquire control of the De Havilland division of Boeing of Canada. De Havilland was a direct competitor of ATR in the market for turbo-prop-powered regional aircraft. Thus, the proposed grouping would have controlled a significant share of the market for forty- to fifty-nine-seater commuter aircraft. Concerned about its possible anti-competitive consequences, the Commission opened an investigation into the proposed operation.

By a vote in the College of nine to four with four abstentions, the Commission decided not to approve the proposed takeover (*Air and Cosmos* 1991). The Commission claimed that the proposed takeover would result in the creation of a 'powerful and unassailable' position in the market for turbo-prop regional aircraft, as the new grouping would possess 50 per cent of the world market and 65 per cent of the Community market in regional aircraft having between twenty and seventy seats (Hawkes 1992: 35). This new grouping, concluded the Commission, could well drive competing firms in the EC's regional aircraft market out of business and undermine the freedom of choice possessed by the air transport companies as well. The decision was immediately criticised by ATR on the grounds that it had been based on a tendentious definition of the relevant market. ATR objected to what it believed to be an arbitrary and unfounded decision to divide the twenty- to seventy-seat regional aircraft market into three discrete segments (twenty to thirty-nine, forty to fifty-nine, and sixty to seventy seats), and a recent analysis of the ruling concluded that it is 'difficult to understand why the Commission bothered with its segmentation approach' (Hawkes, 1992: 37). Moreover, claimed ATR, the Commission neglected to take into account the commercial aspirations of regional aircraft makers in South-east Asia, eastern Europe and Russia. At most, asserted ATR, the new grouping could hope to possess 25 per cent of the real global market. However, despite its threat to do so, ATR decided not to appeal against the decision before the European Court of Justice.

The De Havilland decision led to outbursts from French politicians from all parts of the political spectrum. The then Socialist prime minister, Edith Cresson, described it as 'scandalous' (*Aviation International*, 15 October 1991), while the finance minister, Pierre Bérégovoy, asked, 'does the Commission accept that Europe must arm itself with the means to confront foreign economic competition?' (*Aviation International*, 15 October 1991). Jacques Chirac, leader of the conservative RPR party, commented that 'it is an unjustified and grave decision, contrary to the interests of Europe' (*La Croix*,

8 October 1991). At one level, these sentiments were merely the expression of a wounded and reflexive French nationalism but, at another, they evinced a persistent cross-party belief in the legitimacy of *dirigiste* approaches to industrial policy. For the Socialist party (PS) and a large part of the opposition Gaullist party (RPR), the De Havilland decision represented a rejection of the philosophy of national champions of which France was a leading proponent.

At a bureaucratic level, within the Civil Aeronautical Division (DPAC) of the Ministry of Transport, it was conceded that the De Havilland decision represented a serious setback to the ambitions of French industry. The creation of French aerospace policy had always been treated as a matter of primary national importance. The ruling by Brussels appeared to represent a kind of 'banalisation' of the 'heroic' status which French elites had traditionally attached to aerospace policy making. The French policy community, increasingly led by the commercial strategies of its flagship firm, Aérospatiale, had been trumped by another jurisdictional authority. However, if it is undeniable that the French were particularly upset at seeing their ambitions frustrated by an 'Anglo-Dutch' clique;[9] on the whole they sought to portray the ruling as a blow to Europe's interests. As an official in the Ministry of Transport put it, 'The interest of Europe, in this particular domain, is to globalize . . . and to see if the concentration will benefit Europe' (Interview with DPAC official, Paris, 1993).

One commentator saw the inability of national and business elites to make their case in Brussels in respect of the De Havilland dossier as the product of a general failure to understand the culture of consensual decision making that prevails within the Commission (Muller 1992: 287). A new and powerful actor had confronted the established aerospace policy community and the existing elites had shown themselves ill-prepared to extract the necessary concessions from it. As Pascal Lamy, Executive Director in the office of Jacques Delors, remarked: 'elitist, ambitious, self-sufficient, centralist . . . such is the manner in which France is perceived' (Muller 1992: 287). Prior to De Havilland, France had tended to view the Commission as no more than a vehicle through which it would obtain a perfunctory legal blessing for the industrial, commercial and technological ventures in which it was engaged.

De Havilland highlighted the fact that the Commission had a great deal of potential 'negative' or blocking power. In doing so, it focused minds on the importance for firms of lobbying the Commission thoroughly in advance. It seems, with hindsight, that the French may have failed to anticipate possible Commission objections to the dossier, particularly those concerning the parameters of the market affected by the operation. There were, however, two developments arising from the De Havilland affair which provided a measure of consolation for the French. The first source of belated satisfaction came in respect of the Commission's 1992 policy statement on the aerospace industry, in which it is conceded that 'a merger combining most of the Community's supply capacity in certain sectors of the aircraft industry does not necessarily imply the creation of a dominant position incompatible with the common market' (CEC 1992: 28). The refusal by the Commission to consider the entire global market as the relevant market when deciding whether the new company would have a dominant position had been the principal bone of contention during the De Havilland dispute.

Second, the De Havilland decision led the French government to urge a change in the procedures employed within the Commission for the review of proposed mergers and acquisitions having a European dimension. Under the old procedure, DG IV was solely responsible for making recommendations to the Commission in matters pertaining to competition policy. Such an approach made little allowance for consideration of industrial policy criteria during the examination of proposed mergers and had been the source of intra-Commission tension, pitting DG III (Industry) against the Competition Directorate. As a Commission official pointed out, under the new arrangements requested by Commissioner Martin Bangemann, responsible for DG III:

> There is now coordination beforehand between DG IV and DG III, the two services most concerned with issues relating to industrial concentration, in order to arrive at a consensus. They then go together to the Commission with their recommendation. So this means that the debates are waged at the level of the services and not at the more political level of the Commissioners themselves.
>
> (Interview with official responsible for aerospace matters, DG III, Brussels: 1992)

Henceforth, industrial policy considerations were to enjoy a greater equality with competition criteria.

If the French attitude to the implementation of merger policy by the EU has been ambivalent, the attitude of the British and German governments to the existing merger regulation has been more favourable. Apart from expressing some misgivings about unnecessary bureaucratic procedures and delays involved in the vetting of proposed mergers by the Commission, both countries have argued that a strict application of competition criteria is the only way to ensure that the public interest is met. The Commission, in their view, is entrusted solely with preserving a 'level playing field' in the sector. The British Commissioner, Leon Brittan, co-author of the MCR, a strong proponent of the free market and then responsible for competition, argued at the time of De Havilland that 'having an effective competition policy is as important as any other policy one could pursue' (*International Herald Tribune*, 14 October 1991). Moreover, in Germany, competition rules are more strictly defined and applied than they are at the European level, itself reflecting the fact that the Commission's merger rules represent a compromise between several different national regimes. However, such pro-competition rhetoric may be somewhat misleading. The existence of Article 223 ensures that, in practice, many industrial manoeuvres and concentrations within the defence and aerospace sectors will continue to be undertaken and justified by governments on the grounds of 'national security'.

Technology policy

Periodic acknowledgement of the benefits resulting from collaborative technological research in aerospace has led to occasional joint initiatives since 1945. Thus, the Advisory Group for Aerospace Research and Development (AGARD) was set up by NATO in the early 1950s in order to promote the exchange of technical and scientific information between the different NATO countries. Similarly, the Group for Aeronautics Research and Technology in Europe (GARTEUR) was created in 1973 in order to optimise the research resources possessed by the national aeronautical research establishments of France, Germany, the Netherlands and the UK. GARTEUR, however, lacked a common budget and was never able to incite extensive technological co-operation among the different countries concerned. In general, because of the industry's 'strategic' status, individual states remained reluctant to abandon their control over aerospace research programmes. During the cold war, therefore, national governments remained the principal focus of the lobbying efforts of both aerospace firms and industry trade associations. Continuing high levels of defence expenditure in both France and the UK, a substantial proportion of which was devoted to aeronautical technologies, kept the industry relatively satisfied.

However, in the mid-1980s, President Reagan's planned Strategic Defense Initiative (SDI) prompted a change in the attitudes of member states and companies as regards the benefits of collective research generally, and of research in aerospace in particular.[10] Europe's technological strengths in areas such as aeronautics and electronics were threatened by this massive injection of public capital into America's leading military-industrial firms. French President François Mitterrand, in particular, feared that the shortcomings of Europe's fragmented approach to aerospace R&D would be swiftly exposed by the SDI and by the recently avowed aerospace ambitions of the Japanese. Sensing the moment to be propitious, Commission Vice-President Karl-Heinz Narjes, responsible for industrial affairs, information technology, research and science, approached the heads of the major European aircraft companies in 1987 to seek recommendations regarding appropriate EC action in respect of aerospace research and technology acquisition.[11] The deliberations of this body, which came to be known as the Industry Management Group (IMG), were published in 1988 in the form of the highly influential EUROMART (European Cooperative Measures for Aeronautical Research and Technology) report.[12] The EUROMART report served to awaken both EC and industry officials to the urgent need for collaborative, precompetitive ('upstream'), shared-cost, industrial research in aerospace (CEC 1993: xxxi). It identified nine 'lead projects' which were deemed to be worthy of EU support.

Aware that a new institutional actor was now emerging upon the scene, a variety of interests began to mobilise in Brussels. The German company MBB, which later became DASA after being purchased by Daimler Benz, was, in 1988, the first firm to set up an office in Brussels. MBB served as a kind of conduit permitting several of the large European aerospace firms, many of whom were now persuaded of the need to co-ordinate their research activities, to make their views known to the Commission. Not long afterwards Aérospatiale and the French engine manufacturer, SNECMA, both concerned at the still low profile of aeronautics at the Commission level, established their own offices in Brussels (Interview with AGARD official, Paris, 1994). In response to the increasing importance of the Commission, signalled by its controversial ruling on the proposed ATR–De Havilland merger, most large European aerospace firms now have a permanent representative in Brussels.

Another actor that arrived in Brussels was the Association Européenne des Constructeurs de Matériel Aérospatial (AECMA). AECMA, based in Paris, is the umbrella trade association representing the different national industry associations in the member states (such as the Society of British Aerospace Companies (SBAC) in the UK, the Groupement des Industries Françaises Aeronautiques et Spatiales (GIFAS) in France and the Bundesverband der deutschen Luft-und Raumfahrtindustrie (BDLI) in Germany). Initially, AECMA focused on questions relating to the harmonisation of technical standards in different countries, an ongoing project of the Commission (Interview, AGARD, Paris, 1994). More recently, however, AECMA has moved away from its technical orientation and begun to lobby the Commission on behalf of the European industry through the publication of sectoral strategy papers. AECMA, however, suffers from financial difficulties and depends on the companies which are present in Brussels for its support. In fact, the first AECMA representative in Brussels was seconded from British Aerospace. The result has been that the Commission has tended to look, in the first instance, to the major aerospace companies themselves for help with the formulation of policy initiatives (Hayward 1994a: 359).

Despite the flurry of initial interest, the EC's aeronautical research schemes, contained in the multi-year Framework Programmes,[13] have been a source of frustration for many in the industry. Early expectations were disappointed by the absence of large-scale funding for dedicated and specific aerospace R&D programmes and the frequent inclusion of such research in programmes devoted to generic technologies. The Second Framework Programme (1987–1991), for instance, could summon a budget of only 35 million ECUs for aeronautical-related research, falling under the aegis of Area 5 of the BRITE-EURAM programme (Basic Research in Industrial Technologies for Europe and European Research in Advanced Materials). The Third Framework Programme (1990–1994) represented only a slight improvement with 53 million ECUs allocated as part of the Industrial and

Materials Technology Programme and fell well below industry expectations. As one industry analyst put it:

> The modest amounts to which the firms in the sector may aspire (under these programmes) shows clearly that EU aid to aerospace functions, at best, as a sort of complementary device and does not in any way act as a 'motor' for meaningful technological progress in the European aeronautical industry. The relative weakness of EU assistance to the sector is accentuated by the fact that DG III, which oversees industry policy, has no direct influence on the R&D policies formulated by DG XII.
>
> (Loewenstein 1992: 25–6)

There are two reasons which help to explain why the EU budget is relatively small. First, the EU, under pressure from the UK and Germany, has been discouraged from creating sectoral research programmes as they are seen as implicitly supporting the notion of 'picking winners'. Instead, the Commission has enacted programmes stressing the benefits of basic research and generic technologies which have applications to a variety of sectors. Second, it is widely felt by some of the smaller member states within the EU that aerospace, both as a 'cold war' industry and in relation to Airbus, has already been the beneficiary of considerable public funding. Strong resistance was expressed by these countries to the idea of further spending on large-scale aeronautical research projects by Brussels. Clearly, the smaller states have a vested interest in the kind of smaller scale research that can be performed readily, without the need for dedicated aeronautical research establishments with expensive and sophisticated apparatus.

For a long time the French opposed this view, arguing for more generous project-centred spending on leading-edge aeronautical research activities, an approach which would naturally have favoured the established aeronautical powers. More recently, however, they have begun to show signs of resignation and a reluctant willingness to obtain what they can from the existing menu of aeronautical projects. It should be noted that the Fourth Framework Programme (1994–1998) has attempted to placate critics of the EU's policies for the promotion of aerospace R&D by allocating approximately 230 million ECUs for aeronautical research. This represents 50 per cent of the available Chapter 3 ('Transport Technologies') funding under the Framework Programme. Thus, although many in the industry continue to manifest their dissatisfaction with the degree of priority accorded by the EU to aeronautical research, the recent initiative has been viewed in a more positive light.

Both the struggle to accord greater priority to aeronautical research programmes and the manner in which the aerospace dossier was handled by EU negotiators during the recent round of GATT discussions (see below) has left many convinced that the multifarious nature of aerospace interest representation in Brussels has not served the industry's best interests. Eager to improve their clout within the Commission, the presidents of the major European aerospace firms aligned themselves in 1993 in a new grouping, the European

Aeronautical Industries Council (EAIC) which seeks to bring their collective political and technical muscle to bear on dossiers with a European dimension. This body now meets intermittently with the Commissioner responsible for Industry Policy and the Chairman of AECMA. Despite this development, the problem of divergent national agendas and recurring company jealousies continues to obstruct co-operation of a more enduring nature. As one official remarked, 'speaking with one unified voice to the Commission – this problem is not yet solved' (Interview with official of AGARD Paris, 1994).

Procurement policy

Initiatives to develop a single European weapons market have foundered, for the most part, in the face of opposition from nation states reluctant to abandon their prerogatives in the areas of procurement and arms industrial policies. This situation is gradually changing through the efforts of the Independent European Programme Group (IEPG) which brings together the European Defence Ministers and their National Armaments Directors (NADs). The IEPG, which co-ordinates its activities closely with NATO (North Atlantic Treaty Organisation), has worked since 1976 to open national arms markets to cross-border competition and to promote standardisation in equipment. However, progress has been slow and as of 1992, 'the segment of the arms market opened for IEPG-wide competition is only of the order of 10–20 per cent of national markets for 'hard' defence equipment' (Bauer 1992: 42). In addition, the IEPG has promoted collaboration in defence research with its EUCLID (European Cooperation for the Long Term in Defence) programme which was launched in 1989. In aerospace, EUCLID has sought to promote greater co-operation between IEPG governments in exploring the impact on existing aerospace technologies of the use of composite materials or modular avionics. EUCLID, however, has been hampered by sensitive questions relating to intellectual property and technology transfer, in addition to scepticism raised in connection with the alleged savings of European cooperative research (WEU 1990: 7).

The European Commission's own efforts to aid the opening up of national defence markets continue to be obstructed by Article 223 of the Rome Treaty. Germany, for instance, is hesitant about abolishing Article 223 on the grounds that an emergent common market for arms would favour the UK and France. The significant arms export constraints placed on Germany in the post-1945 period mean that her military-industrial complex is less developed than those of its competitors. EU initiatives have been limited, therefore, to assisting in the creation of the background conditions that may facilitate the emergence of a common European weapons market. The 1986 Single European Act (SEA), for instance, aimed to harmonise the different regimes of technical standards, bidding rules and patent regulations which prevail within EU countries and which act as impediments to a common procurement policy in defence equipment (Bauer 1992: 43). The IEPG and SEA have had some success, as the signing in 1987 of the Anglo-French Reciprocal Purchase Agreement in cross-border tendering demonstrates. Such successes have been overshadowed, however, by larger failures. The European Fighter Aircraft programme, which in theory was to have provided an aircraft for the Air Forces of all the major European states, was hampered by an inability to arrive at a collective staff target (an agreement denoting the aircraft's performance requirements), and industrial rivalries between French and British engine manufacturers. The French decision to build independently the Rafale fighter has doubtless added to the economic costs of both projects.

The Commission has also attempted, as yet with little success, to develop a European company law which would facilitate the creation of large consortia capable of competing for arms contracts on a western European level (interview with AGARD official, Paris, 1994). On balance, although the Common Foreign and Security Policy (CFSP) provisions of the Maastricht Treaty establish the rudiments of a common defence posture among the member states, the Commission's purview is limited largely to influencing civilian sectors which overlap with the defence industry (the so-called 'dual use' industries) and not the defence industry *per se* (as per Article 223). For the moment, it seems that the pace of European integration in the military aerospace sector is more likely to be furthered by the industrial and commercial ventures of firms, in response to changing economic incentives, than by the regulatory activities of supranational entities. In fact, Brussels is likely to remain a peripheral actor until existing state-owned defence and aerospace firms are denationalised, thereby permitting genuine regroupings and consolidation in the sector.

EXTERNAL INFLUENCES ON AEROSPACE POLICY MAKING

EU action in the aerospace sector has been limited to this point, and the Commission has been kept at bay in many areas by national actors eager to retain their control. Three other factors have perhaps exerted a greater influence on the shaping of public policies for the aerospace sector than the EU. These are the GATT talks on aid to large civil aircraft, the end of the cold war, and the trend towards globalisation in the sector.

The GATT and civil aircraft

DG I (Foreign Economic Relations) of the Commission negotiates in the GATT on behalf of the member states participating in the Airbus consortium. It has thus represented their collective interests in the decade-long dispute with the Americans over the forms and levels of public aid provided to large civil aircraft. The Foreign Trade Commissioner consults with the ministers responsible for the commercial aircraft industry in the four states involved (France, Germany, the UK and Spain) and with representatives of the industry itself (including engine and equipment manufacturers). The outcome of the dispute has potentially far-reaching implications for the aircraft industries in the four European countries concerned. Alarmed by the rapid progress in market share that Airbus made in the mid-1980s, the USA began in 1987 to press its claims in the GATT more vigorously. Specifically, the USA claimed that the European system of direct aid (repayable loans) for the manufacture of large civil aircraft is trade-distorting and amounts to a predatory attack on the profitability of American aerospace firms. The crucial question still awaiting resolution is whether European governments will be obliged, as a result of concessions in the GATT negotiations, to move to a US-style, indirect system of aid through research and development funding.

This would be highly damaging to the European industry, imperilling the very structure of support and assistance built up over decades by national governments. The US industry, already operating within a 'GATT-acceptable' regime of aids, would escape relatively unscathed. A truce in the dispute was signed in July of 1992 which put various limits on the aids furnished by European and American governments to their respective industries. However, should this bilateral accord lapse without a new, mutually acceptable arrangement governing such aids being established, it is possible that some version of the general GATT subsidies code will come into effect. Such a code would take a far more restrictive view of the European approach to direct support for civil aerospace. The problem confronting the European industry in making the transition to an indirect regime of aid is that no Europe-wide aeronautical R&D institution currently exists which is comparable to the aeronautical research programmes of the Defence Department and NASA in the USA. Although the Fourth Framework Programme (1994–1998) has increased funding for aerospace research, the absence of the kind of large-scale funding for aeronautics required limits its usefulness as an indirect support regime for the European industry.

Over the last eight years, the GATT has succeeded in prising open tightly knit, national aerospace policy networks. In doing so, it threatens the 'heroic' status traditionally accorded to civil aerospace policy making in the European states considered here. The industry has become uncomfortably aware of the ambivalent manner in which national governmental officials have defended their vital interests in the negotiations with the US industry. In the UK, for instance, the Treasury is thought to be privately disdainful of the size of 'subsidy' which has supported the Airbus consortium over the years. In France, aerospace is alleged to have been sacrificed by officials intent on protecting other important sectors such as agriculture and the audiovisual industry from the depredations of foreign competition. For these reasons, it seems likely that the GATT may be the source of further, largely unwelcome change within national aerospace policy communities in coming years.

The end of the cold war

The easing of East–West tensions since the late 1980s has provoked demands, in Europe and the United States, for reductions in defence spending and for the conversion of military industries to civilian purposes. As perhaps the archtypical 'cold war' industry, aerospace has been particularly affected by the clamour for reduced defence expenditure. In Germany, for instance, concerted public pressure has obliged the government to seek performance modifications and cost reductions (eventually of the order of 13 per cent) to the European Fighter Aircraft (EFA), in which Germany has a substantial stake. Many Germans felt that the Jager 90 ('Hunter' 90), as EFA is known in Germany, was an unaffordable relic from the cold war, ill-suited to new political and strategic circumstances. For some time, in fact, there was considerable uncertainty as to whether Germany would proceed to the final production stage of EFA, although contractual obligations to the Euro-fighter GmbH consortium and the threat of financial penalties appear, for the moment, to have convinced it otherwise.[14] The German Defence Minister's own serious misgivings about the project, allegedly inspired by shorter term political calculations, left many in the German Air Force and aerospace industry feeling confused and betrayed. In a larger sense, DASA has predicted that reductions in the German defence budgets will lead to annual cutbacks in coming years of between 15 and 20 per cent in its business (Hayward 1994b: 87).

In the UK, a series of manpower and equipment cutbacks initiated with the publication of the government's *Options for Change* paper in 1990 fell mainly on the Army and Navy. However, 5000 jobs subsequently went in the aerospace sector when the government decided to cut back on planned Tornado fighter production (Hayward 1994: 87). Both BAe and Rolls-Royce have since announced large redundancies in their military divisions while many of the specialist supplier firms, dependent on the majors, have been compelled to do the same. Although begun before the collapse of the Berlin Wall, the Ministry of Defence's 'value for money' initiative in defence procurement has acquired a new urgency in recent times. The willingness to consider purchases 'off the shelf' from foreign sources, and to impose fixed-price contracts and compulsory performance milestones on programmes awarded to UK aerospace firms, are reflections of the limited resources available in the new strategic and financial environment. Neither the advent of growing numbers of 'out-of-area' conflicts (the war in the Gulf) nor the increase in peacekeeping/humanitarian missions (the UN mission in former Yugoslavia) appears to have applied the brake to the drive for savings in defence equipment budgets. Through their control of the allocation of domestic procurement contracts and their capacity to approve or reject export requests, governments have sought to induce greater collaboration on the part of industry. As their access to research funding from defence ministries is now more regulated, aerospace firms have had to shoulder a greater proportion of the expenses associated with civil aeronautical R&D activities themselves. In both Europe and the USA, then, the scaling back in the weapons buildup and the desire for a 'peace dividend' suggest that the aerospace industry will be put on a more commercial footing in the future as governments find fewer arguments to convince their publics of the need for heavy spending on such items.

Globalisation

The final factor which has contributed to the transformation of the environment in which aerospace policy is made has been globalisation. Globalisation refers to 'the transborder operations of firms undertaken to organise their development, production, financing, and marketing activities' (OECD 1993: 1). In practice, this involves firms organising their activities to take advantage of 'the increased mobility of production factors and the growing number of advantageous locations' (OECD 1993: 1). The most important forms of globalisation are foreign direct investment, certain aspects of international trade and cross-border alliances (joint ventures). Firms in the aerospace sector have shown a particular propensity to engage in strategic alliances and aerospace is now among the most 'globalised' of all industrial sectors. As a senior executive in Daimler-Benz Aerospace, Manfred Bischoff, recently put it: 'all-European solutions are no longer sufficient to safeguard the (industry's) future' (*Financial Times*, 27 January 1995). In response, many European aerospace firms have sought to acquire manufacturing subsidiaries or partners in the USA in order to have a production capacity in the vital 'dollar zone'. In aero-engines, for instance, the French firm SNECMA has pursued a highly successful collaboration with General Electric of the USA, producing the CFM56 engine.

The desire to acquire new technology or access to lower cost capital may also provide a rationale for such ventures. Diversification into the Asian market may be driven by the wish to take advantage of cheaper labour costs, or the need to set up production and customising operations in proximity to expanding aerospace markets (China in particular). Spain's CASA, for instance, has recently embarked upon a collaboration with IPTN of Indonesia to produce a new turboprop regional aircraft. Alliances with firms in eastern Europe and South America are also under way or being contemplated in a variety of product niches within the aerospace sector. Once again, the motivation may be risk sharing, access to cheaper intermediate level components or the desire to penetrate new markets. It might be added that the lengthy recession in the air transport sector, and the dangerously weak financial position of many airlines at present, has given added impetus to the search by aircraft manufacturers for partners with whom to share the risks and costs of the business. Finally, it is evident that such cross-border alliances are not just limited to the larger aerospace firms; many medium and small-sized system and component suppliers within EU states have become vital contractors to international consortia and overseas ventures.

The importance of these changes lies in the fact that state policy makers increasingly lack the expertise and understanding to be of assistance to their national firms as the latter pursue strategies of internationalisation. While governments played a central role in an era when aerospace policies were wedded to national needs and priorities – what Muller has called 'arsenal strategies' (Muller 1989: 212) – they are largely peripheral when there is a requirement for knowledge of global capital markets, international marketing techniques or local taxation laws. Although governments may have important roles to play in the area of export credit financing, power has gravitated to firms as governments have recognised that international market share is the benchmark for success in an era of ruthless neo-mercantilism. Company decisions about employment levels or investment strategies are now as likely to be dictated by 'offshore' incentives and opportunities as they are by the political/business cycles of domestic economies. Furthermore, the hybridisation which results from the creation of quasi-autonomous international holdings renders inadequate national frameworks of regulation, taxation and accountability.[15] Goverments appear to have been relegated to a role of seeking to influence the development of the international trading regime to ensure that rules governing market access favour their own aerospace firms.

CONCLUSION

In spite of the Commission's efforts to develop a role for the EU, the impact of EU action on national aerospace policy has remained limited. The member states have generally been reluctant to cede competence in an area which they regard as inextricably connected with vital security and strategic economic interests. This does not mean, however, that the EU has had no influence on policy or that the member states enjoy absolute freedom in the sector. In the first place, EC action in the areas of competition and technology policy, as well as the collective representation of the member states by the Commission in the GATT, are significant developments, constituting a far from insignificant intrusion on national prerogatives which have hitherto been jealously guarded. Furthermore, European firms are increasingly turning their attentions to Brussels, seeking to explore the new opportunities and meet the challenges presented by the creation of the single European market. Links with national governments are not yet in danger of being severed, but this development signals that companies are looking beyond national horizons for help in confronting the American aerospace industry. It is important to observe, however, that these developments remain restricted to civil aerospace and have not yet spilled over to the military side of the industry.

Second, while the EU has had an admittedly modest impact, wider international developments have had a more marked effect on policy and policy making at the national level. Member states have responded to the changes in the global environment with new policy orientations to meet new demands.

The member states have perhaps retained more freedom and a greater degree of policy control in this sector than in others discussed in this volume. However, even so, policy change reflects the extent to which the EU and wider international developments have circumscribed national autonomy even in this domain.

NOTES

I should like to express my thanks to Pierre Muller and the editors for their comments, Vincent Wright, and officials at AGARD and Aérospatiale for their assistance, and Philippa Hurrell who has offered her support and encouragement throughout my doctoral research.

1 See the contribution of Anthony Masi, Chapter 5, this volume.
2 The aerospace or aeronautical industry comprises firms involved in the manufacture of airframes, jet and turboprop engines, aircraft parts and, more recently, under the heading of space products: guided missiles, space vehicles, space propulsion units, research and communications satellites and related equipment. It also includes the avionics industry which is a specialised branch of the industry engaged in the manufacture of sophisticated electronic components and systems. Aerospace products are further divided into civilian and military usages with different market structures prevailing in each (see Klepper 1991: 184).
3 See especially Kolodziej (1987) and Lovering (1987).
4 The Spinelli Report addressed itself to the civil aerospace industry only.
5 The financial position of the Airbus consortium has been, at times, the source of controversy for the reason that it does not publish a unified set of annual accounts. As a GIE (Groupement d'Intérêt Economique) – the legal formula upon which Airbus was constituted in 1970 – the financial position of the consortium is known only to the partner companies. It is, moreover, impossible to determine the profit/loss position of the consortium from the financial accounts published by the individual firms themselves.
6 DG III (Industry) is the Directorate concerned with the strategic interests of the aerospace industry and has been the principal architect of the few tentative policy initiatives which the Commission has issued in the sector (see CEC 1990, 1992).
7 These measures included proposals to accelerate the harmonisation of technical standards, to create a common European company statute to facilitate future trans-European consolidation in the industry, to promote vocational training such as the expansion of co-operation between aeronautics schools and industry or the harmonisation of aeronautics qualifications, and to promote social dialogue (see CEC 1992).
8 It is important to recall that the personnel and financial resources at the disposal of the Commission are a mere fraction of those allocated to overseeing aerospace activities within the largest member states. At present, the Commission's different services remain highly dependent on national governments for implementation of initiatives taken in Brussels.
9 British Aerospace and Fokker, both manufacturers of regional aircraft, were alleged to have made their opposition to the merger well known to Commission President Jacques Delors. In the vote itself Delors abstained, a fact provoking considerable indignation in Paris.
10 The French and Germans, for instance, were instrumental in the launch in 1985 of the seventeen-nation (now over twenty) EUREKA (European Research Cooperation Agency) initiative which was designed to promote co-operation in the development and launch of new, high-technology products. EUREKA and ESPRIT (European Programme for Research in Information Technology) (set up in 1984)

legitimised a subsequent Community presence in aerospace and paved the way for the creation of aerospace interest representation in Brussels (See Curzon Price 1990: 175–7).

11 These were: Aeritalia SPA, Aérospatiale SNI, Avions Marcel Dassault-Breguet Aviation, British Aerospace PLC, Construcciones Aeronauticas SA, Dornier GmbH, Fokker Aircraft BV, Messerschmitt-Bolkow-Blohm GmbH and Société Anonyme Belge de Constructions Aeronautiques.

12 The study was funded jointly by industry and the Commission.

13 The Framework Programmes were established by the Council of Ministers in 1983 in the hope of integrating all Community aid to R&D into a single, coherent system, capable of ensuring continuity and funding over four-year timeframes. DG XII (Science, Research and Development) oversees the establishment and financing of aeronautical research projects contained within the Framework Programmes (Curzon Price 1990: 178).

14 See *Financial Times* article, 'Eurofighter hits bad weather' 5 September 1994.

15 For development of this point, see Wright (1995).

REFERENCES

Agence Europe (1992) 20 July, Brussels.

Air and Cosmos (1991) 14–20 October, 1348.

Assembly of Western European Union (AWEU) (1975) Mr Warren, Rapporteur to the Committee on Scientific, Technological and Aerospace Questions *The European Aeronautical Industry*, Document 691, Paris, Assembly of Western European Union.

—— (1990) Mr Wilkinson, Rapporteur to the Technological and Aerospace Committee *The Independent European Programme Group (IEPG) and Western European Union*, Document 1228, Paris, Assembly of Western European Union.

Bauer, H. (1992) 'Institutional Frameworks for Integration of Arms Production in Western Europe', in M. Brzoska and P. Lock (eds) *Restructuring of Arms Production in Western Europe*, Oxford: Oxford University Press.

Brzoska, M. and Lock, P. (eds) (1992) *Restructuring of Arms Production in Western Europe*, Oxford: Oxford University Press.

Commission of the European Communities (CEC) (1990) *A Competitive European Aeronautical Industry*, SEC (90) 1456, 23 July, Luxemburg: Office for Official Publications of the European Communities.

—— (1992) *The European Aircraft Industry: First Assessment and Possible Community Actions*, COM (92) 164, 29 April, Luxemburg: Office for Official Publications of the European Communities.

CEC Directorate-General XII (1993) *Synopses of Current Aeronautics Projects Industrial and Materials Technology Programme*, Luxemburg: Office for Official Publications of the European Communities.

Curzon Price, V. (1990) 'Competition and Industrial Policies with Emphasis on Industrial Policy', in A.M. El-Agraa (ed.) *Economics of the European Community*, London: Philip Allan.

Hawkes, L. (1992) 'The EC Merger Control Regulation: Not an Industrial Policy Instrument: The De Havilland Decision', *European Competition Law Review*, 13,1, January/February.

Hayward, K. (1994a) 'European Union Policy and the European Aerospace Industry', *Journal of European Public Policy*, 1,3.

—— (1994b) *The World Aerospace Industry Collaboration and Competition*, London: Duckworth & RUSI.

Johnson, P. (1993) *European Industries Structure, Conduct and Performance*, Aldershot: Edward Elgar.

Jones, C. (1995) 'The Limits of the Policy Community Approach: Policy-Making in the Aerospace Industry in France and Britain, 1979–1992', D.Phil. in preparation, Nuffield College, Oxford University.

Klepper, G. (1991) 'The Aerospace Industry', in D.G. Mayes (ed.) *The European Challenge: Industry's Response to the 1992 Programme*, London: Harvester Wheatsheaf.

Kolodziej, E.A. (1987) *The Making and Marketing of Arms: The French Experience and its Implications for the International System*, Princeton: Princeton University Press.

Loewenstein, A. (1992) 'L'Europe après Maastricht: Une question stratégique', *Cahier Thématique La Politique Industrielle et Structurelle*, Paris: Aérospatiale SNI.

Lovering, J. (1987) 'The Atlantic Arms Economy: Towards a Military Regime of Accumulation?', *Capital and Class*, 33, Winter.

Muller, P. (1989) *Airbus L'Ambition Européenne; Logique d'Etat, logique de marché*, Paris: L'Harmattan.

Muller, P. (1992) 'Entre le local et l'Europe; La crise du modèle français de politiques publiques', *Revue Française de Science Politique*, 42, 2.

Nelson, S. (ed.) (1993) *Treaty Establishing the European Economic Community; The Convoluted Treaties, Vol. II 1957*, Oxford: Nelson & Pollard Publishing.

Organisation for Economic Cooperation and Development (OECD) (1993) *The Globalisation of Industry: Government and Corporate Issues* (Issues Paper of a Symposium), Paris: Industry Committee, OECD.

Wright, V. (1995) 'The State and Major Enterprises in Western Europe: Enduring Complexities', in J. Hayward (ed.) *Industrial Enterprise and European Integration*, Oxford: Oxford University Press.

7   Air transport

Hussein Kassim[1]

The development of a common air transport by the European Union has brought about a radical transformation of the post-war regulatory regime in the sector.[2] Policy development has taken place across a broad front, touching most aspects of the industry, but it has advanced furthest in the area of liberalisation where a regulatory framework for a single market in air services has been created. This has had far-reaching consequences in a sector where governments enjoyed considerable autonomy under a state-centric regime and where most traditionally had used their powers to pursue restrictive and protectionist policies of patriotic interventionism. In these countries, governments have been deprived of the use of, or at least cannot use as freely, the policy instruments which they had previously deployed. However, in the Netherlands and the UK, where historically governments have considered that the national interest was best served by a far more liberal approach, the impact of EU action has been less significant. In the UK, not only did Conservative governments after 1979 embark on liberalisation before the commitment to create a single market was made at the EC level, but the UK actively promoted Community action as a means of extending its own liberal programme.

This chapter will examine the impact of EU action on the content of national aviation policy and the dynamics of national policy making. After a discussion of the post-war regime, the consequences of US deregulation and the policies traditionally pursued by governments in this sector, the main lines of EU policy development will be considered. The impact on policy in the four larger member states – France, Germany, Italy and the UK – will then be considered.[3] The final section will examine the effect of EU action on national actors. Most significant is the extent to which flag carriers have redefined their relationship with the state, departed from their public service mission in favour of a more commercially orientated vocation, and sought to expand their activities beyond narrowly national horizons. No longer dependent on their governments for commercial freedoms in Europe and influenced directly by the development of EU policy, airline companies have both individually and collectively extended their lobbying activities to Brussels, while not abandoning the national level.

THE TRADITIONAL REGIME

Historically, air transport has been governed by a regime founded on the principle, originally enshrined in the Paris Convention in 1941 and reaffirmed by the Convention on International Civic Aviation (the 'Chicago Convention') of 1944, that each state enjoys absolute sovereignty over the airspace above its territory (Cheng 1962, Martin *et al.* 1984, Naveau 1989).[4] In the post-war period, governments used their prerogatives to develop their air transport industries and to support their carriers, intervening extensively and building protective walls around their national aviation markets. Economic fragmentation into distinct national markets was matched by the division of airspace and the management of air traffic control along national lines. Governments acted independently in determining the organisation of national airspace, and in operating air traffic control systems. Consequently, in western Europe, fifty-four control centres, thirty-one technical systems and seventy different computer languages are involved in the management of air traffic (AEA 1989).

Limited international co-operation took place within a number of global and regional aviation organisations. Signatories to the Chicago Convention belonged to the International Civil Aviation Organisation (ICAO), a UN-affiliated body which played a major role in developing non-binding, technical standards for the industry (Naveau 1989, Socher 1991). At the regional level, the main body in Europe was the European Civil Aviation Conference (ECAC), founded in 1954. ECAC was the principle forum within which European states discussed technical and commercial aviation matters (Naveau 1989). ECAC's sister organisation, the Joint Aviation Authorities (JAA), brings together national airworthiness authorities for the purpose of devising Joint Aviation Requirements (JARs) for western Europe. Finally, the European Organisation for the Safety of Air Navigation (Eurocontrol) was created in 1960 to control the upper airspace of its member states. However, its functions were limited until the mid-1980s, when it began to develop an important role in managing air traffic control programmes in association with ECAC (AEA 1995: 38–9). The state-centric nature of the traditional regime was not compromised by the existence and functioning of these organisations, since all were intergovernmental, issuing non-binding recommendations or opinions.

The principle of absolute sovereignty made possible the pursuit of policies of patriotic interventionism. The rights of states to control the movement of air traffic to, from and within their territories found expression in the three regulatory frameworks which governed respectively international scheduled, international non-scheduled (mostly charter) and domestic air services. Control over international scheduled air transport was exercised by governments through bilateral air services agreements (Cheng 1962, Doganis 1991, 1993). The bilateral system grew out of the failure of delegates to the Chicago Convention of 1944, organised to establish a global regulatory system, to reach

Table 7.1 The freedoms of the air

Freedoms defined by the International Air Transport Agreement and exchanged in bilateral agreements

First freedom: the freedom to overfly the territory of another state
Second freedom: the freedom to land for technical reasons in another state
Third freedom: the freedom to carry commercial traffic from the home state to the foreign state
Fourth freedom: the freedom to carry traffic from the foreign state to the home state
Fifth freedom: the freedom for a carrier to carry commercial traffic between two foreign states on a route to or from the home state

Other Freedoms
Sixth freedom: the freedom to operate commercial services between two foreign states via the home state
Seventh freedom: the freedom to operate commercial services directly between two foreign states
Cabotage: the freedom to operate commercial services between two points in a foreign state

---

Source: Based on Doganis 1991

agreement on a multilateral structure for the exchange of the commercial 'freedoms of the air' (see Table 7.1).[5] Instead, these freedoms, defined in the Transport Agreement at Chicago, came to be exchanged on a bilateral basis, following the model included in the Final Act of Chicago and according to the example set by the United Kingdom and the United States at Bermuda in 1946 (Cheng 1962, HMG 1946). These agreements enabled governments to exercise comprehensive and detailed control over air services operating to and from their territories.

In the first place, governments decided how many airlines from each country would be permitted to operate routes between the two countries and designated the companies that would be allowed to perform them. Typically, each country named only one airline ('mono-designation'), its flag carrier, on any one route. Second, the contracting parties specified, usually in the appendices of the agreement, which points in each country could be served by the airlines of the other. Third, the states decided on how capacity was to be shared between airlines of the two countries, usually agreeing on a 50:50 split. Fourth, the bilateral agreement obliged the designated airlines to reach agreement on tariff levels for each route in line with the rates determined by the International Air Transport Association (IATA), which represented the interests of scheduled air carriers. Once the airlines had decided on the rate to be charged, the approval of both states had to be sought ('double disapproval') before the service came into operation.

In order to prevent the use of 'flags of convenience', bilateral agreements contained a nationality clause which limited the attribution of the traffic rights that they granted to companies substantially owned and effectively controlled by nationals of each contracting state.

Bilateral agreements in Europe were usually underpinned by inter-airline accords which contracting governments obliged their companies to sign. Under these accords, the air carriers serving a particular route reached agreement on a range of commercial and technical arrangements, including, for example, flight frequency and sometimes revenue sharing (Doganis 1991: 30–6).

A more liberal system might have developed with regard to international non-scheduled services, since Article 5 of the Chicago Convention required authorisation only from the state of destination. However, in practice, most states imposed strict conditions concerning eligibility and availability of operators (Naveau 1989). In spite of these restrictions, strong, if concentrated, non-scheduled markets developed in the north Atlantic (although this contracted significantly in the 1980s following US deregulation) and in Europe along a north–south axis, connecting Germany, the United Kingdom and Scandinavia with holiday destinations in Greece, Portugal and Spain.[6]

States enjoyed exclusive and absolute control over domestic air services. Governments exercised power with respect to all aspects of commercial activity, controlling market access, the degree of competition permitted on individual routes and the level of air fares. Moreover, governments have been able to impose on airlines the obligation to operate services on routes which, though not commercially viable, were socially necessary, important for reasons of regional development or for maintaining links between the mainland and isolated communities.

Governments exercised control over freedom of establishment in all three categories through the licensing of airline companies. All air carriers had to be licensed, and governments determined the criteria of economic and technical fitness, as well as requiring ownership and substantial control by nationals, which undertakings had to satisfy before they could be registered as airline companies.

The traditional regime thus placed considerable powers in the hands of governments exercised either unilaterally or on a bilateral basis through inter-state negotiation. It afforded them control over virtually all aspects of aviation and equipped them with detailed regulatory instruments. International co-operation was voluntary and limited.

The US challenge to the traditional regime

Between 1945 and the late 1970s, in an era of strict and extensive regulation, governments used their prerogatives to pursue highly restrictive policies. However, this period came to an end when US deregulation breached the system of 'high regulation'.[7] Following criticism of the costs of regulation over a number of years, the Carter administration of 1976 to 1980 deregulated domestic air transport, renegotiated its air services agreements with a number of bilateral partners including some European states (see Driscoll 1981 for a full list) and challenged IATA to 'show cause' as to why it should be exempted from US anti-cartel legislation (Doganis 1991).

The new US approach represented a milestone in air transport policy and regulation. First, domestic deregulation yielded significant benefits to passengers in the form of lower fares and competition in quality of service, although the consolidation of the industry and the development of hub-and-spoke networks began to erode these benefits some years later.[8] It demonstrated that commercial aviation could be exposed to market pressures (Baumol *et al.* 1982) and that strict regulation was not a *sine qua non* for the existence of a reliable air services network. Second, the USA's new foreign aviation policy introduced a number of innovative concepts and practices to international aviation. The new bilaterals expanded access, allowed multi-designation, granted fifth freedom rights, incorporated non-scheduled services which were permitted unlimited freedoms, removed capacity restrictions, and introduced a system of double disapproval for fares under which tariffs became operative unless both governments expressed disapproval. Third, the US government's challenge to IATA effectively led after 1979 to a downgrading of that body's operations. IATA could no longer require that fares agreed at its conferences be enforced by its members (Doganis 1991). Finally, the US called for a non-tariff zone on the North Atlantic. It signed a Memorandum of Understanding (MOU) with twelve members of the European Civil Aviation Conference in 1982, which introduced a new concept in tariff setting. Zones of flexibility were established in relation to a reference fare, and governments were not permitted to disapprove of tariffs that fell within these zones, irrespective of the conditions set down in bilateral agreements.

US deregulation profoundly affected attitudes towards the regulation of air transport across the world, and in Europe in particular. European governments in ECAC reflected on the state of the industry in the light of the US experiment. In the UK, the Conservative Party and consumer groups looked to follow the American example. Elsewhere, there was less enthusiasm, even if developments in US aviation were closely monitored and its experiment constituted a point of reference in debates about the future of the industry and its regulation.

NATIONAL AVIATION POLICY IN EUROPE; PATRIOTIC INTERVENTIONISM IN THE SKIES

In Europe, most countries historically pursued restrictive and interventionist air transport policies. These were justified on a number of grounds. First, air transport was considered to engage the state's responsibility for ensuring the nation's security. Second, commercial aviation was an infant industry. Third, possession of a flag carrier acquired a near mystical significance, signalling national independence and becoming a symbol of sovereignty (Sampson 1984: 115–20). Fourth, governments believed that the public interest could not be met by the free market. Private operators, motivated by profit maximisation, would not be willing to serve isolated communities on unprofitable routes. Thus a reliable and extensive air services network could only be guaranteed by state intervention. Finally, governments used their air carriers as instruments for non-aviation policy objectives, especially in the areas of foreign policy, defence, industrial policy and employment.

Support and sponsorship of the flag carrier – the national champion of the air – formed the central pillar of national aviation policy. Flag carriers were typically brought into being by the state and partly or fully publicly owned. The French government, for instance, played an important part in the creation of Air France in 1933, and was instrumental in the formation of Air Inter in 1954. In the UK, the government formed Imperial Airways out of a merger of four existing carriers in 1924, nationalised the company in 1939, dismembered it in 1946 to form three new public corporations – British Overseas Airways Corporation (BOAC), British European Airways (BEA) and British South American Airways (BSAA) – and merged BOAC and BEA in 1974 to form British Airways (BA). The national airline was supported from the public purse through a range of direct and indirect subsidies, cheap loans, tax exemptions and various other dispensations. It enjoyed privileges guaranteed by statute and was insulated from competitive pressures behind protective walls. Typically, flag carriers were granted monopolies on international routes and on domestic networks, and their presence in the non-scheduled sector through subsidiaries (for example, Air France's Charter and Lufthansa's Condor Air) protected by restrictive charter policies. They were granted dominant positions at the major national airports, privileged access to landing slots and favourable ground handling arrangements. Moreover, the flag carrier was supported by a battery of minor measures. Civil servants were obliged, for example, to use the national carrier for trips abroad. Finally, aviation as a whole typically benefited from exemptions from, or special treatment under, national competition rules (OECD 1988: 38–53). Thus restrictive practices and concerted actions not tolerated in other economic sectors were permitted in air transport.

The policies traditionally pursued by France, the Federal Republic of Germany and Italy approximated closely to the protectionist model. All boasted state-owned flag carriers, even if the precise mode of ownership and control varied between them. The French state had a 99 per cent stake in Air France, while 82 per cent of Lufthansa's equity was held by the state and a small number of public investors. Alitalia was unique among flag carriers in that it was not a public enterprise in its own right, but a subsidiary of the state holding company, the Instituto per la Riconstruzione Industriale (IRI), which held a 99 per cent stake in the airline.

In all three countries, mono-designation on international scheduled routes was the general rule (ECAC 1982: 105). Lufthansa and Alitalia enjoyed a near monopoly of international routes, while the French government divided the international routes served by its carriers between Air France and the privately owned carrier, UTA (Esperou 1984, Folliot 1991).[9] In the area of non-scheduled services, France (Freud 1987) and Italy adopted restrictive policies in support of their flag carriers, though Germany adopted a more liberal policy. In all three countries, the domestic network was operated as a monopoly; by Air Inter in France, by Lufthansa in Germany and by Alitalia through its subsidiary, ATI, in Italy.

The Netherlands and the UK were unique in Europe in pursuing liberal aviation policies.[10] In particular, both followed a multi-airline policy, negotiating rights where possible for more than one of its air carriers to provide services on international routes (ECAC 1982: 105). Moreover, the UK pioneered low-cost air travel in the 1960s and 1970s, and operated a particularly liberal charter policy. It was also the only country in Europe to establish an independent regulatory authority for aviation, the Civil Aviation Authority (CAA), which was created in 1971 (Baldwin 1985). Furthermore, the UK had the greatest number of independent airlines in Europe, as well as the strongest consumer lobby.

Thus, the liberal British tradition in aviation was well established before the first Thatcher government, elected in 1979, embarked on a series of major reforms (Barnes 1988). First, the autonomy and power of the CAA was increased (Tritton 1990). Second, the domestic network was partially deregulated (Barnes 1988). Third, it took the radical step of privatising its flag carrier, British Airways (Ashworth and Forsyth 1984). A new chairman, Sir John (now Lord) King, was appointed to prepare the company for privatisation in 1981. The company's management was overhauled, the workforce reduced from 54,000 to 36,000, the fleet rationalised and a new commercial ethos instilled. British Airways became a publicly listed company in 1987. It has since been Europe's most successful carrier, profitable even during the industry's worst ever crisis in the early 1990s (Lehman Brothers 1993: 7).

Finally, the UK sought to revise its bilateral agreements with a number of its European partners on liberal terms (Abbot and Thompson 1991, Barrett 1987, Pelkmans 1986). However, the government came to realise that the liberalisation of the international regime could not be brought about by bilateral renegotiation alone and looked to the EEC as the means for multi-lateralising its programme (Interview with former UK Department of Trade official, 24 August 1992). It formed an active coalition with the Commission and the Netherlands in the transport working group of the Council, and sought, through informal contacts, to assuage the fears of France and Germany about liberalisation (Interviews with former UK Department of Transport officials, 24 August 92 and 19 February 93). The British Presidency played a major part in securing the commitment of the Twelve in 1986 to the creation of the single market in air services and was instrumental in the introduction of the market access proposal that was to form a key component of the first air transport liberalisation package (Interview with a Commission official, 13 July 92). Thus policy change in UK aviation pre-dated EEC action in this domain, was implemented by an ideologically motivated government determined to 'roll back the frontiers of the state' and was partially inspired by the US experience.

Governments and airlines

Since their commercial opportunities were dependent on the state and negotiations between states, airline companies sought to protect or further their interests through contact with governments. Airlines cultivated relationships with the transport, finance, trade, industry and foreign affairs ministries, as well as the relevant advisory councils or regulatory bodies, such as the Conseil Supérieur de l'Aviation Marchande (CSAM) in France or the CAA in the UK, members of parliament, political parties, chambers of commerce, airport authorities and consumer groups (Van den Polder 1994). They also maintained links with ECAC and other international aviation bodies.

Some airlines enjoyed a greater degree of influence than others. Flag carriers had close relations with, and privileged access to, the highest levels of government and national aviation authorities, so that in some countries it was difficult to tell where the management of the airline ended and the state began. In contrast, independent and charter airlines tended to be outsiders and had to work more assiduously to obtain their objectives.

Flag carrier status did, however, carry some disadvantages. Being in the public sector meant that they had to compete with other state-owned companies for financial resources,[11] and were vulnerable to political pressure and interference. Managerial continuity was not assured, and political appointees to the top executive positions were not necessarily chosen for their experience of either business or aviation. Moreover, the relationship between public enterprises and the state tended to be under constant discussion and subject to periodic revision.

Furthermore, flag carriers rarely enjoyed autonomy in commercial matters. In the first place, governments often imposed obligations on them. For instance, in Germany, Lufthansa was obliged to provide maximum route coverage and a high frequency of services, while the Italian flag carrier, Alitalia, was compelled to grant discounts to passengers belonging to particular social categories. Second, it was not unusual for governments to take decisions which were costly to the flag carrier. For example, in the 1960s and 1970s Air France was compelled to operate aircraft which were out of date (Caravelles) or unsuitable (Concorde). It was also 'encouraged' to move to the newly constructed Roissy-Charles de Gaulle airport in 1974, thereby disconnecting it from Orly airport, the hub of the domestic network and the airport preferred by passengers (Attali 1994: 23). Third, state ownership usually implied for public enterprise a lack of autonomy in decision making concerning labour. This was partly a function of government weakness in the face of trade union pressure. Particularly in France and Italy, governments tended to back down in the face of industrial action and to make successive concessions, so that national carriers were powerless to change work practices or determine the level of salaries. This was an important factor, given that European labour costs have been significantly higher than in the US (CAA 1993, Comité des Sages 1994). Redundancies in the public sector were politically sensitive, and flag carriers often found their hands tied by government when attempting to address the problem of overstaffing. The fact that British Airways had been privatised at a time when the rights of organised labour were coming under attack in the UK and that it was no longer in the public sector gave it a flexibility not enjoyed by Air France, Alitalia or Lufthansa.

The traditional regime was thus characterised by the dependence of airline companies on governments and by close relations between state and flag carrier, even if this was not always harmonious. There was a degree of national variation. However, the general pattern was one of protectionism, collusion and anti-competitive practice.

THE DEVELOPMENT OF A COMMON AIR TRANSPORT POLICY[12]

The development of a common air transport policy did not commence until the mid-1980s. A majority of the member states were opposed to EEC action. They had no desire for their autonomy to be diminished nor did they see the use of creating a further forum for managing aviation, particularly when other dedicated, experienced and more inclusive bodies existed. They also feared the implications of the implementation of the liberal economic principles of the Treaty of Rome for their traditional policies (Estienne-Henrotte 1988). The signatories to the EEC Treaty had committed themselves to the elimination of barriers to trade and were enjoined to abstain from measures which hindered the attainment of Treaty objectives. Specific provisions outlawed discrimination against EEC nationals (Article 7), prohibited restrictive practices (Article 85), the abuse of dominant position (Article 86) and the granting of special or exclusive rights to public undertakings (Article 90), and provided for the control of state aid (Articles 92–4). In addition, member states were required to take all appropriate steps to eliminate agreements with third countries that were incompatible with the Treaty (Article 234).

The conservative majority in the Council argued that Article 84 (2) of the EEC Treaty, which dealt directly with air transport, gave the Council the right to decide by unanimity when, and indeed whether, action should be taken.[13] However, this view was opposed by the Commission and the European Parliament, as well as by the UK government. With only the UK and the Netherlands supporting Community involvement in air transport, no progress was possible. However, the deadlock was broken in the mid-1980s by the judgment of the European Court of Justice in the 'Nouvelles Frontières' case that the competition rules did apply to the air transport sector,[14] the initiation of legal proceedings against EC flag carriers for their alleged infringement of

Community competition rules by the Commissioner for competition, Peter Sutherland, and the efforts of the Dutch, Belgian and British Council presidencies (Kassim 1996). The outcome was the adoption in December 1987 of the first air transport liberalisation package, which represented the first major step in the development of the common air transport policy (Council 1987). Further liberalisation measures followed in due course, and other initiatives were launched in the areas of harmonisation, infrastructure and foreign policy in order to develop a balanced policy.

Liberalisation

The liberalisation component of the Community's air transport policy has had the greatest impact on state autonomy. It has advanced in the form of market-building, market-regulating and market-strengthening measures.

Market building

The regulatory framework of the single internal market has developed through the adoption of three air transport liberalisation packages. The traditional regulatory structure has been loosened, offering new freedoms to airline companies and limiting the discretionary power of governments (see Table 7.2). Rather than imposing a new EC-wide regime, the first two packages aimed to liberalise the provisions relating to capacity, market access and tariff setting of existing bilateral agreements, rather than abruptly introducing a new multilateral system. The first package obliged national authorities to grant traffic rights to carriers on international routes where traffic surpassed a particular threshold. It thereby introduced the principle of multi-designation, removing the right of the state of destination to deny access to more than one foreign EC carrier on busy routes and introduced limited fifth freedom rights. With respect to capacity sharing, it widened the permissible range from the traditional 50:50 to 55:45 until September 1989 and 60:40 thereafter. A zonal system on the MOU model (see above) was introduced for tariffs whereby discount or deep discount fares falling within a particular range were to be considered approved if the relevant national authorities did not raise objections within thirty days of the fares being filed by the airlines. Airlines were thus given greater freedom to set their own fares and no longer had to seek governmental approval from two states.

The second package, adopted by the Council in June 1990, extended the measures agreed three years earlier (Council 1990). The thresholds triggering multi-designation were lowered and fifth freedom rights were made slightly easier to acquire, capacity sharing restrictions were further eased and the zonal tariff system extended.

The third package, however, intended to complete the creation of the single market, was far more radical (Council 1992). With respect to market access, multi-designation was permitted on all routes, restrictions on fifth freedom

Table 7.2 From the Chicago regime to the single market

Policy	Chicago regime	First package	Second package	Third package
Fares	Agreed by both governments	Zonal system: automatic approval of discount and deep discount fares within defined range	Zonal system extended; conditions on availability of discount fares relaxed	Airlines set own fares; safeguards on availability of discount fares relaxed
Licensing	National rules	No change	No change	EU criteria for ownership, airworthiness and economic fitness
Access				
• relations between state and own airlines	Governments full discretion	No change	No change	Subject to EU regime
• relations with foreign carriers	Negotiated bilaterally	Subject to EC rules	Subject to EC rules	Subject to EU rules
• multiple designation (country to country)	Negotiated bilaterally case by case	Yes under EC rules	Yes under EC rules	Yes under EC rules
• multiple designation (city pairs)	Negotiated bilaterally	Automatic above defined thresholds	Thresholds lowered	Full access allowed
• safeguard provisions			Provision for regional development	Provision for regional development
• fifth freedom	Rarely	Permitted for 30% traffic p.a.	Permitted for 50% traffic p.a.	Permitted without quota constraint
• cabotage	Never granted	No change	No change	Full cabotage rights under EU regime from 1 April 1997
Capacity	Generally 50:50	55:45%, then 60:40	60:40, plus additional 7.5% p.a.	No limits, but safeguard can be triggered

Source: Council 1987, 1990, 1992.

rights were lifted and domestic markets were to be opened to other EC carriers from 1 April 1997. Moreover, whereas the first and second packages had limited the power of governments with respect to carriers from other member states, the third applied to a government's rights with respect to its own carriers. However, member states retained the right to deny access exceptionally to congested airports and to allocate traffic on a non-discriminatory basis between airports in the same airport system. Concerning the setting of tariffs, airlines were permitted to set fares freely according to their own commercial judgement, with intervention only if they were excessively high or low. With regard to capacity, all restrictions were removed, although safeguard measures permitting emergency action to be taken in the event of financial catastrophe were introduced.

The third package also introduced an EC-wide licensing regime. This was intended to overcome the obstacle to the freedom of establishment posed by the nationality clause in bilateral agreements and the system of national licensing. The new regulation introduced a Community-wide airworthiness certificate and established Community ownership and control criteria which allowed any carrier that satisfied them to operate services anywhere in the Community. Finally, the package abolished the distinction between scheduled and non-scheduled services.

Market regulating

Progressive liberalisation was matched by a corresponding evolution of the competition rules (Balfour 1994, De Coninck 1992). The December 1987 package included a regulation which implemented the competition rules of the EEC Treaty in air transport, as well as a regulation allowing the Commission to grant block exemptions from these rules for certain specified activities. This latter measure enabled airlines to continue to co-operate in areas where the consumer would benefit and made it easier for companies to adjust to market pressures.

Community rules regarding concentrations and state aid, which had hitherto been a dead letter in respect of air transport, were now applied for the first time. No longer were these matters strictly a national concern. Until 1990, when the Merger Regulation came into effect, concentrations were treated under Article 86 of the EEC Treaty (Council 1989a). Three air transport operations were considered in the first period: the British Airways buy-out of British Caledonian in 1988, Air France's takeover of UTA in 1989, which also gave it control of Air Inter,[15] and KLM's absorption of Transavia (Balfour 1994). The Commission gave its conditional approval to all three. In the first two cases it negotiated agreements with the airlines concerned and their respective governments, under which commitments were undertaken by the parties to ensure that competition was maintained in the affected markets. Thus British Airways agreed not to appeal in the event that the UK Civil Aviation Authority decided either to transfer some of its route licences to other carriers or to reduce the number of its slots at London's Gatwick airport.[16] Under the 'Brussels Accord' of October 1990, Air France was compelled to dispose of its holding in the French independent carrier, TAT, and to give up its rights and freeze its capacities on specified domestic routes, while the French government undertook to allocate traffic rights to Air France's competitors on a number of international and domestic routes (CEC 1990a).[17]

The Commission maintained the same approach in dealing with the cases in which it intervened under the merger Regulation. Thus, with respect to Air France's purchase of a shareholding in Sabena, BA's acquisition of a 49 per cent stake in TAT and its takeover of Dan-Air, it gave its approval, but insisted that certain conditions were observed (Balfour 1994: 1037–8).

The regulation of state aid is essential for the creation of a genuinely competitive market in air services, since liberalisation might otherwise trigger a 'subsidy race' (CEC 1984), producing anti-competitive effects. However, since it touches upon intimate relations between state and flag carrier, the area is highly sensitive politically. Largely due to this fact, the Commission, which enjoys considerable power under Articles 92–4 of the EEC Treaty in regard to state aid, had hitherto adopted a flexible approach.

Under Article 92 (3) of the EEC Treaty, member states are obliged to inform the Commission of any intention to grant state aid (CAA 1993: 113–16). When a case is referred to the Commission, it decides whether the state, in awarding the capital injection, loan, guarantee or concession, has acted as a private investor would have done under normal market principles.[18] If it decides that a private investor would have so acted, the Commission rules that state aid is not in question and that the operation represents a normal transaction between shareholder and company. The operation thus receives clearance. If the Commission concludes that a private shareholder would not have acted in this way, state aid is at issue and a formal procedure is normally opened. In this case, the important question is whether the operation involves a form of state aid which is compatible with the Common Market. If it decides that it is not, the transaction will not be permitted. However, if the Commission considers that a common interest is served or that regional development is promoted, the operation will be approved, subject to conditions specified by the Commission after investigation and in consultation with the relevant parties.

The Commission has acted pragmatically in the cases which it has treated so far. In two controversial cases concerning Air France in 1991 and 1992, it decided that state aid was not at issue and issued no formal decision (CEC 1991a, 1992a, 1992b). In both instances, the Commission indicated in press releases that Air France presented a good investment opportunity. In other cases, involving Sabena in 1991 (CEC 1991b), Iberia in 1992 (1992c) and Air France (1994a), Aer Lingus (1994b), Olympic Airways (1994c) and TAP in 1994 (1994d), the Commission concluded that state aid was at issue, but approved the operations subject to certain specified conditions.[19] It had generally required that the aid in question forms part of a restructuring package, that it is granted on a 'one time, last time' basis, and that the government should in future distance itself from intervention in the management of the company concerned. It has also placed limitations on what the capital can be spent on, ruling out investment in other EU carriers, the acquisition of aircraft or increasing capacity. In the Air France case, it decided that the aid should go to Air France alone, and thus not to Air Inter, the other company in the group (Balfour 1994).

The Commission has taken the general view that although its 'aim is to create a level playing field from 1993. . . some airlines carrying the financial burden of the past must have the chance for a fresh start, provided that this does not adversely affect the situation of competitors' (CEC 1992b: 3).[20] However, it has suggested in a revised set of guidelines on state aid adopted in 1994 that 1 April 1997 should be regarded as a deadline for state support (CEC 1994e). It has also warned that in future it will be necessary to 'think the unthinkable' (1992b: 6): that flag carriers might be lost through bankruptcy or merger.[21]

Market strengthening

The EU has also acted to remove sources of market distortion. In 1989, following consultation and close co-operation with ECAC, the Community introduced a code of conduct covering computer reservation systems (CRSs) (CEC 1989b). CRSs are powerful marketing and ticket distribution tools which were first developed in the USA (Katz 1988). Their use has created fears that the airlines who own CRSs may discriminate against air carriers who pay for their flights to be displayed on them. The code of conduct, which was updated in 1993, aims to ensure that the system owners do not abuse their position. Action has also been taken with regard to airport landing slots, which have become increasingly scarce at some airports. A code of conduct directing that slots are allocated according to non-discriminatory and transparent procedures was introduced in 1993 (Council 1993a).

Harmonisation

Community action with respect to harmonisation has covered a number of areas.[22] One particularly interesting development has been the establishment of a procedure whereby the technical standards (JARs) formulated by the JAA automatically become Commission proposals (Council 1991). If approved by the Council they are incorporated into Community law, thus becoming binding in the member states.

Infrastructure

Until recently, member states resisted Commission efforts to promote EU involvement in matters concerning airports or air traffic management systems, preferring to retain national control in this area or to continue their co-operation in traditional forums, such as ECAC and Eurocontrol. Since 1991, however, they have been increasingly willing to use the EC/EU for funding research under its own auspices or by other organisations,[23] and for promoting a more coherent approach to air traffic control management in Europe through commitments to procure compatible technology (Council 1993b). Further EU involvement is assured under the Trans-European Network programme (TENs) to integrate transport, including air transport, infrastructure.

External policy

Although the EU has developed limited external policy functions and exported the Community's air transport regime to the EFTA countries, the question of whether the Union's role in external matters should be developed any further is strongly contested. The Commission has long contended that commercial aviation relations with third countries form part of the Community's commercial policy for which the Commission has exclusive competence (CEC 1990b). It argues that there are legal and pragmatic reasons as to why it should negotiate air services agreements with third countries.[24] However, the overwhelming majority of member states oppose the Commission on both grounds, and hold that the negotiation of bilateral agreements should remain a national responsibility and that insurmountable practical difficulties would beset attempts by the Community to negotiate on behalf of the Fifteen.

THE IMPACT OF EU ACTION

The development of the common air transport policy has had very significant implications, although the impact of EU action has varied between member states as well as between policy areas. The UK has been least affected, while France, Germany and Italy have increasingly had to abandon their conservative aviation policies with varying degrees of completeness, enthusiasm and difficulty. With respect to the behaviour of national actors and the relationship between government and airline companies, a general change has come about.

Although EU action concerning harmonisation and infrastructure has affected the member states, the consequences of the development of the common air transport policy have been most far-reaching in the area of liberalisation. Government discretion over freedom of establishment and market access, to fix capacity shares and to interfere in the setting of tariffs has been removed or tightly circumscribed. Moreover, aviation is now subject to EC competition rules which govern agreements between airlines, dominant position, mergers and state aid, public service obligations and monopoly rights, as well as more general regulations which prohibit discriminatory practices. As a result, governments have been deprived of many of the instruments which previously made possible policies of interventionism.

The impact on national policy

Of the four larger member states, the UK has been least affected by EU-led liberalisation. Although UK governments had supported British flag carriers, they had been prepared to allow independent airlines to compete on international routes wherever it was able to negotiate traffic rights. It had a liberal charter policy, had liberalised its domestic market and privatised British Airways. For France, Germany and Italy, however, the implications of EU action have been considerable, even if in only one of the three, namely Germany, has the state's shareholding in the flag carrier been significantly reduced (see Table 7.3). Traditional policy orientations have been discarded and old practices abandoned, largely as a consequence of the single market and in anticipation of the full opening of a domestic aviation market on 1 April 1997, but also due to factors such as the changing intellectual climate concerning regulation and pressure on public spending.

Neither France nor Italy have been enthusiastic about EU liberalisation of air transport. France in particular has repeatedly expressed its objections to what it perceives as Anglo-Saxon 'ultra-liberalism' (see Attali 1994: 151–70). It has generally acted in the Council as the spokesman for the conservative camp, and called consistently for the pace of liberalisation to be slowed.[25] Despite its resistance, however, France has not been able to safeguard its traditional policy objectives. Historically, these have consisted of five elements: the support and protection of Air France; the avoidance of Franco-French competition on international routes (*'une ligne, une compagnie'*); the reservation of the domestic network for Air Inter; a restrictive charter policy, and the imposition of public service obligations on carriers, to ensure the maintenance of communications links with isolated communities. However, only the last element has remained relatively unscathed.

France has attempted to persist with its national champion strategy. Although in 1993 the government of Edouard Balladur included Air France in a list of twenty-one companies earmarked for privatisation, successive governments have intervened in and for the company, while state ownership and financial support of the airline have continued. Governments of both left and right have not distanced themselves from the management of the company. With respect to the 1989 merger, for example, the then Prime Minister, Michel Rocard, claimed to have 'piloté' (piloted') the operation (Vinçon 1991: 215). In autumn 1993, the failure of the Balladur government, in the face of industrial action, to support the implementation of the restructuring plan 'CAP 93', led to the resignation of the President of the company, Bernard Attali, although since the appointment of Christian Blanc as his successor, the company has been allowed greater autonomy. Governments have also tried to protect Air France against competition from foreign carriers. Thus in the

'Battle of Orly', the French government attempted unsuccessfully to prevent British Airways and Air UK from inaugurating services between London and the hub of the French domestic network at Paris's Orly airport. Under pressure from both the Commission, which ruled in April 1994 that the French authorities were acting in contravention of the provisions of the third package (CEC 1994f), and London, the French transport minister agreed to allow the carriers to begin their services to Orly from 13 June.[26]

As the Orly episode demonstrates, the French government does not enjoy the autonomy it previously did in protecting its flag carrier. This is further underlined by the fact that the financial relations between the state and public enterprises are regulated by the Commission, and even when it approves of a proposed operation, the Commission can impose conditions on carrier and government. As in the case of its 1994 decision, the Commission can impose restrictions which not only limit government discretion with respect to the company, but also impose organisational changes. Thus, for example, the Commission's stipulation that the state should benefit Air France only within the Air France group has led to changes in the organisation of the group. More broadly, under the Brussels Accord, the requirement that the French government should grant traffic rights to competitors of Air France underlined the fact that states can no longer exercise control over their aviation markets.

Other elements of the traditional policy pursued by France have been challenged. In the first place, the principle of *'une ligne, une compagnie'* can no longer be maintained, since the French government does not have the discretion to determine which French companies should be granted traffic rights on international routes. Second, the French government has been unable to sustain Air Inter's domestic monopoly, despite the fact that in 1993 it renewed the company's rights until April 1997. Under the October Accord, the French government was obliged to grant traffic rights to companies on internal routes to compete with Air Inter, but few new entrants survived. More recently, TAT, in which British Airways has a 49 per cent shareholding, referred the French authorities' refusal to allow it to operate services on two of the country's most lucrative domestic routes to the Commission. In its decision of April 1994, upheld by the European Court of Justice six months later on appeal by the French government, the Commission ordered France to open Orly-Toulouse and Orly-Marseilles immediately (CEC 1994f, *Financial Times*, 29 November 1994: 18). Apparently wishing to avoid further confrontations with the Commission, the French authorities have granted traffic rights to a number of other carriers since the beginning of 1995 (*Le Monde*, 4 May 1995: 26). Finally, France had traditionally adopted a restrictive charter policy, but under the third package the distinction between scheduled and non-scheduled services has been abolished, effectively making companies that formerly operated charter services eligible for the full range of traffic rights.

Italy, like France, was not enthusiastic about EU liberalisation. Although Alitalia had been partially privatised in 1985, this was motivated principally

Table 7.3 Ownership of European flag carriers in 1988 and 1995

Airline	Country	Ownership (%)	
		1988	*1995*
Aer Lingus	Ireland	State 100	State 100
Air France	France	State 99.38	State 99.3
Alitalia	Italy	State 67	State 86.4
		Private 33	
British Airways	UK	Private 100	Private 100
Iberia	Spain	State 100	State 100
KLM	Netherlands	State 36.9	State 38.2
		Private 63.1	Private 61.8
Lufthansa	Germany	State 74.31	State 35.68
		Public Institutions 7.85	Public Institutions 4.97
		Private 17.84	Private 59.35
Luxair	Luxemburg	State 20.91	State 23.11
		n.a.	State-owned bank 13.41
			Luxair Group 13.18
Olympic Airways	Greece	State 100	Lufthansa 13
Sabena	Belgium	State 54.72	State 100
		Private 45.28	State 61.8
SAS	Sweden	State 50	Finacta 37.5[1]
	Denmark	Private 50	State 50
	Norway[2]		Private 50
TAP	Portugal	State 100	State 100

Sources: Button 1991:88 and AEA *Yearbook 1995*
Notes:
1 A consortium of Air France and a number of Belgian banks
2 The Scandinavian Airways System (SAS) is a joint company in which three national carriers, SILA (Sweden), DDL (Denmark) and DNL (Norway) held in 1995 the following stakeholdings respectively: 42.85%, 28.57% and 28.57%

by the need to tackle the public debt rather than by liberal inclination (Rapp and Vellas 1992). As a consequence of the development of the single market from 1988, Italy has been compelled to modify its traditional policy, although it has continued to use its diminishing powers to protect its flag carrier. The state has distanced itself from the management of the company, and allowed its managing director, Roberto Schisano, the freedom to restructure the company without government interference (see Table 7.3).

Germany has substantially revised its aviation policy. Although initially re-luctant, it has become increasingly liberal since the mid-1980s, even if it has not betrayed the same evangelical zeal as the Netherlands and the UK. Under Jurgen Weber, president of the company since 1991, Luftansa has undergone a radical transformation, restructured under the three-year 'Programm '93' and run like a private enterprise. In 1994, Lufthansa's ties with government were loosened decisively in a rights issue which saw the state's shareholding fall from 51.4 to 39 per cent. Although the EU was a key factor in prompting change in Germany's aviation policy, the latter must be seen in the context of a wider restructuring of the public sector which began in 1982, when the CDU/FDP coalition initiated a privatisation programme (Rapp and Vellas 1992).

The Impact of EC action on national policy actors

The emergence of the EC as a regulatory authority in the air transport sector has had important consequences for actors in the air transport sector. First, the traditionally collusive relationship between flag carrier and state is in the course of redefinition in France, Germany and Italy. Airlines have had to become independent, commercially orientated and profitable, since governments no longer have the power or the instruments to offer them financial support or protection. Companies have responded to the challenges brought by the new regulatory environment with varying degrees of conviction and success. All have undertaken extensive restructuring programmes, involving large-scale redundancies, comprehensive organisational changes and route and fleet rationalisation, aimed at transforming bureaucratic and inefficient companies into commercially orientated and profitable enterprises. In France and Italy, the transition has not been easy and the process in France in particular has been accompanied by bitter industrial disputes and strike action.

Second, the creation of a single European market has led flag carriers to consolidate their domestic positions, take shareholdings in other airline companies and engage in a range of co-operative, often transnational, arrangements. Although alliances and co-operative arrangements are not new phenomena in the industry, the number and nature of the new partnerships is unprecedented (see Table 7.4). These involve joint marketing, code-sharing – where the same flight involves different airlines flying under the same flight code – franchising and, in some cases, equity participation (AEA 1995, *Airline Business* 1995).

Third, EU policy has affected the traditional balance of power between different categories of airline. Although flag carriers are still able to benefit commercially from the advantages that have accumulated over decades, they no longer enjoy the regulatory protection, statutory privileges or financial support which was afforded to them in the past. Conversely, independent carriers are less constrained, since governments can no longer deny them traffic rights on a discretionary basis.

Finally, EU action has had an impact on interest intermediation. The fact that states no longer have the power to dispense grace, favour or commercial opportunity, and the new role played by the European Union and especially the European Commission, has led airlines to direct their lobbying activities to the institutions of the EU. Collectively, interests are represented through

Table 7.4 Major partnerships of selected flag carriers

Airline	Shareholdings %	Alliances	Other operations
Air France	Air Charter 80 Air Inter 76 Air Austral 34 Air Tchad 33.7 Middle East Airlines 28.5 plus smaller stakes in various African airlines	Air Canada[1] Aeromexico[1] Vietnam Airlines[2] Japan Airlines[3]	Merger with UTA Bought shareholding in CSA (Czechoslovakia), but negotiated re-sale of stake Negotiated sale of stake in Sabena
Alitalia	Avionova 45 Eurofly 45 Malev 30 Air Europe 27.6	Malev[3] British Midland[3] Continental Airlines[3]	
British Airways	British Asia Airways 100 Brymon European 100 BA Regional 100 TAT 49.9 Deutsche BA 49 GB Airways 31 Air Russia 25 USAir 24.6 Qantas 21	Cityflyer Express[4] Maersk Air[4] Loganair[4] Manx Airlines[4] TAT[4] Deutsche BA[4] GB Airways[4] Brymon European[4] USAir[3,5,7] Qantas[6]	Merger with British Caledonian Merger with Dan-Air
Lufthansa	Condor Flugdienst 100 Lufthansa Cargo 100 Lufthansa CityLine 100 EuroBerlin 49 SunExpress 40 Lauda Air 39.7 Business Air 38.4 Cargolux 24.5 Luxair 13	United Airlines[3,5] Canada[3,5] Varig[3] Thai Airways[5] Lauda Air[3] Business Air[3] Luxair[3,5] Cargolux[5,6] Finnair[5]	

Source: AEA 1995

Notes: 1 alliance agreement; 2 equipment sharing; 3 code sharing; 4 franchising; 5 joint sales-/marketing agreement; 6 joint operations; 7 frequent flyer programme

three Euro-level federations: the Association of European Airlines (AEA), which represents the larger companies, the European majors; the Association des Compagnies Aériennes de la Communauté Européenne (ACE), the European section of the International Air Carriers Association (IACA), representing non-scheduled carriers, and the European Regional Association (ERA), which speaks on behalf of regional airlines. However, since there is considerable divergence within these organisations, many companies lobby on an individual basis. In Brussels, relationships are cultivated with the relevant Directorate-Generals of the European Commission, notably, DG VII (transport) and DG IV (competition), and advisory bodies to the Commission, such as the Joint Aviation Committee, as well as the European Parliament, especially members of the EP Transport and Tourism Committee, the Economics and Social Committee, and the permanent representation of their member state (Van den Polder 1994).

Despite the increased importance of Brussels, national governments have not been abandoned. Even if they are bypassed by carriers making direct contact with EU institutions and are no longer the 'gatekeepers' for national interests, airlines rely on national officials to provide early warning of policy initiatives, as well as up-to-date information about the progress of proposals through the machinery of the Council. They also attempt to ensure that their interests are defended and advanced by their government in Council negotiations. It is worth noting that outside Europe commercial opportunities still depend on interstate negotiation and good relations with government need to be maintained.

CONCLUSION

The development of the common air transport policy has radically transformed the Chicago system in Europe. A multilateral regulatory system has been constructed, under which EU member states no longer enjoy absolute autonomy and where countries which had previously pursued conservative aviation policies have been compelled to liberalise. Thus, while France, Germany and Italy have abandoned or modified their traditional orientations, the content of UK policy has been relatively unaffected, even though, like the other three, its government no longer enjoys ultimate authority over aviation. Governments have been deprived of the power to intervene extensively in their aviation industries, while air carriers no longer depend on their own state for their commercial opportunities.

Policy change in France, Germany and Italy has been largely prompted by EU action, though in Germany and in Italy specifically national factors – the coming into office in 1982 of a government committed to restructuring the public sector in the case of the former, and pressure on public funds in the latter – have also played a part. Important too, though a factor whose influence it is more difficult to assess, was US deregulation which introduced free market thinking into the sector and the 'paradigm change' of the late 1970s/1980s which threw into question the role of the state in industry and which 'rediscovered the firm' (Wright 1995).

In other areas of aviation, the impact of the EU has been significant, even if not radical. Despite the efforts of the Commission, EU action with respect to external relations has been limited and national autonomy undiminished, since the member states have opposed proposals that would prevent them from conducting their own bilateral negotiations. Concerning harmonisation and infrastructure, the situation is more complex. The Community has developed a role alongside the long-standing, competent – and intergovernmental – organisations in the sector. It has evolved a largely complementary relationship, channelling funding to, encouraging participation in and enforcing the recommendations of, projects or processes initiated elsewhere, as well as attempting to promote a more co-ordinated approach to particular problems in its own right. Insofar as it supports the work of the relevant intergovernmental bodies, EU action has not promoted policy change on the part of the member states, but in some areas, such as VAT and the harmonisation of personnel licences, state autonomy has undoubtedly been affected.

NOTES

1 The author would like to thank the officials, past and present, from national administrations and the Commission, as well as the airline executives and interest group representatives, who generously offered their assistance in granting non-attributable interviews during the course of the research for this chapter. Thanks are also due to John Peterson, who offered comments on the first draft.

2 Although as Christopher Chataway, chairman of the UK Civil Aviation Authority, has noted, 'The new regulations have not, of themselves created a more competitive industry in Europe. Rather, they have set the conditions whereby a more open, competitive market can be brought about' (CAA 1993: iii).

3 The relationship between governments and their flag carriers is discussed in Kassim 1995.

4 Article 1 of the Chicago Convention reads, 'Each state has complete and exclusive sovereignty over the airspace above its territory'. A full text of the Chicago Convention and its associated treaties can be found in Martin *et al.* (1984).

5 Although agreement was reached on the multilateral exchange of the non-commercial first and second freedoms.

6 Charter accounted for 30 per cent of the total airline output (expressed in revenue passenger kilometres of the Community) of the Twelve in 1993 (CAA 1993: 2).

7 The term 'high regulation' was used by Button and Swann (1991).

8 See the following for discussions of the consequences of US deregulation: Bailey *et al.* 1985; Morrison and Winston 1986; Joskow 1988; Moore 1986; Wheatcroft and Lipman 1990.

9 According to the terms of a settlement, which Bernard Attali (1994), former president of Air France, has called the 'Yalta franco-française', UTA served south, central and west Africa, Singapore and Australia and New Zealand, while Air France served the rest of the world.

10 In the UK, for example, the position of British Airways at Heathrow airport was until 1991 protected by traffic distribution rules, which prevented new airlines from gaining access to the airport.

11 As a result, many national airlines were undercapitalised. See Vinçon (1991) for discussion of this problem in relation to Air France.

12 For detailed discussion of Community action and aviation policy in Europe, see Balfour 1994, Button and Swann 1989, McGowan and Seabright 1989, McGowan and Trengrove 1986.

13 Article 84 (2) originally read, 'The Council may, acting by unanimity, decide whether and to what extent and by what procedure appropriate provisions may be laid down for sea and air transport.' Qualified Majority Voting was introduced by the SEA.

14 *Ministère public v. Lucas Asjes and others*, Joined Cases 209–13 (1986) ECR 1425. The Court's ruling thus clarified the situation following the uncertainties that

remained after the 'French Seamen's' case (*Commission v. French Republic*, Case 167/73, (1974) ECR 359–79).

15 Air France already owned a 32 per cent stake in Air Inter, while UTA held a 35 per cent holding in the domestic carrier. Thus, when Air France bought UTA, it acquired control of Air Inter.

16 See (1989) 4 CMLR 258.

17 For full details, see ITA Press (1990), 131, 2, 16–30 November.

18 This is the so-called 'market economy investor principle'. See CAA 1993:114–16 for further discussion.

19 Somewhat suprisingly, although it decided that state aid was at issue in the case of Iberia, the Commission did not issue a formal decision.

20 The Commission's pragmatic approach has not been welcomed by all. In October 1994, the UK government, British Midland and six other airlines led by British Airways filed suit with European Court of Justice against the Commission's 1994 decision concerning Air France. The state aid given to the company in 1994 has been estimated to be 'almost equal to all the entire losses made by all the world's airlines in 1993' (Sir Michael Bishop, chairman of British Midland, quoted in the *Financial Times*, 5 October 1991: 1).

21 Unofficially, a Commission official has expressed the view that '[t]he biggest barrier to air transport liberalisation in Europe is this crazy idea that every member state has to have its own airline. . . . People still assume that there is something glorious about flying, but airlines are just glorified bus companies' (quoted in the *Financial Times*, 29 July 1994: 2).

22 EU policy also covers Value Added Tax, noise limitation, compensation to passengers for denied boarding and the harmonisation of personnel licences.

23 The EU is a major contributor to ECAC programmes, such as the Airport/Air Traffic Systems Interface (APATSI) project, and to Eurocontrol's Assistance Services (EAS), which provides technical support to the countries of eastern Europe.

24 For example, it argues that the single market will not have been completed until all EU carriers have the right to fly from any point within the Union to any country within which a member state has a bilateral agreement. It has also strongly criticised the member states who have individually negotiated 'open skies' bilateral agreements with the US for giving away EU assets and for failing to win the benefits which might have been secured if the EU had negotiated as a bloc.

25 It was largely due to French lobbying that the freedoms granted to foreign EC airlines under the first two packages were not extended to home carriers – the so-called 'UTA clause' – and that the liberalisation of domestic markets was put back to 1997. France also called for a relaxation of Community rules during the Gulf crisis.

26 However, the French authorities sought to impose limits on the size of aircraft that could be used and the number of flights that could be made, as well as a ceiling on the number of passengers that could be carried each year.

REFERENCES

Abbott, K. and Thomson, D. (1991) 'Deregulating European Aviation: The Impact of Bilateral Liberalisation', *International Journal of Industrial Organization*, 9, 125–40.

Airline Business (1995) 'Alliances', June, 27–67.

Ashworth, M. and Forsyth, P. (1984) *Civil Aviation Policy and the Privatization of British Airways*, London: Institute of Fiscal Studies.

Association of European Airlines (AEA) (1989) 'Towards a Single System for Air Traffic Control in Europe', Brussels: AEA.

—— (1995) *Yearbook 1995*, Brussels: AEA.

Attali, B. (1994) *Les guerres du ciel: cinq ans aux commandes d'Air France*, Paris: Fayard.

Bailey, E., Graham, D. and Kaplan, D. (1985) *Deregulating the Airlines*, Cambridge, MA: MIT Press.

Baldwin, R. (1985) *Regulating the Airlines: Administrative Justice and Agency Discretion*, Oxford: Clarendon Press.

Balfour, J. (1990) *Air Law and the EC*, London: Butterworth.

—— (1993) 'The Control of State Aids in the Air Transport Sector', *Air and Space Law*, 18:4–5, 199–204.

—— (1994) 'Air Transport – A Community Success Story?', *Common Market Law Review*, 31, 1025–1053.

Barnes, F. (1988) 'The Impact of Partial Deregulation in the United Kingdom Domestic Air Transport Market', in OECD (1988) *Deregulation and Airline Competition*, Paris: OECD.

Barrett, S. (1987) *Flying High: Airline processes and European regulation*, Aldershot: Avebury.

Baumol, W.J., Panzer, J. and Willig, R. (1982) *Contestable Markets and the Theory of Industry Structure*, New York: Harcourt, Brace, Jovanovich.

Button, K.J. and Swann, D. (1989) 'European Community Airlines – Deregulation and its Problems', *Journal of Common Market Studies*, June, 27:4.

—— (1991) 'Aviation in Europe', in K.J. Button (ed.) *Airline Deregulation: International Experiences*, London: David Fulton Publishers.

Cheng, B. (1962) *The Law of International Air Transport*, London: Steven & Sons Ltd.

Civil Aviation Authority (CAA) (1993) *Airline Competition in the Single European Market*, CAP 623, Cheltenham: CAA.

Comité des Sages (1994) *Expanding Horizons: A Report by the Comité des Sages for Air Transport to the European Commission*, Brussels: Commission.

Commission of the European Communities (CEC) (1979) 'Contribution of the European Communities to the Development of Air Transport Services', *Bulletin of the European Communities*, Suppl. 5, Luxemburg: Office of Official Publications of the European Communities (OOPEC).

—— (1984) Civil Aviation Memorandum no. 2, 'Towards the Development of a Community Air Transport Policy', COM (84) 72 final, Brussels: Commission.

—— (1990a) Press Release IP (90) 870, Brussels: Commission.

—— (1990b) COM (90) 17 final, Brussels: Commission.

—— (1991a) IP (91) 1024, Brussels: Commission.

—— (1991b) OJ L 300, 48, Luxembourg: OOPEC.

—— (1992a) IP (92) 587, Brussels: Commission.

—— (1992b) Report by the Commission to the Council and the European Parliament, SEC (92) 431, 19.3.92.

—— (1992c) IP (92) 606.

Council (1987) Regulation 3975/87 and Regulation 3976/87 (competition), Directive 87/601/87 (fares), Decision 87/602/87 (access and capacity), OJ L 374, 31.12.87, 1–26.

—— (1989a) Regulation 4064/89, OJ L 395, 30.12.89, corrected OJ L 257, 21.9.90.

—— (1989b) Regulation 2299/89, OJ L 220, 29.7.89, amended Regulation 3089/93, OJ L 278, 11.11.93 and corrected regulation 3089/93, OJ L 17, 25.1.95.

—— (1990) Regulation 2342/90 (fares), Regulation 2343/90 (access), Regulation 2344/90, OJ L 271, 11.8.90, 1–16.

—— (1991) Regulation 3922/91, OJ L 373, 31.12.91

—— (1992) Regulations 2407/92 (licensing), 2408/92 (access), 2409/92 (fares), 2410/92 (competition) and 2411/92 (competition) OJ L 240, 24.8.92.

—— (1993a) Regulation 95/93, OJ L 14, 22.1.93.

—— (1993b) Directive 93/65, OJ L 187, 29.7.93.

De Coninck, F. (1992) *European Air Law: New Skies for Europe*, Paris: ITA Press.

Doganis, R. (1991) *Flying Off Course: The Economics of International Airlines*, London: Harper Collins.

Doganis, R. (1993) 'The Bilateral Regime for Air Transport: Current Position and Future Prospects', in OECD *International Air Transport: The Challenges Ahead*, Paris: OECD

Driscoll, E.J. (1981) 'New Trends in the International Bilateral Regulation of Air Transport', *International Business Lawyer*, 158,

Espérou, R. (1984) 'La politique française de transport aérien', *Annuaire française du transport aérien 1981–2*, Gardanne: Bibliothèque de l'Association pour le development ment de l'Institut de Formation Universitaire et du Récherche du Transport Aérien, Université d'Aix-Marseille à Gardanne.

Estienne-Henrotte, E. (1988) *L'application des règles générales du traité de Rome au transport aérien*, Brussels: Editions de l'Université de Bruxelles.

European Civil Aviation Conference (ECAC) (1982) *Report on Competition in Intra-European Air Services*, Doc. no. 25, Paris: ECAC.

European Commission (1994a) OJ L 254, 30.9.94, 73 and OJ L 258, 6.10.94, Luxemburg: OOPEC.

—— (1994b) OJ L 54, 25.9.94.

—— (1994c) OJ L 279, 28.10.94, 29 and OJ L 260, 8.10.94, 27.

—— (1994d) OJ L 273, 25.10.94, 22.

—— (1994e) Application of Articles 92 and 93 of the EC Treaty, OJ C 350, 10.12.94, 5–20.

—— (1994f) OJ L 127, 19.5.94, 32–7.

Folliot, M. (1991) 'La libéralisation de la politique aéronautique française', *Revue française de droit aérien et spatial*, 173:1

Freud, M. (1987) *Charters Interdits*, Strasbourg: Buet et Reumeaux.

HMG (1946) *Final Act of the Civil Aviation Conference and Agreement between the Government of the United Kingdom and the Government of the USA Relating to Air Service between their Respective Territories*, Cmnd. 6747, London: HMSO.

Institut des Transports Aériens (ITA) (1993) *World Data Guide*, Paris: Institut des Transports Aérien's.

Joskow, (1988) 'Deregulation and Competition Policy: The US experience with Deregulation in the Air Transport Sector', in OECD *Deregulation and Airline Competition*, Paris: OECD.

Kassim, H. (1995) 'National Champions of the Air – Still Carrying the Flag?', in Jack Hayward (ed.) *National Enterprise and European Integration: from National to International Champions*, Oxford. OUP.

—— (1996) 'Theories of Integration and their Limits: European Community Policy Development in the Air Transport Sector, 1957–1992', D. Phil. thesis, University of Oxford, in preparation.

Katz, R. (1988) 'The Impact of Computer Reservation Systems on Air Transport Competition', in OECD *Deregulation and Airline Competition*, Paris: OECD.

Lehman Brothers (1993) *European Airlines: A Turbulent Decade*, London: Lehman Brothers Securities, 14 September.

McGowan, F. and Seabright, P. (1989) 'Deregulating European Airlines', *Economic Policy*, 9, 283–344.

McGowan, F. and Trengrove, C. (1986) *European Aviation: A Common Market?*, London: Institute of Fiscal Studies.

Martin, P., McLean, D., Martin, E. and Margo, R. (1984) *Shawcross and Beaumont Air Law*, 4th edn, London: Butterworths.

Moore, T. (1986) 'US Airline Deregulation: Its Effects on Passengers, Capital and Labor', *Journal of Law and Economics*, April, 1–29.

Morrison, S.A. and Winston, C. (1986) *The Economic Effects of Airline Deregulation*, Washington DC: Brookings Institute.

National Consumer Council (NCC) (1986) *Air Transport and the Consumer: A Need For Change?*, London: HMSO.

Naveau, J. (1989) *International Air Transport in a Changing World*, Brussels, Martinus Nijhoff.

Organisation for Economic Co-operation and Development (OECD) (1988) *Deregulation and Airline Competition*, Paris: OECD.

Pelkmans, J. (1986) 'Deregulation of European Air Transport', in H.W. de Jong and W.G. Shepherd (eds) *Mainstreams in Industrial Organisation*, Dortrecht; Martinus Nijhoff.

Rapp, L. and Vellas, F. (1992) *Airline Privatisation in Europe*, 2nd edn., Paris: Instut de Transport Aerien.

Reynolds-Feighan, A. (1995) 'European Air Transport Public Service Obligations: A Periodic Review', *Fiscal Studies, 16:1, 58–74.*

Sampson, A. (1984) *Empires of the Sky: The Politics, Contests and Cartels of World Airlines*, London: Hodder & Stoughton.

Socher, E. (1991) *The Politics of International Aviation*, Basingstoke: Macmillan.

Tritton, C. (1990) 'Existing and Prospective Community Law and Civil Aviation: A UK Perspective', in P.J. Slot and P.D. Dagtoglou (eds) *Towards a Community Air Transport Policy*, London: Kluwer.

Van den Polder, R. (1994) 'Lobbying for the European Airline Industry', in R.H. Pedlar and M.P.C.M. Van Schendelen (eds) *Lobbying the European Union: Companies, Trade Associations and Issue Groups*, Aldershot: Dartmouth.

Vincent, D. (1987) 'Le rôle de la Commission dans la mise en place du marché unique', Ecole Nationale des Ponts et Chaussées, *Liberalisme et déréglementation*, Paris: Presses Ponts et Chaussées.

Vinçon, S. (1991) *Rapport de la commission de contrôle chargée d'examiner la gestion administrative, financière et technique de l'entreprise nationale Air France*, Senat, Second Ordinary Session 1990–1, Document no. 330, 16.5.91, Paris: Journaux Officiels.

Wheatcroft, S. and Lipman, G. (1990) *European Liberalisation and World Air Transport*, London: Economist Intelligence Unit.

Wright, V. (1995) 'The State and Major Enterprises in Western Europe: The Enduring Complexities', in Jack Hayward (ed.) *National Enterprise and European Integration: from National to International Champions?*, Oxford: OUP.

8   Energy policy

Francis McGowan

ENERGY POLICY – A CONSTRAINED CONSTRAINT

Energy policy in the European Community has been characterised by a struggle between the Commission, on the one side, and the member states and their industries, on the other. Over the years, the Commission has proposed a number of schemes to create a common energy policy, but without success. While governments and national firms have often differed on the details of national policies in this area, they have sought to maintain their autonomy and have been opposed to any transfer of responsibility to international authorities, not least to the Community itself. Increasingly, however, a Community dimension has emerged, on the basis of a mixture of promotional and regulatory activities, with the latter in particular providing the Commission with an important bargaining chip. Thus, while the Commission has been constrained by the reluctance of member states to pool sovereignty in a common energy policy, it has been able to act as a constraint upon governments and firms, not least because of the autonomy it enjoys on the basis of initiating policy, and the extent to which it had been able to exploit its role in broader areas of policy, such as competition and environment. This chapter explores the changing dynamics of the energy policy debate at the national and international as well as the European levels. However, before examining this process, it is necessary first of all to examine the question of energy policy: what are its aims? And how has it traditionally been organised?

WHAT IS ENERGY POLICY?

Energy policy is concerned with the coal, electricity, gas and oil industries, as well as newer technologies such as nuclear power, renewable energy and activities to enhance the efficiency of energy supply and consumption. Any attempt to define 'energy policy' more analytically runs into all the problems associated with the word 'policy'. Policies can be defined as what governments do or what governments say they do, manifesto commitments or *post hoc* rationalisations, specific initiatives or by-products of other actions.[1] In this chapter we confine ourselves to a simple distinction between official energy policy and unofficial policies affecting the energy sector. Official energy policy can be defined as a clearly elaborated and explicitly formulated strategy by government for the management of existing and future energy balances. In many cases there will be commitments to specific technology/investment choices and the co-ordination of activities among the energy supply industries themselves. Unofficial policies for the energy sector concen those policies which governments adopt for a variety of reasons, but which impinge upon the energy industries and energy balances, whether intentionally or incidentally. This distinction also operates at the EC level, where much of the first twenty years of the Community's history were spent trying to develop an official common energy policy, largely without success, but where other policies now exert a strong influence on the conduct of governments and energy industries (Daintith and Hancher 1986).

The orientation of official energy policies, and the balance of other policies affecting the energy sector, has shifted over the decades. For much of the post-war period there was an emphasis on fostering national energy resources and managing the transitions to a more diverse energy balance, on the basis of a preoccupation with supply security (particularly since the oil crisis of the 1970s and early 1980s). A key role in policy making was played by planning methodologies: forecasting, target setting and the introduction of interventionist policy mechanisms. The other strand of policy has been strategic in another sense, involving the use of the energy sector to fulfil broader macro- or micro-economic objectives: the development of new technologies, control of balance of payments and inflation and the pursuit of social equity. Both objectives have been pursued through influence over the energy supply industries themselves, resulting from outright ownership or the bestowal of special privileges and rights within energy markets such as the granting of exclusive rights of monopoly franchises.

More recently, the emphasis on supply security and strategic importance, along with the claim that energy is a 'special case', has begun to weaken in the face of the radical changes in energy markets. These include, in particular, the fall in energy prices in the mid-1980s and the more favourable supply–demand balance in energy resources markets, technological changes, such as the advent of information technology and the changing economics of various energy supply options and broader political changes. As a result, other policy concerns such as the protection of the environment or the promotion of competition have begun to impinge upon the energy sector (McGowan 1990). These challenges also involve a shift in interests which have been involved in energy policy making. In the past, the energy companies were the main targets and the beneficiaries of the policy. As they were closely tied to government, through ownership or other privileged links, this outcome is perhaps not too surprising. However, it would be wrong to say that policy was simply 'captured' by producer interests, since policy was not exclusively carried out for their benefit. On the consumer side, large users often enjoyed special arrangements, while there was a political imperative to maintain prices to the bulk of consumers at low levels and to even out differences in costs between different regions. Beyond this, national industries serving the energy sector were protected by preferential purchasing arrangements.[2] Thus, while policy was being driven largely by the interests of the energy industries, the benefits of policy were redistributed quite widely, arguably approximating some level of 'National Interest'. By shifting both the priorities and the mechanisms of policy, the new concerns of energy policy have reconfigured the interests represented: environmental objectives are given greater prominence, as are liberalisation measures. The consequent redistribution of costs and benefits is still being fought over in most countries.

For the most part, energy policy has been a domestic concern, with governments intervening directly or through national firms to manage energy markets in an attempt to maintain some degree of sovereignty. For most governments in EU countries, energy had been regarded as too important to leave to international markets or to surrender too much in co-ordination within intergovernmental arrangements. Such concerns appear to fly in the face of the realities of energy markets. As Table 8.1 shows, most member states consume considerably more energy than they produce. In 1960, the countries which comprised the Twelve produced energy equivalent to just under 70% of their needs. By 1970, less than 40% of needs were produced. In the 1980s and 1990s the situation had improved to around 50%, largely as a result of increased energy efficiency and the development of domestic energy resources. It is likely, however, that with increased demand and declining output from local sources, dependence on imported energy is likely to increase again.

It has been difficult for countries to insulate themselves completely from developments within international energy markets, as the oil shocks demonstrated. It is true that, through a mixture of taxes, subsidies, tariffs and quotas, governments have maintained energy prices above, below or in parity with 'world prices' for traded energy commodities to the extent that they choose them to be, often as part of efforts to support existing or emerging domestic energy supply options.[3] The underlying vulnerability has remained, however. The issue of how far supply security can be equated with self-sufficiency and how far countries need to be self-sufficient in energy resources is highly debatable, but for countries with only a limited resource, decisions regarding the treatment of those resources, whether they be fossil fuels, nuclear power or renewable energies, will most likely be more sensitive than in a country with substantial and diverse resources.

That vulnerability may help to explain the rather *dirigiste* approaches adopted in most member states over much of the last forty years. Of course, all the EC countries have market economies and all – or nearly all – claim that their policies towards the energy sector are based on the principles of the free market. However, notwithstanding the different ways in which 'the free market' is interpreted in different countries (Albert, 1992, Hart 1992 and

Table 8.1 European energy requirements, 1960–90 (m tonnes oil equivalent)

	1960 Total energy production			1970 Total energy production			1980 Total energy production			1990 Total energy production		
	Domestic energy production	Supply	As a % of supply	Energy production	Supply	As a % of supply	Domestic energy production	Supply	As a % of supply	Energy production	Supply	As a % of supply
Belgium	14.0	23.3	60	7.1	40.3	18	8.0	46.1	17	12.6	48.3	26
Denmark	1.0	9.0	11	0.3	20.2	1	0.7	19.5	4	9.9	18.3	54
France	50.9	85.1	60	42.6	147.3	29	47.0	190.7	25	104.8	221.2	47
Germany	127.1	144.5	88	174.7	304.6	57	184.0	359.2	51	184.8	355.1	52
Greece	0.4	2.6	15	1.7	8.1	21	3.7	16.0	23	8.8	22.1	40
Ireland	1.5	3.9	38	1.4	6.3	22	1.9	8.5	22	3.4	10.6	32
Italy	21.8	48.1	45	21.1	110.7	19	20.0	139.2	14	25.6	154.7	17
Luxemburg*	0	3.3	0	0	4.2	0	0	3.6	0	0.0	3.6	0
Netherlands	11.2	22.5	50	29.2	49.9	59	71.8	65.6	110	59.8	154.7	90
Portugal	1.7	3.4	50	1.4	6.0	23	1.5	10.3	15	2.1	3.6	13
Spain	12.0	18.3	66	9.7	38.4	25	15.8	68.7	23	31.2	66.4	35
UK	116.1	161.8	72	101.8	207.7	49	197.8	201.2	98	207.5	88.0	98
European Community**	357.7	525.8	68	391.0	943.7	41	552.2	1128.5	49	650.5	211.8	53
											1216.5	

Source: International Energy Agency

Note: * Luxemburg produces less than 0.1 m tonnes oil equivalent
   ** This table covers all current members of the EC; in 1960 and 70 there were 6 members;
in 1980 there were 10 and by 1990 there were 12

Shonfield 1965), the extent to which the energy policies pursued in most countries could be said to be operated on the same basis as most other sectors of the economy is highly questionable. Energy had been treated as a strategic resource, and accordingly, energy policy has for the most part been interventionist, explicitly or implicitly correcting for a host of market failures (Helm *et al.* 1989), as well as meeting other policy objectives. Far from being run along the lines of the free market, the energy sector has been one of the few elements of a planned economy in many otherwise capitalist countries.[4]

The planning orientation is best demonstrated by the high priority given to forecasting as a tool of policy making. While such techniques are common in many industrial policy concerns, the time horizons – often thirty or forty years – have been much longer than in other sectors, as is the degree to which they have been used as a guide to investment decisions (Baumgartner and Midttun 1987). The 'long-termedness' of energy policy is also reflected in the chosen technologies, notably nuclear power, which are characterised by long lead times in constructions and in operating life.

The need to manage uncertainty in energy markets helps to explain the persistence of energy policy priorities and techniques throughout much of the post-war period: institutional memory of market disruption and a perception that energy import dependence leaves economies exposed have been, and remain, powerful incentives for most governments. However, it is important not to ignore other explanatory factors including the community of expertise which has generated much of the conventional wisdom on energy policy and planning, on the one hand,[5] and the self-interest of politicians and public officials and the related desire to use energy policy as a surrogate for regional development or social security, on the other. Whatever one's interpretation of the motivations, however, most countries were characterised by a similar mix of official and unofficial energy policies, even if there were important differences in how policy was carried out and priorities chosen.[6]

The differences have probably been exacerbated by the changes within the energy policy debate. The political factors which have been important influences in shaping the new debate – the growth of the green movement, on the one hand, and the growing influence of neo-liberal ideas on economic management, on the other – have varied in their impact from country to country, compounding the existing specificities of resource endowment, industrial structure and political economy. Table 8.2 identifies a number of the characteristics of national policy in the four larger member states.

Prior to the 1980s, British energy policy conformed to the norm of a strong concern for supply security and for broader policy objectives. The state has had a direct influence on the energy sector for may decades, dating back to its purchase of a stake in what was to become British Petroleum, its establishment of a public corporation to manage the electricity grid and, most importantly, the post-war nationalisation of the coal, electricity and gas industries (Cairncross 1986). Although it was not until the 1960s that a formal statement of energy policy was published (Ministry of Fuel and

Table 8.2 Diversity of energy balance and industry structures

	EC	UK	France	Italy	Germany
GDP (b. $1.985)	3108.4	523.3	619.3	503.8	840.7
Population (millions)	347.2	57.9	57.4	57.9	80.6
Domestic Energy Production (m tonnes oil equivalent)	649.5	213.4	111.6	27.5	161.0
coal	187.3	49.8	11.2	1.4	100.3
oil	122.8	96.9	3.6	4.8	4.1
gas	145.6	45.6	2.8	14.7	13.7
electricity	193.8	21.1	94.1	6.6	42.8
Total Energy Supply (m tonnes equivalent)	1235.9	216.2	231.2	159.2	340.3
coal	267.0	60.2	22.8	13.5	106.5
oil	544.9	83.4	89.9	94.9	134.6
gas	229.1	50.2	28.1	41.1	56.8
electricity	193.8	21.1	94.1	6.6	42.8
Electricity Production (GWh)	1958.7	325.2	458.2	222.7	533.3
coal	766.1	203.7	38.8	25.8	311.0
oil	211.5	27.7	9.5	116.0	13.2
gas	136.1	8.7	3.0	35.2	32.9
nuclear	678.8	78.5	338.4	0	158.8
hydroelectricity	160.0	5.5	67.9	42.2	17.4
other	6.2	1.0	0.6	3.5	0.2
Energy utility structure	Diverse	Privatised and competitive	Publicly owned centralised and monopolistic	Publicly owned, semi-centralised and monopolistic	Mixed ownership decentralised and monopolistic

Source: International Energy Agency, author's analysis

Power 1965, 1967), unofficial energy policy was carried out through the state's role as the shareholder in the British energy industry. The energy industry's conduct was overseen by the Treasury and the Ministry of Fuel and Power (later the Department of Energy). The Treasury was important in determining the general regime within which the industry operated, as part of a wider system of controls over nationalised industries covering issues of productivity as well as investment and finance. The Ministry was more closely involved with the strategic aspects of energy policy (Pearson 1981).

The wider role of energy in the British economy was a constant feature of government intervention. The immediate task for the nationalised energy sector was reconstruction, both of itself and of the economy as a whole. Later, it was used to help develop new technologies (such as nuclear power) and resources (such as North Sea oil and gas). In these cases, the government was involved as part of a triumvirate with the energy firms and the supplier engineering firms.

Overall, the record of energy policy in the UK must be judged as mixed. By the beginning of the 1980s the UK was almost unique in Europe in enjoying self-sufficiency in energy within a balanced portfolio of fuels, yet there were serious shortcomings in the performance of the energy industries themselves. For every success, such as the development of a natural gas network or the transformation of coal industry productivity, there was a failure, such as the nuclear power programme. The energy industries themselves proved to be monolithic and inefficient (Surrey 1986). Arguably, the problems of British energy policy could be summarised as a failure of government to intervene where it should have done (productivity) and interfering where it should not (choice of technologies).[7]

Given the mixed record, it is perhaps not surprising that a radical government committed to rolling back the state should seek to redefine energy policy. Under the so-called 'Lawson doctrine', the government decided that, in future, market forces would be the main determinants of energy balances, and that privatisation and liberalisation of the energy sector would be priorities (Department of Energy 1982, Lawson 1992). In fact, the implementation of the Lawson doctrine took many years: the 1980s were characterised by classic traditional energy policy interventions (on nuclear power and on gas development) while many of the initial moves to encourage markets proved to have a very limited impact (Roberts *et al.* 1991, Vickers and Yarrow 1988).

None the less, by the early 1990s, British energy policy had been transformed. The major energy utilities are now in private hands and moving towards more competitive market structures. The government does not intervene in the way it did in previous decades; for example, over the crisis in the coal industry following electricity privatisation (Department of Trade and Industry 1993) and leaves major decisions in some areas to regulatory bodies. The key demonstration of this change was the closure of the Department of Energy after the 1992 election and the transfer of responsibilities to Industry and Environment. These ministries still have to grapple with some difficult issues, such as the future of nuclear power (Industry) and meeting commitments on controlling emissions from energy sources (Environment). Indeed, the latter concern has almost reinvented energy policy by obliging the government, which has sought to present itself as 'green', to take issues of energy efficiency and renewables seriously (Department of the Environment 1990).

In many respects, French energy policy developed along similar lines to the UK with long-standing participation in the oil sector (Feigenbaum 1985), widespread nationalisation after the Second World War and the use of public firms for energy policy objectives. Responsibility for the energy industry has been shared by the Ministry of Industry, within which the Directorate for Energy resides, and the Ministry of Finance. The former has been responsible for the strategic development of the industry and the latter has been involved in questions of finance and investment and pricing. However, the nature of the French political system and particularly, the close links between government and industry, have led to a much more coherent pursuit of energy policy goals than in the UK. At times, it has appeared that French energy industries have been better able to dominate thinking on key energy policy decisions than their British counterparts.[8]

The massive nuclear programme of the 1970s and 1980s demonstrates the coherence of French energy policy both in terms of the close links between government and industry and the consistency of policy over time. This programme was driven by the lack of alternative indigenous resources, aside from some gas and coal; the French energy resource base is confined to a declining coal industry and some small gas fields, and proved much more effective in delivering cheap electricity than any other nuclear programme in Europe or the rest of the world (Thomas 1987). The programme also illustrates the strength of the French energy industries, a strength which has more recently been demonstrated by the hitherto successful resistance of the French energy sector to pressures from those seeking to introduce greater competition or to encourage environmental protection.

At first glance, the history of Italian energy policy appears to fit into the pattern found in the UK and France. In practice, however, the gap between intentions and outcomes has been much larger than in the rest of Europe, notwithstanding some important successes. Under fascism, the state became a major participant in the energy sector but it was only in the post-war period that this role was effectively exploited, for example, in the development of the country's gas resources. This success proved rather unusual, as the state oil and gas company and later the state electricity company, which was nationalised only in the 1960s as part of the 'opening to the left' by the Christian Democrats, were primarily used as instruments of patronage by all the political parties (Feigenbaum *et al.* 1993).[9]

Energy policy has been managed by the Ministry of Industry. Regulation of investments was carried out by the Interministerial Committee for Economic Planning (CIPE) and of prices by the Interministerial Committee for Prices (CIP). In theory, policy was determined in the formulation of an overall National Energy Plan. However, while this was revised regularly over the decades, its forecasts and recommendations have rarely been realised. Instead, the government has used the energy sector as a means of pursuing other goals, for instance, limiting price increases to control inflation. Implementing every policy has also been made difficult by the planning process in Italy, one which allows local environmentalists to block investments in new power stations. The Italian environmental movement has been able to exploit these rules much more effectively than environmentalists in France and the UK, though it would be wrong to suggest that they have been able to influence the overall balance of energy policy beyond this veto. Pressures to open up to competition are relatively weak. Although legislation has been adopted to encourage greater competition very few attempts to exploit it have succeeded. It may be, however, that the proposed privatisation of the energy industries, along with pressure from both regional parties to decentralise as well as a more activist national anti-trust authority, could open the way to more scope for competition in the energy sector (de Paoli 1991).

In historical terms, German energy policy appears to be the exception to the tradition of centralised energy policies, utilising publicly owned energy industries. The Federal government does not have any ownership stakes in the energy sector, the last being divested when it sold its stake in the industrial conglomerates VEBA and VIAG, while energy policy has explicitly celebrated the reliance on free market mechanisms, for example, in the area of pricing. In practice, however, German energy policy has been in many ways as interventionist as any other in Europe, particularly in the last ten years with the rise of the environmental movement. Even the impression of separation between firm and state is undermined by the extensive ownership stakes of the Laender and municipal authorities (Feigenbaum *et al.* 1993, Hardach 1980).

For much of the post-war period, German energy policy was guided by a long-established consensus between government, the producer industries and the engineering equipment sector, summed up in the pre-war Energy Act of 1935 in security of supply and low energy prices in return for monopoly rights (Helm and McGowan 1989, Padgett 1990). From the 1960s, this was taken to involve a commitment to the then strategic technology of nuclear power, though the consensus was subsequently extended to coal through the 'Contract of the Century', signed in the early 1980s, which provided support to the hitherto declining domestic industry. The policy was not without its opponents but it was not until the Chernobyl accident that the consensus broke down, following the Social Democrats' decision to support a phasing out of nuclear power. Over the 1980s, moreover, the coal industry came under criticism not because of cost, even though by then it was three times the price of imported coal, but because of environmental problems: first acid rain, and more recently, the greenhouse effect (Boehmer-Christiansen and Skea 1990). This growing environmental dimension made itself felt on energy policy at a sub-national level. The Laender and municipal authorities began to develop their own energy policies, emphasising conservation and recycling.

The debate on German energy policy is now characterised by real tensions between those who wish to take the new environmentalist agenda further, and those who wish to restore the old consensus on nuclear power and coal. Talks in 1993 designed to foster a new consensus proved unsuccessful. At the same time, the pressures for addressing the special conditions enjoyed by some German firms have grown: while attempts by the anti-trust authorities to open up the sector to competition have largely failed, most recently in the wake of unification there seems to be growing interest in opening up the industry, both from those who seek to challenge the major firms and the major firms themselves.

The evolution of energy policies in the UK, France, Italy and Germany suggests, if anything, an increasing diversity of approaches, even if starting from common principles and facing similar challenges. All four countries shared a common set of values regarding energy policy. There was, perhaps, rather more rhetoric about the 'free market' in Germany than in other countries, but this was belied by quite extensive intervention at the Federal, and later the regional and municipal levels of government. There was a strong consensus among those countries regarding both the techniques for analysing energy balances, namely long-range forecasting and planning with high levels of growth predicted, and the technologies which would meet future needs, principally, nuclear power.

The main differences concerned the effectiveness with which the latter policy was pursued. The UK and France both overcame opposition to nuclear power, but only France developed a full and successful commitment to the technology. Germany was able to formulate an effective programme, but widespread political opposition has foreclosed further development. Italy was not able to develop an effective programme due to a combination of policy failure and public opposition. All the countries relied on a mix of government intervention in alliance with energy industries to tackle questions of supply security and wider strategic goals. On the face of it, Germany was again an exception given the more limited role of the state as an owner, at least at a federal level, but major German energy firms, such as Ruhrgas, VEBA and RWE, have been closely involved in the development and implementation of policy. The alliance has arguably been the most effective in France, with the nuclear case again the prime example, but the partnership between government and the oil and gas industries in the UK, and arguably Italy, secured the development of major natural resources. Divergences in the performance of public enterprise do exist, however, and cast doubt on the extent to which energy policy was effectively pursued.

Nor should the different resource bases be ignored. All four countries have sought to exploit natural resources, particularly after the energy crises. However, as table 8.1 and 8.2 indicate, endowments differ considerably and affect the detail of energy strategy. There is no doubt that the UK's good fortune in possessing a well-balanced portfolio of energy resources has affected its subsequent energy policy, particularly in the last ten years, while the other countries have had much more limited supplies of water, gas and coal, and have adopted very different approaches to the management of those limited resources.

Changes over the last ten years have exacerbated the differences between the states. One might expect that these new issues would have encouraged a convergence of policies, but, if anything, the opposite has been the case, not least because of the differences in emphasis between countries and in the pace of change. Although preferences for different sources of energy have been evident for some time, the growth of environmentalism and neo-liberalism in the 1980s has confirmed the divergent policies.

At the political level, the impact of environmentalism and neo-liberalism on energy policy has depended both upon the overall political influence of these movements and the special characteristics of the energy sector. It could be argued that the neo-liberal challenge has been so far resisted by the French and by the German energy industries, as evidenced by the maintenance of energy monopolies in both countries and the continuation of massive financial support for the German coal industry. While the Italian energy industries have not been able to prevent change, given the scale of political upheavals and economic problems, they have been able to exploit political differences in the country to slow the pace of change. The neo-liberal pressures appear to have had the greatest effect in the UK, where the stronger commitment to liberalisation and privatisation has effectively nullified competing energy policy agendas, notably supply security, and overturned the old interests of the energy industries. In the case of gas and electricity, however, this has been achieved more by co-optation – the benefits of private ownership – than by confrontation.

The impact of environmentalism has taken very different forms in the four countries. In Germany, the influence of environmentalism might be considered comparable to neo-liberalism in the UK in its challenge to the traditional energy policy agenda. However, a judgement on the real influence of environmentalism will depend on how strongly one views both the overall clout of the German environmental movement and the compatibility of supply security and environmental protection. Both favour, for example, energy efficiency and renewables, but differ on issues of coal and nuclear power. The compatibility of green issues with a liberalised energy policy has been tested in the UK. British environmental movements have been able to exploit the turbulence in energy policy and the government's green rhetoric, for example, through promoting renewable energy sources and energy efficiency. They have not been able to overcome the energy industries' successful opposition to major policy changes, such as the carbon tax; however, in Italy, environmental concerns have largely made themselves felt in a local setting through successful opposition to large energy projects, such as new power stations. French environmentalists, while at times politically influential, have not been able to refocus energy policy.

The impact of these new agendas, then, has been to alter significantly energy policy in some states more than others: Germany, with environmental concerns, the UK with the neo-liberal turn and, in a less dramatic fashion, Italy with both. The French appear to have maintained greater continuity, but it is not clear for how long this will last. For all four countries, the European dimension has been increasingly influential.

THE CHANGING GLOBAL SETTING

The divergence between European states has taken place in the context of much broader changes in the energy sector, particularly in terms of the level at which energy firms and markets are organised. The exercise of autonomy may be harder to sustain as the international context becomes more important for national energy policy making. Energy markets and firms are becoming more global, while many of the preoccupations of recent years, such as trade liberalisation and environmental protection, are inherently international. The issues which have arisen domestically, therefore, also appear on an international agenda.

The corollary to the traditional defensiveness of energy policy strategies in the EU has been a limited role for international co-ordination in the sector. The main institutional innovation was the creation of the International Energy Agency (comprising the OECD countries except, until 1990, France) to handle supply disruptions in the oil market, to monitor developments in the energy sector and to review members' energy policy (Keohane 1984). There has also been the development of a non-proliferation regime, which has involved the management of trade in nuclear equipment and materials, though the effectiveness of the regime has frequently been called into question (Walker and Lonnoth 1983). In the past, energy has figured in the communiqués of western summits and UN debates, but with limited follow-up.

The question of appropriate authority structures for energy policy, however, is again being raised as the broader process of globalisation in the world economy begins to impinge upon the sector.[10] The oil industry has of course been the quintessentially global industry, notwithstanding a wave of nationalisations from the 1950s to the 1970s – a wave which has since been reversed as foreign investment and joint ventures have blossomed. However, other energy sectors are now increasingly characterised by international firms, a process driven by privatisation in both developed and developing countries.[11] Overall, the national firm could become an endangered species in the energy sector.

Other internationalising pressures can be seen on the demand side as the international markets for energy resources grow. Coal is following oil onto the international market with a limited range of countries exporting their lower cost resources to importers, many of whom are scaling back their own higher cost industries. The gas and even the electricity markets have also become more open to trade. Moreover, for some large users, energy price conditions have become an important criterion in corporate strategy. Such consumers of energy are likely to look increasingly beyond their national borders for supplies of energy and to question policies which may constrain their ability to seek out the lowest cost source of supply.

As a result of these changes, governments may find their autonomy in the energy sector is becoming even more limited, arguably as much as it is in other areas of the economy, such as steel, electronic components or finance. If the traditional mechanism of energy policy, the publicly owned energy corporation, is no longer to hand, governments may have to reconsider both their objectives for, and their approach towards, energy policy. Governments' scope for action may also be changing because of obligations to international agreements, particularly in the areas of trade liberalisation and environmental protection. Even if their own energy policies have not moved in the direction of greater competition/transparency and sensitivity to environmental impacts, commitments made in international fora may oblige them to do so.

Traditionally, trade liberalisation has not focused on the energy sector. The Gatt talks, for example, have largely ignored national conduct in this area. However, the Gatt rules on subsidies and on procurement may well impinge more directly on the energy sector. The new World Trade Organisation (WTO) is likely to pursue these issues further, particularly if it develops a competence in the area of competition policy (Hoekmann and Mavroidis 1992).

The WTO is also likely to deal with trade-related environmental issues, though the compatibility of free trade and environmental protection is a highly contested issue.[12] Indeed, just as the global forum is seen as the main focus for trade reform, so it is regarded as the only effective framework for negotiations on the major environmental challenges facing the Earth. Getting an agreement on such issues is not easy. The negotiations on the relatively straightforward problem of controlling ozone depletion began in the early 1980s, although a scientific debate extended back considerably further, and took some years to be finalised (Weale 1991). The issue of abating greenhouse gas emissions will be much more difficult to agree. Even so, the fact that the debate is taking place suggests that decisions on the environmental consequences of energy use are being taken seriously at a global level (Grubb 1990).

THE DEVELOPMENT OF EC POLICY

It is clearly too early to judge how far these institutional developments will constrain national governments and regulate energy firms and markets. It could be argued that such changes may be necessary: if firms and markets are globalising, should there not also be at least some element of global regulation? However, while the development of international authority structures might be thought desirable, the very real differences in interests and perceptions between governments are likely to limit the prospects for such initiatives. The stronger pressures at a global level will be those in energy market and corporate structures. International governance might be considered as an ideal accompaniment to these developments, but, aside from some limited 'regulatory' roles, such as opening up market access and attempting to limit emissions, it is likely to remain the most idealistic component. In this context, regional policy solutions may be more realistic, obtaining what it may no longer be possible to secure at a domestic level. On the face of it, the European Community should be particularly well suited to its task.

There is no doubt that energy should have played an important part in the Community's affairs: two of the three treaties on which the EC is based are concerned with energy specifically: the ECSC and Euratom Treaties were devoted to coal, which then dominated energy balances, and nuclear power, which was seen as the future. A common market for other energy sectors was, by implication, addressed in the Rome Treaty. The gap between intentions expressed in the Treaties and the outcomes, however, has proved a large one for energy, and the Commission's attempt to secure the agreement of member states to a Community energy policy of any sort, let alone one reflecting the ideals of the treaties, were for many years unsuccessful (McGowan 1994).

Throughout the 1950s and 1960s attempts to develop policies for energy industries were ignored or rejected by member states, who sought to retain control over the energy sector. The crisis of 1973–4 should have provided an opportunity for an EC role but instead proved to be a further instance of the Community failing to co-ordinate policy. Member states pursued their own policies or worked through the IEA (van der Linde and Lefeber 1988). In the wake of these failures, the Commission attempted to develop a more strategic yet more modest approach to the management of energy supply and demand, involving the setting of target objectives (such as the reduction of energy imports as a proportion of total energy needs to the improvement in energy intensities). In these cases, however, the main concern was to change the structure of energy balances rather than the structure of energy markets (CEC 1988a).

By the mid-1980s, therefore, the Commission had succeeded in establishing a place in energy policy making, but it was far from being central to national policy agendas, consisting instead of information-gathering, target-setting and, most significantly, R&D. These activities could hardly be thought to constitute a comprehensive Community energy policy. From that time on, however, the scope for a wider, if unofficial, Community role in energy policy began to increase. This shift was partly as a result of changes within the Community itself. The Single European Act marked the turn-around in the fortunes of the Community and was paralleled by renewed activism on the part of the Commission. That dynamism was most clearly seen in two areas, market liberalisation and environmental protection, which were in any case impinging on national policy agendas. These proved to be areas to which the policy techniques of the Commission and the competencies and the commitments of the relevant Directorates, DGIV and DGXI, were well suited. Thus, the Commission was able to play an increasingly visible role in proposing policy and regulating the Community economy, including the energy sector.

The catalyst for market liberalisation was undoubtedly the single market programme, and while this initiative touched on energy only tangentially, in relation to the issues of taxation and procurement of equipment, the idea of a single market for energy took off on the back of the success of '1992'. In 1988, the Commission published its initial analysis of what needed to be done to bring about such a market. The measures included a reorganisation of the energy utility markets to permit greater integration and competition, greater transparency of energy prices and an abandonment of the special links between energy industries and their local suppliers. The Commission stressed the need to bring the conduct of the energy industries into line with principles of EU law (particularly with regard to the competition provision) (CEC 1988b).

The Commission's liberalising activism has been seen across the energy sector. In the oil sector it has sought to open up licensing procedures and has completed its long-running policy of breaking the monopolistic position of state-owned oil companies in Mediterranean states. In the coal sector, it has sought to tackle both the subsidies given to the industry and the privileged supply links between national industries and key consumers, principally the electricity industry. Application of competition rules has largely been carried out case-by-case, as a result of rulings laid down on the basis of European law, either where member states have sought clarification or approval of reform measures, or from disputes between member states being referred to the European Court of Justice. The Commission itself is taking a number of member states to the Court, challenging their trading monopolies in electricity and/or gas. So far, however the Commission has chosen not to use its powers under Articles 90 to impose directly liberalising measures in the energy sector (Hancher and Trepte 1992).

The Commission's interest in the environment is not new. Its involvement in environmental issues dates back to the early 1970s, although its formal competence was only recognised in the Single European Act. The significance of EC environmental policy for the energy sector has paralleled the ascent of the issue up the political agenda in an increasing number of member states (Owens and Hope 1990). Policy in the 1980s focused on legislation to tackle the emission of NOx, Sulphur Dioxide and particulates from power and industrial plant and motor vehicles (Boehmer, Christiansen and Skea 1990). The current concerns are with emissions which contribute to the greenhouse effect. In 1991 the member states agreed to stabilise emission of carbon dioxide by the year 2000. The Commission's approach focuses on the introduction of an energy tax to encourage greater energy efficiency and to discourage the use of fossil fuels. However, the cornerstone of this policy, a proposal to levy a tax on fuels according to their contribution to the carbon dioxide emissions, appears to have failed, due mainly to British hostility.

There are other aspects to the Commission's energy policy agenda. It continues with its support for energy efficiency and renewables through research budgets, though this is only a small element, and other measures designed to encourage their use, such as recommendations for preferential terms for renewable sources of supply. It has developed policies for supporting the development of energy infrastructures, primarily in less developed areas of the Community. It has also sought to develop its responsibilities in the area of security by seeking to join the International Energy Agency and to play a more active role in crisis management.

Such a variety of activities would suggest that the Commission still anticipates a formal Community competence in energy policy. Its attempts to formalise its role in the Treaty on European Union were unsuccessful. Although the Commission was able to insert a (relatively weak) commitment to a Community role, in the very last stages of the negotiations a number of member states indicated their objections and obtained its removal from the text that was finally agreed. The Commission was able to insert a commitment in the Treaty to reconsider the treatment of energy at the Intergovernmental Conference in 1996[13] however, and it is now in the process of making the case for a Community energy policy role. At the beginning of 1995, it produced a Green Paper on energy policy and the issue is one of the Commission's priorities in the 1995 Work Programme (CEC 1995).

Whether or not the Commission is successful in securing a formal competence in energy policy, it is clear that it will continue to develop policies which act as constraints on how policy is pursued at a national level. The growth of this 'regulatory' role is likely to remain the Commission's most potent means of influencing national policy. The Commission is particularly well suited to operating in a regulatory mode (Bulmer 1994, Majone 1994). Moreover, most of the developments have been in the areas of competition and the environment, where a clearer Community competence has emerged which effectively cuts across sectoral concerns. In these cases, it is possible to identify a more rounded perspective, based on broader principles (the benefits of competition or the need to protect the environment) than sectoral priorities and supported by strong legal bias (indeed, the role of the Court in defining the scope of regulation has been of considerable importance) (McGowan and Seabright 1995).

The emergence of the Commission's regulatory role on energy matters has reinforced its position in other respects. In particular, it has prompted many inside and outside the energy industries to take the Commission seriously. This is best illustrated by the refocusing of lobbying activities towards Brussels. The creation of specifically European associations for the electricity, gas, oil, renewables and conservation industries, the establishment of European branches in large energy firms' government affairs departments and the increase in complaints and cases on energy matters taken to the Commission and the Court are symptomatic of the growing attempt to influence European institutions. Indeed, groups within member states are just as likely to try European conduits as a way of changing national policies; for example, environmentalists have addressed complaints concerning government support for the nuclear industry in the UK to the Commission.

Governments too can no longer ignore the Commission's activities in the energy sector. Whether it is the British seeking approval for privatisation plans, the Germans negotiating on Commission objections to coal subsidies or the French and Italians defending themselves against allegations of anti-competitive behaviour in the electricity sector, national authorities must take account of the European dimension in almost all aspects of energy policy.

The Commission's role in regulating for the environment is arguably less of a constraint upon national policy making, if only because it has emerged on the basis of Council decisions, most of which require unanimity. In a sense, the member states have been careful to ensure that their room for manoeuvre on energy policy is not constrained by Community environmental regulations. When the Single Act was signed, member states attached a Declaration which states that the new environmental rules would not affect their ability to develop their energy sectors. Similarly, in the Maastricht Treaty, member states were able to secure unanimity as the method of decision making on environmental rules affecting the energy sector. Despite these limitations, however, there is still scope for the Commission to intervene regarding the way in which agreed decisions are implemented in member states.

The competition rules are a source of greater restriction, as there is greater discretion allowed to the Commission in determining how far national conduct is in line with the Treaty. Increasingly, the Commission is intervening on issues of market structure and conduct and the provision of government support in the energy sector. Some of these policy actions have a relatively long history (the attempts to curtail subsidies to the coal industry and the reform of oil monopolies). However, in the last few years the extent of Commission activities has increased markedly – a development not unconnected with its desire to develop the internal energy market.

The case which demonstrated the Commission's scope for constraining national conduct was its intervention in the British electricity privatisation programme. It is perhaps ironic that the Commission should tackle a country which was in the process of reform, and therefore moving in the 'right direction', but an industry which was actively undergoing change was an easier target for the Commission than one which maintained the *status quo*. Tackling the *status quo* would mean confronting the industry across most of the Community. The Commission addressed two issues following notification from the UK government; namely the arrangements made for the nuclear sector and the more general arrangements regarding competition after privatisation. The Commission's action obtained a very different regime for the treatment of nuclear power in the privatised industry. Other interventions have focused on the nature of trading monopolies in the electricity and gas sectors, the provision of subsidies for new projects and a series of joint ventures between the French utility, EdF, and energy intensive industries.

The results of these interventions were variable, and in many cases it has been clear that the Commission has been under considerable political pressure, and in some cases the Commission's bark has been worse than its bite. Indeed, it would be wrong to suggest that the regulatory activities of the Commission are 'unconstrained'. There are clear limits to Commission interventions. At one level there is a question over whether the Commission should intervene, where the political calculation is related to the likely reaction of national governments, and whether or not Commission action would be seen as illegitimate. At another level, once the decision to act is taken there is the risk that its initiatives will be rejected in the Council and overturned by the Court.

CONCLUSION

It is nearly forty years since the first Community initiatives in energy policy were proposed, but a coherent policy remains elusive. Each of the energy sub-sectors has been affected by Community policies, but, beyond a set of promotional activities in such fields as information, research and regional planning, the policies are largely invoked on the back of the internal market and the application of competition rules, on the one hand, and environmental protection, on the other. Thus, a number of member states continue to resist the transfer of sovereignty on energy policy to the Community. Yet they cannot ignore the Community as a constraint to their own autonomy. The rather confused division of labour which results however, risks not only conflicts between member states and the Commission, but in conflicts between the various strands of energy policy. It may be that the pressures of different policy objectives, and the need both to reconcile these and to rationalise and regulate derogations from them, will push the Community towards a *de facto* energy policy, raising a number of questions about accountability and democracy. Ironically, the problems will result from the failure of member states to consider and debate a coherent and common energy policy for the Community.

NOTES

1 See, for example, the discussion on the meanings of 'policy' in Hogwood and Gunn 1984: 13–19.
2 This was true of all energy industries but has been most fully documented in the electricity sector; see Epstein 1971.
3 While it is of course debatable how far one can talk of a world price for energy products, the scale of the divergence in energy prices between member states reflects national preferences (in the form of covert subsidies or overt taxes) rather than market conditions. See CEC 1984.
4 The 'distortions' in national policies are dealt with in the annual review of the International Energy Agency, various.
5 At least in the 1970s, the elite consensus on the priorities for energy policy and the techniques of analysis was such that one might be tempted to refer to an epistemic community of sorts. It is harder to identify such a community at present however. On this concept, see Haas 1992.
6 Whether or not this constitutes a form of policy convergence is debatable. See Bennett 1991.
7 Since the early 1980s, the Monopolies and Mergers Commission has published assessments of nationalised industries. See, for example, Monopolies and Mergers Commission 1981. On the specific issue of nuclear technologies choice see Rush *et al.* 1977.
8 On the question of the French energy sector's autonomy see Hayward 1986 and Lucas and Papaconstantinou 1985.
9 On the development of the Italian energy sector see Posner and Woolf (1967) and Clough (1986). See Lucas and Papaconstantinou 1985 on appointments.
10 For an account of globalisation, see Ohmae 1992. One attempt to deal with the concept from a political science perspective can be found in Grant 1992.

11 For an account of that process in what has traditionally been the most national-
istic part of the energy sector, see McGowan 1993.
12 On the growing importance of environmental issues in trade policy debates, see
Kulessa 1992. For a critique of free trade on environmental grounds, see Hines
and Lang 1993.
13 See 'Declaration on Civil Protection, Energy and Tourism' in the Treaty on European Union.

REFERENCES

Albert, M. (1992) *Capitalism against Capitalism*, London: Whurr.
Baumgartner, T. and Midttun, A. (eds) (1987) *The Politics of Energy Forecasting*,
Oxford: Clarendon.
Bennett, C. (1991) 'What is Policy Convergence and What Causes it?' *British Journal
of Political Science*, 21, 2.
Boehmer-Christiansen, S. and Skea, J. (1990) *Acid Politics: Environmental and Energy
Policies in Britain and Germany*, London: Belhaven Press.
Bulmer, S. (1994) 'The Governance of the European Union', *Journal of Public Policy*,
London: Belhaven Press.
Cairncross, A. (1986) *Years of Recovery*, London: Methuen.
Clough, S. (1986) *Economic History of Modern Italy*, New York: Colombia University
Press.
Commission of the European Communities (CEC) (1988a) *The Main Findings of the
Commission's Review of Member States' Energy Policies*, Luxemburg: Office for Of-
ficial Publications of the European Communities.
—— (1988b) *The Internal Energy Market*, Luxemburg: Office for Official Publications
of the European Communities.
—— (1984) *The Application of the Community's Energy Pricing Principles in Member
States*, Luxemburg: Office for Official Publications of the European Communities.
—— (1995) *For a European Energy Policy*, Luxemburg: Office for Official Publications
of the European Communities.
Daintith, T. and Hancher, L. (1986) *Energy Strategy in Europe: the Legal Framework*,
Berlin: de Gruyter.
de Paoli, L. (1991) 'Organisation and Regulation of the Italian Energy System',
ENER Bulletin, No. 9.
Department of Energy (1982) 'Speech on Energy Policy', *Energy Paper*, 51.
Department of the Environment (1990) *This Common Inheritance*, London: HMSO.
Department of Trade and Industry (1993) *The Prospects for Coal – Conclusions of the
Government's Coal Review*, London: HMSO.
Epstein, B. (1971) *The Politics of Trade in Power Plant: The Impact of Public Procure-
ment*, London: Trade Policy Research Centre.
Feigenbaum, H. (1985) *The Politics of Public Enterprise: Oil and the French State*,
Princeton: Princeton University Press.
Feigenbaum, H., Samuels, R. and Weaver, O. (1993) 'Innovation, Co-ordination and
Implementation in Energy Policy', In R. Weaver and B. Rockman (eds) *Do Institu-
tions Matter? Government Capabilities in the United States and Abroad*, Washing-
ton: Brookings.
Grant, W. (1992) 'Economic Globalisation, Stateless Firms and International Gov-
ernance', University of Warwick Department of Politics and International Studies,
Working Paper 105.
Grubb, M. (1990) *Energy Policy and the Greenhouse Effect*, London: RIIA.
Haas, P. (1992) 'Introduction: Epistemic Communities and International Policy
Co-ordination', *International Organisation*, 46,1.

Hancher, L. and Trepte, P. (1992) 'Competition and the Internal Energy Market' *European Competition Law Review*, 13,4.

Hardach, K. (1980) *The Political Economy of Germany in the Twentieth Century*, California: University of California Press.

Hart, J. (1992) *Rival Capitalists*, Ithaca: Cornell University Press.

Hayward, J. (1986) *The Market Economy and the State*, Brighton: Harvester Wheatsheaf.

Helm, D., Kay, J. and Thompson, D. (eds) (1989) *The Market for Energy*, Oxford: Clarendon Press.

Helm, D. and McGowan, F. (1989) 'Electricity Supply in Europe: Lessons for the UK', in D. Helm, J. Kay and D. Thompson (eds) *The Market for Energy*, Oxford: Clarendon.

Hines, C. and Lang, T. (1993) *The New Protectionism*, Earthscan.

Hoekmann, B. and Mavroidis, A. (1992) 'Competition, Competition Policy and the Gatt', *World Economy*, 17, 2.

Hogwood, B. and Gunn, L. (1984) *Policy Analysis for the Real World*, Oxford: OUP.

International Energy Agency (various) *Energy Policies and Programmes of IEA Countries*, Paris: IEA/OECD.

Keohane, R.O. (1984) *After Hegemony: Co-operation and Discord in the World Political Economy*, Princeton: Princeton University Press.

Kulessa, M. (1992) 'Free Trade and Protection of the Environment', *Intereconomics*, 27, 4.

Lawson, N. (1992) *The View from Number 11*, London: Bantam.

Lucas, N. and Papaconstantinou, D. (1985) *Western Europe Energy Policies: A Comparative Study of the Influence of Institutional Structure on Technical Change*, Oxford: Clarenden Press.

McGowan, F. (1990) 'Conflicting Objectives in European Energy Policy', in C. Crouch and D. Marquand *The Politics of 1992: Beyond the Single Market*, Oxford: Blackwell.

—— (1993) 'Reforming the Electricity Sector: The North as a Model, the South as a Market', in Pearson, P. (ed.) *Electricity in the Third World*, Guildford: SEEC.

—— (1994) 'Energy Policy', In A.M. El Agraa (ed.) *The Economics of the European Community*, Brighton: Harvester Wheatsheaf.

—— and Seabright, P. (1995) 'Regulation in the European Community and its Impact on the UK', in M. Bishop, J. Kay and C. Mayer *The Regulatory Challenge*, Oxford: OUP.

Majone, G. (1994) 'The Rise of the Regulatory State in Europe' *West European Politics*, 17, 3.

Ministry of Fuel and Power (1965) *Fuel Policy*, London: HMSO.

—— (1967) *Fuel Policy*, London: HMSO.

Monopolies and Mergers Commission (1981) *A Report on the Operation of the Board of its System for the Generation and Supply of Electricity in Bulk*, London: HMSO.

Ohmae, K. (1992) *The Borderless World*, London: Fontana.

Ostry, S. (1990) *Governments and Corporations in a Shrinking World*, Washington: Council for Foreign Relations.

Owens, S. and Hope, C. (1990) 'Energy and the Environment – The Challenge of Integrating European Policies', *Energy Policy*,17.

Padgett (1990) 'Policy Style and Issue Environment: The Electricity Supply Sector in West Germany', *Journal of Public Policy*, 10, 2.

Pearson, L. (1981) *The Organisation of the Energy Industries*, Basingstoke: Macmillan.

Posner, M.V. and Woolf, S. (1967) *Italian Public Enterprises*, London: Duckworth.

Roberts, J., Elliot, D. and Houghton, T. (1991) *Privatising Electricity*, London: Belhaven.

Rush, H., MacKerron, G. and Surrey, A. (1977) 'The Advanced Gas-cooled Reactor: A Case Study in Reactor Choice', *Energy Policy*, 15, 2.

Shonfield, A. (1965) *Modern Capitalism*, Oxford: OUP.

Surrey, A.J. (1986) 'The Nationalised Energy Industries', in J. Gretton and A. Harrison (eds) *Energy UK*, Newbury: Policy Journals.

Thomas, S.D. (1987) *The Realities of Nuclear Power*, Cambridge: Cambridge University Press.

van der Linde, J.G. and Lefeber, R. (1988) 'IEA captures the Development of European Energy Law', *Journal of World Trade* 22, 5.

Vickers, J. and Yarrow, G. (1988) *Privatisation – An Economic Analysis*, Cambridge, Mass: MIT.

Walker, W. and Lonnroth, M. (1983) *Nuclear Power Struggles*, London: Allen & Unwin.

Weale, A. (1991) *The New Politics of Pollution*, Manchester: Manchester University Press.

9   Water

Jeremy Richardson[1]

LEARNING TO LIVE WITH THE EU? POLICY CHANGE IN THE UK AND THE EUROPEANISATION OF WATER

It is impossible to assess the impact of the European Union on water policy in the UK without acknowledging the importance of endogenous changes. There has been a series of endogenous, that is, intra-sectoral, policy and organisational changes – particularly the effects of privatisation and the institution of a completely new regulatory regime after 1989 (Maloney and Richardson 1995). In addition, these 'shocks' to the sector have taken place in the context of a major shift in the *political salience* of water policy at both the national and European levels over time It is therefore somewhat difficult to isolate EU factors and to assess their impact, if only because so much change has been taking place in the sector over a long period of time. The whole sector has been undergoing a series of both incremental and radical changes – legislative, institutional, and cultural – since the mid-1970s. In particular, the move towards a privately owned system in England and Wales (the Scottish system is about to undergo major changes) has had implications for the way in which the UK is currently responding to EU water policy. In part, this is because the network of actors involved at the national level is now more extensive and complex and less consensual, and in part because privatisation has exposed the difficult question of how to finance improvements more clearly than in most other EU states. To some degree, the challenge of Europeanisation – familiar in other policy areas – has arrived in the water sector alongside the destabilisation and erosion of a hitherto relatively stable policy community. Europeanisation of the sector may be seen as the second part of a 'pincer movement' on the sector as a whole.

Although it will be argued that the UK's history and traditions of environmental management have generally made the UK a difficult European partner in the water sector, it should be noted that many of the financial and economic issues currently causing controversy in the UK will inevitably surface sooner or later in many other EU states. For particular reasons, the UK may have recognised the erosion of national autonomy somewhat earlier than other member states. As the other member states do so, the 'politics of water' at the European level may begin to change. Privatisation and the new regulatory regime in England and Wales have hastened the examination of issues which have possibly remained less visible elsewhere in Europe. It can be argued, therefore, that the UK's position in terms of policy bargaining at the EU level could well improve over time as her partners face some of the (as yet) hidden or disguised costs of meeting EU legislative requirements. Even so, for the UK to become a really powerful actor in the formulation of EU water policy will require some difficult adjustments of culture and tradition on the part of the Department of the Environment and the water industry at a time when the latter is becoming more independent of its former political master. Essentially, the UK has maintained a 'policy style', both in terms of content of policies and in terms of policy formulation, which is often quite different to 'continental' traditions. As in the field of social policy (Mazey 1994), it will be difficult for the UK to convince its partners that it is they who are out of step. For the UK to increase its influence over the formulation of European level water policy will probably require a degree of accommodation, by the UK, of some of the fundamental approaches to pollution control and environmental management adopted by her European partners. If this can be accepted, then the UK has some advantages – in terms of the co-ordination of national responses and of national actors – which it may then be able to exploit (Mazey 1992; Mazey and Richardson 1993).

Many of the UK's difficulties in coping with the Europeanisation of water policy are commonly attributed solely to the UK's general position in resisting a federal European Union, yet the history of national water policy in the UK has undoubtedly made a major contribution to the 'European problem' as it is now perceived. In particular, the increasingly tight financial regime for the industry, instituted in the UK throughout the 1970s and 1980s, is a major cause of the current difficulties with European legislation. These changes were not related to water problems *per se*. They were the result of general economic difficulties, IMF intervention and a general shift in the climate of opinion against further expansion of public expenditure. Indeed, it might be argued that had it not been for the strict financial regime, the UK would be no more 'uncomfortable' with EU water policy than, say, Germany, France, Holland or Denmark. It was the funding policies pursued under public ownership that were one of the main causes of the quite severe backlog of investment in water supply and sewage treatment infrastructure – not an overburdening European 'super-state'.

Thus one needs to take account of the history of the water sector, prior to the erosion of national autonomy and sovereignty, before trying to assess the impact of Europeanisation. The increasingly tight national financial regime – in terms of restriction on investment, prices and required rates of return – had two important effects. First, as suggested above, it inevitably caused a deterioration in the physical infrastructure which would have to be dealt with sooner or later. Second, it was important in causing leading figures in the industry to seek privatisation of the industry. This was despite the fact that the government originally had no intention of privatising the industry and had made no internal preparations for such a major policy change (Richardson *et al.* 1992). Thus the transfer of the ten regional water authorities (RWAs) in England and Wales from the public to the private sector had nothing to do with Europeanisation. The 'politics of privatisation' was a case of national politics caused by specific national circumstances, not a response to the European challenge. The European factor emerged only after the initial decision to privatise, when it was realised that the specific form of privatisation originally proposed – in particular the nature of the regulatory framework for the privatised industry – could not be decided without taking note of the role of the EC. Hence EU legislation did influence considerably the actual form of privatisation.

Prior to privatisation, the sector had been one of low political salience, fairly routine and 'private' policy making – effectively the RWAs had the franchise for public policy within the financial constraints set by the Treasury – and rather low salience for EU matters. The privatisation process itself, however, increased the considerable potential for EU influence and forced a major reconsideration of the initial privatisation proposals. The consequences of that rethink are very evident today since it produced a completely fresh regulatory regime for the newly privatised industry. In its original White Paper in 1986, the government had accepted the industry's argument that the RWAs should be privatised *in toto*, including their regulatory functions. In so doing, it followed the standard pattern in its privatisation programme in order to avoid breaking up industries, and to privatise in a manner acceptable to both the existing industry managers and, crucially, to potential investors. The Department of the Environment failed to recognise that the transfer of regulatory functions, then exercised by the RWAs in the traditional British self-regulatory style, to the private sector would be unworkable, although privately, the industry itself had identified this as a potentially serious problem under EC law.

In the event, the government faced a deluge of opposition from bodies such as the Council for Protection of Rural England (CPRE), the Institute for European Environmental Policy (IEEP), the Country Landowners' Association (CLA), the Institute of Water and Environmental Management (IWEM), the Confederation of British Industry (CBI) and the trade unions. Thus the traditional tightly drawn policy community was challenged by a group of actors not usually central to water policy. Many of these actors used the threat of European law as their entry ticket to the water privatisation policy process. The question of whether the proposed privatised RWAs (WSPLCs) could be deemed to be 'competent authorities' under EC law proved crucial. For example, Nigel Haigh, Director of the IEEP and the leading authority on the implementation of EC environmental law in the UK, wrote to *The Times*, questioning whether the privatised water companies would constitute 'competent authorities'. He pointed out that, unless this was resolved, the government could at any time be challenged in the European

Court (*The Times*, 13 May 1968). The CPRE also commissioned its own legal advice from Professor Francis Jacobs. His conclusion was that

> the European Court, if the question were raised before it, might well decide that at least in relation to some of the functions assigned to the 'competent authorities' by the EEC directives in the field of water pollution, the UK could not properly assign them to the WSPLCs.
>
> (Jacobs and Shanks 1988: 18)

As Nigel Haigh has since argued,

> if the Government presented a Bill to parliament giving powers to the WSPLCs to act as 'competent authorities' for implementing EC Directives, then it would be open to a public interest body (such as the CPRE) to raise the matter in a national court who would then refer the matter to the European Court under article 177. The CPRE made it clear that they would do this. The Government therefore knew that they could not avoid protracted proceedings before the European Court which at least would cast a pall of uncertainty over any attempts to float the WSPLCs on the stock exchange. It was this point that shook them.
>
> (Private correspondence, 28 May 1991)

The European Commission had itself eventually issued a carefully worded warning that the proposed transfer of pollution control functions to the private sector might be inconsistent with EC legislation (OJ L 129, 18 May 1996, p.23). In the event the new Secretary of State for the Environment, Nicholas Ridley, abandoned the privatisation proposals and shifted the whole policy process away from policy community politics to a process of 'internationalised policy making' within the Department. After a period of internal deliberations, Mr Ridley, who himself was already concerned about the general principle of private bodies having public regulation functions, decided to remove the environmental regulatory function from the proposed WSPLCs and to set up a new water environmental regulator, the National Rivers Authority (NRA).[2] It was his view that 'so important a power of decision over the activities of others should not be placed in private hands' (Richardson *et al.* 1992: 168).

The end result was that privatisation not only transferred the ownership of the water industry in England and Wales totally to the private sector (there already existed a small private water company sector), but it also created a new regulatory framework for the industry. Thus the *origins* of privatisation had nothing to do with Europeanisation, but the *form* of privatisation was directly influenced by European considerations. National autonomy was so constrained that a major element of privatisation policy had to be recast.

The 1989 Water Act also enabled the UK to finally incorporate and rationalise much EC law into British law. The central core of the regulatory system is three agencies: the National Rivers Authority, responsible for environmental regulation; the Office of Water Services (OFWAT), responsible for price regulation; and the Drinking Water Inspectorate (DWI), currently within the DOE, responsible for drinking water quality. There is little doubt that, without the effects of EC law, this complex regulatory framework would not have emerged. Its current relevance is that the now considerable degree of public conflict that has arisen between the NRA and OFWAT, and their respective constituencies, has raised the political salience of the *effects* of EU water laws and exposed the conflicting objectives of water policy as a whole. Prior to privatisation, these conflicting objectives were internalised within the industry or were confined to the restricted policy community of 'water actors' and were generally not subject to public scrutiny or debate. The UK now has an especially visible regulatory regime, operating in the context of very high political salience, increased European level mobilisation of interests, and considerable increases in investment and costs, and hence in price to the consumer. The UK is therefore now an extreme if not unique case of the visible impact of the EU on a policy sector.

In the light of the history of the sector, however, the current intense British debate is misdirected on at least two counts: first, the Labour Opposition tends to focus on the costs of privatisation; and second, the government tends to focus on the costs of 'Europe', and has been joined in this view by the Director General of OFWAT, Ian Byatt. Thus it is now common to attribute the massive investment programme now under way, with its associated price increases to consumers, solely to 'Brussels'. For example, the government has argued that 'compliance with European directives has played a major part in deciding the composition of the substantial investment programmes of some £30 bn on which the water companies have put in since privatisation' (Maclean 1993: 8.1). Industry spokespersons have also emphasised the cost effects of European directives, but are perhaps more ready to recognise that the UK's infrastructure investment record in the past was not good by European standards. (No doubt, being now in the private sector makes it easier for them to admit to the failings of the system under public ownership.) For example, the Director of the WSA, Janet Langdon, has argued that the 'cost of water has been increasing since the 1980s due to two factors – catching up on the lack of investment in water infrastructure since the second world war and the quality standards required by the EC Directive and by customers' (Langdon 1993: 5.2).

Similarly, it could not be argued that the UK had been subject to an *impositional* policy style by the European Community in the past, since much of the policy framework now in place was agreed by unanimity and not under qualified majority voting. In other words, the intergovernmental model could have been used to defend national autonomy. Not for the first time, the UK finds itself objecting to the costs of implementing policies to which it agreed some years ago. In part, therefore, current difficulties are due to lack of foresight by the UK – and, indeed, by many of her European partners – at the policy formulation and policy decision phases of the European policy process. National governments did not adopt a rational actor model because

they failed to recognise the significance of the game in which they were supposed to be the key players. Prior to privatisation, the UK had been gradually
sliding down the European 'league table' in terms of environmental and water
quality indicators and investment, just as it had in many other policy sectors
quite unrelated to water policy, such as education and training, and even
infant mortality rates. Thus it is too easy to 'blame' Europeanisation for, say,
increased water charges today, unless it is argued that raising environmental
and drinking water standards was not necessary in itself and that renewal of
the old infrastructure was unnecessary. If the UK had decided to raise its
standards of its own volition in response to increased scientific knowledge
and domestic interest group pressures, then the costs and charging implications, so much debated today in the context of 'complying with European
law', would have had to be faced as part of a *national* policy programme. One
needs to be cautious, therefore, in assuming 'cause and effect' when evaluat-
ing the impact of Brussels. Much of the action now being taken might well
have happened in any case. Even so, there is no doubt that the general effect
of European legislation has been to force the *pace* of investment in new water
infrastructure in the UK, by constraining policy choice – that is, 'do nothing'
has been removed as an option because of the UK's membership of the EU.
As Haigh argues, the Bathing Water Directive, for example, has 'had a considerable impact in the UK. It has led to the commitment of substantially
greater expenditure on sewage treatment and disposal than would otherwise
have occurred' (Haigh 1994: 4.5–7). The implication here is, of course, that
the British would have been quite happy to continue swimming in their own
sewage, had it not been for EU law.

The question of costs, and therefore, of prices to the consumer, has
emerged post-privatisation as the overriding issue in much of the public
debate. Yet in *comparative* terms, the UK may be in the process of catching up
on prices commonly charged for water elsewhere in Europe. Low investment
in the past produced low prices. As investment levels are raised to meet higher
standards and simply to replace decayed Victorian infrastructure, prices (or
taxes) are bound to follow. As the special 'Water Tariffs' Working Group of
Standing Committee of the International Water Services Association (IWSA)
found in 1992, British water prices are relatively low by international standards (see Table 9.1).

The British case is therefore a complex amalgam of exogenous and
endogenous factors. Within this complex amalgam, the EU is undoubtedly
now the principal source of exogenous change. It provides the main legislative
framework and source of future legislative change under which the water
industry operates, and has become the central focus of much of the policy
debate. To a very considerable degree, the question of national autonomy in
this field is outdated. The nation states lost sovereignty long ago and some of
them are now trying to regain it.

It would be wrong to see the UK as simply a 'laggard', however. The UK
has moved to adopt a general system of integrated pollution control with the

Table 9.1 International comparison of drinking water prices

Comparison of annual water charges for a family of two adults and two children living in a house and consuming 200 m^3/year (expressed in ECUs as at 8 November 1991)

Country/city	Annual charge (ecu)	Country/city	Annual charge (ecu)	Country/city	Annual charge (ecu)
Austria		Germany		Malaysia	
Linz	98	Frankfurt	255	Kuala Lumpur	25
Salzburg	152	Geldenwasser	300	Netherlands	
Vienna	165	Hamburg	245	Amsterdam	130–160
Belgium		Munich	162	The Hague	180
Antwerp	104	Stuttgart	275	Utrecht	87
Brussels	228	Hungary		Spain	
Liège	143	Budapest	33	Madrid	129
Denmark		Miskolc	111	Barcelona	138
Aarhus	111	Pecs	133	Seville	79
Copenhagen	92	Italy		Alicante	71
Odense	100	Bologna	75	Murcia	150
Finland		Milan	20	Switzerland	
Helsinki	144	Naples	95	Berne	97
Tampere	156	Rome	41	Geneva	326
France		Turin	38	Zurich	251
Banlieue: Paris	225	Japan		United Kingdom[1]	
Lyon	234	Nagoya	63	Bristol	103 (189)
Marseille	185	Osaka	39	Cardiff	149 (264)
Nice	232	Sapporo	87	London	94 (136)
Paris	111	Tokyo	69	Manchester	95 (199)
Germany		Yokohama	63	Newcastle	
Berlin	154	Luxemburg		Upon Tyne	100 (210)
Dusseldorf	240 ·	Luxemburg	206		

Note: [1] Data for the UK are unmetered with metered in parentheses.
Source: Achtienribbe *et al.* 1992: 360

setting up of the Environment Agency and in this regard is in advance of OECD recommendations that this should be a generally accepted approach (Haigh 1992: 3.11). Another example of policy innovation where the UK is more advanced than some of its European partners in the water sector was the adoption of single purpose authorities based on the principle of integrated river basin management in 1973/4. Many EU states have yet to grasp the inherent logic of this approach to the management of a scarce resource.

THE DEVELOPMENT OF EU WATER POLICY

Water policy was developed quite early at the EC/EU level, with the first major proposals being adopted between 1973 and 1975 (at the same time, coincidentally, as the sector was being reorganised in the UK). Now, twenty years later, a range of directives and decisions are in place, covering both freshwater and marine pollution (Haigh 1992: 4, 2-1). These deal with such issues as surface water for drinking, bathing water, waters for shellfish and freshwater fish. Exposure or product standards for drinking water were added in 1980. It was in the discussions over EC proposals to limit the discharge of dangerous substances into water that the fundamental differences between the British and continental approach were most evident: the Commission proposed to limit pollution of the most dangerous substances by emission limit values, while the UK sought a policy of quality objectives which would allow varying emission standards. A compromise was reached whereby both limit values and quality objectives were allowed, with member states – in practice only the UK – free to adopt quality objectives provided they could satisfy the Commission through an agreed monitoring procedure that quality objectives were being attained (Haigh 1992: 4.2–1).

EU environmental legislation is now a classic example of how the Commission has successfully extended and expanded its area of competence. The original Treaty of Rome did not include references to environmental policy. The Commission, as a key policy actor, has been an effective policy entrepreneur in the use of the Treaty in order to develop its environmental competence. For example, it has used Article 100 of the Treaty, covering the harmonisation of laws in member states directly affecting the establishment or functioning of the common market. Also, Article 235, concerning measures which 'prove necessary to attain . . . one of the objectives of the Community', has been used in the absence of specific delegation of power by the Treaty. Until 1987, all Community environmental legislation was based on one or the other (or both) of these articles (EEC 1992). It was the passage of the SEA in 1987 that formalised the power of the EU in the environmental field. Article 100a lays down criteria for environmental protection legislation affecting the internal market and allows legislation to be adopted by qualified majority voting (QMV) in the Council. Articles 130r, 130s and 130t lay down the goals, means and procedure for the adoption of legislation regarding the environment but require unaninimity (EEC 1992).

By 1987, some 200 items of environmental legislation had been agreed under articles 100 and 235 (Haigh 1994: 2.1). The passage of the Maastricht Treaty further strengthened the power of the EU in the environmental field. Under Article 2 of the Treaty, one of the EU's basic tasks is defined as promoting 'sustainable and non-inflationary growth respecting the environment'. Environmental policy has to be based on the 'precautionary principle'. The SEA's provision that environmental policy should be integrated into other EU policies was also reinforced (Haigh 1994: 2.3). In addition to legislation, the EC has so far produced five Environmental Action Programmes, indicating the general direction of EC/EU environmental policy. The Fifth Environment Programme is especially interesting: it places great emphasis on the active involvement of all parties concerned with the environment on a

Table 9.2 Principal EU instruments governing water

Council Directive 73/404/EEC	Detergents
Council Decision 75/437/EEC	Marine Pollution from Land-based Sources
Council Directive 75/440/EEC	Surface Water for Drinking
Council Directive 76/160/EEC	Bathing Water
Council Directive 76/464/EEC	Dangerous Substances Discharges
Council Directive 77/585/EEC	Mediterranean Sea
Council Decision 77/586/EEC	Rhine River
Council Decision 77/795/EEC	Exchange of Information about Surface Fresh Water
Council Directive 78/659/EEC	Fresh Water for Fish
Council Directive 79/869/EEC	Drinking Water Measuring Methods
Council Directive 79/923/EEC	Shellfish Waters
Council Directive 80/68/EEC	Groundwater
Council Directive 80/778/EEC	Water for Human Consumption
Council Decision 81/420/EEC	Mediterranean Sea
Council Decision 82/176/EEC	Mercury Discharges
Council Directive 82/242/EEC	Testing of Detergents
Council Decision 83/101/EEC	Mediterranean Sea
Council Decision 83/513/EEC	Cadmium Discharges
Council Decision 84/132/EEC	Mediterranean Sea
Council Directive 84/156/EEC	Mercury
Council Decision 84/358/EEC	North Sea
Council Directive 84/491/EEC	Hexachlorocyclohexane Discharges
Council Decision 85/613/EEC	Marine Pollution by Mercury and Cadmium
Council Decision 86/85/EEC	Oil Spills
Council Directive 86/280/EEC	Dangerous Substances Discharges
Council Decision 87/57/EEC	Marine Pollution from Land-based Sources
Council Directive 90/656/EEC	Transitional Measures in Germany

Source: EEC 1992

voluntary and preventative basis, and on the detailed consultation of interested parties in the preparation of major decisions.

The EC itself has identified some twenty-seven items of EC water legislation which had been passed by 1990. The list, not surprisingly, consisted of some measures which are relatively minor and narrow in scope, such as Directive 82/242/EEC, Testing of Detergents, to legislation which is of major importance in the water industry and beyond, such as Directive 80/778/EEC, Water for Human Consumption. Since then, further legislation, both major and minor, has been developed. For example, the Council adopted Directive 91/676/EEC on nitrates from agricultural sources and Directive 91/271/EEC on urban waste water. Both are major pieces of legislation with considerable cost implications.

EC/EU water legislation is now at least as comprehensive as many national systems of water regulation. The full list, up to 1990, is shown in Table 9.2.

Moreover, as discussed below, the 'mature' phase of EU policy making has now been reached, wherein old legislation is subject to periodic review.

POLICY THEORY, POLICY INSTRUMENTS AND RELUCTANT BRITISH COMPLIANCE?

EU water policy falls into a category where the UK is often at odds with its European partners. Unlike, say, EU competition policy or EU aviation policy, where the UK has played a leading role in driving these policy sectors forward at the EU level, water policy is more like EU social policy. The general picture is one of the UK reaching a reluctant compromise on some policy issues with occasionally more serious difficulties leading to cases taken to the European Court of Justice against the UK. The UK's current objective has been to slow down the pace of further reform and to seek greater flexibility under the subsidiarity principle. Ideally, the government would like to see some repatriation of water laws so that it can reassert a degree of national autonomy over this policy sector.

In what is regarded as the standard work on the impact of environmental policy on the UK, and from which this section draws heavily, Nigel Haigh has captured the essence of the UK's 'problem' with the EU. He quotes a report of the Royal Commission on Sewage Disposal in 1912 as follows: 'A chemical standard can be applied in any one of two ways – either to the contaminating discharge itself or to the stream which has received this discharge' (Royal Commission on Sewage Disposal 1912). As Haigh argues, 'the choice between the two types of standard quoted above has been the cause of a long-running dispute between the UK and other Member States over water pollution' (Haigh 1992: 3.1).

It might be thought that the dispute over whether emission standards or environmental quality standards are the most appropriate policy instruments for controlling pollution merely reflects differences of 'policy style' (Bulmer 1983, Richardson 1982, George, Chapter 2, this volume). However, as Haigh argues, to characterise the difficulties between the EU and the UK simply in these terms is misleading, not only because in practice the UK has a mixture of policy instruments in place, but also because '[the] catalogue of available tools for controlling pollution shows that the Community has used them all' (Haigh 1992: 3.7). The UK's difficulties have been only partly due to differences in what Haigh terms 'pollution theory'. One theory is that 'emission standards need be no more stringent than required to meet . . . quality objectives. The emission standards will therefore quite logically vary from place to place' (Haigh 1992: 3.8). The opposing theory, sometimes actually adopted by the UK, is reflected in the German concept of *Vorsorgeprinzip*, or the principle of anticipation and foresight. 'This holds that the point of emission is the logical point to set up controls and they should be as stringent as available technology permits' (Haigh 1992: 3.9). In practice there has been intensive bargaining, usually leading to greater flexibility and longer periods for compliance as a result of the UK's lobbying efforts. This pattern seems more akin to a model treating the British state as a kind of interest group, which finds it impossible to block a policy yet is able to bargain at the edges.

Much of the British argument has been, quite plausibly, that physical conditions are quite different in the UK and that it makes no economic sense to adopt expensive policy instruments specifically designed to meet quite different conditions elsewhere in Europe. A related argument, also adopted by the UK, has been the general question of costs and, more recently, its welfare and distributional consequences. Again, it might be argued that this is a more 'rational' policy style, which tries to relate policy instruments to known risk and to recognise the concept of opportunity cost in the use of scarce resources. Matching investment to risk assessment is, of course, *politically* difficult in policy areas of high political salience and where the focus of policy is something as emotive as 'pure' water. It is relatively easy for the scientific and environmental community to present demands for action against pollution, and relatively difficult for policy makers to engage the public in debates about risk assessment.

While Haigh is undoubtedly right to emphasise the mixed nature of policy instruments in terms of the dichotomy between emission standards or quality standards at both the European and British level, the UK's position has been constantly cautious with respect to the ways in which the EU should behave, almost irrespective of the particular policy instruments under debate. In a sense, the centre of gravity of the UK's approach has been rather different from its European counterparts. This is bound to leave the UK as the 're-luctant partner'. Almost any speech by a British minister or official is characterised by its use of caveats. For example, in his address to the *Financial Times* Conference on the European water industry in March 1993, David Maclean MP (Minister of State for Environment and Countryside) argued that 'in fixing standards we must have regard to what is practically achievable by all states within a realistic timetable. Achievability must include whether society, particularly consumers, can bear the cost' (Maclean 1993: 8.1). Illustrating the importance which the government can place on consumers' rights when necessary, he warned his audience that consumers were now taking a key interest in what their charges cover and were asking for increases in their bills to be justified 'in terms of value for money as well as on medical and scientific grounds' (Maclean 1993 : 8.1). Turning to future policy, he emphasised that it was 'essential that all concerned including the Commission are fully briefed on the costs of meeting any proposed standards' (Maclean 1993: 8.2). There was no point in pursuing 'scientific perfection' without recognising that the consumer/taxpayer does not have a bottomless purse. Governments and suppliers did 'not have the luxury of being able to think about improvements in one hermetically sealed box and the practical consequences and costs in another' (Maclean 1993: 8.2)

A second very important theme raised by the minister, and one which preoccupies many polluting industries across Europe (Richardson 1994), concerned the question of the role and use of scientific research and evidence. The government was looking to ensure that these directives reflect the latest scientific thinking. Present parameters reflect the state of knowledge of now more than a decade ago. However, recognising that this line of argument could well be a hostage to fortune, he stressed that this did not *necessarily* mean that standards would become more stringent. In doing so, he was echoing the fears of industries, such as the agro-chemical and water industries, that the advance of scientific knowledge might be the driving force of a sort of regulatory escalator; that regulation would follow science. The risks of a purely science-based policy approach lie in handing over power to unaccountable scientific communities in what Habermas called a 'scientisation of politics' (Habermas 1971). Governments then become vulnerable to demands for tighter and tighter regulation, requiring more and more money. This danger is particularly acute when environmental groups dramatise scientific findings, producing a 'megaphone' effect for science. Policy makers, of course, want to choose which science they cite and turn to rival epistemic communities for support. Thus, in the minister's view, 'for many pesticides, nitrates and polycyclic aromatic hydrocarbons current scientific and toxicological thinking points to Drinking Water Directive standards being wrongly set' (Maclean 1993: 8.2).

The important question of the level at which decisions should be made has also been a central concern of the British government. There has been a steady twin-track European lobbying strategy. The first is to slow down the rate of policy change, as suggested above. The second involves pressure to either 'repatriate' certain policy decisions or to maximise the degree of flexibility allowed to member states in the implementation of EU water legislation. Both are well-known interest group strategies, commonly adopted by member states in EU bargaining. The repatriation/flexibility strategy might be seen as a fall-back position in the UK's Euro-water strategy. If the first option does not deliver the policy pay-off most desired, the second comes into operation.

The main weakness of this strategy is that it has some potentially cross-sectoral consequences. While the UK may seek greater national autonomy in water and other environmental legislation, it is clearly less than happy if, for example, the French seek a similar degree of flexibility in subsidising Air France. Playing multi-dimensional games requires a degree of sophisticated calculations of pay-off costs across a whole range of policy sectors. Even so, British environmental ministers are left with little option if they wish to reduce or slow down the cost effects of European water legislation, however inconsistent the UK's position in other policy areas may seem to its European partners.

Referring specifically to Article 3 (3) of the Treaty of European Union, the Minister argued that the new emphasis on subsidiarity was one of the most significant recent developments. Essentially, the EU should 'exercise a certain degree of humility in taking a view about what can be better done at the Community rather than the national level' (Maclean 1993: 8.1). The difficulty with this, however, is that although it may suit the British government in the case of water, it may run counter to its broader European strategy.

Thus, in matters such as public procurement, the UK would be seen in the vanguard of those wanting to bring about a level playing field. Yet the Minister had a specific concern about the Public Procurement Directives, including the Utilities Directive, and the use of mandatory European standards for contracts over a prescribed threshold. In a rather revealing passage he argued that

> the objective of opening up a single market in Europe and EFTA countries is not to achieve a total uniformity in practice and products across all members states. . . . As long as products meet the essential requirements of the Construction Products Directive, *due account must also be taken of different geographic and climatic conditions, ways of life and the technical traditions of each state.*
>
> (Maclean 1993: 8.2, emphasis added)

This argument is, of course, not unrelated to the type of argument used by other member states, for example, in protecting traditional methods in the brewing industry, cheese manufacturing and systems for the transport of live animals to which the British government has raised strong objections.

An increased emphasis on the need for effective European level *monitoring* and *enforcement* is also apparent in the UK's Euro-water strategy. The British government has been pressing for improved monitoring of what is *actually* happening in all the member states. With considerable justification, it believes that part of the explanation of the UK's poor reputation at home and in Europe in the water sector is due to the UK's more effective and open systems of measurement and monitoring of environmental and water quality standards. As the then chairman of the Water Services Association has argued, outside the UK there is often relatively little information on the actual implementation of water directives and little to match the level of detailed information available on the thousand or so water catchment zones designated in the UK (Courtney 1992: 4.2). His views are shared by the British government which, in its memorandum to the Director General of Water Services, published in October 1993, argued that the UK's monitoring and record keeping 'are among the best and most publicly available in Europe' (DoE 1993: 5). Similarly, the Chief Inspector of the Drinking Water Inspectorate has expressed the hope that other member states in the European Union will adopt the Inspectorate's approach to drinking water quality monitoring and reporting. Thus he has argued that:

> If there were to be an equivalent standard of sampling, analysis and reporting, it would then be possible to make objective comparisons between Member States on quality and on compliance with the EC Directive. I hope that the benefits of the experience gained by the Inspectorate through the full and consistent overseeing of the implementa-

tion of the Regulations will be recognised by the EC Commission in
drafting revisions to the EC Drinking Water Directive.

(DWI 1994: xiv)

Linked to this view has been the UK's pressure for the setting up of the
European Environmental Agency and for a more rigorous 'effectiveness
auditing' system. Even without this, the UK is unlucky to be painted as the
'dirty man of Europe'. Thus the Minister for the Environment and the
Countryside, David Trippier, pointed out in 1992 that, although the UK had
by then been taken to the ECJ twice for non-compliance with environmental
legislation, the Commission had taken over a hundred cases to the ECJ
against other member states in relation to environmental legislation (Trippier
1992: 1.1). While continuing to emphasise that responsibility for enforcing
Community legislation should remain with individual member states, he
argued that 'the Commission should seek to ensure that every member state
has not only legislation in place transposing Community Directives, but also
regulatory bodies with the necessary duties, expertise and resources to ensure
full compliance' (Trippier 1992: 1.1). The British government had therefore
put forward the concept of an 'audit inspectorate' to operate at Community
level. He argued that:

> This would follow a model already established in fields like fisheries and
> veterinary control. It would be a small but highly competent unit, respon-
> sible for assessing each member state's own arrangements, and giving the
> Commission the information which it currently lacks to ensure that Com-
> munity legislation is being consistently and effectively enforced. There is
> strong and growing support for this concept of an 'Audit Inspectorate',
> and we hope that the Commission will come forward with a concrete pro-
> posal soon, so that we shall be able to give it a high priority during the UK
> Presidency.
>
> (ibid.)

In the absence of a generally accepted and universally applied monitoring
and measurement system, the British government is going to remain trapped
on the classic 'indicator problem'.

Finally, the British government's ultimate fall-back position is identical to
that adopted by all polluting industries, as well as by the water supply and
waste disposal industries, to press for more time to implement laws, thus
spreading the cost, and the incidence of charges, over a longer period of time.
For example, it has calculated that if the investment required for the Urban
Waste Water Directive between 1995 and 2000 were rephased over a ten-year
period, that is halving the requirement for 1995–2000, price limits between the
latter dates might be reduced by an average of about 1.5 per cent (DoE 1993:
10).

It would appear that the more that the UK can shift the European policy
debate to these questions, as it is trying to do with some degree of success (see

below), the more likely it is for the UK to exercise influence over policy reformulation and innovation, especially now, in times of economic difficulties within the EU as a whole. Indeed, Haigh suggests that 'the need to consider both approaches to pollution control is being increasingly accepted in the UK and elsewhere, and featured in the (EC) fourth action programme on the environment' (Haigh 1992: 3.11). Thus there may be a degree of policy theory convergence, both in terms of a continuation of a mixed policy instruments approach and in terms of cross-national policy learning (Rose 1993).

IMPLEMENTING EC LAW: SOVEREIGNTY CRUMBLES

Space does not permit other than a brief summary of some of the more salient EC water legislation and the effect of the legislation in the UK. (An excellent and continually updated review of the whole of EC water legislation, the UK's political response, and effects of EU legislation in the UK, is provided by Haigh 1994.)

Surface water for drinking

The Water Act 1989 provided the opportunity for EC law to be brought formally within UK law. Considerable upgrading of treatment plants has taken place, though Haigh concludes that it might be a mistake to attribute this to EC law, since many of the improvements would have been planned anyway. 'The most that can be said is that the Directive has drawn attention to some deficiencies and may have hastened improvements' (Haigh 1992: 4.3–4).

Drinking water

Passage of the Drinking Water Directive proved problematic, not only because of UK problems. The UK was particularly concerned about regulations on lead, because of the special problem faced in the UK and the potential difficulty in complying. The compromise which was negotiated increased the degree of flexibility and extended the period of compliance for the various parameters. The UK was the only government to suggest that the nitrate parameter, now causing severe problems in other EU states, such as Holland and Germany as well as in the UK, would present difficulties (Haigh 1992: 4.4–4). Although the UK has, under the 1989 Water Act, made formal provision for the implementation of the Directive, it has still caused problems. Indeed, in 1987 the Commission took the UK to the ECJ, which on 25 November 1992 ruled that the UK had failed to adequately incorporate the Directive into UK legislation (Haigh 1992, 4.4–6). A significant proportion of the UK's drinking water supply was then in breach of the EC Directive with respect to at least some of the parameters, and the UK argued that more time was needed to comply.

The Drinking Water Directive has undoubtedly presented the water industry in the UK with a very serious exogenous 'shock', causing both compliance problems and forcing the belated introduction of massive investment programmes. It has also played a disproportionate role in gaining for the UK, possibly undeservedly, a bad reputation in the sector. Haigh concludes that:

> The Directive has therefore had considerable impact on legislation and practice in the UK. It has led to greater public scrutiny of water supplies, for it has been necessary for water undertakers to apply for derogations and delays and this has clearly exposed problem areas. The Directive has resulted for the first time in the setting of detailed statutory quality standards for drinking water, and ensured that consumer and environmental interests were not overlooked in the privatization of the UK water industry. In particular, it has ensured that water supply companies' undertakings to improve the quality of those supplies of drinking water below EC standards were made more rigorous than they otherwise might have been.
>
> (Haigh 1992, 4.4–10)

Bathing Water

This Directive has also proved problematic for the UK, sometimes with hilarious results. Along with the debate in the UK over non-compliance with the Drinking Water Directive, the bathing water issue has been one of high political salience, strongly influenced by the very existence of EU legislation. Thus the very fact of EU legislation strengthens considerably the political position of environmentalists (and even of surfers) as it puts both the water companies and the government on the defensive. It is one thing not to have a law at all, but quite another for a government to be in breach of it. For a newly *privatised* industry to be in breach of it is even worse in terms of public perceptions. The main conclusion of a long and difficult saga is that the UK has often been in breach of the Directive and has been subject to a series of Commission actions to force UK compliance.

The UK decided initially that in designating bathing beaches in compliance with the Directive, bathing waters with fewer than 500 people in the water at any one time should not be identified, that any stretch with more than 1500 people in the water per mile should be identified and that those with between 750 and 1500 per mile were open to negotiation! Blackpool, one of the UK's most popular seaside resorts, was assessed at between 750 and 1500 and by agreement between the water authority (as it then was) and the District Council was not identified (Haigh 1992: 4.5–5). The total exercise resulted in only twenty-seven bathing waters being communicated to the Commission in 1979 compared with 8000 in the rest of the EC, thirty-nine of which were in landlocked Luxemburg (Haigh 1992: 4.5–5). Since then there has been a gradual improvement in the UK's record – not surprising in view of the very high level of adverse publicity following the earlier poor results. For example, in July 1993 the UK was praised by the European Commission for tackling pollution at coastal beaches after years of being dubbed the 'dirty man of Europe' (*Water Bulletin*, 2 July 1993). However, it should be noted that the 3 per cent improvement on the previous year, raising the success rate of beaches tested from 76 per cent to 79 per cent, involved only 455 of the UK's beaches – and still left over 20 per cent failing EU standards. Moreover, the UK suffered the embarrassment of a successful prosecution before the ECJ in July 1993 over the pollution levels at Blackpool (and Southport).

We should be cautious, however, in seeing the UK as the *only* member state to have difficulties. As Haigh points out, the Commission had, by June 1989, begun legal proceedings against eleven of the Twelve, with Portugal granted a derogation until 1993. For example, in August 1993 the Consumers' Association complained that Mediterranean beaches, including ones which had been awarded the prestigious Blue Flag, are contaminated with sewage. The Association considered that official figures released by the EC could not be trusted and that the reporting procedure was 'farcical' because it relied on data supplied by governments (*Water Bulletin*, 6 August 1994). In its 1994 report, the Association reported that, although the UK came close to bottom of the most recent Euro-bathing water statistics, with only Germany lower, its position was probably better than it looked because not all the league table results were reliable. For example, half the countries – France, Germany, Greece, Italy and the Netherlands – failed to test all the beaches sufficiently often to make the results valid. Others – Italy and Greece – admitted to EC officials that they ignored the results of tests after rainfall. UK bathing waters are tested come rain or shine (*Water Bulletin*, 17 June 1994).

Even so, faced with a letter from the Commission under Article 169, the British government has had to make very substantial changes to the investment programme, for example, in November 1989 a £1.4 billion long sea outfall programme was announced with a further £1.5 billion programme announced in March 1990. This did not prevent the Commission from bringing an action before the ECJ that month and the issuing of a Reasoned Opinion in July 1990 (Haigh 1992: 4.5–7). The UK lost the ECJ case (Case C-56/90).

The Urban Waste Water Directive

This Directive has proved problematic for many EC states. Essentially it is intended to bring about considerable improvements in the treatment of domestic sewage, industrial waste water and rainwater run-off – so called urban or municipal waste water. There are vast differences in degrees of treatment between the member states. The UK's position is interesting in two respects. Yet again the UK was brought into line, despite its reservations. However, the EC/EU was not the only source of exogenous pressure on the UK: some of the Directives discussed above were influenced by the OECD and by the WHO (Richardson 1994). In this case, pressure from the North

Sea littoral states was also important, as well as pressure from the EC and from domestic public opinion (Haigh 1992: 4.6–5). As Haigh argues, these pressures produced a major U-turn in UK policy: the government agreed to the general use of secondary treatment prior to discharge into the sea, thus abandoning the UK's earlier position that the disposal of crude sewage at sea was acceptable, because the sea could cope. It also announced the ending of the dumping of sewage sludge at sea, necessitating the future construction of expensive, and possibly environmentally damaging, incineration plants on land (Haigh 1992: 4.6–5).

DOMESTIC CONFLICT AND THE CONTINUED EUROPEANISATION OF THE UK WATER POLICY PROCESS

As Stephen George has suggested, the UK has been regarded as an awkward partner since it joined the EC in 1973 (George 1990: 1). This is especially true in the field of water policy, yet it would be quite wrong to see the UK as unique in this respect. There is little doubt that some of the problems which the UK has faced in complying with EU law are being replicated elsewhere in the Union. Certainly, many European states, notably Germany, France and Italy, are facing quite steep increases in water charges. The UK has not been alone in pressing for more flexibility and longer lead times for the implementation of EU policy. Moreover, the UK has, however reluctantly, instituted a massive investment programme in the water industry, tackling both the backlog of investment caused by financial restraint from the mid-1970s onwards and the new requirements of legislation. Domestic pressure, and the willingness of domestic pressure groups and individuals to see the EU as an alternative policy-making area (Mazey and Richardson 1992), have undoubtedly reinforced the pressures from the EC and, through 'whistle blowing', have been the cause of specific EU actions against the UK. Thus all the key actors – the DoE, the Water Services Association, the regulators and the environmentalists – have begun to refocus their attention to the EU level. This is also true for other EU states. For example, the Commission received over 12,000 letters from Germany alone concerning possible revisions to the Drinking Water Directive.

In the UK, however, the domestic pressures are developing a new degree of complexity. First, as would be predicted by interest group theory, countervailing action is emerging from those groups who lost out as a result of the new policy settlement. For example, the CBI, in its response to OFWAT's paper on meeting the costs of continual environmental improvement in water, has pointed out that the driving force for higher levels of expenditure in the water industry is the standards set in legislation (*CBI News*, October 1993: 23). More generally, the CBI has attacked the European Commission's proposals to impose stricter liability on business to pay for pollution damage. Even bankers are joining the lobby against this proposal, fearing that they will be liable for pollution costs incurred by their borrowers (*Financial Times*, 3 September 1993). The Treasury, too, has begun to show concern about the inflationary potential of Euro-legislation on water, although the Chancellor has so far failed to arouse much interest from his colleagues in the Council of Ministers. More hopefully from the British government's perspective, the *scientific* debate is becoming more pluralistic. Bearing in mind our earlier point concerning what Habemas called the scientisation of politics, the expert scientific community is clearly not monolithic. There is therefore potential for mobilising rival epistemic communities. For example, in July 1994 a Dutch microbiologist told a House of Lords Select Committee that the methodology laid down for the proposed updates of the bathing water directive were neither practicable nor did they reflect advances in scientific thinking (*Water Bulletin*, 29 July 1994).

Second, OFWAT has emerged as an institutionalised countervailing power to the hitherto powerful lobby of environmentalists and the NRA. OFWAT's stance is not inconsistent with the government's broad Euro-strategy outlined earlier. For example, the Director General, Ian Byatt, has argued that what matters to customers and citizens is not the work done (the 'inputs'), but the results achieved (the 'outputs'). 'Such outputs should, moreover, emanate from what the customers want and are ready to pay for – not what the producers – or regulators, *including the European Commission* – say they ought to have' (Byatt 1993: 4.1, emphasis added). For example, the OFWAT National Customer Council (ONCC) pledged itself to 'put pressure on the Director General of Water Services and the British Government to keep prices down and on the EC to limit obligations on companies which are drawing up bills faster than customers are willing to pay' (ONCC, 5 July 1993). It specifically urged the government to renegotiate the timetable for implementation of the Urban Waste Water Treatment Directive 'which is the major factor behind huge increases in bills forecast for the next ten years' (ONCC, 13 July 1993).

In contrast, the chairman of the NRA, Lord Crickhowel, has been anxious *not* to see a reduction in the pressure for improved standards, either from the EU or from the DoE in its capacity as the body responsible for setting national water quality objectives. In a counter-move intended to avoid the accusation that it had been 'captured' by environmentalists, the NRA commissioned its own survey of water customers – 'a survey of Mr Byatt's customers' as Crickhowell put it – which showed high support for quality and environmental issues and, indeed, for EC legislation with 91 per cent of respondents feeling that EC agreements were 'a good thing' (Crickhowel 1993). Referring specifically to the possibility of the UK securing a relaxation of EC environmental obligations, he expressed doubts. He pointed out that the government had stated quite clearly that 'there must always be satisfactory implementation of the requirements of community legislation while they remain in place. He also reminded his audience 'that while they remain in place the NRA will carry out its duty to monitor and enforce those obligations, using its scientific and professional skills in a realistic but not excessive way' (Crickhowel 1993). Concerning the government's belief, expressed in its paper, *Water Charges – The Quality Framework (DoE 1993)*, that some modification of the Waste Water directive was desirable, he remained doubtful: 'in the NRA we do not detect much sign as yet that Brussels or our European colleagues are much inclined to make substantial changes, and as the Government's Paper makes clear, any discussions are bound to take time' (Crickhowel 1993). However, there are signs that the Commission may be adopting a more consensual policy style under the Fifth Action Programme, including attempts to assess the charges and advantages of implementing policies (Garvey 1993: 1.3).

PROSPECTS FOR A EUROPEAN CONSENSUS

To what extent does the emergence of a slightly more cautious and cost-conscious approach by the Commission represent a major policy opportunity for the UK? It is applying pressure to the Commission to reconsider and delay directives on water quality, particularly for a review of sewage treatment, following the EU's agreement to review the drinking water directive and to cost its proposals fully. One of the government's difficulties is that any retreat by the EU will provoke an environmental backlash, supported by the Labour opposition. The government will be seen as not caring about environmental and health issues. Moreover, at the EU level, environmentalists are undoubtedly a more effective lobby than at the UK level (Mazey and Richardson 1992) and are able to challenge the member states in the policy process.

There are also significant institutional obstacles in Brussels. There is no reason to assume that the Commission will be any less of a policy entrepreneur and policy broker than in the past (Mazey and Richardson 1994). Its present caution in this regard is more likely to represent a tactical shift than a strategic change. Moreover, the European Parliament has always been a significant 'player' in EU environmental policy (Earnshaw and Judge 1995, Judge 1993) and its Committee on Environment, Public Health and Consumer Protection will be vigorous in defending what has already been gained. For example, the Committee's Chairman, Ken Collins MEP, warned delegates at the Commission's major conference on drinking water (23 September 1993) that there could be no change in the Directive 'without proper consultation of the democratic institutions of the EC, and in particular without the full participation of the EP and my committee'. As he put it:

> we do know that some member states have neglected their water industry investment, have failed to comply, have infringed the Directive and yet now want to lower the standards and so forgive their past failures. If the same approach were applied to the Ten Commandments, the history of the world would surely be different.
>
> (Collins at Drinking Water Conference, 1993)

He also warned of the legal minefield facing those states who wished to see a lowering of standards, and reminded his audience that the Drinking Water Directive had been agreed unanimously by all the ministers under Article 100, because they had recognised that water was a resource central to the establishment and functioning of the internal market. If future revisions were to proceed under Article 100a, he pointed out that the EP would then be *central* to the final decision because of the co-decision procedure.

Moreover, the UK's EU partners sometimes have very different arrangements for the water sector, especially in terms of its funding. Thus as Neil Summerton of the DoE has observed, the old British system, prior to water privatisation, of making decisions in smoke-filled rooms in the Treasury is still the norm in many other parts of Europe. Elsewhere in Europe, he argued:

> water charges are a matter of political determination – often by municipalities rather than central governments. Some countries continue to subsidise price from tax revenues in a variety of ways. Others cross-subsidise between consumers in different places rather as we do. In principle, the situation for them, as for us, has however been crucially changed by the existence of the urban waste water treatment directive. That imposes a stiff timetable for improvement and therefore for investment to achieve it. Everywhere this measure is proving more expensive than was assumed when it was negotiated, with some notable price effects. But the different funding system means that there is no need for other governments to admit this yet.
>
> (Summerton 1993)

He has captured perfectly the situation facing the UK and the potential for it to influence its European partners, as follows:

> Pace is the main issue. It is already clear that many of our partners are finding the timetable in the (waste water) directive an immense burden – which is not surprising as they have poor systems, in some cases poorer than ours. It is clear that some of our partners are going to find the existing timetable impossible financially as well as practically.
>
> (Summerton 1993)

In fact, the UK is in good company in experiencing problems in complying with EU water laws. For example, one commentator had described the Netherlands' record on EEC environmental directives as 'curious' (Bennet 1986: 89). He writes that:

> serious problems of implementation have arisen, evidenced by the delays in formally complying with virtually every Directive. Moreover, not only was delay recurrent, it was often a persistent symptom, extended in some cases to several years. It was with good reason that the Netherlands was

twice taken to the European Court for failing to implement the bathing
water and surface water for drinking Directives.

(Bennet 1986: 90)

Germany has also had difficulties. Thus Rüdig and Kramer note that the
Federal government's decision to delay the implementation of the pesticides
aspects of the Drinking Water Directive raised public attention, Environmental groups started to campaign on the issues and the European Commission criticised Germany for not implementing the Directive properly (Rüdig
and Kramer 1994).

There may thus be a window of opportunity for the UK to reverse its ill-
fortune in the field of EU water policy, because its partners are also in financial difficulties. This will present opportunities to form *ad hoc* cross-national
coalitions on specific issues – such as the successful Anglo-French demand to
exempt sewage sludge incineration from the Hazardous Waste Incinerator
Directive agreed in July 1993. In the longer run, however, the British government, if it is to avoid the difficulties of the past, must achieve at least four
things. First, it will need to come more into line with the continental style of
environmental regulation, as in other policy areas. Second, it will need to suc-
ceed in its campaign to secure elsewhere in Europe something like the British
approach to monitoring and enforcement. Failure to do so will leave the UK
exposed to a 'double disbenefit' – weak influence over policy formulation yet
a national tradition of providing reliable data on actual conditions. Third, it
will need to secure a means of influencing the EU agenda-setting process –
particularly the process by which scientific ideas are translated into public
policy via the activities of epistemic communities, advocacy coalitions and
the operation of very loose issue networks at the Euro-level (Richardson
1994). Finally, it will need to address the equally difficult task of ensuring
that the Europeanisation of British water policy networks which is now
developing quite rapidly (Maloney and Richardson 1995) does not leave the
government without allies in the European policy process.

None of these tasks is likely to prove easy. The balance sheet shows some
gains and some losses in this overall strategy. Clearly, there is a sense in which
the British argument about costs and benefits is being won at an intellectual
level in Europe. Gone are the days when the Commission really could ignore
costs. Not only have some (relatively minor) Euro-regulations been removed,
but also, as a senior Commission official has pointed out, the Commission's
style and approach to legislation has changed over the last few years, reflecting
'a considerable change in attitude in how the Community's policy is to be
realised. It provides greater flexibility for member States to take action which
is appropriate for a particular situation' (Garvey 1993: 1.2). Moreover, cost
pressures in France, Germany, Italy and elsewhere are becoming increasingly
apparent, although it would be wrong for the UK to assume a necessary linkage between rising costs to consumers and rising opposition to Euro-
legislation.

At the time of writing, in early 1995, the Commission's proposals for revising the Drinking Water Directive are being considered. The British government can take some satisfaction from the fact that the Commission has proposed a reduction in the number of parameters from sixty-seven to forty-eight – representing the deletion of thirty-two 'inappropriate' parameters and the inclusion of thirteen new ones. It also emphasised the importance of subsidiarity and flexibility and the setting of minimum monitoring standards. However, it also proposed the adoption of the WHO guidelines on lead contamination of water – recommending a reduction to 10 microgrammes per litre instead of the existing 50 microgrammes per litre. Although spread over fifteen years, the proposal would cost 20 billion ECUs (£15.7 billion) across the EU as a whole, and 3 billion ECUs (£2.4 billion) in the UK. The Commission has also proposed new standards for the use of disinfectants to treat water.

On the debit side so far as the UK is concerned, there is still no sign of a major policy shift at the European level. For example, Ionnis Paleokrassas, the EU Environment Commissioner, has vigorously defended EC environmental legislation, particularly the controversial Urban Waste Water Directive, against British criticism. Moreover, he has pointed out that the Directive was agreed unanimously in 1991 (*Water Bulletin*, 23 July 1994). Specifically referring to British appeals to reduce strict pesticide limits, the Commissioner warned that the problems to be addressed were very real and that deferring action would mean that 'our difficulties become greater' (*Water Bulletin*, 8 October 1993). Signs of further trouble for the UK emerged in December 1993 after the British press had been briefed by the Prime Minister's press service, following the European Council meeting on 10–11 December. Headlines followed, such as 'UK kills European Water Laws' and 'EC Backs Down on Water Rules'. In subsequent correspondence between Jacques Delors and Ken Collins, it was confirmed that no such agreement had been reached. As Delors put it in his letter: 'you are correct in pointing out that the minutes of the Brussels European Council do not mention any agreement upon these matters; the reason is simple; there is no such agreement' (letter to K. Collins, 12 January 1994). Thus 'Europeanisation' is certain to continue to present a strong challenge to the UK and it seems safe to predict that a continuation of the erosion of national autonomy will result.

This autonomy will be eroded in two ways. First, as already indicated, the British government will be increasingly engaged in cross-national coalition formation. Inevitably this will involve compromises and complex trade-offs, as other member states attempt both to achieve their national goals and to satisfy the needs of domestic politics. Second, although domestic water policy in the UK is led by the so-called 'quadrapartite four' of the DoE, NRA, OFWAT and the Water Services Association (WSA, representing the industry) there is no guarantee that this coalition of interests can act collectively in response to the European challenge. The differences between the NRA and OFWAT are there for all to see, and there have already been tensions between the NRA and the DoE over the former's independent Euro activities. Moreover, those actors not part of this policy community will focus their attention increasingly on Brussels. Not being part of the quadrapartite four means that they are free to develop their own Euro-strategies and to participate in a variety of Euro networks of policy actors. Clearly, the DoE is trying to facilitate the co-ordination of 'the British' in this sector, and convenes regular meetings of 'interested parties'. The difficulty is that everyone knows that the DoE cannot guarantee to deliver any agreed Euro strategy, even if it were possible to reach agreement on one. Hence the Europeanisation of the sector is likely to continue, making it very difficult for any one actor to act 'rationally'. In essence, all the players are participating in a rather fast-moving and unpredictable Euro game.

NOTES

1 The author wishes to acknowledge the support of the Anglo-German Foundation for this research.
2 The NRA is now part of the Environment Agency, but the term NRA will be used throughout this chapter.

REFERENCES

Achtienribbe, G., Horner, V., Papp, E. and Wiederkehr, Z. (1992) 'International Comparison of Drinking-water Prices', *Journal of Water SRT – Aqua*, 41,6: 360–3.

Bennet, Graham (1986) *European Community Environmental Policy in Practice. Vol. 2. Netherlands: Water and Waste. A Study of the Implementation of the EEC Directives*, London: Graham & Trotman.

Bulmer, Simon (1983) 'Domestic Politics and European Community Policy-Making', *Journal of Common Market Studies*, 21,4: 349–63.

Byatt, Ian (1993) 'Economic Regulation – the Way Ahead', address to *Financial Times* Conference on The European Water Industry, 15–16 March 1993.

Courtney, William (1992) 'Prospects for the UK Water Industry', address to *Financial Times* Conference on the European Water Industry, 10–11 March.

Crickhowel, Lord (1993) 'Water Service Quality and Water Bills', address to *The Economist* Conference on Water Policy, 9 November.

Department of the Environment (DoE) (1993) *Water Charges: The Quality Framework*, London: DoE.

DWI (1994) *Drinking Water 1993. A Report by the Chief Inspector, Drinking Water Inspectorate*, London: HMSO.

Earnshaw, David and Judge, David (1995) Early Days: The European Parliament, Co-decision and the European Union's Legislative Process Post-Maastricht', *Journal of European Public Policy*, 2,4: 624–49.

EEC (1992) *European Community Environmental Legislation, Vol. 7, Water*, Brussels: EEC.

Garvey, Tom (1993) 'Regulation: Water Pollution – Water Policy in the European Community', address to *Financial Times* Conference on The European Water Industry, 15–16 March.

George, Stephen (1990) *An Awkward Partner. The UK in the European Community*, Oxford: Oxford University Press.

Habermas, Jurgen (1971) *Toward a Rational Society. Student Protest, Science and Politics*, London: Heinemann.

Haigh, Nigel (1992 and 1994) *Manual of Environmental Policy: The EC and the UK*, London: Longman.

Jacbs, F. and Shanks, M. (1988) 'Joint Advice re: Water Authority Privatisation', unpublished report commissioned by the Council for the Protection of Rural England, London: CPRE.

Judge, David (ed.) 'Predestined to Save the Earth? The Environment Committee of the European Parliament', in Judge, David (ed.) *A Green Dimension for the European Community. Political Issues and Processes*, London: Frank Cass, pp. 186–212.

Langdon, Janet (1993) 'The Cost of Drinking Water and the Customer', address to *Financial Times* Conference on The European Water Industry, 15–16 March.

Maclean, David (1993) 'Keynote Address', address to *Financial Times* Conference on The European Water Industry, 15–16 March.

Maloney, William A. and Richardson, Jeremy (1995) *Managing Policy Change in the Britain. The Politics of Water*, Edinburgh: Edinburgh University Press.

Mazey, Sonia (1992) 'The Adjustment of the British Administration to the European Challenge', paper presented to Conference on Administrative Modernisation in Western Europe, University of Perugia, Italy, July.

—— (1994) 'The Development of EC Equality Policies: Bureaucratic Expansion on Behalf of Women?', paper presented to Conference on National Policy-Making and the EC, Oxford, 14–15 January.

Mazey, Sonia and Richardson, Jeremy (1992) 'British Pressure Groups and the Challenge of Brussels', *Parliamentary Affairs*, 45,1: 92–127.

—— (eds) (1993) *Lobbying in the EC*, Oxford: Oxford University Press.

—— (1994) 'The Commission and the Lobby', in G. Edwards and D. Spence *The Commission of the European Commmunity*, London: Longman.

ONCC (1993a) 'New National Council Calls on Government to Halt Water Price Rises', *Press Release*, ONCC, 5 July.

—— (1993b) 'Water Consumer Body Urges Government to Re-negotiate Sewage Treatment Directive', *Press Release*, ONCC, 12 July.

Richardson, Jeremy (ed.) (1982) *Policy Styles in Western Europe*, London: Allen & Unwin.

—— (1994) 'EU Water Policy-Making: Uncertain Agendas, Shifting Networks and Complex Coalitions', *Environmental Politics*, 3,4: 139–67.

Richardson, Jeremy, Maloney, William and Rüdig, Wolfgang (1992) 'The Dynamics of Policy Change: Lobbying and Water Privatisation', *Public Administration,* 70, 2.

Rose, Richard (1993) *Lesson-drawing in Public Policy: A Guide to Learning across Time and Space*, Chatham, NY: Chatham House.

Royal Commission on Sewage Disposal (1912) Eighth Report.

Rüdig, Wolfgang, and Kramer, Andreas (1994) 'Networks of Co-operation: Water Policy in Germany', *Environmental Politics*, 3, 4.

Summerton, Neil (1993) 'Water: Paying for Quality', address to *The Economist* Conference on Water Policy, 9 November.

Trippier, David (1992) 'Opening Address', address to *Financial Times* Conference on The European Water Industry, 10–11 March.

10 High technology

Mark Thatcher[1]

THE EUROPEAN COMMUNITY AND HIGH TECHNOLOGY: THE IMPORTANCE OF THE NATIONAL AND INTERNATIONAL CONTEXT[2]

'High technology' sectors provide an excellent case study to analyse the importance and impact of European Community (EC) policy making: first, they are economically strategic, due not only to their sheer size, but also to the dependence of other sectors on their supply; and second, national governments and suppliers have traditionally attempted to play a central role in the regulation and development of 'high technology'. In the 1980s and 1990s, however, EC activity greatly expanded in 'high technology' sectors, and EC policy appears to mark a sharp break with traditional post-war national industrial policies.

In assessing the impact of the EC on national policy and policy making, this chapter examines the direct impact of EC regulation: the extent to which EC legislation represented and required changes to the existing organisation of high technology sectors of member states. It also looks at the indirect effects of EC regulatory reform: the ways in which EC decisions affected the expectations and strategies of national actors, resulting in reforms being undertaken at national level. It argues that, although EC action differs considerably from national policies before the 1980s and its expansion has been considerable, its impact needs to be analysed in the light of trends in policy already under way in member states during the 1980s and early 1990s, including both the effects of specifically national factors and also international factors unrelated to the EC. It shows that the direct effects of EC legislation were limited because several elements of EC reforms had already been introduced by member states; this is most applicable to the UK, where most EC legislation required no change in existing national regulation, but is also relevant for other countries, where a movement of regulatory reform similar to that undertaken by the EC had already begun.

EC action also produced indirect effects, in particular, it aided changes in ideas and actors' strategies. Nevertheless, this indirect impact must also be examined within the context of developments at the national and international level, an exercise which reveals the limits of the effects of EC policy on actors' strategies. On the one hand, reforms within EC member states were often related to specific national conditions, which included the aims of governments, financial pressures on public suppliers and the degree of domestic opposition to change. On the other hand, transnational forces also offered pressures for regulatory reform; these included the changing technological and economic character of high technology, lobbying for change by multinational companies and the American administration, calls by business users for modified national regulation and new ideas concerning competition and regulation. Detailed analysis shows that the 'indirect' effects of EC measures on regulatory reform in large measure consisted in policy makers within member states using EC regulation to justify reforms desired for a variety of national and international factors largely unrelated to the EC.

EC policy in high technology has included both regulatory activity and EC programmes in research and development; this chapter examines EC regulatory policy, as this appears to require member states to modify national policies and to remove much of their freedom of action. (For discussion of research and development policy, see John Peterson, Chapter 12, this volume.) Within 'high technology', it looks at the area that has seen greatest EC regulation, namely information and communications technology, and in particular, the telecommunications infrastructure and traditional telecommunications services; new, advanced services which combine computing/ information technology and telecommunications;[3] customer premises equipment (CPE) which consists of terminals attached to telecommunications networks,[4] and the manufacture of equipment for the telecommunications infrastructure. High definition television (HDTV) is also examined with respect to the setting of EC norms for satellite transmission.[5]

The impact of EC regulation in the UK, France, Germany and Italy is analysed by looking at four aspects of high technology: the framework of policy making in high technology, including its organisation and the strategies and relationships of actors; the extension of competition and the rules governing supply; equipment manufacturing, and HDTV. First, however, policies in the UK, France, West Germany and Italy before the 1980s must be examined, together with EC regulation after 1980.

NATIONAL INDUSTRIAL POLICIES IN HIGH TECHNOLOGY PRIOR TO THE 1980s

Before the 1980s, the regulation of high technology sectors was determined almost entirely at national level in EC member states. International bodies were concerned with international services and had no powers to impose their decisions on national authorities. Nevertheless, regulatory frameworks and national policies were marked by a high level of similarity in most European countries (Cawson 1990, Foreman-Peck and Müller 1988). The telecommunications sector was dominated by public telephone operators (PTOs) which were publicly owned and were generally either joined with the postal service in a government posts, telephone and telegraph (PTT) department or were licensed by the government.[6] The main PTOs were the Post Office in the UK, the *Deutsches Bundespost* in West Germany and the DGT (*Direction Générale des Télécommunications*) in France; in Italy, the supply of telecommunications services was very fragmented and several PTOs existed, the most important of which were ASST (*l'Azienda di Stato per i Servici Telefonica*) and SIP (*Società Italiana per l'esercicio telefonica*). Broadcasting of television was generally undertaken by separate organisations from PTOs. National policy involved only a limited group of actors, notably PTOs, television broadcasting organisations, the government (particularly the PTT and Finance Ministries), and equipment manufacturers. Regulatory bodies independent of the government or PTO generally did not exist and there was virtually no competition. Users and potential or existing CPE and service suppliers were weak and had few formal rights.

PTOs enjoyed a monopoly over the building and operation of public telecommunications networks, the supply of almost all telecommunications services and the supply of most CPE.[7] PTOs were national organisations, deriving the vast majority of their income from their domestic markets. They performed a number of industrial policy and fiscal functions. Their tariffs were set not only to influence the level of demand for telecommunications, but also for wider purposes, such as raising revenue, reducing inflation or cross-subsidising certain services or types of user. Tariffs therefore often diverged from costs. PTO investment was altered according not only to plans for telecommunications, but also to wider fiscal aims. New services were planned in order to aid equipment manufacturers or to assist regional development. PTO profits were sometimes used as a source of funds for the government or to subsidise chosen firms and their research and development.

In the manufacture of equipment for high technology sectors, PTOs and governments supported 'national champions', which were generally privately owned. These firms included GEC and Plessey in the UK, CGE/Alcatel in France, Siemens in West Germany and Telettra and Italtel in Italy. 'National champions' were effectively guaranteed orders by a very closed public procurement process. Moreover, they were protected by the establishment of specific national standards, creating a 'non-tariff barrier' against foreign firms, who, with no guarantee of orders, would have had to invest heavily to produce equipment to the national standard and who faced a situation in which it was unlikely that they would win a large enough market share to recover the high development costs. The clearest example of national standards was in television transmission in the 1960s, when most of Europe adopted the PAL norm, whereas France adopted the SECAM standard; specific national norms were also used, however, in the markets for CPE and equipment for the telephone network.

THE CHANGING INTERNATIONAL CONTEXT OF HIGH TECHNOLOGY

From the 1970s, and particularly in the 1980s and 1990s, traditional national industrial policies in western Europe were confronted by powerful trans-national forces which transformed high technology. These forces comprised a technological and economic transformation of high technology, international regulatory reform and new ideas concerning competition. Three main effects for European high technology policy can be identified: powerful incentives for wider competition in the supply of services and terminal equipment; strong pressures for concentration and internationalisation, particularly in the manufacture of equipment for telecommunications networks; and finally, an increase in the economic importance of appropriate supply of high technology services and equipment.

The technological and economic characteristics of high technology have been transformed in the period since the 1960s. The driving force behind change has been the 'marriage' of telecommunications, broadcasting and computing, together with rapid technological progress in all three fields. On the supply side, a large number of diverse 'advanced services' and types of terminal equipment have developed. Examples include facsimile services and equipment, electronic mail and data services, ranging from data transmission networks to sophisticated financial dealing and processing services. The monopoly supply of these advanced services and terminal equipment by PTOs became increasingly difficult to sustain from the 1980s onwards: not only were such services and equipment extremely diverse, but it became difficult to separate them from computing services and equipment, a field traditionally outside public monopolies in most west European countries. New methods of switching[8] and transmission, particularly digitalisation,[9] and new materials such as optical fibre cable, provided another supply-side change. They enabled the development of new services, and also the transmission of telephony, data and images (including eventually television) in digital form and using the same telecommunications network. Moreover, they altered the cost structure of high technology, reducing entry costs for setting up a tele-communications network and the costs of long-distance transmission relative to shorter distance communications, whilst at the same time aiding the linkage of several telecommunications networks. These changes assisted the extension of competition; they also meant that if PTOs maintained previous price structures, they could be undercut on long-distance services. However, competition threw up new regulatory questions concerning norms and standards. Compatible standards were needed to allow different pieces of equipment and services to be used together, and to avoid purchasers becoming 'locked into' supply by a particular firm by sunk costs and incompatible equipment, which would prevent real competition. Finally, on the supply side, the cost structure for manufacturing equipment for telecommunications networks altered. Greatly increased costs of research and development meant that much larger markets were needed for profitability. Hence powerful pressures for concentration arose, as markets in individual European countries became too small to support even one equipment manufacturer.

On the demand side, the uses of high technology equipment and services became more diverse and also more widespread. Applications were made in a number of fields including banking (cash withdrawal systems and financial data processing), tourism and travel (information and reservation systems), the financial market (dealing systems) and manufacturing (computer assisted manufacture and design). The range of applications not only made monopoly supply by a PTO difficult to maintain, but also meant that high technology increasingly became economically 'strategic', since its supply had implications for a wide range of economic sectors. The success and even survival of firms in certain sectors became greatly influenced by the supply of high technology services and equipment. The dependence of businesses on the appropriate supply of high technology services created a new and important potential group of actors in policy making.

Regulatory changes in countries outside western Europe, notably the United States and Japan, offered another transnational pressure for change. In the United States, the 'computer settlements' of the 1960s and 1970s allowed competition in certain advanced services. Then, in 1982, came the 'Bell Settlement': the giant American PTO, AT&T, was broken up into regional PTOs ('Baby Bells') and had to face competition in long-distance and international communications, but was allowed to expand into equipment manufacturing. For western Europe, the United States offered not just an example but also sources of pressure for liberalisation, as computer companies such as IBM and PTOs, especially AT&T, sought to expand abroad, supported by the American administration and Congress. At the same time, new ideas concerning the benefits of competition also appeared from the 1970s onwards, particularly from North America. Economists began to question 'natural monopolies', and instead offered theories of 'contestable markets' to justify competition being permitted (Baumol *et al.* 1982). Gradually, beliefs concerning the benefits of competition began to spread in western Europe via, it has been suggested, an 'epistemic policy community' (Cowhey 1990). Thus the international environment of high technology provided powerful pressures for change in traditional national policies in western Europe.

THE EXPANSION OF EC REGULATION IN HIGH TECHNOLOGY

Before the 1980s, the EC played almost no role in high technology (Sandholtz 1992: 92–9, Schneider and Werle 1990). However, this greatly altered in the 1980s and early 1990s. The Commission developed increasingly wide-ranging plans for high technology, which were followed by a series of regulatory measures. Within the Commission, policy was led by DG XIII, responsible for Telecommunications, Information, and Research, and DGIV, the competition Directorate. The expansion of EC regulation was accompanied by the strengthening of the legal powers of the EC in high technology. Telecommunications were included in the Internal Market programme, and hence were covered by majority voting under the Single European Act of 1987. More importantly, following two decisions of the European Court of Justice in telecommunications,[10] the Commission was able to use Article 90, concerning 'public enterprises', to issue Directives without the approval of the Council or European Parliament, in order to allow competition.[11]

With respect to national institutional frameworks, the EC laid down few stipulations in high technology. Indeed, the issuing of Directives rather than Regulations meant that the method of implementing EC legislation was left to member states. Moreover, member states were free to choose the ownership and administrative status of PTOs. Nevertheless, EC Directives insist that regulatory decisions be made by bodies independent of suppliers and that they be taken according to public, non-discriminatory and 'objective' criteria.

In contrast, wide-ranging EC legislation obliging member states to allow competition and outlawing national monopolies granted to PTOs was passed or, by 1994, was in the process of being passed. This began with the 1988 'Terminals Directive', issued under Article 90, which allowed competition in the supply of all types of CPE (CEC 1988). Then in 1990, a Services Directive was issued, again by the Commission acting under Article 90 (CEC 1990). This obliged member states to abolish 'special and exclusive rights' and allow competition in the supply of all services except 'reserved services', namely voice telephony and telex services. More comprehensive action followed in 1993: the Council accepted that from 1998 EC rules would permit competition in voice telephony and telex services in most EC countries,[12] and hence existing national PTO monopolies would be ended. Moreover, it was agreed that in 1995 the Commission would examine whether competition in 'the infrastructure' (i.e. building and operating telecommunications networks, and the use of other infrastructures, notably cable television networks, for telecommunications) should be permitted. In fact, in November 1994, the Council had accepted that competition in the provision of telecommunications infrastructure, including the use of cable television networks for telecommunications, would be permitted from 1998; this represented a compromise over timing, as it rejected Commission plans for limited competition to begin in 1995. The Commission has also introduced legislation to allow competition in satellite services and equipment, and in 1994 it issued a Green Paper arguing for the maximum extension of competition in mobile telecommunications services and networks (Commission 1994).

EC regulation also aimed at ensuring that competition in supply would be 'fair' and 'effective'. A series of Directives laid down conditions governing access to the telecommunications infrastructure for service providers. Matters covered included the right of service providers to connect equipment to the infrastructure, and the principle that tariffs must be based on 'objective criteria', notably costs (Council 1990a).[13] In order to ensure that competition was not limited by nationally determined licensing requirements, EC legislation only allowed member states to require suppliers to meet minimum standards or 'essential requirements', which were specified by the EC, and to do so in a manner that was proportional, non-discriminatory and scrutinised by the Commission. One method of meeting the EC's 'essential requirements' was to comply with EC approved norms and tests. Many EC standards in high technology are established by the European Telecommunications Standards Institute (ETSI), established in 1988.[14]

In equipment manufacturing, the aim of EC policy was to open national equipment markets to competition from firms other than 'national champions'. Legislation was passed dealing with public procurement in telecommunications: a Directive in 1990 laid down procedures for tenders to ensure that selection procedures were fair and non-discriminatory and that norms and quality criteria were not used to favour certain suppliers (Council 1990b). The EC also introduced mutual recognition of licences between member states for CPE (Council 1991a).

HDTV was the major exception to the policy of avoiding mandatory EC standards. A Council Directive in 1986 imposed the 'MAC' standard for all direct broadcasting of television by satellites over a certain power for a period of five years, after which the Directive could be renewed (Council 1986). 'MAC' was a set of European standards, developed for HDTV within a EUREKA programme.[15] It was intended that an intermediate MAC standard, D2-MAC, would offer enhanced quality for specially adapted television sets, while remaining compatible with existing sets. In the long term, a high definition MAC standard (HD-MAC) would be developed, which would permit much higher quality pictures to be transmitted.

The development of MAC, however, encountered a series of problems (Cawson 1995, Dai *et al.* 1993). The cost of large screen television sets suitable for D2-MAC was high and demand for them was correspondingly low. At the same time, broadcasting in MAC was expensive and large public subsidies were deemed necessary in order to persuade broadcasters to offer a sufficiently wide range of programmes to make consumer purchases of large screens worthwhile. The development of improved conventional television transmission (PAL-Plus) threatened to compete with D2-MAC. Although the MAC Directive was renewed in 1992 this was only after a long struggle, and the Directive did not cover low power satellites, such as Astra, which were now being used to broadcast satellite television operating the old PAL standard. Then, after the failure to obtain the UK's agreement to large-scale subsidies for the broadcasting of programmes in D2-MAC, the Commission announced in 1993 that MAC would be abandoned as the mandatory EC standard, effectively ending the MAC project.

Thus EC activity in high technology greatly expanded in the 1980s and 1990s, to cover much of information and communications technology. EC regulation, based on 'fair' and effective competition, offered a distinct approach to traditional national industrial policies in Europe.

THE IMPACT OF EC REGULATION ON THE UK, FRANCE, GERMANY AND ITALY

In analysing the development of national high technology policies in the UK, France, Germany and Italy, the most striking overall feature is the similarity of the direction of change in all four countries. The trends include the extension of competition, reforms in the organisational position of PTOs (leading to privatisation), the internationalisation of suppliers, especially through the formation of alliances (a process most marked for equipment supply, but also increasingly apparent in the strategies of PTOs) and, in HTDV, the failure of the MAC norm. In looking at changing national policies, the role of transnational pressures for change can be seen. These pressures have included lobbying by the USA administration and American companies, the belief in the growing inevitability of competition and the need for national suppliers to prepare for this, and the requirements of business users.

However, similarity of trends has been combined with differences in the impact of EC regulation between the four countries. These differences are closely linked to contrasts between countries in the pace, timing and form of change at the national level. The direct impact of EC regulation has varied with the extent to which member states had already introduced similar legislation themselves or, in the case of equipment supply, internationalisation had largely produced effects intended by EC public procurement Directives. Thus, for instance, the direct impact of EC regulation was very limited in the UK, where similar measures were in place before EC Directives, but was somewhat more significant in the other three countries, where certain elements of EC legislation were new.

The indirect impact of EC regulation has also varied according to the extent to which actors' strategies had already adapted to a world of competition and internationalisation, and also the degree of domestic opposition to reforms. Hence, in France, Germany and Italy, EC regulation played a significant role in altering the strategies of actors who became convinced of the need to prepare themselves for greater competition. It also provided an important resource for policy makers to overcome domestic opposition to reforms. In contrast, the strategies of actors in the UK were already in the process of changing, and hence the indirect impact of EC measures was less important. Nevertheless, in assessing the effects of EC regulation, the part played by national and transnational factors, unrelated to the EC, is crucial: often EC regulation was used to justify reforms due to non-EC factors. Finally, the impact of the EC on national strategies must also be analysed in the context of the preparedness of each member state for greater competition. This has been closely related to whether a country was a 'policy leader', such as the UK, which had already introduced policy changes before EC action, or a 'policy laggard', such as Italy, which had failed to prepare for the change and hence sought to delay EC regulatory reforms in order to create a period to catch up.

The UK

Comprehensive reorganisation of telecommunications and related sectors and the extension of competition occurred in the UK during the 1980s and early 1990s. Reforms took place before EC legislation, and almost no consideration was given to EC policy. They were driven by a combination of factors unrelated to the EC, including the aims of the Conservative government, fiscal pressures, new ideas concerning competition and the impact of the Office of Telecommunications, Oftel (Thatcher 1993, 1995).

The institutional and administrative structure of telecommunications was altered during the 1980s. British Telecom (BT) became a public corporation, separate from the Post Office, in 1981. BT was privatised in 1984, through the sale of 51 per cent of the shares. The government's remaining stake was sold in 1990 and 1993. An independent regulatory agency, Oftel, was established in 1984 to regulate the telecommunications sector, and BT in particular. The existence of Oftel meant that later EC requirements for the separation of regulation and supply were already satisfied by the UK. Indeed, the UK had moved a further step forward by making Oftel independent of the government.

The organisational changes introduced at national level were accompanied by modifications in policy formation and the strategies of actors. New actors emerged, notably Oftel, while the role of users widened and became more significant. After privatisation, the government respected BT's autonomy: it did not intervene in BT's internal decision making and largely ended its role as intermediary in relations between BT and its suppliers, and its constant dealings with both. In the new organisational framework, the strategy of BT altered. One element was internationalisation. During the 1980s this largely occurred outside Europe, notably by BT acquiring stakes in North American companies. But, during the 1990s, BT sought to expand in Europe, both by establishing subsidiaries and by becoming a 'global operator', especially through an alliance with the USA operator, MCI, beginning in 1993. BT lobbied at national and EC levels for the extension of competition in other EC member states. Furthermore, BT altered its relations with its traditional suppliers and turned to new, foreign firms for equipment. The British suppliers, especially GEC and Plessey, responded by concentration and internationalisation: GEC and Plessey formed a joint telecommunications equipment subsidiary, GPT, in 1988, followed by GEC and Siemens making a successful bid for Plessey in 1989, under which Siemens took a 40 per cent stake in GPT. These changes in actors' relationships and strategies therefore took place before EC action, in response to prior national policies.

The 1980s and 1990s saw the introduction of competition into almost the entire telecommunications and advanced services fields in the UK prior to EC legislation requiring it. BT's monopoly over CPE supply was ended during the early 1980s, while the supply of advanced services was permitted by the 1984 VANS (Value Added Network Services) licence and the 1987

VADS (Value Added Data Services) licence; competition was introduced in the supply of satellite services in 1988, partly due to lobbying by the USA firm PanAmSat, with the support of the American administration. Competition in voice telephony was allowed through the establishment of a duopoly between Mercury and BT in 1982, unrestricted resale of leased line capacity in 1989 and the ending of the BT-Mercury duopoly in 1990. Indeed, the UK went further than required under EC legislation by permitting several infrastructures to be built and operated, first with the BT/Mercury duopoly, and then with the decision to allow other network operators to establish and operate their own telecommunications infrastructures. The influence of the EC over these policy developments appears to have been very limited, since both the government and Oftel favoured greater competition, and did not require inspiration by the EC.

The EC's aim of 'fair' and 'effective' competition was also not new for the UK. Oftel had already made this one of its central objectives. As a result, Oftel had introduced rules similar to many of the measures contained in later EC legislation. Thus, for instance, the limiting of standards to 'essential requirements' represented little change, as mandatory standards for much of CPE and advanced services had been ended in the late 1980s. The conditions of access to the infrastructure were already regulated by British measures: BT's licence required interconnection with other operators' networks, whilst Oftel had laid down the rules for interconnection, notably between BT's network and other suppliers, and had established the general principle of cost-based pricing in the supply of services, especially when competitive pressures were weak. Furthermore, to ensure 'fair competition', licences, notably the one given to BT, stipulated that certain businesses must be separated and prohibited cross-subsidisation between services. EC requirements that regulatory decisions be public and according to non-discriminatory criteria had also largely been introduced by Oftel before EC legislation.

In equipment manufacturing, the EC's rules in 1990 for public procurement did represent limited change. BT, Mercury and other new PTOs were covered by EC tender requirements, and although Oftel already scrutinised purchasing decisions, using various criteria, it focused on benefit for the consumer (Oftel 1985). Nevertheless, the opening of the British equipment market preceded EC action, taking place in two ways. First, foreign suppliers had entered the market. BT had turned to new suppliers, such as Ericsson, from which it bought public switches after 1985. Second, the equipment manufacturing sub-sector had been restructured and internationalised via the German-based firm Siemens taking a 40 per cent stake in the main British equipment manufacturer, GPT, in 1988.

The main exception to the congruence between British and EC regulatory reforms was HDTV. Two operators had been licensed for the direct satellite broadcasting of television in the UK: SKY Television, which used the existing PAL transmission system, and BSB, launched in 1990, which used a D-MAC format. SKY was able to use PAL because the EC's 1986 MAC Directive only

covered satellite transmission over a certain power level, whereas SKY programmes were transmitted using a low-powered telecommunications satellite,
Astra. In November 1990, faced with mounting losses, BSB 'merged' with,
but in practice was taken over by, SKY. The result was the use of PAL and the
abandonment of BSB's D-MAC transmissions. British users bought PAL
satellite equipment. The government refused either to prevent SKY's takeover of BSB or to oblige SKY to use MAC for its broadcasts, deciding to
leave the matter to 'the market'.

For the UK, EC regulation was generally perceived as following the British
'example', not leading it. Indeed, British firms appeared well-placed to
benefit from EC legislation on competition, having already adjusted to competition domestically. In particular, BT seemed to occupy the position of a
privately owned 'national champion', able to expand into other EC markets
and compete more effectively than other PTOs, thanks to its private company
status, tariff rebalancing, high profits and lack of politically imposed
burdens. The British government welcomed EC activity to widen competition
and establish EC rules for 'fair and "effective" competition', even though this
meant increased Community and Commission powers. The major exception
was HDTV. The MAC norm posed a threat to SKY, and the extension of the
ban of PAL to Astra on the renewal of the original MAC Directive in 1992
would have meant that the equipment purchased by SKY subscribers was
unusable. The UK's stance was strengthened by the fact that the HDTV
project did not involve a leading role for British companies. The British
government fought hard against the MAC norm and EC measures to
subsidise programmes and transmission using MAC (Cawson 1995).

France

EC measures ran counter to the model of French industrial policy in the
1970s and early 1980s, and in particular the launching of *'grands projets'*
involving public and private actors and often underpinned by public monopolies (Cohen 1992). It might thus be expected that EC regulation, based on
'fair' and 'effective' competition, would have greatly altered French policy in
high technology. But, whilst EC regulation has had a significant direct, and
especially indirect, impact on French policy, this has been tempered by three
factors: reforms similar to the EC's measures or following the same direction
of change had already been implemented in France; factors largely unrelated
to the EC lay behind many of the modifications introduced, and the implementation of regulatory reform may limit the degree of change in practice.

Comprehensive institutional reform in France faced the determined opposition of powerful interests. This applied especially to France Télécom, which
was, until 1990, part of the civil service, being formally a unit within the PTT
Ministry and which combined the roles of supplier of services, regulator and
policy maker. The trade unions and employees of France Télécom fiercely
opposed modifying France Télécom's *statut* as part of the civil service. In

1986, the Right came into government pledged to make the DGT (*Direction Générale des Télécommunications*, as France Télécom was then known) into a 'public telecommunications company', a form of public corporation. However, fear of the reaction of the trade unions prevented this from being implemented and only the DGT's name was altered (to France Télécom). After 1988, under Rocard's premiership, another attempt at reform was undertaken. After a long period of consultation and debate, various reforms were implemented in 1990. France Télécom's organisational position was altered, so that it became an *exploitant public* (a special form of public corporation) and ceased to perform regulatory functions.

Until the 1990s, privatisation of France Télécom had been ruled out. But, during the 1990s, and especially after the return of the Right to government in 1993, preparations were made for greater change. Discussions began over reforms whereby France Télécom would become a limited company and would be partially, if not entirely, privatised. The idea of an independent regulatory body was also mooted. Athough a bill was promised for 1994, it did not materialise.

The government and France Télécom's senior management used EC measures to justify wider reforms in the late 1980s and early 1990s (Prévot 1989: 133–6, *Le Monde*, 13 October 1990 and 6 July 1993). They argued that France Télécom needed greater autonomy to meet the competition and separation of regulation and supply 'imposed' by the EC. Moreover, France Télécom pursued an active strategy of internationalisation. It has sought to form a close alliance with Deutsche Telekom, and also with the USA operator, Sprint, through the formation of joint ventures. It has made plans for a deepening co-operation with these PTOs, including the possibility of exchanges of shareholdings with Deutsche Telekom. Commercial autonomy and privatisation appear useful, if not essential, for this strategy. The internationalisation of France Télécom has been linked, at least in part, to the effects of EC legislation opening up national markets to competition, and to the threat from BT, perceived as a common danger to both France Télécom and Deutsche Telekom.

However, the limits of the impact of EC action on the framework of policy making in France must be noted. First, the reforms implemented thus far have been modest. Under the changes introduced in 1990, the government retained a wide range of powers over France Télécom, notably including over its financial framework, objectives and strategy, and the nomination of a majority of its board members. No independent regulatory body has been established and so the PTT Ministry remains the regulator. Further reform and privatisation of France Télécom face obstacles, including strong opposition from the trade unions and many employees. Second, factors other than EC regulation and its effects also played a part in bringing about reform. Elements of the political Right had a long-standing desire to reform France Télécom. Furthermore, the management of France Télécom favoured greater autonomy, since it resented France Télécom being used as a source of funds to further French industrial policy. Moreover, from the mid-1980s, much of France Télécom's senior management believed that international competition was inevitable, irrespective of EC action, and that internationalisation was essential; hence attempts at internationalisation had begun before EC measures, albeit mostly outside Europe. Furthermore, a central motivation behind plans to privatise France Télécom is the prospect of raising valuable funds to ease the problem of the government's budget deficit. The third limiting factor is that institutional reform does not guarantee ensuing modifications in the relationships between actors, especially as the PTT Ministry remains the regulatory authority. Thus, for instance, after 1990, France Télécom has continued to serve as a source of funds for government-inspired objectives, whilst the equipment manufacturer Alcatel has maintained close links with the French government and France Télécom, despite becoming a private company in 1987 (Sally 1993).

With respect to the impact of EC legislation extending competition, most elements of the 1988 Terminals Directive and 1990 Services Directive had already been implemented by France. Thus, for instance, the public monopoly over the supply of CPE had been limited before the 1980s, and remaining elements were abolished in the early 1980s. Competition was permitted in telematic services in 1982,[16] and in other advanced services under a decree of 1987. Nevertheless, some elements of EC legislation did represent change for France and hence offered some examples of the impact of EC regulation. The Services Directive meant an extension of competition to certain services for France, notably data transmission networks and the resale of leased line capacity. EC rules concerning 'essential requirements' and norms, access to the infrastructure and the criteria for regulatory decisions are more wide-ranging and rigorous than previous arrangements. More generally, EC measures on 'fair' competition appear to remove important areas of discretion previously available to the PTT Ministry to limit or influence competition. Most importantly, competition in fixed line voice telephony and provision of the telecommunications infrastructure had not been introduced before the 1993 and 1994 EC agreements.

Nevertheless, the impact of EC regulation on France in terms of changes in the rules on competition required by EC legislation must be assessed in the wider context of French policy. A movement towards greater competition had already been under way before EC measures, under the influence of various factors. There had been a desire to allow a wider range of sources of information, particularly by sections of the Left after 1981, and also a growing belief that competition in new services (but not necessarily in voice telephony and the basic infrastructure) was inevitable and beneficial. Moreover, pressure had arisen for competition in advanced services and CPE from business users, especially those in information intensive sectors, such as computing and banking. France Télécom had begun to prepare for a further extension of competition, notably to voice telephony from the mid-1980s, by gradually moving its tariffs closer to costs. Finally, the actual operation of new regulatory frameworks in practice is not clear. Although restrictions on the supply of CPE do seem to have been largely removed, French implementation of competition in advanced services has been slow and reluctant. For instance, the government established a complex procedure for obtaining licences to offer public data services and France Télécom has used its tariff structure to discourage the creation of private data networks which might compete with its own services (Roussel 1993). Regulation remains in the hands of the *Direction Générale de la Poste et des Télécommunications* (DGPT), a division of the PTT Ministry, and its commitment to 'fair' and 'effective' competition remains unproven.

Although EC rules on public procurement were new for France, the opening of the equipment market had begun to take place along similar lines to the UK. New suppliers had entered the French market; in particular, France Télécom's second largest supplier, CGCT, was sold in 1987 to a consortium including Ericsson. In addition, French firms internationalised. Alcatel became an international, European group after 1987 through its purchases of most of ITT's telecommunications subsidiaries and the Italian firm, Telettra. The influence of EC regulation on these developments was limited, especially as international expansion and exports had been major objectives of French policy in equipment manufacturing since the 1970s.

The difficulties of separating EC regulation from national decisions and attempts to use the EC to solve other, largely unrelated, problems are best illustrated by French policy towards HDTV. During the late 1970s, the DGT announced that it would launch telecommunications satellites. Its arch rival, the television broadcasting organisation Télédiffusion de France (TDF) then pressed for a similar programme of television satellites, known as TDF1 and 2 (Cohen 1992: 307–51). Rapidly, however, it became clear that the TDF satellites were unnecessary and were not economically viable. HDTV seemed to offer a solution to their use. It also provided commercial opportunities for the publicly owned firm, Thomson, which maufactured equipment, particularly television sets, and which was experiencing large losses and fierce competition, especially from Japanese producers. HDTV offered the prospect of new products and markets for Thomson. France Télécom was the main instrument used to promote HDTV and the MAC norm in France. When it took over TDF in 1989, it was obliged to accept responsibility for the TDF satellite programme, and also for promoting equipment, transmission and programmes using the MAC norm. The hope was that the simultaneous launching of D2-MAC equipment, programmes and transmission would create a viable market, especially for services using the TDF satellites and for Thomson's HDTV television sets, albeit a market initially co-ordinated by public actors, especially France Télécom. However, this strategy came to an end when the EC's attempts to impose MAC collapsed.

The strategy of French governments and France Télécom until the 1990s was to accept the principle of EC legislation, but to seek to restrict the Commission's, and especially DG IV's, role in extending competition to include provisions in EC regulation limiting competition through norms and to maximise the discretion left to national authorities. Moreover, until 1993, France vigorously opposed competition being allowed in voice telephony or the infrastructure, by far the largest areas of telecommunications. However, in the 1990s, and especially after the Right returned to government in 1993, the French strategy altered: EC legislation to widen competition to voice telephony and the infrastructure was accepted; indeed, France allied itself with the UK and Germany in 1994 in pressing for the EC to permit limited competition in the infrastructure from 1995. One set of reasons for the change in the French strategy related to the failure of the French government's attempts to prevent the extension of competition by the Commission under Article 90, and also a growing belief in the inevitability of competition. Another was that the government and France Télécom's management were able to use EC regulation as a justification for reforming France Télécom, including privatisation, and for the strategy of internationalisation. They believed that rapid reform of France Télécom's administrative status and the formation of alliances, especially with Deutsche Telekom, would enable France Télécom to compete successfully in Europe and elsewhere, and particularly to face the threat from BT. In contrast to telecommunications, the French attitude to the EC's HDTV programmes was highly enthusiastic. The French government was the most vociferous among the member states in pressing for the compulsory MAC standards and the accompanying action plans, and the last government to accept that the attempt to launch a MAC standard had failed and should be ended.

Initially, the impact of EC measures on France was very limited. The extension of competition required by EC legislation was circumscribed due to earlier national modifications; France Télécom remained a publicly owned organisation retaining a very significant monopoly and, with HDTV, France appeared able to continue '*grands projets*', albeit at the European level. In the 1990s, the impact of EC regulation grew, as it facilitated an extension of competition and increased pressures for reform of France Télécom, whereas the HDTV project failed. Nevertheless, the effects of EC regulation were primarily to amplify and accelerate existing trends towards greater competition and internationalisation, to offer a supplementary pressure for changes to France Télécom's organisational status and commercial strategy and to provide a justification for reforms which formed part of a modified national strategy, itself only very partially linked to EC policy. Hence EC regulation formed one pressure among several in French policy making.

Germany

Traditionally, Germany was one of the most closed markets in Europe. Policy making was dominated by central government and the PTO, the *Deutsches Bundespost* (the DPB), certain electronics companies, notably Siemens, and the *Länder* (Haid and Müller 1988, Humphreys 1990). EC legislation might therefore be expected to have had a major impact. Closer examination, however, reveals that EC regulation had a limited effect and that the role of other factors proved more significant.

Until 1989, the DPB was a federal administration, and combined postal and telecommunications services. Pressures for reform grew from the mid-1980s, but these were largely independent of the EC. The most important were new ideas concerning the organisation of telecommunications and the belief that the DBP's organisational position needed to be changed to allow it to cope with the wider competition that was being permitted, both for certain services within Germany and internationally. Nevertheless, there was strong opposition to major organisational change from the trade unions, the SPD and some *Länder* (Cawson *et al.* 1990, Schmidt 1991). After a long process of consultation and several concessions by the government, limited organisational changes were introduced in 1989. The Deutsches Bundespost was split into three corporations, including Deutsche Telekom, with the latter gaining limited autonomy, while the PTT Ministry became a separate regulatory body. But further changes appeared blocked. The PTT Minister from 1982 to 1992, Christian Schwarz-Schilling, ruled out either ending Telekom's monopoly over voice telephony and the infrastructure, or privatisation of Deutsche Telekom.

However, in what appears to be a remarkably rapid shift, in 1993, further, far-reaching changes were decided. Telekom (together with the other two branches of the old Bundespost) was to become a company by 1995. It would therefore operate under private law and would enjoy much greater autonomy. In addition, an independent regulatory body would be set up. Telekom was to be partially privatised by sale of a minority stake thereafter, although the government was to keep a majority share for at least five years. These changes were accepted after protracted negotiations between the government and several parties, including the opposition SPD, whose support was needed for the two-thirds majority in both houses of the Bundestag required to amend the Constitution.[17] The trade unions did not oppose the direction of change, even though a loss of 30,000 Telekom jobs was envisaged and Telekom employees would cease to be civil servants.

In the process of change, EC measures were an aid to those wishing to undertake reform. It was argued, especially by Telekom's top management, that EC measures to extend competition in European markets meant that Telekom needed to restructure its organisation in order to face competition and be able to undertake expansion abroad. Nevertheless, the changes of the early 1990s owed more to non-EC factors. The most important was the effect of reunification. An estimated DM60 billion was required in investment in the former East Germany over the period between 1990 and 1997. As a result, Telekom had to borrow very large sums, but faced rising interest charges and a falling capital base, and required an injection of capital.[18] At the same time, under the 1989 reforms, Telekom was obliged to subsidise the losses incurred by postal services and to hand over revenues to the government, the two elements costing no less than DM6.5 billion in 1992, which eliminated Telekom's profits. Moreover, the failure to modernise the telecommunications network in the Eastern *Länder* was leading to calls for more radical change, notably allowing competition in the provision of the infrastructure and to the illegal creation of alternative telephone networks to Telekom's. Where competition was permitted, Telekom found itself disadvantaged. The clearest example was in new digital mobile telephony (*Les Echos*, 15 March 1993). As a result of these pressures, Telekom's management, notably its head, Helmut Ricke, pressed urgently for privatisation (*La Tribune de l'Expansion*, 28 September 1992, and *Financial Times*, 26 October 1993). Finally, the privatisation of Telekom appeared to offer a useful source of funds to reduce the rising Federal Government Budget deficit. These factors, largely unrelated to EC regulation, were the driving force behind the acceptance of much greater change than the limited reforms of 1989.

In the extension of competition and rules governing supply, EC measures did have some impact on Germany. In the early 1980s, EC reforms provided pressure for wider competition: in CPE supply, the EC Commission challenged the Bundespost's extension of its CPE monopoly to cordless telephones and modems (Ungerer and Costello 1988: 169–70); subsequently CPE supply was liberalised. The Services Directive allowed greater competition than that permitted in the 1989 Restructuration Law, and it and the ONP Directives were clearer with respect to the rights of suppliers. The most significant extension of competition arising from the application of EC rules came with the 1993 EC agreement to allow competition in voice telephony and with the decision to end PTO monopolies over the infrastructure, both areas falling within Telekom's monopoly under the 1989 law.

Nevertheless, closer examination reveals that other, non-EC factors were more significant in the extension of competition than EC legislation. Competition had already been extended before EC legislation or was introduced concurrently to it. Thus, for instance, the removal of restrictions on the supply of CPE had begun in 1986, the 1989 PTT Restructuration Law permitted competition in most 'advanced' services, and in 1989 several suppliers were permitted in satellite services and a second mobile telephone service was licensed (Schmidt 1991). Furthermore, the extension of competition was linked to non-EC factors. The opening of CPE and advanced services supply to competition followed the beliefs of the CDU/CSU–FDP coalition government, particularly the reform-minded PTT Minister, Schwarz-Schilling, lobbying by American firms such as IBM and ATT, the threat of retaliation by the United States and the wishes of German firms, especially in the computing field (Schmidt 1991, and *Financial Times*, 31 July 1986 and 2 June 1987). The 1993 EC agreement on the extension of competition in voice telephony and its possible introduction for infrastructure only came after German support for these measures, which itself was linked to pressures for the privatisation of Telekom and the entry of new operators to provide the capital investment required for modernisation.

In equipment manufacturing, EC rules on public procurement represented some move away from the traditionally very close relationship between the Deutsches Bundespost and Siemens. However, the opening of the German market was already occurring, partly as a result of the financial presures on Telekom in the early 1990s, but also due to the sale by ITT of a majority stake in SEL, the second largest supplier to Telekom, to the French-based group CGE in 1987. Further 'Europeanisation' took place when in 1988 Siemens joined forces with the British-based group GEC-Plessey.

The clearest example of the difficulties of imposing European measures against the opposition of powerful domestic interests is provided by HDTV. German policy makers in the late 1980s faced pressure not to follow the MAC norms. In particular, equipment manufacturers feared that they would lose their domestic market to other firms. Moreover, they were working on PAL-Plus, an advanced version of their existing transmission standard, PAL. Nevertheless, the German government continued to accept the MAC norm. The main reason for this, however, was pressure from France, which made the issue an important element in Franco-German co-operation, rather than the role of the EC Commission. It was only due to very strong French lobbying that the German government did not succumb in 1990 to domestic pressures to abandon D2-MAC and concentrate on PAL. Moreover, despite the decision to adhere to MAC, several cable and satellite companies decided to transmit using PAL and German organisations, including the public broadcasting organisations ARD and ZDF, participated in the development of PAL-Plus, which offered a potential competitor to D2-MAC and helped to undermine it (Dai *et al.* 1993).

The German government's approach towards EC regulation was to accept measures widening competition. During the 1980s, this was because EC measures had already been implemented at the national level and/or because they helped to reduce pressures, notably American ones, for greater German action to open up markets. After 1990, Germany accepted more sweeping EC measures to extend competition into voice telephony and the infrastructure; indeed, Germany sided with the UK and France in 1994 in pressing for an early start to competition in the infrastructure. Again, however, the position of the German government was linked to national and international factors. The 1993 agreement on extending competition to voice telephony illustrates the use of EC action for domestic ends: it was reached in large part thanks to German support, but the German position altered after the decision to privatise Telekom had been taken, because competition in voice telephony provided a useful accompanying measure to privatisation. German support in the 1990s for a rapid extension of competition was part of the new strategy of the German government and Telekom's senior management: greater competition would be accompanied by the privatisation of Telekom, its preparation for competition and the formation of international alliances, notably between Telekom and France Télécom, in order to capture European and international markets.

Change in German high technology policy has thus been more the product of factors operating at the national level (especially the effects of reunification, but also pressure from users and the decisions of manufacturers) and international factors (especially American lobbying in the 1980s) than EC regulation, which represented a supplementary pressure for change. In the face of these pressures, the strategy of the German government and Telekom's management altered: as in France, competition was to be accompanied by the privatisation and internationalisation of the German PTO. The most important function of EC regulation was to aid the introduction of the new strategy of German policy makers.

Italy

The organisation of Italian high technology until the 1990s possessed a number of special features. First, supply was fragmented, with no less than six different PTOs, and there was no equivalent of British Telecom or France Télécom. Second, the administrative status of these entities varied, ranging from partially privately owned licensees to fully owned subsidiaries of a holding company for telecommunications (notably the STET, itself owned by the public holding company IRI), to ASST, which formed part of the PTT Ministry. Third, a very high degree of intervention by political parties took place, especially in the case of ASST, for purposes such as patronage, regional development and the creation of employment for party supporters (Foreman-Peck and Manning 1988).

EC reforms offered an important pressure for organisational reform, as the fragmented structure of the sector would leave Italian suppliers vulnerable to outside competitors. Plans for the concentration of suppliers into one entity and the granting of considerable commercial autonomy to this entity were made from the mid-1980s. Nevertheless, only limited changes were implemented during the 1980s, and it was only in the 1990s that the process of reorganisation made headway. In 1992 ASST was separated from the PTT Ministry and became part of the IRI group, and IRI began a partial privatisation of STET by announcing the sale of a 16 per cent share in the latter to raise capital. More wide-ranging organisational modifications followed, notably the creation of a Telecom Italia in August 1994, which regrouped all the service providers. The privatisation, total or partial, of Telecom Italia is planned.

However, pressures other than EC policy were important in the reform process. One was lobbying by business users. During the 1980s, companies, especially large ones such as Fiat or Olivetti, called for modernisation, claiming that Italy's dated and fragmented system was inefficient and harming their operations. Another factor was that the holding companies, STET and IRI, found that action was needed to raise capital, both to pay for expansion and modernisation and to support the manufacturing sub-sector, faced by rising costs and a domestic market that was too small (*Financial Times*, 28

November 1988, 12 November 1991 and *La Tribune de l'Expansion*, 4 May 1992). Moreover, new management at STET pressed for greater autonomy, especially from control by politicians, in order to be able to operate in a more commercial manner. These factors meant that, after long discussion of reform, which had begun in the early 1980s, and despite the reluctance of the Christian Democrats, the process of reorganisation of the sector was begun in the late 1980s and the early 1990s. However, it was only after sweeping political changes, notably the destruction of the Christian Democrats as a political force, that more significant reforms were undertaken and that serious preparations for privatisation were begun. Furthermore, the major attraction for political leaders was that privatisation would provide revenue to aid Italy's grave budgetary difficulties. Thus EC measures provided impetus for a reorganisation process under way in Italy for several other reasons.

In terms of competition, EC regulation represented a very considerable change for Italy, where public monopolies remained at the end of the 1980s and in the early 1990s. Hence its implementation will require major regulatory reforms. Nevertheless, the impact of the EC must be assessed in the context of two other factors. The first is the implementation of EC regulation. The 1990 Services Directive contained exceptions for certain countries with 'underdeveloped infrastructures' concerning competition in certain services, such as data transmission, which were specifically designed to appease several member states, including Italy. Moreover, EC legislation dealing with matters such as interconnection or rules for 'fair' competition had largely still not been transposed into Italian law by 1993. The second factor is that other sources of change existed apart from EC regulation. The most important immediate source of change was lobbying by business users. During the 1980s, companies argued for the removal of restrictions on services and equipment. They frequently set up private networks to avoid the problems of the public switched network and thus in practice public monopolies were broken. Hence EC measures combined with domestic pressures for the extension of competition.

As in other European countries, the equipment market was opened not only through changes in purchases, but also through international alliances and takeovers. In 1989 a 20 per cent stake in the STET's manufacturing subsidiary, Italtel, was sold to ATT, in the hope of profitable co-operation with the latter, while in 1990 a majority stake in Fiat's public switching manufacturing subsidiary, Telettra, was sold to Alcatel. The major factors for these moves were the increasing costs of manufacturing and the Italian market being too small to recover these costs, rather than the EC, which played little direct role in the restructuring (*Financial Times*, 28 November 1988, 12 November 1991, and *La Tribune de l'Expansion*, 4 May 1992).

Thus overall, EC regulation provided an additional pressure for change, which combined with national and international forces for change. Nevertheless, policy reactions to pressures for reform were slow, and in the mid-1990s Italy still appeared ill-equipped to implement reforms and Italian suppliers seemed badly placed to face international competition. The management of Italian high technology suppliers was caught during the 1980s and 1990s between domestic and international pressures for greater competition and domestic (especially political) barriers to a reorganisation of supply which was necessary to prepare for competition. The Italian government strove, at the EC level, to delay the extension of competition, in order to provide more time to reorganise Italian suppliers. Hence domestic policy and political inertia appeared to have limited the impact of all pressures for change, including the EC.

CONCLUSION

EC activity in high technology expanded significantly during the 1980s and 1990s. By the mid-1990s, it covered the majority of the telecommunications sector, advanced services and satellite broadcasting. Moreover, the EC differed from international organisations, in that its rules were binding on member states and concerned most of the sector and not merely international services. Furthermore, EC regulation represented a very different approach to previous industrial policies and organisation of the sector. It outlawed much traditional national industrial policy: public monopoly rights were ended; users and suppliers of services and CPE were given rights; regulation was to be independent and 'fair'; standards were set at a minimum level, determined by the EC, and suppliers were left free on how to meet these minimum requirements; and finally, rules to open public procurement to firms other than 'national champions' were instituted.

Closer analysis, however, reveals limits to the direct impact of EC activity on national policy as many elements of EC legislation had already been introduced at the national level before EC action. The extent to which this had occurred varied between the four countries examined and between the different pieces of EC regulation. Thus, for instance, almost all the EC rules on competition, independent regulation and the removal of most mandatory norms and standards had already been carried out in the UK prior to EC legislation. In the other three member states, certain elements of EC policy had already been introduced or were in the process of being put into effect; the most common were competition in the supply of customer premises equipment and advanced services. Moreover, the equipment manufacturing sub-sector had already internationalised and indeed Europeanised in the four countries examined before rules on public procurement were introduced. Compliance with EC rules did necessitate some alterations in France, Germany and Italy; this was the case with respect to provisions such as allowing competition in voice telephony and the infrastructure, which account for by far the largest component of telecommunications revenue, rules on public procurement and the separation of supply and regulation. Nevertheless, important elements of EC regulation, particularly those passed during the 1980s, were anticipated by the member states.

EC action also had indirect effects. EC regulation provided useful ammunition for those national policy makers seeking reform, often led by heads of PTOs and certain politicians on the political Right. It provided a justification for reforms including the alteration of the institutional basis of publicly owned suppliers, privatisation, the extension of competition and the ending of public monopolies and the internationalisation of markets and suppliers. Such reforms met opposition, notably from trade unions and some political parties, such as the SPD in Germany and the Christian Democrats in Italy, and an 'external' source of pressure, EC legislation, was used to argue that change was inevitable or necessary.

This indirect impact, however, must also be assessed in the context of other non-EC factors. First, discussion of reform and lobbying for change at the national level had begun before EC regulation was introduced. EC action provided a supplementary justification for change. Second, EC measures were used to implement reforms desired for reasons largely unrelated to the EC. Thus, for example, privatisation offered receipts for fiscally hard-pressed governments and allowed the financial and capital investment needs of PTOs such as in Germany and Italy to be met outside the public sector. The needs of users, especially in information-intensive sectors, created pressures for better supply and increased competition, and multinationals and foreign governments lobbied for the opening of markets. In equipment manufacturing, the difficulties of sustaining firms reliant solely on a domestic base rendered apparent the benefits of international alliances and the opening of national markets to new suppliers. Hence EC activity, although offering a useful political resource for national interests advocating change, was only one of several pressures for change.

By the mid-1990s, considerable contrasts still existed between the four countries, notably in terms of the ownership and administrative organisation of PTOs and competition in voice telephony and the infrastructure. A number of national factors are responsible for these contrasts, including the history of high technology in each country, the position and aims of governments during the 1980s and 1990s, the power of opponents of change, the readiness of PTOs to meet competition and the configuration and competitiveness of domestic manufacturers. Certain trends, however, appear to be common to all four countries studied, resulting in the narrowing of national differences. These include increased institutional autonomy for PTOs and movement towards privatisation, the extension of competition, the weakening of national norms, the opening of equipment markets and internationalisation, especially of equipment manufacturers, but also increasingly for PTOs.

These general trends across the four countries, and indeed elsewhere in the world, and the role of non-EC factors in justifying change, suggest that other forces modifying regulation in high technology must be considered. New ideas concerning the benefits and practicability of competition in high technology have spread across countries, especially from the United States

(Cowhey 1990). Multinationals such as IBM and AT&T, often supported by the American administration, lobbied to be allowed to enter European markets, especially those that combined telecommunications and computing/electronics such as those for CPE and advanced services, especially as the computing/electronics market lay outside traditional PTO monopolies (Cawson *et al.* 1990, Hills 1986). Business users, particularly in information-intensive sectors, who depend on the supply of high technology services and CPE, have pressed for the ending of restrictions and greater competition in supply. The managements of PTOs have, in turn, pressed for organisational reforms (increased autonomy and often privatisation) which enable them to face increased competition and to internationalise. At the same time, governments have realised that privatisation of PTOs provides valuable funds in a period of budgetary stringency. In equipment manufacturing, rising fixed costs, especially of research and development, have provided a powerful pressure for internationalisation. Underlying many of these factors has been the technological and economic transformation of high technology, notably the weakening of sectoral boundaries between telecommunications, computing/electronics and the audiovisual sector,[19] the widening of the applications of high technology in the economy and the changing cost structure of supply.

Much of the EC's regulation in high technology was part of a movement of regulatory reform concerning high technology in the four countries studied, a movement itself driven by deeper forces for change. The importance of the congruence between EC and national and international factors is best illustrated by the HDTV saga. The EC's norms ran counter to trends in the UK, which therefore fiercely resisted the renewal of the 1986 MAC Directive, whilst German broadcasters began to develop their own rival standard to D2-MAC. Moreover, the EC's chosen norms seemed to become technologically obsolete in the late 1980s and early 1990s, and to require considerable and unprofitable expenditure by national bodies. Despite the enormous sums and prestige invested by the EC Commission, and persistent lobbying by France, the result was the abandonment of the MAC norm in the 1990s. HDTV would indicate that when EC measures attempt to run counter to national and international trends, they fail and are abandoned.

In high technology, EC action had its greatest impact when combined with other powerful forces and interests, both national and international, pressing in the same direction. These non-EC factors have meant that much EC legislation either required little change at the national level or provided a useful justification for changes desired or seen as inevitable for reasons linked to non-EC national or international factors. Indeed, these characteristics of EC regulation are central in explaining the acceptance by member states of the EC's role in high technology regulation, which either placed few new demands on them or otherwise offered a political instrument to justify and implement changes against domestic opposition (Thatcher 1995). But, at the same time, the role of non-EC factors means that the impact of EC activity has been limited, since EC action either followed changes that had already been introduced by the member states or it strengthened arguments made by protagonists for reform, advocated for reasons unrelated to the EC.

NOTES

1 This chapter was completed during ESRC Research Fellowship ref. H53627502595 which the author gratefully acknowledges.
2 Reference to the European Community is made throughout this chapter, since high technology policy has taken place primarily within this pillar. However, the European Union is referred to where appropriate.
3 These services are extremely varied; they include data transmission and processing services, electronic information and telematic services and electronic payments and data interchange systems.
4 Advanced forms of such equipment increasingly involve the combination of office equipment, computing/information technology and telecommunications, as terminals are linked together, or linked to databases, via telecommunications networks.
5 HDTV is a complex field, overlapping telecommunications and audiovisual policy, involving both regulation and research and development, with policy being undertaken within the framework of EUREKA and also by the EC; among the many analyses see Cawson 1995, Dai *et al.* 1993, Peterson 1991, Sandholtz 1992 and Matthew Fraser, Chapter 11 this volume.
6 The notable exception was in the UK, where the Post Office became a public corporation in 1969.
7 Telecommunications services consisted almost exclusively of voice telephony, telegraph and telex services until the 1970s and the 1980s, when new, advanced services and types of CPE began to be supplied.
8 Signals in telecommunications have to be 'switched', from the line of the sender to that of the recipient.
9 Transforming communications into binary form, the same form as used in computers.
10 The Terminals Directive case of 1990 (*France v Commission of the European Communities*, Case 202/88 [1990] ECR I-2223) and the Services Directive case (joined cases C271, C201, and C289/90, *Spain, Belgium, Italy v Commission of the European Communities*, [1992] ECR I-5833) of 1992, in which the Court largely upheld the powers of the Commission and its wide view of the scope of Article 90 in banning publicly granted monopolies against a challenge by certain member states.
11 Article 90(1) forbids member states from introducing or maintaining measures conflicting with other articles of the Treaty, and specifically 'special and exclusive rights', such as a monopoly, that are contrary to competition rules in the Treaty.
12 Longer transition periods were allowed for certain countries.
13 The Open Network Provision (ONP) Directive of 1990, a framework Directive setting out general principles, followed by Directives dealing with specific services.
14 Although legally ETSI is a private body, owned by different types of members (PTOs, equipment manufacturers and users), the EC Commission was instrumental in its creation and sub-contracts standards-setting to ETSI.
15 EUREKA Programme EU95.
16 In France, also known as 'Minitel'; these services allow access to computer databases, through use of a screen and transmission of signals from the user to the database via the telecommunications network.
17 Article 87 specified that the Bundespost, and hence Telekom, must be publicly owned.

18 The sums were becoming dangerous: with revenue of DM54 billion in 1992, Telekom faced debts of DM100 billion, the servicing of which took up 12% of income (*The Economist*, 30 October 1993).
19 See also Matthew Fraser's chapter on broadcasting in this volume, which identifies similar forces at work.

REFERENCES

Baumol, W.J., Panzar, J.C. and Willig, R.D. (1982) *Contestable Markets and the Theory of Industry Structure*, San Diego: Harcourt Brace, Janovitch.

Cawson, A. (1995) 'High Definition in Europe: Why the Flagship of European Technology Policy Hit the Rocks', *Political Quarterly*, 66 (2): 157–73.

Cawson, A., Morgan, K., Webber, D., Holmes, P. and Stevens, A. (1990) *Hostile Brothers*, Oxford: Clarendon Press.

Cohen, E. (1992) *Le Colbertisme 'high tech'*, Paris: Hachette.

Commission of the European Communities (CEC) (1988) Commission Directive 88/301/EEC, Luxembourg: Office for Official Publications of the European Communities OJ L 131, 27.5.88, 73.

—— (1990) Commission Directive 90/388/EEC, Luxemburg: Office for Official Publications of the European Communities, OJ L 1922, 24.7.90, 10.

—— (1994) *Green Paper on a Common Approach in the Field of Mobile and Personal Communications in the European Union*, COM (94) 440, OOPEC: Brussels.

Council (1986) Council Directive 86/529/EEC, Luxemburg: Office for Official Publications of the European Communities, OJ L 311, 6.11.86, 28.

—— (1990a) Council Directive 90/387/EEC, Luxemburg: Office for Official Publications of the European Communities, OJ L 192, 24.7.90, 1.

—— (1990b) Council Directive 90/531/EEC, Luxemburg: Office for Official Publications of the European Communities, OJ L 297, 29.10.90, 1.

—— (1991a) Council Directive 91/263/EEC, Luxemburg: Office for Official Publications of the European Communities, OJ L 128, 23.5.91, 1.

—— (1991b) Council Directive 90/5311/EEC, Luxemburg: Office for Official Publications of the European Communities, OJ L 297, 29.10.91, 11.

Cowhey, P.F. (1990) 'The International Telecommunications Regime: The Political Roots for High Technology', *International Organization*, 44(2): 169–99.

Dai, X., Cawson, A. and Holmes, P. (1993) *Competition, Collaboration and Public Policy: A Case Study of the European HDTV Strategy*, Sussex: Mimeo.

European Commission (1995) *Green Paper on the Liberalisation of Telecommunications Infrastructure and Cable Telecommunications Networks*, Luxemburg: Office for Official Publications of the European Communities, COM (94) 682, 25.1.95.

Foreman-Peck, J. and Manning, D. (1988) 'Telecommunications in Italy', in J. Foreman-Peck and J. Müller (eds) *European Telecommunication Organisations*, Baden-Baden: Nomos.

Foreman-Peck, J. and Müller, J. (eds) (1988) *European Telecommunication Organisations*, Baden-Baden: Nomos.

Haid, A. and Müller, J. (1988) 'Telecommunications in the Federal Republic of Germany', in J. Foreman-Peck and J. Müller (eds) *European Telecommunication Organisations*, Baden-Baden: Nomos.

Hills, J. (1986) *Deregulating Telecoms: Competition and Control in the United States, Japan and the UK*, London: Frances Pinter.

Humphreys, P. (1990) *Media and Media Policy in West Germany*, New York, Oxford and Munich: Berg.

Oftel (1985) *British Telecom's Procurement of Digital Exchanges*, London: Oftel.

Peterson, J. (1991) 'Technology Policy in Europe: Explaining the Framework Programme and EUREKA in Theory and Practice', *Journal of Common Market Studies*, XXIX, 3: 269–90.

Prévot, H. (1989) *Rapport de synthèse*, Paris: PTE Ministry.

Roussel, A. -M. (1993) 'French Telecom Opens Up to Competition (Slowly)', *Data Communications*, October: 8–11.

Sally, R. (1993) 'Alcatel's Relations with the French State: The Political Economy of a Multinational Enterprise', *Communications et Stratégies*, 9: 67–95.

Sandholtz, W. (1992) *High–Tech Europe*, Berkeley, Los Angeles and Oxford: University of California Press.

Schmidt, S. (1991) 'Taking the Long Road to Liberalization. Telecommunications Reform in the Federal Republic of Germany', *Telecommunications Policy*, 15, 3: 209–22.

Schneider, V. and Werle, R. (1990) 'International Regime or Corporate Actor? The European Community in Telecommunications Policy', in Dyson, K. and Humphreys, P. (eds) *The Political Economy of Telecommunications*, London and New York: Routledge.

Schreiber, K. (1991) 'The New Approach to Technical Harmonization and Standards', in L. Hurwitz and C. Lequesne (eds) *The State of the European Community*, Harlow: Longman.

Thatcher, M. (1993) 'Examining explanations of public policy making: Industrial policy in Britain and France in the case of the telecommunications sector, 1969–1990, D.Phil. thesis, University of Oxford.

—— (1995) 'Regulatory Reform and Internationalisation in Telecommunications', in Hayward, J.E.S. (ed.) *Industrial Enterprise and European Integration: From National to International Champions in Western Europe*, Oxford: Oxford University Press.

Ungerer, H. and Costello, P. (1988) *Telecommunications in Europe*, Luxemburg: CEC.

11 Television

Matthew William Fraser

TELEVISION WITHOUT FRONTIERS: DECODING THE EUROPEAN UNION'S BROADCASTING POLICY

When once asked for his opinion on European television, Jacques Delors quipped: 'It's a French or British viewer watching an American programme on a Japanese television set.' The former EU president's frustrated comment on the state of the European television industry summed up perfectly why, in the early 1980s, the European Commission decided to take policy action in the broadcasting field.

When the Commission first announced its 'Television Without Frontiers' policy in 1984, it was an essentially pro-market project whose objective was to develop a pan-European broadcasting market by encouraging the emergence of new commercial operators. This was to be accomplished through a minimalist approach to harmonisation of national standards in areas such as advertising, copyright payments, right-of-reply provisions and the protection of minors against pornography. The Commission was convinced that the explosion of new media technologies, and the resulting incapacity of nation states to regulate them, would necessitate a supranational approach. The Commission, moreover, saw the television industry as part of a broader, EU-led industrial strategy in the high-tech sector: European television programme producers would create the software, while the European consumer electronics industry furnished the hardware, and an EU standard for 'high definition' television and digital satellite delivery would be set. For the Commission itself, this broadcasting initiative was an expression of its own institutional ambition to intervene in a new policy area.

The Commission's policy was therefore an essentially neofunctionalist strategy aimed at accelerating European integration by unleashing the commercial dynamism of transnational actors in previously closed national television markets. It was a well-timed strategy in the early 1980s, when state monopolies in broadcasting systems were being threatened by the commercial opportunities created by new technologies such as cable and satellite. The Commission correctly predicted these developments. It overestimated, however, the speed with which changes would occur. The long-awaited communications revolution would not arrive in Europe until the mid-1990s. The Commission, moreover, underestimated the capacity of national governments and interest groups to resist, albeit temporarily, the profound changes taking place in the broadcasting sector. Indeed, the 'Television Without Frontiers' policy quickly ran into the very national obstacles that it was hoping to dismantle. As in the telecommunications sector, nation states in Europe jealously insisted on maintaining control over a national *chasse-gardée*, particularly as television has traditionally been considered an indispensable instrument of national unity, and in some cases of political control. Furthermore, state-owned television networks and their production unions have traditionally benefited from tight, corporatist-style arrangements with their national governments, and these interest groups, too, felt threatened by a liberalised, pan-European television market.

In 1986, the Commission was forced to redraft its broadcasting policy in order to appease these national (mainly French) lobbies, who were demanding a more *dirigiste* approach to protect European television from massive imports of American programmes. Specifically, a minimum 60 per cent quota on European programmes was imposed on television channels. The revised policy met vigorous opposition, both in Europe and abroad. First, the Council of Europe, the EC's institutional rival which considered cultural matters to be its exclusive jurisdiction, opposed the Commission's foray into broadcasting. Second, and perhaps more importantly, the United States objected to an EC 'industrial' policy which threatened to curb imports of American films and television programmes. In the end, the combined pressure from the USA, the Council of Europe, the free-trade-orientated EC governments (mainly Britain) and a number of powerful lobbies forced another last-minute revision of the policy. In 1989, the *dirigiste* aspects of the Directive were watered down before it was adopted by the Council of Ministers.

In 1994, after five years of clear non-compliance with the Directive by member states, the Commission announced a 'reform' of the Directive in an effort further to liberalise EU broadcasting regulation at a time of rapid globalisation of the audio-visual industry. In early 1996, that reform was still being debated within EU institutions, but with the addition of Austria, Sweden and Finland to the European Union the forces of liberalisation appeared to enjoy a clear majority. The Directive was now, after more than a decade of institutional and multilateral rivalry, taking on the ideological pigmentation of the original pro-market document of 1984.

It will be argued in this chapter that EU broadcasting policy was intended chiefly to challenge state authority over the broadcasting sector, but it failed – in the short term – due to the power of the member states to maintain control over their sectoral policy networks. National governments were also able to thwart the EU policy inside the Council of Ministers, where a drawn-out process of intergovernmental bargaining eventually led to the last-minute compromise that fudged the Directive's orientation. This assertion of state autonomy *vis-à-vis* the EU proved insufficient and short-lived, however, as international political and economic pressures eventually forced national governments to adopt the same deregulatory policies they were opposing, albeit for different reasons, at the EU level. In the mid-1990s, the EU's so-called 'big bang' telecommunications policy further pushed the European communications sector towards deregulation by 1998. In the meantime, the Directive has done little to promote a pan-European broadcasting market, much less a European cultural identity.

NATIONAL BROADCASTING POLICY IN EUROPE: HEROISM OR MUDDLE?

In the 1980s, broadcasting in Europe underwent a veritable revolution. While its consequences have been political and economic, its underlying structural cause was essentially technological. The introduction of new technologies marked a rupture between so-called 'old media' and 'new media' (Negrine and Papathanassopoulos 1990: Ch 2). Until about 1980, most Europeans were still familiar with the old media technologies, particularly terrestrial television with its mere handful of off-air channels picked up by aerial. In the 1980s, however, the new media revolution introduced – at first slowly and then rapidly after 1990 – cable television, video-cassettes, direct-to-home broadcast satellites, digital video compression, and eventually total multi-media convergence. Each of these two phases had its own essential character-istics and each, moreover, attracted a set of dominant sectoral actors who forged a normative consensus about the legitimacy of these media, and thus benefited from a quasi-exclusive right to exploit them.

The old media order was, in the first place, public service orientated and state-controlled. This was in part technologically determined: since the off-air Hertzian band offered a limited number of over-the-air frequencies, televi-sion channels were deemed a scarce public resource and therefore submitted to the same public utility principles as gas, petrol, water and telecommunica-tions. Second, old media systems remained, for cultural and linguistic reasons, essentially national in scope and character. Futhermore, terrestrial television signals could travel only short distances and hence remained within national borders. Third, the old media tended to be politicised due to the pressures inherent in state control. Finally, the old media were essentially non-commercial. Most public television networks were financed by licence fees levied on television sets, and consequently were not dependent on adver-tising revenues.

The technological explosion of the 1980s transformed these four basic characteristics of the European broadcasting landscape. Cable and satellite television offered consumers a multitude of new private channels, while video-cassettes and satellite television brought competing conduits for home entertainment. In 1980, for example, there were only two commercial televi-sion networks in the twelve EU countries. A decade later, there were thirty-two private channels and thirty-one public channels (Brants and Siune 1992:

102). The content of television, due to the pressures of advertising, consequently became more commercial in character. This new commercial orientation – stressing consumerist reflexes rather than the citizenship values which public television tends to reinforce – was part of the broader ideological paradigm change from the Welfare State to a free-market model.

The main consequence of this paradigm shift was a serious challenge to state-owned broadcasting monopolies. Responses by states varied, at least initially, according to national policy styles and political cultures. In many cases, governments responded willingly to what they saw as the new deregulation consensus by announcing bold, pro-market policy initiatives. Some policies, with a keener eye on national objectives, favoured creating 'national champions' capable of competing, and flag-waving, in the global media market. But such bravado was often undermined by incoherent policies reflecting contradictory ambitions – or 'heroic muddle', as it has been aptly described (Dyson and Humphreys 1985: 162–379). On the one hand, proactively liberal governments, such as Britain's during the Thatcher years, saw their pro-market fervour tempered by entrenched interests within traditional broadcasting elites; on the other hand, states with a strong *dirigiste* tradition, such as France, adopted a state-led approach, but were forced to make concessions to sectoral pressures exerted by the new commercial operators.

When Margaret Thatcher became Prime Minister in 1979, the new media technologies were just beginning to take off in Europe. The timing could not have been better: the new media technologies offered a perfect commercial vector for Thatcher's much-vaunted 'enterprise culture'. In addition, the new commercial possibilities of the broadcasting sector gave Thatcher the opportunity to shake up the existing broadcasting establishment whose power the Prime Minister profoundly resented. Not only was Thatcher convinced that the BBC and ITV networks were politically hostile towards the Tories, but she was also determined to break the BBC–ITV duopoly's privileged market position.

Media policies during the Thatcher era had two main characteristics. First, policy making was highly centralised, often restricted to the Cabinet Office, or discussions between the Prime Minister and a few 'dry' ministers, frequently the Trade and Industry Secretary. As Jeremy Tunstall put it: 'A maverick field like communications policy – which knows no boundaries – is tailor made for Prime Ministerial interference' (Tunstall and Palmer 1990: 221). A Cabinet Committee on the Media officially existed, but in fact it never met. Second, broadcasting policy under Thatcher was 'industry-led'. The government not only adopted policies aimed at favouring the emergence of new private sector actors, but it also exclusively consulted private sector lobbies – who were viewed as 'outsiders' by the BBC–ITV elite – before drafting policies.

Thatcher's centralised, industry-led approach was a calculated snub to the traditional broadcasting policy community, which was dominated by the closed world of the BBC–ITV duopoly and officials from the sector's sponsoring ministry, the Home Office. The British broadcasting establishment corresponded to the classic definition of a policy community: it was a discreet, informal network of like-minded individuals who were acutely conscious of their 'insider' status. Most came from Oxbridge, and were attached to establishment values emphasising the virtue of public service, professionalism and self-regulation. In his book on the BBC, Tom Burns has called it a 'social-industrial complex' (Burns 1977: 42).

Throughout the 1980s, Thatcher showed a persistent determination to break the BBC–ITV establishment. Thatcher's satellite television policy showed all the hallmarks of her government's centralised, industry-led media policy. Satellite television offered the Thatcher government an ideal industrial project that would be led by industry and financed solely by private funds. The project, called UNISAT, was to be led by a consortium of companies, including the former state-owned British Telecom and British Aerospace, both now privatised. When the government turned to the question of television programmes, however, the choice of a software partner was unexpected: the BBC. However contradictory, the partnership with the BBC was meant to add a 'buy British' philosophy that would reinforce the project's political appeal. Still, the presence of the BBC, which was keen to launch a satellite channel as a way of preventing the market entry of potential competitors, led to the consortium's collapse. Opposed by a government-sponsored programme consortium called the 'Club of 21' – made up of private companies such as Thorn-EMI, Virgin and Granada – the BBC pulled out of the project in 1985. The result was that the project, plagued by prohibitive costs, technical problems and infighting among interest groups, failed to get off the ground for several years.

Satellite television was a perfect example of a bold Thatcherite policy that got bogged down in its own policy contradictions, principally due to confusion about the state's role in promoting the industry. On the one hand, the government felt the need to pursue an industrial strategy to promote British industries. On the other, it wanted to pursue a policy compatible with the Thatcherite *laissez-faire* principle. In the end, the satellite television policy combined a bit of both – and consequently failed.

It was not until the early 1990s, after the money-losing Sky TV and BSB channels merged to form BSkyB that satellite television took off in Britain. Indeed, the most ironic twist in the satellite television policy flip-flop was the BBC's important role in the process. The BBC would eventually enter into a joint venture with BSkyB owner Rupert Murdoch in a satellite television sports channel. The BBC, moreover, later launched its own satellite channel, called UK Gold, in tandem with the ITV station Thames.

Thatcher was more successful in her attempt to prise open the tight world of the BBC–ITV duopoly. The Prime Minister made no secret of the fact that she opposed the ITV network's monopoly on commercial revenues (due to the absence of the BBC in the advertising market). She announced that, as part of the Tory government's new Broadcasting Act (1990), the

ITV stations would be put up for auction. In so doing, Thatcher hoped to break up the ITV side of the traditional broadcasting establishment by bringing in new commercial operators. The political advantage of the manoeuvre was that the new ITV owners, grateful for having won lucrative television franchises, presumably would be more favourably disposed towards the Conservatives.

This time Thatcher's strategy produced more immediate results. Following the 1990 Broadcasting Act, the sixteen ITV stations were put up for sale. The following year, four of the existing ITV franchises, including the big Thames station, vanished overnight when their owners lost their licence renewal bids. Several other franchises were, as Thatcher had hoped, sold off to new commercial operators from outside the broadcasting establishment. The most powerful player in the new ITV landscape was Carlton television's owner Michael Green, a broadcasting outsider with close personal ties to Thatcher through his friendship with the Trade and Industry Secretary, Lord Young. Granada's new owner, an unknown Irish businessman called Gerry Robinson, promptly fired Granada president, David Plowright, a pillar of the broadcasting establishment. Many observers none the less noted the conservative nature of the process. Fewer bidders than expected had come forward, and most of the licences were won by their erstwhile holders. Moreover, some Thatcher-backed candidates saw their bids turned down by the new regulatory body in charge of the bidding, the Independent Television Commission.

There could be no doubt, however, that the ITV franchise affair dealt a serious blow to the existing BBC–ITV establishment. In the early 1990s the BBC was unquestionably attempting to adjust – or at least be seen to be doing so – to the new commercial realities of Britain's broadcasting sector. It's entry into commercial satellite broadcasting was a sign that the public network, like ITV, was changing with the times. While developments in the UK broadcasting sector foreshadowed the pro-market trend elsewhere in Europe, during the 1980s the corporatist reflexes of established actors were sufficient to at least buffer, and delay, the effects of deregulation.

After more than a decade in power, Thatcher realised, to her everlasting regret, that the BBC and ITV networks would have to be a part of whatever changes the Tories hoped to impose on the broadcasting sector. Her heroic, deregulatory approach to broadcasting policy also came into conflict with her personal desire to maintain political control over the broadcasting system, even over the content of television programmes. This was due not only to Thatcher's suspicion of the BBC and ITV as ideologically hostile to her, but also to her stern moral views about what should, and should not, be aired on television (Davidson 1992: 6–12). This fundamental contradiction – between *laissez-faire* and political control – led the Tories to pursue muddled broadcasting policies. As the *Financial Times* put it: 'UK broadcasting policy has simply failed to keep up, marked as it was with the self-contradictions of the Thatcher era: her desire to deregulate on the one hand, but her taste for an ever sterner moral and political oversight on the other. The result was muddle and U-turn' (Hargreaves 1993).

When out of office, Thatcher said, for her part, in her 1993 memoirs:

> Broadcasting was one of a number of areas in which special pleading by powerful interest groups was disguised as a high-minded commitment to some greater good. So, anyone who queried, as I did, whether a licence fee was the best way to pay for the BBC, was likely to be pilloried as at best a philistine and at worse undermining its consititutional independence.
>
> (Thatcher 1993: 264)

French media policies in the 1980s were, like the British experience, 'heroic' in their inspiration but in reality got muddled for reasons of political expedience, lack of coherence and contradictory objectives. President François Mitterrand shared Thatcher's penchant for a highly centralised form of decision making and political control of the broadcasting system; but whereas Thatcher encouraged industry-led initiatives, the French government favoured a state-centred approach to policy initiatives in the audio-visual sector.

Still, the French Socialists could not resist the deregulatory fervour sweeping western democracies at the time. While the French government did not follow the British example of privatising its state-owned telecommunications company, it opted to liberalise radio and television. This was in fact less contradictory than it might have seemed. Mitterrand had long suffered politically as an opposition figure under Gaullist control of the media. In 1981, his policy of liberalisation was partly intended to shake up, indeed to clean out, the old Gaullist broadcasting establishment. In that respect, Mitterrand, like Thatcher, cleverly exploited the principle of deregulation to remove perceived enemies in the broadcasting elite.

France's traditional broadcasting policy community was, like Britain's, dominated by public television. Relations between the state and the television industry were, as in Britain, based on corporatist arrangements. Unlike Britain, however, France had a strong, state-backed movie industry, and its production lobbies maintained.intimate contacts with the Ministry of Culture. The television lobbies, notably the private networks and producers after 1986, tended to deal with the Ministry of Communication. The result was that, with the Elysée and the Prime Minister's office, Matignon, perched above these two ministries, broadcasting policy often suffered from bureaucratic fragmentation. Neither presidential co-ordination nor the omnipresence of *énarque* technocrats placed strategically throughout this fragmented administrative structure could impose coherence on the decision-making process.

Throughout the 1980s, the French government switched from a heroic, state-driven policy approach to a more improvised approach that was sensitive to industry and commercial considerations. France's satellite television policy illustrated that transition. Like Britain, France was eager to seize the industrial opportunities afforded by Direct Broadcasting by Satellite (DBS) television. France was particularly eager to launch a DBS project as a defensive move against Luxemburg's medium-powered, commercial satellite projects, which it condemned as a 'Trojan horse' for American television programmes. But France's DBS project fell victim to the familiar administrative quarrels between the Direction Générale des Télécommunications of the telecom department and TDF, the state-owned satellite agency (Cohen 1992: 130). Each had its own satellite project. A compromise was eventually found by going forward with both projects at once, which only aggravated the DGT–TDF rivalry, as each was using its own satellite (De Closets 1992: 423). In 1985, the entire DBS scheme suffered a serious setback when Mitterrand created new private television terrestrial networks. With new terrestrial channels offerred to the public for free, why would viewers subscribe to costly satellite services? The DBS project, moreover, suffered from the classic French obsession with *hardware* aspects of industrial policy – transponders, high-tech tubes and costly satellite launches. The policy overlooked the all-important *software* questions of DBS-delivered television programmes and who was going to provide them. Luxemburg's Astra satellite had not overlooked those questions, and hence quickly took the lead in the DBS market.

After the neo-Gaullist election victory in 1986, Prime Minster Jacques Chirac immediately set about overturning the Socialists' broadcasting policy, but proved more than willing to play by the same rules. The licences for the new networks, La Cinq and M6, were revoked and given to friends of the neo-Gaullists – notably press baron Robert Hersant, who became the controlling shareholder of La Cinq. Chirac was ready to jettison the delay-plagued DBS project altogether, but at the last minute was persuaded by the industry lobby's warning that British, Japanese and Luxemburg satellites would soon relegate France to a second-rate power if it did not move forward with its own national DBS project. It was just the kind of argument – heavy on lofty symbolism about France's national *grandeur* – to which the French government, particularly the neo-Gaullists, were sure to be sensitive (Noam 1991: 305). Chirac in fact decided to save the satellite project by raising the stakes: France would develop satellites as part of the new high-definition television revolution. Thus a French *grand projet*, projected on to the European stage, was being exploited to disguise a French policy muddle at home. The French-developed HDTV standard, called D-MAC, would be promoted as a European standard – just as France had attempted to impose its SECAM terrestrial television standard on Europe in the 1960s. The HDTV satellite project was, not surprisingly, handed over to state-owned France Télécom (Cohen 1992: 335). France managed to convince the European Commission of the D-MAC technology's merits as an EC-wide standard, but EC governments and television networks were decidedly less enthusiastic. It took several years for the EC's HDTV project finally to unravel in the early 1990s, when the D-MAC standard was finally rejected due to British opposition.

In 1987, Chirac did what Margaret Thatcher would have liked to do with the BBC when he privatised France's biggest public network, TF1. The sale of TF1 – to construction industry magnate Francis Bouygues – dramatically transformed French television, both on and off the screen. On the screen, the other French television networks – including the public channels – became more aggressively commercial as a response to TF1's sudden conversion to popular television programming to attract high ratings. Off the screen, the sudden arrival of new commercial operators radically altered France's broadcasting policy community, with TF1 as a major player. In addition, with a large private network legally obliged to buy privately produced programmes, an independent production sector sprang up. Consequently, the old broadcasting establishment of public networks and their in-house production unions were suddenly challenged by the arrival, in the space of only two years, of four private networks – TF1, La Cinq, M6 and Canal Plus – and a new private producers' lobby. Each camp, moreover, had its own sponsoring bureaucracy – the Ministry of Communications for the private sector and television networks, the Ministry of Culture for the public sector and directors' and actors' guilds. The administrative summit, Matignon and the Elysée Palace, was reserved for 'national champion' players with high-level contacts such as Canal Plus president, André Rousselet, who had been President Mitterrand's closest adviser for more than thirty years.

This dichotomy only further fragmented an already divided policy process. By the early 1990s, French media policies, despite ideological differences, resembled the heroic muddle of Thatcherite policies in Britain. The French government was caught between conflicting priorities of political *dirigisme* and a perceived need to liberalise broadcasting so that 'national champions' could compete internationally. Furthermore, the increasing rivalry between the old and new media players, and the resulting transformation of the broadcasting policy community, rendered certain policy initiatives contradictory. In sum, the French government seemed constantly to be intervening in the broadcasting sector to announce its own retreat.

THE EUROPEAN COMMISSION'S INITIATIVES IN BROADCASTING

No reference to broadcasting was made in the Treaty of Rome. It took thirty-four years, with the signing of the Maastricht Treaty in December 1991, for the word 'culture' to figure in the treaty.

Early attempts at pan-European broadcasting integration were instigated not by the European Commission but by independent organisations and a few national governments. The European Broadcasting Union (EBU), a non-governmental television programme-sharing consortium created in 1950, was an early form of *institutional* integration. The EBU's usefulness for EU integration was limited, however, because it represented only public television networks, including some from countries beyond the EU. Furthermore, the

EBU was essentially a cartel and as such defied the free-market, pro-competition ethos that was driving European integration.

Other efforts to integrate Europe's broadcasting systems have been made through *technical* standards, but these projects have tended to reflect specific national ambitions. France, for example, attempted to impose its colour television picture standard, SECAM, throughout Europe. The SECAM technology ran into direct competition from the German PAL standard, however, while the United States and Canada adopted the NTSC standard. When other EC countries, such as Britain, refused to accept SECAM, France gave up its west European ambitions and resorted to selling the technology throughout eastern Europe, thanks to an accord signed by Charles de Gaulle with the Soviet Union (Noam 1991: 295).

By 1980, the European Commission was keen to impose a *regulatory* form of integration on European broadcasting markets. But since the Commission had no formal basis for intervening in broadcasting, its first priority was to strengthen the EC's legal legitimacy in the sector. To this end, the European Court of Justice became an important institutional ally. In 1974, the Court had ruled that a television programme was by definition a 'service' as defined by the Treaty of Rome, and moreover, that such services had a 'transnational' character. Six years later, it ruled, in the 'Debauve' case, that the EC had the right to ensure a 'minimal harmonisation' of state broadcasting legislation with a view to facilitating the free circulation of audio-visual products (ECR1980). This jurisprudence imposed a constraint on the Commission that would prove fateful for the 'Television Without Frontiers' policy: since television programmes were considered a 'service', the EC was obliged to avoid a *cultural* definition of audio-visual products and insist instead on a strictly *economic* definition. As Jacques Delors declared in 1985: 'Under the Treaty of Rome, the EC does not have the means to impose a cultural policy. It will therefore have to tackle the problem from an economic point of view' (Negrine and Papathanassopoulos 1990: 57).

Given this purely economic definition of audio-visual products, it is not surprising that the EC broadcasting policy was drafted within the Commission's powerful DG III, responsible for internal market questions and industrial affairs. DG X, which is in charge of cultural matters, actually played a minor role in the policy process leading to the Directive's adoption in 1989, though it was later given the difficult task of implementing the Directive. The tension between the two DGs was essentially ideological: the DG III tends to be ultra-liberal and pro-market, while the DG X is more culturally orientated as it must deal with sectoral interest groups such as unions representing television and film producers, directors and actors. This fragmentation within the Commission also explains the lack of coherence of the Directive itself. As each DG had its own ideological orientation and interest group constituency, it was difficult to develop a coherent policy that would be universally supported by the wide variety of concerned interest groups. But between the small DG X, which is staffed mainly with generalists, and the large, horizontal DG III with its battalion of economists and legal experts, the latter was from the outset clearly in charge of the broadcasting policy.

In the early 1980s, few broadcasting interest groups were even active at the EU level. The European advertising lobby, however, was very active in Brussels. The Commission's close relationship with the advertising lobby began in 1975, when the DG III was drafting an EC policy on advertising standards. The policy ended up reflecting the interests of the advertising industry. The European Association of Advertising Agencies (EAAA) even succeeded in convincing Commission officials to define advertising as a 'public service' (Mattelart and Palmer 1991: 535–56).

When DG III officials began to consider drafting a television policy, they again turned to the advertising lobby, now called the European Advertising Tripartite (EAT). The EAT naturally saw television as a vector for commercial messages. This view suited the Commission, as it was obliged to advance an economic definition of television programmes as a 'service'. The resulting alliance between the DG III and the EAT corresponded moreover to the Commission's neofunctionalist ambitions: advertisers were ideal instruments of European integration because they were transnational commercial actors. The advertising lobby was a particularly ideal partner because the European media advertising market was under-exploited commercially, largely due to the domination of non-commercial state monopolies in broadcasting. In 1980, for example, total advertising expenditures in the EC were $18.7 billion, while television advertising was only $2.9 billion – only a quarter of expenditures in the USA advertising market despite comparable population sizes.

While the European advertising lobby was well organised in Brussels, the only comparable broadcasting organisation was the European Broadcasting Union, but at the time its head office was in Geneva. In any case, the EBU was not invited to play an active role in the policy process, for it was, as previously noted, a programme cartel that represented state-controlled public television networks. The Commission in fact sought to limit the EBU's role in a policy initiative that was chiefly aimed at encouraging the expansion of a *private* television industry. Television producers' associations were also absent in Brussels, except as *ad hoc* groups composed of national associations and formed around specific issues. Since the European Commission had no history of intervention in the broadcasting field, most national interest groups saw no need to establish lobbies in Brussels – until the 'Television Without Frontiers' Green Paper appeared in 1984 (CEC 1984).

TELEVISION WITHOUT FRONTIERS: EURO POLICY MUDDLE?

The Commission's 'Television Without Frontiers' Green Paper dealt with four main areas: the new television technologies; the commercial potential of these technologies; the legal competence of the EC to take action in the broadcasting sector, and the role of television in the process of European integration. The most salient aspect of the Green Paper was its interest in the question of television advertising. This was, apart from reflecting the interests of the EAT, an extension of an electoral debate in Germany opposing Social Democrat defenders of non-commercial public television against conservative advocates of commercial channels (Humphreys 1988: 185ff.). The Green Paper, drafted by German legal experts in DG III, called for the speedy creation of commercial television. It recommended, specifically, that a 20 per cent ceiling be put on television advertising – at that time the highest legal level permitted in a EC country (Luxemburg).

National reaction to the Green Paper was almost universally hostile. Many interest groups, notably television directors' and producers' associations, complained that the EC policy was too pro-market and failed to treat television programmes as *cultural* products. Others frankly observed that the Commission had been captured by the advertising lobby (Guillou 1988: 65). While the new private television networks saw no problem with the Green Paper on the question of advertising limits, licence fee-supported public broadcasters were naturally less enthusiastic.

The Commission evidently had made two fundamental errors in drafting the Green Paper. First, it relied too heavily on input from the advertising lobby and as a result excluded other important sectoral interest groups. This oversight was largely due to the fragmented policy-making structure within the Commission itself. Second, the Commission underestimated the power of the public broadcasting lobby, the EBU. The EBU was particularly hostile to the EC initiative, whose position in favour of commercial broadcasting challenged the EBU's very *raison d'être* as a programme consortium for public networks. Commercial television, particularly satellite television, threatened to undermine the EBU's main function as a cartel that buys sports and information programming on behalf of it members (Noam 1991: 291).

In 1985, the European Commission was renewed with Jacques Delors as president. Within a year, the Commission announced its broadcasting Directive, also called 'Television Without Frontiers' (CEC 1986). The Directive took a much more protectionist stance than the Green Paper. First of all, it tightened up some of the Green Paper's light-touch provisions, such as the 20 per cent advertising ceiling, which was lowered to 15 per cent. The Directive also imposed two different quotas on television networks: a minimum quota of 60 per cent on 'European' programmes, and a production quota obliging networks to devote at least 10 per cent of their programming budgets to the purchase of programmes from independent producers. These measures were inspired by identical quotas in France, whose former socialist finance minister was none other than Monsieur Delors.

This sudden policy shift, from pro-market position to a more protectionist approach, can be explained to a large extent by the hostile reactions to the Green Paper. Much of the outcry had come from France's heavily regulated and state-financed film and television lobby, which claimed that the lack of French-style quotas imposed on European television networks would incite broadcasters to buy cheap American products. The quota did in fact anger EC television networks: as television was becoming increasingly commercial in the late 1980s, many networks were indeed buying large quantities of popular American programmes to maintain high ratings. In France, however, private networks in 1986 had only just been created and therefore had little influence on the French position concerning the Directive. France had, after the USA, the world's second largest audio-visual industry in terms of exports, and so any restriction on the inflow of American programmes promised, in theory, to increase French audio-visual exports within the EC. Not surprisingly, an outspoken critic of the Directive was the powerful Hollywood lobby, the Motion Picture Export Association of America. Its president, Jack Valenti, a former White House adviser under Lyndon Johnson, vociferously denounced the European broadcasting policy as 'protectionist' and pressured EU governments to vote against it.

The debate was further complicated by the institutional rivalry between the Commission and the Council of Europe, which in 1986 had drafted its own broadcasting 'convention'. The Council of Europe's broadcasting policy reflected the organisation's non-binding, intergovernmental approach to European integration. That sat well with the certain EC countries, especially the UK, which was adamantly opposed to the Directive's more supranational approach. The Thatcher government, heavily pressured by the Reagan administration to oppose the Directive, warned the Commission that it would recognise only the Council of Europe's authority in broadcasting unless the Directive's quotas were removed.

This sudden surge of national and international opposition to the Directive had the effect of shifting the EC decision making process away from the Commission and towards the Council of Ministers. As a result, the broadcasting policy, which had been a Commission-led, functionalist-inspired initiative, now became a process of intense intergovernmental bargaining. In this new context of crisis, the Commission's role was reduced from that of a corporate actor to that of an embattled mediator (Nguyen 1988: 106). The Commission was particularly caught between the European Parliament, where a majority of MPs embraced France's position in favour of high protectionist quotas, and the Council of Ministers where the only country resolutely behind the quotas was France (Dupagne 1992: 99–122).

The Council of Europe's foray into the debate proved fatal for the Directive. Faced with anti-Directive opposition by EC member states within the Council of Ministers, in 1988 the Commission decided to cede to Britain's pressure. Thus the Directive's provisions were watered down to make them compatible with the Council of Europe's non-binding convention. Specifically, the 60 per cent quota was altered to state that a 'majority' of European programmes would have to be broadcast by television channels, but only 'where practicable'.

France initially fought this compromise within the Council of Ministers, but quickly realised that it was isolated on the issue. In the spring of 1989,

France finally agreed – after a stormy exchange between Paris and Brussels that was played out in the press – to accept the compromise. France imposed one condition, however: that the EC agree to subsidise the audio-visual production industry. A fund, called Eureka Audiovisual, was therefore created to operate in tandem with the nascent MEDIA project, which had been allotted a $247 million budget over five years starting in 1990. The Eureka fund was accorded a five-year budget of roughly $180 million.

The Directive was adopted on 3 October 1989. Only Belgium and Denmark voted against it. At the Council of Ministers meeting in Luxemburg, Germany and the UK obtained a last-minute insertion: the European 'majority' quota would be 'politically binding' but not 'legally binding' on EC member states. This meant essentially that enforcement of the quota could not be upheld by the European Court of Justice.

THE IMPACT OF EU BROADCASTING POLICY

The impact of the 'Television Without Frontiers' policy on national broadcasting policies was very limited, at least in the short term. The elaboration and adoption of the policy was influenced, at the most critical moments, by essentially national agendas. Consequently, the policy was designed to produce – with the exception of the outstanding issue of programme quotas – a minimal impact on national broadcasting systems. In the longer term, however, the EC broadcasting policy has served as a legal instrument which, in tandem with international market forces, would begin pushing EC national governments towards increasing deregulation in the sector.

National opposition to the Directive initially was varied, though most of it came from northern EC governments. Denmark categorically refused to recognise the EC's legitimacy in the broadcasting sector, mainly because the Danish government wished to maintain closer cultural links with Scandinavian countries belonging to the Nordic Council. The UK, for its part, took the view that the EC policy threatened to 'interfere' in the traditional independence of British television networks. Germany, on the other hand, claimed it could not accept a EC broadcasting policy because German television was the exclusive domain of the regional *Länder*. Luxemburg, whose CLT network is the most commercial broadcaster in Europe, naturally opposed the quotas. Ireland and the Netherlands tended to be sensitive to American pressures against the Directive (the US government had threatened to exclude the Dutch electronics giant, Philips, from an American 'high definition' television project if the Dutch government voted in favour of the Directive). Belgium's French-language producers sided with the French position, but the Belgian government opposed the Directive because it offered no funding projects for regional television production, which Belgium's Flemish producers had been demanding.

Southern countries – Spain, Italy, Portugal and Greece – supported the Directive, if only half-heartedly, because they shared France's tradition of heavily state-regulated broadcasting systems. As relatively poor countries, they were also hoping that EC funds would flow to their weak audio-visual production industries. But as deregulation took off in the late 1980s, even these governments were increasingly pressured by new private broadcasters, who were heavily dependent on cheaply purchased American programmes. This was particularly true in Italy, where Silvio Berlusconi's private stations were successfully competing with the three state-owned RAI channels.

Most of the debate over the Directive, however, was dominated by an ideological stand-off between the UK and France. The British government's insistence on preserving national control over its broadcasting system was motivated by three factors. First, the Thatcher government was ideologically hostile to European integration and so naturally opposed the EC's policy initiative in a politically sensitive sector. Second, the British government was acutely sensitive to the US opposition to the Directive's quotas (the USA threatened to stop buying British television programmes if the UK voted in favour of the Directive). Third, the UK's media policies tended to be formulated, despite Thatcherism, in the closed neo-corporatist world of the BBC–ITV Home Office establishment, and consequently showed little interest in policies beyond the UK's borders (Tunstall 1984: 324).

This last point explains why the British government managed to ignore a major contradiction in its position against the EU quotas. The Thatcher government opposed the quotas on the grounds that they violated the time-honoured British principle of broadcasting 'independence'. Yet similar quotas constitute one of the central pillars of the British broadcasting system. Indeed, the BBC–ITV duopoly has long been used to a high (86 per cent) quota on British programmes. This quota was set, largely to placate unions, after a so-called 'gentlemen's agreement' when the ITV network was created in the 1950s (Collins 1990: 155). In the early 1980s, moreover, the new independent television production sector benefited from a similar measure: Channel 4 was obliged to buy 25 per cent of its programmes from independent producers. Thanks largely to these neo-corporatist arrangements, the UK's BBC–ITV dominated broadcasting sector has always been well protected against foreign television programmes. When UK broadcasters have looked to the outside world, they have tended, for linguistic reasons, to turn towards the United States and Commonwealth countries such as Australia and Canada.

The BBC–ITV duopoly had other reasons for opposing the Directive. Both networks were launching new satellite channels, partly as a way of blocking the entry of other commercial operators, but also to get a head start in transnational satellite services in the global market. They knew, like other broadcasters, that satellite television would entail a heavy reliance on cheap stocks of readily available American programming. As the European quotas threatened to undermine the commercial viability of satellite channels, they had to be opposed. This put the BBC–ITV duopoly in the contradictory position of defending their regulated, quota-based privileges in the UK while denouncing similar European measures proposed by the European Commission. However contradictory, it turned out to be a shrewd tactic. The early joint ventures between the BBC and Thames in 'UK Gold', and between the BBC and Rupert Murdoch in a satellite sports channel, showed how the UK's changing television landscape could produce the most unexpected alliances. In 1994, the BBC turned its back on Murdoch and joined up with the Pearson media group to launch two pan-European satellite channels – one all news, the other devoted to entertainment – as a way of competing with Murdoch's Sky TV on the Continent.

France's tireless defence of a protectionist Directive was a scarcely veiled attempt to impose its own broadcasting model at the European level. This strategy of policy hegemony was typical of France's attitude towards the EC (Mény 1989: 387–99). In this case, however, it entailed a fundamental contradiction which was precisely the opposite of the UK paradox: while France was attempting to impose a *dirigiste* model at the EC level, the French government was in fact *liberalising* its domestic broadcasting system. The French strategy was aimed at unleashing 'national champions' like Canal Plus through deregulation at home, while imposing EC regulations as protection for French transnational broadcasters in the global market. There was even talk in France of promoting an 'Airbus audio-visuel' for Europe.

Still, if France was pursuing a 'national champion' policy for its big television networks and communications groups, it none the less had to deal with corporatist lobbies from the film and television production industries. Indeed, the French broadcasting policy network remained surprisingly dominated by these lobbies throughout the 1980s. Their influence made France's concession on the EC quotas difficult to sell at home. Thus after conceding on the quotas in Brussels, the French government attempted to placate domestic lobbies by increasing its *national* quota on French-language television programmes from 40 per cent to 50 per cent. In other words, France attempted to *re-nationalise* the EC policy with tougher restrictions applied domestically. The European Commission promptly opposed this move, and succeeded in rallying to its side French commercial television networks and producers, which created an *ad hoc* lobby called 'Télévision de demain'. The French government eventually backed down by lowering the French-language quota to 40 per cent to open the door to more non-French EC programmes. It was a victory for the Commission, thanks to its alliance with French sectoral actors who favoured, at least in principle, a lighter national regulatory regime. The episode proved that, in the face of deregulation and pressures from commercial lobbies, even classic corporatist reflexes were no longer working in France.

Since the Directive went into effect on 3 October 1991, its implementation has been largely a history of national non-compliance. The Commission has instigated infringement proceedings against most EU member states, the most delinquent of which has been the UK. On a number of occasions, the Commission has warned the UK that its broadcasters have not been respecting the 'majority' quota on European programmes, particularly satellite channels such as Murdoch-controlled BSkyB and Ted Turner's non-domestic channels operating in Europe with UK licences. Murdoch and Turner have cleverly invoked the Directive's legal opt-out clause, which states that the quotas must be respected 'where practicable'. According to BSkyB, adherence to the EU quotas is not 'practicable' because the satellite channel is still not profitable. The Turner group claims that respecting EU quotas on his Cartoon Network and all-film TNT channel is similarly not 'practicable', because cartoons and films are overwhelmingly American. Unimpressed, in March 1994 the Commission began a legal action against the UK government. The UK was accused of failing to comply with the 'Television Without Frontiers' Directive by granting British link-up licences to satellite channels to non-EU channels such as Turner's TNT and Cartoon Channel. The Commission argued that satellite channels should not be given a licence based on the country of up-link alone, which is the UK practice, but should have their place of business established in a member state. In the three years since the UK's Broadcasting Act was passed in 1990, the ITC regulatory body granted more than sixty satellite non-domestic licences. Once again, the UK has been cast in the role of the 'Trojan horse' for American cultural imperialism.

The question of television advertising and sponsorship has been another implementation obstacle. For one thing, the European advertising lobby, which was instrumental in drafting the early Green Paper version of the EU policy, later became sceptical about imposing pan-European advertising standards on different national cultures. Television channels meanwhile have not been abiding by the 15 per cent ceiling on advertising. The Commission's DG X – which has been put in charge of the Directive's implementation – has warned Italy, Spain, Greece, Germany and Denmark about flouting the Directive's rules on advertising limits. But there seems little the Commission can do except take its case before the European Court of Justice, which it is reluctant to do. As a media law expert from the UK told the *Wall Street Journal*: 'This is a good example of quite a widespread problem in European law. To get a Directive through, member states are happy to accept ambiguous wording. But they are only postponing the problem to when they transpose it into national law' (*Wall Street Journal* 1994).

Other issues, such as copyright and right-to-replay provisions, proved so contentious due to conflicting national practices that they had to be removed altogether from the Directive and dealt with separately. The EU funding programmes, EUREKA and MEDIA, have been greeted with mixed reactions by interest groups. Both programmes are French-style funding bodies which have inspired everything from total indifference to open hostility. The British government wanted the MEDIA fund to be closed down (Collins 1994: 89–102). In truth, neither fund was particularly effective in its first five years, due largely to the small amounts involved. For example, the $50 million that MEDIA dispensed annually from 1989 to 1994 is approximately equivalent to the budgets of two Hollywood films. If the funding bodies have not succeeded in creating a healthy pan-European audio-visual industry, they have helped to reinforce the EU's legitimacy *vis-à-vis* interest groups as the dispenser of subsidies, however modest.

The Commission has also been pursuing a competition policy in the audio-visual sector. In the past, merger controls in the media have been a strictly national matter, though laws have varied widely from country to country. In France, no single investor could own more than 25 per cent of a television network, though after coming to power in 1993 the neo-Gaullist government increased that ceiling to 49 per cent. In the UK, there are no ownership restrictions in the cable market, and the 1990 Broadcasting Act dramatically relaxed ownership regulations on the private ITV franchises. These moves towards fewer restrictions have been interpreted as a possible pre-emptive strike against media ownership regulation at the EU level. In 1992, the Commission published a Green Paper on 'Pluralism and Media Concentration' whose aim was to give the EC powers to curb undue concentration in the sector. The tension between national and EU initiatives is thus patent: France and the UK and other countries are loosening concentration rules, while the EU appears to be moving towards tightening regulations.

So far, however, the European Commission's rulings on anti-competitive practices have been inconsistent. In 1990 the satellite sports channel Screensport (in which W.H. Smith was a major shareholder) complained to the Commission that its competitor Eurosport (jointly owned by Rupert Murdoch's Sky TV and European Broadcasting Union members such as the BBC) was prohibiting its access to sporting events. The basis of the complaint was that, despite the partnership with Murdoch, the EBU was a public broadcasting consortium that was abusing its cartel power to inhibit competition for the rights to transmit sporting events. In early 1991, the Commission accepted Screensport's argument and struck down the EBU-Sky partnership as anti-competitive. In 1993, Eurosport was relaunched by France's TF1 and Canal Plus networks in tandem with the big American television network, ABC.

In the case of United International Pictures (UIP), however, the Hollywood film cartel in Europe, the Commission has been more indulgent. UIP was created in 1981 by three big Hollywood studios (MGM, Paramount, and Universal) to jointly distribute their films in foreign markets. Throughout the 1980s, the Commission complained that UIP was a cartel and therefore violated Article 85 of the Treaty of Rome. In 1988, however, the Commission granted UIP a five-year exemption on the grounds that it provided 'economic benefits' to Europe's audio-visual sector. That assertion was disputed by members of the EC film industry, who pointed out that UIP had invested nothing in European audio-visual production. None the less, when UIP's exemption expired in July 1993, the Commission was so divided on the matter that, benefiting from a lack of decision, UIP was accorded a *de facto* extension of its exemption. On the other hand, in November 1994 EU competition commissioner Karel Van Miert, after launching a full inquiry into the German consortium, Media Services – owned jointly by three large groups (Bertelsmann, Deutsche Bundesposte Telekom (DBT) and Kirsch-gruppe) – vetoed the merger. The Commission had been worried that the proposed consortium, which specialises in pay-television services, would impose its decoding standard on the pay-television market and this would constitute a breach of fair competition rules. DBT, which dominates the German cable television market, already owned a significant stake in the Luxemburg-based firm that operates the Astra satellite; and Bertelsmann and Kirch are part owners of Germany's only pay-television channel, Premiere.

CONCLUSION

National non-compliance and limited enthusiasm for the EU's bold vision of a dynamic pan-European broadcasting market is a sign that, in the first several years of the Directive's implementation, governments are reinterpret-ing EU rules, often in imaginative ways, to suit their own purposes. The EU, with no regulatory body backed up by the threat of legitimate physical con-straint, can do little to impose its authority on national television networks and transnational operators.

Still, while early signs are not encouraging, the EU broadcasting policy may well be redeemed by future developments in the global audio-visual industry. As cable and satellite channels finally start to take off in the mid-1990s, national governments are realising that they are powerless to impose their authority on the transnational actors who dominate these markets. The example of Ted Turner's satellite channels offers a perfect illustration of this dilemma. In 1993 when Turner launched, thanks to a UK link-up licence, the TNT and Cartoon Network, the channels were beamed across Europe from the Luxemburg satellite, Astra. The French and Belgian governments, furious at the UK's indulgence towards Turner's media interests in Europe, promptly banned their regulated cable companies from offering the two American channels to their subscribers on the grounds that they failed to respect the EU's 'majority' quota on European programming. The controversy over the Turner channels put the European Commission in an awkward situation. If it failed to resolve the issue at the European level, it would risk seeing its authority diminished if countries like France decided to react by taking measures at the national level. The fact that France and Belgium invoked the EU policy was a sign, however, that they were confessing their own incapacity to regulate the new television technologies and were counting on the Com-mission to take necessary legal action before the European Court of Justice.

In late 1993, the GATT negotiations, in which the EU audio-visual indus-try won a temporary 'exemption' from the multilateral trade accord, gave a decided boost to the EU's legitimacy in the broadcasting sector. The USA had demanded, among other things, that American audio-visual products not be restricted by quotas and that the 'Television Without Frontiers' Direct-ive should not apply to new television technologies. At stake in the GATT negotiations was the very principle of subsidies for film and television production. While most European countries – and the EU itself with its MEDIA and Eureka funds – subsidise their audio-visual industries, the Hollywood industry receives no subsidies in the USA. The USA therefore was calling for the audio-visual sector to come under the 'market access' and 'national treatment' provisions of the GATT, which in effect would have put an end to European subsidies. The GATT talks cast the EU in the role of a supranational state undertaking negotiations within the framework of an international regime. The GATT accord was not merely about co-ordinating policy to correct a market failure, but about the distributional consequences brought about by the emergence of the EU as a single actor looking to protect its own interests in a strategically important sector that the USA traditionally has dominated (Krasner 1990: 363). In the end, the EU, under tremendous pressure from France, refused to apply the GATT provisions to films and television programmes, which meant a virtual exemption.

In early 1994, the Commission published a new broadcasting Green Paper as part of a comprehensive overhaul of its audio-visual policy. To most observers, this 'reform', which was still moving through EU institutions during the spring of 1996, was a thinly disguised effort to refashion the Directive into a more pro-market, 'light-touch' regulation policy. Failing all else, the new Green Paper was a timely pretext for Commission officials to consult interest groups in an attempt to do what it had failed to do in the past, namely to forge a broadcasting policy network at the EU level. But while extending the MEDIA fund's subsidies promised to attract certain sectoral interests, the general thrust of the reform appeared to be taking a deregulation approach to bring EU rules in line with global market conditions. This, too, could be interpreted as an attempt to placate certain interest groups, namely the big television networks and satellite channels. In short, the EU's policy in the future seems to be based on a double policy carrot: locked-in funds for television programme producers and lighter-touch regulations for the television programme broadcasters. In this context, the controversial European quota seems incompatible with an increasing tendency in favour of deregulation.

Even a liberalised EU regulatory regime may prove to be 'too little, too late' to command compliance from transnational groups such as Sky TV, Canal Plus, Fininvest and Bertelsmann. At present, these groups appear to be exploiting *national* deregulation in order to launch themselves on the global market via transatlantic alliances with big American media groups – a strategy of *reculer pour mieux sauter*.

Still, if the member states have lost much of their regulatory capacity in the rapidly globalising broadcasting market, the EU has not yet succeeded in recuperating that dispersed authority to its own institutional advantage. One solution may be the establishment of a EU regulatory agency, perhaps for both the audio-visual and telecom sectors. The Commission's 'big bang' telecom policy, announced in June 1994, made precisely that proposal. If such a body were set up, the EU's legitimacy in broadcasting/telecom would be considerably reinforced *vis-à-vis* existing national regulatory regimes, which could eventually even be dismantled. Given the politically sensitive nature of broadcasting, EU member states will likely resist, at least in the short term, any such attempt to set up a supranational regulator.

REFERENCES

Brants, K. and Siune, K. (1992) 'Public Broadcasting in a State of Flux', in K. Siune and W. Truetzschler *Dynamics of Media Politics*, London: Sage.

Burns, T. (1977) *The BBC: Public Institution and Private World*, London: Macmillan.

Chippindale, P. and Franks, S. (1991) *Dished! – The Rise and Fall of British Satellite Broadcasting*, London: Simon & Schuster.

Cohen, E. (1992) *Le Colbertisme high tech*, Paris: Hachette.

Collins, R. (1990) *Television: Policy and Culture*, London: Unwin Hyman.

—— (1994) 'Unity in Diversity? The European Single Market in Broadcasting and the Audiovisual, 1982–92', *Journal of Common Market Studies*, 32, 1.

Commission of the European Communities (CEC) (1984) 'Television Without Frontiers', Green Paper on the establishment of the Common Market for broadcasting, especially by satellite and cable, Communication from the Commission to the Council, Luxemburg: Office for the Official Publications of the European Communities, COM (84) 300, Final,14 June.

CEC (1986) COM (86), 146 final, 30 April.

Davidson, A. (1992) *Under the Hammer: The ITV Franchise Battle*, London: Heinemann.

De Closets, F. (1992) *Tant et plus!* Paris: Grasset & Le Seuil.

Delwit, P. and Gobin, C. (1991) 'Etude du cheminement de la directive Télévision sans frontières: synthèse des prises de position des institutions communautaires', in G. Vandersanden (ed.) *L'espace audiovisuel européen*, Brussels: Université de Bruxelles.

Dupagne, M. (1992) 'EC Policy-making: The Case of the Television Without Frontiers Directive', *Gazette* (Netherlands), 49.

Dyson, K. and Humphreys, P. (1985) 'The New Media in Britain and in France – Two Versions of Heroic Muddle?', *Rundfunk und Fernsehen*, 33.

Eureka Audiovisual (1992) *Key Figures of the European Audiovisual Industry*, Supplement 4, EEC, Brussels, March.

European Court of Justice (ECR) (1980) 'Arrêt Debauve', affaire 53/79 of 18 March ECR Recueil.

Gudin, C.-E. (1990) 'Existe-t-il un marché européen de la télévision?', *Revue des affaires européennes*, 1.

Guillou, B. (1988) 'L'Europe des images: la diversité plus forte que l'unité?', *Médiapouvoirs*, Paris.

Hargreaves, I. (1993) 'Why the BBC Should be Privatised', *Financial Times*, 13 November II–1.

Humphreys, P. (1988) 'New Media Policy Dilemmas in West Germany: From Ideological Polarisation to Regional Economic Co-operation', in K. Dyson, and P. Humphreys *Broadcasting and New Media Policies in Western Europe*, London: Routledge.

Krasner, S. (1990) 'Global Communications and National Power', *World Politics*, October.

Mattelart, A. and Palmer, M. (1991) 'Advertising in Europe: Promises, Pressures and Pitfalls', *Media Culture and Society*, 13.

Mény, Y. (1989) 'The National and International Context of French Policy Communities', *Political Studies*, XXXVII.

Negrine, R. and Papathanassopoulos, S. (1990) *The Internationalisation of Television*, London: Pinter.

Nguyen, D. (1988) 'Options for the European Community: Arbitrator, Mediator or Actor?', *Intermedia*, June.

Noam, E. (1991) *Television in Europe*, New York: Oxford University Press.

Papathanassopoulos, S. (1990) 'Broadcasting and the European Community: The Commission's Audiovisual Policy', in P. Humphreys and K. Dyson *The Political Economy of Communications*, London: Routledge.

Schneider, V. and Werle, R. (1990) 'International Regime or Corporate Actor? The European Community in Telecommunications Policy', in P. Humphreys and K. Dyson *The Political Economy of Communications*, London: Routledge.

Thatcher, M. (1993) *The Downing Street Years*, London: HarperCollins.

Tunstall, T. (1984) 'Media Policy Dilemmas and Indecisions', *Parliamentary Affairs*, 3.

Tunstall, J. and Palmer, M. (1990) *Liberating Communications*, London: Blackwell.

Wall Street Journal, (1994) 'EU Laws on Broadcasting Spur Wave of Local Battles', 25 January, 4.

12 Research and development policy

John Peterson[1]

The role of the European Union (EU) in research and development (R&D) policy now extends to virtually every conceivable technological sector. The budget for the EU's technology Framework[2] programme is higher than that of any other single EU programme besides the Common Agricultural Policy. Using language that only a Eurocrat could love, the European Commission (1992b: 19) claims that, '[a]mong the strong points, generally recognised as the main result achieved, one may cite the "Europeanisation" of research ("communitarisation", or introduction of the community dimension into research activities). Another strength of European R&D programmes is that they tend to be less driven by inertia than national programmes. Since they are relatively new, EU programmes are less captive to "historical incrementalism and prior commitments" and thus are freer to focus on "newer, faster moving areas" of technology' (UK Cabinet Office 1993b: 84). Indeed, Sharp (1991: 395) claims that European programmes 'have in fact effectively eclipsed national programmes of high technology support'.

In key respects, this chapter seeks to refute Sharp's thesis. It contends that the extent to which national R&D policies have been 'Europeanised' has been greatly exaggerated. It argues principally that the impact of growing EU activity on national R&D policies has in fact been surprisingly modest. EU funding has increased and EU programmes are often more focused on 'leading edge' technologies than are national programmes, but research policies remain highly nationalised in Europe, and thus illustrate a more general, global paradox:

> Notwithstanding dramatically intensified international integration, science and technology continue to be supported through a process that is primarily national ... the underlying fact is that the resources allocated for [science and technology], public or private, are still dominantly national in terms of their purpose and their policy setting.
>
> (Skolnikoff 1993: 115–6)

To explain why most R&D in Europe remains 'dominantly national' in orientation, the analysis below proceeds in four sections. First, the significance of R&D for industrial policies and the logic of European collaboration are outlined. The second section sketches the historical development of EU R&D policy. Third, European Union and national R&D policies are considered in comparative perspective. Finally, the fourth section assesses the impact of expanded EU actions on national policies and policy making structures in Germany, France, Italy and the United Kingdom (UK).

WHY R&D MATTERS, STATES INTERVENE AND EUROPE COLLABORATES

The increasing importance of R&D for industrial policy stems primarily from the way in which the end of the Cold War has altered the meaning of 'security' for industrialised states. Economic power has supplanted military power as the prime guarantor of national well-being. Technological prowess has become a more critical source of national economic power. Recent evidence suggests that innovation in commercial technologies is becoming a more important prerequisite of military power (see Sandholtz *et al.* 1992, Crawford 1994). R&D matters because it is an important tool for defending and developing market power, and thus safeguarding national security.

Krugman (1994) remains sceptical about the extent to which markets have become 'globalised' (Humbert 1993). He also questions the inevitability of pitched battles between 'competition states' (Cerny 1990, Peterson 1993a) or regional blocs (Sandholtz *et al* 1992, Howells and Wood 1993) for technological ascendancy. However, for better or worse, technological competition in the 1990s is as much between states as between firms (Stopford and Strange 1992). Governments intervene because competition between firms is 'imperfect' in many technology-intensive industries: market failures arise from high barriers to entry, huge economies of scale and steep learning curves. Of course, governments may not intervene wisely. But they do intervene, particularly when oligopolistic markets for critical technologies are dominated by foreign firms. For example, allegations that Japanese producers of semiconductors were engaging in predatory pricing in the 1980s led to a range of western public policy responses (Flamm 1990, Ziegler 1991).

A common policy response is to offer public R&D subsidies. Government funds for research can be justified on the grounds that technological development is cumulative in nature and competitive advantage derives mostly from 'learning by doing' (Sharp and Pavitt 1993). Catching up and keeping up with technological change, let alone stealing a march on the competition, requires large, continuous investments in R&D which markets do not deliver. To remain competitive, semiconductor manufacturers must invest an astonishing 35 per cent of their total revenues in R&D and capital investment (Lie and Santucci 1993: 116).

European governments often choose to pool their investments into critical technologies for three fundamental reasons. First, common R&D programmes allow them to fund expensive projects jointly which none could fund on its own. Second, when governments subsidise collaboration across borders it encourages firms to exploit the EU's internal market: firms which collaborate become familiar with market opportunities beyond their national borders, they elevate their aspirations and treat the internal market as their 'home' market. Third, collaboration allows the EU to match the scale of large, collaborative projects under way in Japan and the United States (see Peterson 1993a: 2–10, Sandholtz 1992: 125–31). The logic of collaboration in Europe has encouraged the construction of a distinctive EU policy for research.

THE DEVELOPMENT OF A EU R&D POLICY

Aside from the nuclear field, the Treaty of Rome established no legal basis for the development of a common European R&D policy.[3] National governments resisted most Commission proposals for collective R&D action until the early 1980s. By this time, the market shares of most European technology producers were in free-fall. For example, American firms had captured nearly 80 per cent of the European market for computers by 1982 (Woolcock 1984: 315–31). National technology policies clearly were failing to boost or even maintain European competitiveness in technology-intensive industries.

The Commission responded by bringing together Europe's largest electronics firms to form the 'Big 12 Roundtable'. The Commission-Big 12 alliance was a critical and largely collective actor in lobbying national governments to create the European Strategic Programme for Information Technology (ESPRIT) in 1982 (Peterson 1991, Sandholtz 1992: 173–80). ESPRIT earmarked 11.5 million ECUs in Community funding to subsidise R&D projects involving firms from at least two member states. The perceived success of ESPRIT's first phase and continued lobbying by 'national champions' in technology-intensive industries led European governments to accept that more and larger collaborative R&D programmes were needed to respond to large-scale initiatives already under way in the USA and Japan. The first Technology Framework programme for 1984–7, with a price tag of 3.8 billion ECUs, signified a substantial expansion of Community-funded R&D activity.

The picture became more complicated in 1985. The Commission proposed a vastly increased budget of 10.3 billion ECUs for the Framework programme's second phase (1987–91) at the same time as the Reagan administration sought European partners for its Strategic Defense Initiative (SDI). As an alternative to the politically loathsome idea of French participation in SDI, François Mitterrand proposed the creation of the European Research Co-ordinating Agency (EUREKA) as a purely intergovernmental initiative with no centralised funds or supranational powers. EUREKA appealed to British and West German governments which strongly objected to the Commission's proposed budget for Framework II.

Initially, the Commission viewed EUREKA as an unwelcome distraction from the development of the EU's own *acquis* in research policy. For their part, the French insisted that EUREKA would complement the Framework programme by funding 'downstream' or 'near market' research, which aimed to produce marketable products and processes quickly. Meanwhile, the Commission had to be mindful of Community competition laws, which restricted the Framework programme to 'upstream' or 'pre-competitive' R&D,[4] designed to define new technical standards or develop enabling technologies for products which were still years away from marketability. Eventually, EUREKA grew to rival the Framework programme in size by the early 1990s. The Commission had to learn to live with it.

Still, the Commission managed to convince national governments that an expanded Framework II programme was needed to 'flank' the freeing of the internal market. Thus the Single European Act (SEA) amended the Treaty of Rome to provide a much stronger legal basis for a Community research policy. Overall multi-annual budgets for the Framework programme still required unanimous agreement from the Council of Ministers. But the Community now had a legal mandate to 'strengthen the scientific and technological base of European industry and to encourage it to become more competitive at an international level'. For the Commission:

> The hope was that, if the Council could be persuaded to agree to a blueprint research strategy, the building blocks could be slapped into place rapidly thereafter, without the need for a perpetual return to debates over first principles and the eternal wrangles over money.
>
> (Holdsworth and Lake 1988: 414)

In the event, negotiations on the Framework programme remained laborious and time-consuming. As net contributors to the EU's general budget, Germany and the UK remained the harshest critics of the Commission's proposed R&D spending. Smaller member states, which lacked large, integrated national champions of their own, pushed the Commission to earmark more funding for small, inexpensive R&D projects – or 'type B' projects – in which their own national firms had a chance to participate (Sandholtz 1992: 177).

In some respects, the Commission's frustrations were compounded by the Maastricht Treaty. The Framework programme's budget remained subject to unanimous voting on the Council. The new co-decision procedure, which effectively gave the European Parliament (EP) veto powers, threatened to complicate negotiations further. On the other hand, Article 130h of the Maastricht Treaty committed EU member states to 'coordinate their research and technological development activities so as to ensure that national policies and Community policies are mutually consistent' (Council and Commission 1992: 56).

For the Commission, the meaning of the Maastricht Treaty for research was that 'the coordination of national policies essentially ceases to be entrusted solely to the good intentions of Member States ... Article 130h represents an important opportunity' (CEC 1992b: 26–7). Despite its earnest language, the Commission's power to influence national research policies

Table 12.1 Total EC/EU spending on R&D 1987–93 (million ECUs)

1987	1988	1989	1990	1991	1992[1]	1993
939	1135	1412	1706	1749	2790	2556

Note: 1 Includes budget plus carryovers
Source: CEC 1992b

remains weak. However much lip-service is paid in treaties or political declarations to the goal of creating a truly integrated EU research strategy, such a strategy remains a rather dim and distant prospect.

EU AND NATIONAL R&D POLICIES IN COMPARATIVE PERSPECTIVE

Europe's total combined R&D effort is modest compared to those of its main competitors. Only about 2 per cent of total European GDP is invested in research, compared to about 2.9 per cent in the USA and 3 per cent in Japan. The Commission's first post-Maastricht statement on R&D insisted that the EU's R&D effort was both underfunded and poorly integrated (CEC 1992b: 32–7). Far more of what is spent on R&D in Europe is spent by the EU than was the case five years ago (see Table 12.1). Spending on research accounts for about 3.8 per cent of the EU's total budget, up from 2.6 per cent in 1988 (CEC 1992b: 19).

Moreover, a significant amount of 'national' spending on R&D now occurs through EUREKA. It funds only collaborative projects involving research organisations from at least two member states. Table 12.2 charts rapid increases in the number and value of EUREKA projects since 1987.

Increased EU activities in R&D and the expansion of EUREKA might be viewed as evidence of the 'Europeanisation' of research and the homogenisation of national research policies. Yet spending on collaborative R&D is still dwarfed by spending on purely or largely national activities. While EU expenditure on research has effectively doubled since the late 1980s, it has done so from a very low base. EU spending still equals only 4.5 per cent of total national spending on civilian R&D. Moreover, national efforts remain uneven and dissimilar even among large EU member states (see Table 12.3).

Table 12.2 The evolution of EUREKA 1987–93

	1987	1988	1989	1990	1991	1992	1993
Ongoing projects (no.)	165	212	292	369	478	539	816
Value (billion ECUs)	4.0	3.8	6.4	7.8	8.4	9.4	15.3

Source: EUREKA Secretariat 1993

Table 12.3 National R&D spending

	R&D Spending as % of GDP (1991)		Public R&D as % of total (1989)	Defence R&D as % of total public R&D (1990)
	Total	*Public spending*		
Germany	2.6	1.1	32.8	12.8
France	2.9	1.4	48.1	38.5
UK	2.1	0.9	36.5	45.2
Italy	1.4	0.8	49.5	6.8
EU 12	2.0	1.0	40.0	24.3

Sources: Eurostat 1992, 1993, UK Cabinet Office 1993a

As a percentage of GNP, France spends substantially more on research than does Germany, and far more than the UK or Italy. French public spending on R&D is nearly 50 per cent more than the EU average, while public budgets in Italy and the UK are comparatively miserly. About half of the total value of all R&D in France and Italy is paid for by public sources, compared to about one-third in the UK and Germany. The UK and France spend far more on defence R&D than do other EU member states.

Despite the heterogeneity of their national R&D efforts, the EU's four largest member states do form a powerful bloc when their research interests converge. Taken together, Germany, France, the UK and Italy account for nearly 90 per cent of all national spending on industrial R&D in the EU (see Table 12.4). Their command of such a large share of Europe's technological resources makes them powerful players in EU R&D policy making.

Consensus among the four largest member states on the need to pool national efforts in information technology (IT) and communications was reflected in the large shift of EU funding to these sectors after 1987 (see Table 12.5). Both ESPRIT and the RACE (Research in Advanced Communications

Table 12.4 National shares of total EU/industrial R&D (1990)

Country	Share (%)
Germany	31.7
France	23.3
United Kingdom	20.7
Italy	12.2
Others	12.1

Source: French MRE 1992

Table 12.5 EU R&D spending by sectors: the first three Framework programmes

	I (1984–87) (%)	II (1987–91) (%)	III (1990–94) (%)
Information and communications	25	42	39
Industrial technologies and new materials	11	16	16
Energy	50	23	14
Biotechnology	5	9	13
Environment	7	6	9
Human capital and mobility	2	4	9
Total cost (billion ECUs)	3.8	5.4	5.7

Source: Skoie 1993

in Europe) programme primarily benefited large electronics firms from larger member states. Apart from the Dutch firm Philips, all members of the 'Big 12 Roundtable' were domiciled in the UK (ICL, GEC and Plessey), France (Thomson, Bull and CGE), Germany (Siemens and Nixdorf) or Italy (STET and Olivetti). The largest four member states received more than three-quarters of all EU funding for IT and communications technologies under Framework II (Stubbs and Saviotti 1994: 163).

However, the Commission learned that it had to accommodate the preferences of smaller member states in order to secure unanimous acceptance of its proposals for the Framework programme on the Council. *Juste retour* remained the most powerful 'rule of the game' even as the Framework programme expanded. The need to satisfy smaller states was reflected in increased funds for industrial technologies (such as robotics and new materials) and biotechnology under Framework III, as well as the exponential growth of the Human Capital and Mobility programme, which seeks to increase cross-border exchanges of researchers. Markets for many industrial technologies and biotechnology featured relatively low barriers to entry. Research organisations in smaller member states thus had a chance to compete for EU funding. The Human Capital and Mobility programme promoted the transfer of technology, knowledge and researchers between large member states and the EU's less technologically advanced regions.

In short, by the early 1990s the Framework programme was no longer viewed as a clear-cut means for compensating large, richer member states for their net contributions to the EU's structural and cohesion funds, which primarily benefit small, poorer EU countries. Doubts persisted in larger member states about the EU's ability 'to design and manage programs of industrial support without succumbing to the redistributive politics that have plagued many such undertakings in the United States' (Mowery 1993: 46). These doubts surfaced when the Commission's proposed 13.1 billion ECU budget for Framework IV (1994–8) was blocked by France, Germany and the UK in late 1993. For its part, the EP sought to exploit its new co-decision powers by insisting, along with smaller member states, on an even larger budget. Eventually, a compromise figure of 12.3 billion ECUs – with the possibility of an extra 700 million ECUs as a 'top-up' – was accepted by the French, British and Germans in early 1994.

The redistributive politics of the Framework programme help explain why large EU states have embraced EUREKA with such enthusiasm. Europe's two most ambitious collaborative projects were launched as EUREKA projects and primarily funded from national coffers: the Joint European Silicon Structures Initiative (Jessi) into advanced semiconductors and the High Definition Television (HDTV) project to develop the next generation of television equipment (Peterson 1993b). EUREKA harmonises national R&D policies only marginally. National governments have unchallenged control over all funding decisions and are free to contribute as much or as little funding as they wish to any EUREKA project which involves their domestic firms.

By contrast, after long and arduous negotiations on the Framework programme's overall budget and priorities, the Commission retains considerable discretion in decision making about the actual division of EU funds between projects and, by extension, member states. Skoie (1993: 20) claims that 'on the whole decisions are taken by the Commission's administrative staff – there lies the real decision-making power'. In particular, the Commission has wide latitude to determine the content of 'type B' projects. Often, 'a type B project amounts to little more than an interesting idea which may unfold into a well-defined project.... In effect, type B projects help to accommodate specific interests and demands', especially those of small states (Molina 1993: 40). While type B projects are the most tangible symbol of the redistributive politics of the Framework programme, critics charge that the Commission more generally favours programmes which are unfocused. Programmes with vague objectives or priorities invite an avalanche of applications for available funds. 'Over-subscription' is then used by the Commission 'as a tool to argue the case for more funds' (UK Cabinet Office 1993b: 23).

Usually, the Commission can count on the support of private actors when it argues for increased funds for R&D (see Peterson 1995). Since its early success in aligning with the Big 12 in the early 1980s, the Commission has maintained very close links to industry. Especially at the policy development stage, private actors may play a crucial role in decision making through their participation in the various 'panels of experts' which advise the Commission.

To a significant extent, large electronics and telecommunications firms, such as Philips and ICL, now focus their lobbying on Brussels as much as their national capitals for two main reasons. First, ESPRIT and RACE represent more of a genuine pooling of national R&D than do other EU programmes. About 12 per cent of all spending on IT in the Union is funded through the Framework programme. Second, the Commission has substantial discretion of its own within both ESPRIT and RACE. By contrast, most other Framework sub-programmes feature many firms competing for a relatively small amount of funding. Notable exceptions exist, but the vast majority of European firms in technology-intensive industries focus most of their lobbying activities on their national governments, as opposed to the Commission or EP. More funds are available from national programmes and they are usually easier to secure than EU funds. Even when firms want to influence the Framework programme, they often seek to do so by working through national channels.

Two wider points emerge from this discussion: first, in light of their very high share of total European spending on research, large member states have relatively weak means for controlling EU R&D policy; and second, larger member states generally agree that too much EU R&D funding is distributed according to political, as opposed to technological, criteria. Suspicions persist that the Commission is more interested in expanding its general industrial policy *acquis* than in funding the most promising R&D or in responding to criticisms of the Framework programme (see CEC 1992a). Larger EU states, with the exception of Italy, remain reluctant to expand the Framework programme. Furthermore, as the following section makes clear, the development of a truly 'Europeanised' R&D policy faces administrative and structural obstacles at the national level, as well as political obstacles at the EU level.

A REVIEW OF NATIONAL POLICIES

Germany

The claim that Germany's R&D policy has been more successful than that of any other EU member state is uncontroversial. German public research laboratories, particularly the Fraunhofer Gesellschaft, are world-class. The share of national R&D spending which is privately funded is higher in Germany than anywhere else in Europe. Industrial, 'downstream' research accounts for about 70 per cent of all German R&D (Conrad 1993: 99). Many German firms view the Framework programme, with its traditional emphasis on pre-competitive R&D, as having limited relevance to them. Germany remains a large net contributor to the Framework programme's budget.

German R&D structures, as much as German success, have deterred an integration of domestic with EU strategies. The national R&D ministry, the BMFT (Bundesministerium fur Forschung und Technologie) is the federative agent for most national R&D initiatives. However, R&D policy is a matter of shared responsibility between the federal government and the individual Länder, which account for nearly 40 per cent of total German public R&D spending. The Länder have significant autonomy to determine their own research policies (BMFT 1991: 29; Gotz 1992). Thus German R&D policy 'lacks a substantive vision and orientation which would allow the integration of its various activities' across the 'distinct [decision-making] communities' of the Federal Republic, let alone those of the EU (Conrad 1993: 102).

Besides nuclear fusion, the sector where German R&D efforts are most Europeanised is IT. But even here, the BMFT spent nearly 700 million ECUs on national IT support between 1984 and 1993. The collaborative Mega-Projects into advanced semiconductors, which linked Siemens with Philips, were conducted as EUREKA projects and primarily funded through national channels. The participation rate of German firms in ESPRIT is low and the BMFT has done relatively little to try to increase it (Mytelka 1993: 60–2). As a BMFT official with intimate knowledge of EU R&D policy observes:

> There is influence on national policy-making in that one tries not to dupli-
> cate things which are already done here in Brussels. But it's not a process
> whereby one first looks at what is done here and then decides to concen-
> trate on other areas . . . I'm not sure that the major decisions in Germany
> to support IT or not are really influenced deeply by the things the Com-
> munity is doing. And I think I could say the same about . . . all areas of
> R&D.
>
> (Interview 1993)

For their part, German research organisations tend to view the Framework programme's relatively centralised and bureaucratic decision-making procedures with contempt. Until recently, doubts about the quality of EU-funded R&D fostered the assumption in Germany that the most important and promising R&D projects should be carried out nationally. This assumption has come under challenge because of the fiscal strains caused by German unification. Between 1989 and 1991, total German expenditure on R&D fell from 2.88 to 2.66 per cent of GDP (Stubbs and Saviotti 1994: 143).[5] Germany's powerful Ministry of Finance imposed strict new limits on public spending for research.

The BMFT has thus been forced to take account of R&D funded through the Framework programme as never before. It must do so if only to defend itself against Finance Ministry charges that public money should not be allocated for what is already being funded – with a large German contribution – through the EU. In a backhanded way, the Finance Ministry has encouraged both the BMFT and German research organisations to seek opportunities for participation in EU-funded R&D more systematically.

France

EU R&D policy is considered a matter of national importance in France, far more than in Germany, for three reasons: first, France is more committed than any other EU Member State to nuclear energy, a sector which features significant EU activities; second, EU R&D policy is viewed as a partial antidote to the traditional and costly isolation of French research organisations

Table 12.6 The Framework programme: French contributions and receipts (million ECUs)

	1988	1989	1990	1991	1992
Contributions	210	256	295	363	391
Receipts	243	310	361	444	533

Source: French MRE 1992

from those in other European countries (Peterson 1993a: 75–9); and third, the scale of EU actions often matches the high ambitions of French R&D policy. As a national official from another large Member State puts it:

> The French want to do everything: in all domains, all sectors. They are totally unselective and they won't give up any sector. They want to have EuroDisney and a European HDTV standard and more funding for IT. The rest of us are much less ambitious.
>
> (Interview 1993)

France has probably done more than any large EU Member State to harmonise its domestic R&D policy with actions taken at the European level. By contrast with Germany, France is a net beneficiary of the Framework programme. As the EU's R&D budget has grown in size, the net gains for France have accumulated (see Table 12.6). Laredo and Callon (1990) conclude that EU funds have facilitated a significant increase in French doctoral theses, as well as a type of R&D ('basic technological research'), which was previously unknown in France and which straddles the time-honoured division between basic and applied R&D.

These gains help to explain the shift to a 'very pro-European' national policy in France in the 1980s. French firms and laboratories were urged to seek EU R&D funds, particularly after the Chirac governments slashed national funding between 1986 and 1988 (Mytelka 1993: 62). Both the inter-ministerial Comité National d'Evaluation de la Recherche and the publicly funded R&D policy assessment unit, the Observatoire des Sciences et des Techniques were created in 1989–90 primarily to co-ordinate French R&D actions with those undertaken by the EU or within EUREKA.

The French rate of participation in ESPRIT is now higher than that of Germany. More generally, 11 per cent of all industrial R&D undertaken in France is funded through 'foreign sources' (French MRE 1992: 24). French organisations participate in nearly 40 per cent of all ongoing EUREKA projects. Far more projects are led by French firms than by firms from any other Member State (Peterson 1993a: 25–7). Yet several factors mitigate against the 'Europeanisation' of French R&D policy. One problem is that lines of ministerial responsibility for national and EU R&D policies are blurred and inter-agency animosity is rife (Sharp and Holmes 1989: 9–11).

The Ministère de la Recherche et de l'Espace (MRE) is charged with co-ordinating the R&D actions of most domestic French ministries. It presides over the largest national public R&D budget in the EU. However, the Ministry of Foreign Affairs – not the MRE – is primarily responsible for negotiations on the Framework programme. One upshot is that the French, in the words of a Quai d'Orsay official, are often 'not that interested in objectives of [EU] research. The key is that we get out of the budget what we put in' (interview 1993). Once negotiations are complete, the Framework programme is the joint responsibility of the French Ministry of Industry and the MRE, between whom rivalries are not infrequent.

A second factor is the recent decentralisation of the domestic R&D policy-making process in France. Wide disparities in technological development between French urban areas and regions led Socialist governments in the 1980s to delegate significant powers to determine regional industrial development strategies to the Agence Nationale de Valorisation de la Recherche (ANVAR). In 1992, the Direction de l'Innovation de la Technologie et de l'Action Regionale was created to reorient public funds for R&D away from the Paris region, where nearly 60 per cent of the French R&D effort is concentrated (French MRE 1992: 30, 41). The growing role of these agencies makes it more difficult for the MRE to lead from the centre in integrating the French research effort with that of the EU.

French policy makers tend to find the redistributive element in the Framework programme particularly intolerable. The French are strong proponents of the Colbertiste view that the most urgent and important goal of EU R&D policy should be bolstering the competitiveness of European, especially French, producers of critical technologies such as semiconductors and computers, notably Thomson and Bull, in the face of daunting competition from the USA and Japan. As the originators of EUREKA, the French are keen supporters of the programme, which offers the benefits of collaboration across borders without the need to compromise national goals. Put simply, despite the considerable 'Europeanisation' of their national R&D policy, the French have sought to use new European programmes to pursue their national ambitions far more than they have compromised their own goals for the sake of European solidarity.

United Kingdom

The traditional British aversion to increased EU spending on R&D has not wavered since the Framework programme was first created. However, the link between changes in the UK's national R&D policy and expanded EU actions has, at least in budgetary terms, been direct. In most EU member states, projects funded through the Framework programme are considered 'additional' to those undertaken at the national level. By contrast, many Union actions are treated in the UK as effective substitutes for national actions in the same technological sectors. After increases in EU R&D funding were agreed at the

Edinburgh summit in late 1992, proportionate reductions in the UK's national R&D budget were announced almost immediately.[6] The Major government has continued the Thatcherite practice of 'clawing back' from the R&D budgets of corresponding individual British departments about half of the total British contribution to the EU's R&D budget.

The practice of 'clawing back' is partly a consequence of the long-standing principle that decisions on support for innovation should be made autonomously by different British government departments on a 'customer-contractor' basis (Gummett 1991: 34). In the words of one UK official, 'the UK has never had an R&D "policy" in the way that term is understood in other Member States and by the Commission' (interview 1993). The idea that overarching national R&D priorities (let alone European ones) do not and should not exist remains entrenched.

The Office of Science and Technology (OST), created within the Cabinet Office in 1986, is viewed by the Major government's critics as a poor substitute for the large and powerful R&D ministries of France and Germany. However, the government continues to resist calls to place all public R&D:

> under the control of a single centralised department, [thus] breaking completely the carefully nurtured and fundamental view that individual departments should be committed themselves under their own volition, to the R&D necessary to underpin their own policy. . . . [Centralisation] would be a very odd doctrine, unique in the world; even the Germans with their large Science and Technology Ministry don't do that, and the French and others are moving in the opposite direction.
>
> (Waldegrave 1993: 8)

Whatever its handicaps, however, the UK is a substantial net beneficiary of the Framework programme. The EU accounts for about 6 per cent of total UK public spending on civil R&D (UK Cabinet Office 1993b: 84). The Major government has been anxious to publicise the fact that the UK does far better out of Union R&D (in net budgetary terms) than Germany.[7] British organisations have forged more collaborative links through the Framework programme than have organisations from any other Member State (see Table 12.7).

As in Germany, the IT sector is where the UK's national actions are most highly integrated with those of the EU. More generally, 'it is increasingly

Table 12.7 Total collaborative links between research organisations under the Framework II programme within and between each member state

United Kingdom	17,583
France	16,929
Germany	15,766
Italy	9,695

Source: UK Cabinet Office 1993b: 15

difficult in many areas to conceive of British science policy independently of the European Community' (Gummett 1991: 36). A study commissioned by the UK Cabinet Office (1993b: 90) suggested that EU-funded R&D had:

> re-orient(ed) the research community to the point where it regards itself as part of an emergent European scientific community . . . Europeanisation has reached deeply into the fabric of research and development in the United Kingdom.

If this reorientation has occurred, British governments have done rather little to encourage it, beyond cutting funds for national programmes. The government's 1993 White Paper on Science and Technology contained remarkably few references to EU research actions (HMSO 1993). Both major opposition parties have criticised the Major government for failing both to develop a coherent national R&D strategy or to co-ordinate national with EU actions in any systematic way (see Moore 1993, Foster 1993). In White-hall, the Framework programme is viewed with a mixture of apathy and con-tempt. Most British ministries loathe increases in EU R&D funds since the practical effect is to reduce funds available for national programmes. As EU spending has increased, national public R&D support in the UK has fallen by 1.3 billion ECUs in real terms since 1986 (Mulvey 1993). Declining national funding helps explain the relatively low level of British participation in EUREKA (UK Cabinet Office 1993b: 78). More generally, the UK lacks both a national R&D 'strategy' as well as a ministry with the means and muscle to co-ordinate UK-funded actions with those of the EU. If British R&D policy has been 'Europeanised', it has happened more by default than design.

Italy

Post-war R&D policy in Italy has reflected the general weakness of its gov-ernments. The perceived need of the governing Italian political parties to reward their industrial clienteles has led successive governments to offer a largely patternless set of ill-targeted industrial subsidies. Italian public spend-ing on R&D effectively doubled between 1984 and 1991 (Eurostat 1993: 55). Yet growth in the R&D budget was more a product of the growing insecurity of the major Italian political parties than any conscious or overarching strategy.

The Ministry for Scientific and Technological policy (MST) shares responsibility for Italian R&D policy with the Ministry for Industry. Thus, for example, proposals for support from the Italian Fund for Innovation, created in the late 1980s, were evaluated by the Ministry of Industry. How-ever, if proposals were for projects which included non-Italian European partners, they were considered jointly with the MST (Napolitano 1988: 382). More generally, Italian R&D policy has reflected the general picture of the Italian administrative state painted by Cassese (1993: 320–1):

The decision-making process is characterised by numerous authorities which take part in every procedure. Every decision, even the most insignificant, needs approval from two regulatory bodies, the Treasury and Court of Accounts, which, in order to exercise control, have branches in every ministerial department.

More specifically, R&D policy has suffered from a style of Italian policy making in which 'decisions are so thoroughly checked *ex ante*, there is hardly any *ex post facto* control. Efficiency and results seem not to carry any weight. Attention is focused on procedure itself rather than outcome' (Cassese 1993: 321). Furthermore, although the MST does have a sub-directorate for the co-ordination of national R&D actions with those of the EU, it lacks any effective means for the evaluation of national R&D needs or activities. Italian policy makers often still cite the EC's Forecasting and Assessment of Science and Technology (FAST) reports, issued in the early 1980s, as one of the most recent assessments of Italy's R&D needs.

Given its chaotic national R&D policy, a better-funded and expanded EU R&D policy is viewed with enthusiasm in Italy. Unlike their German counterparts, many Italian industrialists view the EU's decision making procedures as less onerous and bureaucratic than those which govern domestic support. In particular, Italy's large and vibrant coterie of small firms has benefited from the growth of the Community's programmes for industrial technologies.

Italy tends to support, almost by instinct, the ideas that EU R&D spending should be increased and that the Commission should be given more resources for technology assessment. Italian officials insist that 'we are aware that there is a bureaucracy problem, but there will be no European Union without a centralised administrative body. And the research evaluation process is a part of this philosophy' (interview 1993). Put simply, an integrated European R&D policy is viewed as a desirable substitute for a national Italian policy which has produced few success stories. This point is evidenced both by consistent Italian support for increased funds for the Framework programme as well as by Italy's high rate of participation in EUREKA (EUREKA Secretariat 1993: 5). However, the lack of a coherent 'R&D policy' and the continued use of research funding as a tool of political patronage in Italy are likely to continue to deter the harmonisation of Italian and EU research strategies.

CONCLUSION

The logic of common European R&D programmes is clear. They encourage cross-border industrial linkages, allow governments to share the costs of expensive projects and give Europe the chance to match the scale of Japanese and American efforts. Yet governments in most large EU member states continue to guard their national R&D policy prerogatives jealously. The estimated amount spent on the Framework programme and EUREKA between 1990 and 1994 (12 billion ECUs) was modest when compared to the total spent on national industrial support (67 billion ECUs) during the same period (see Findlay 1991).

Of course, many national programmes are not really designed to promote technological development. Sharp (1991: 395) estimates that as much as two-thirds of all national industrial support goes to declining industries to protect employment. By contrast, the Framework and EUREKA programmes have:

> been able to define new areas of support. Moreover, in many of these sectors it now makes sense to think in 'European' rather than national terms. For these reasons, although in money terms the [European] programmes might be dubbed 'small beer', their influence is considerable and it can be fairly said that the focus of technology policy in Europe has now, in the early 1990s, shifted from national governments to Brussels.
>
> (ibid.)

However, this contention is problematic on two grounds. In the first place, the growth of EUREKA can in no way be equated with a 'shift to Brussels' in the focus of European R&D policies. If anything, EUREKA's growth represents the desire of national governments to check and control such a shift. Most EUREKA projects are 'national' projects with some type of European dimension which is often weak or tenuous (see Mariti 1993: 200; Peterson 1993a: 73–102). Second, the line between 'European' and 'national' R&D support has become blurred. EU and national funds are combined increasingly within single projects. However, we cannot assume that national R&D policy makers think in 'European as opposed to national terms' when national policies are made. In R&D as in other policy areas, national governments tend to view the EU as a forum for the pursuit of national goals by other means.

This point was illustrated by national responses to Commission proposals in 1993 to contract out the management of specific Framework sub-programmes. The Commission argued that it could concentrate more on policy development if 'concertation networks' of research organisations managed EU projects. The Germans, with their much-envied research institutes, enthusiastically supported the idea of decentralising project management while admitting that their position was 'a pretty isolated one' (interview 1993). The French made positive public noises about the idea, but expressed private reservations about the desirability of giving the Commission more resources and, by extension, autonomy in 'policy development'.

Italy appeared to concur with smaller states in arguing that decentralisation was a code word for renationalisation. With Italy's recent domestic political experience in mind, one official suggested, 'For us, Europe is a sort of impartial body which has to stay impartial. . . . If we're going to have a European Union, we can't risk having independent agencies or decentralised bodies which give no guarantee of impartiality' (interview 1993). For their part, the British appeared reluctant to tamper with a system which brought them net benefits. One UK insider suggested:

> These ideas for decentralisation have been pushed by the Germans, who've not done that well out of Framework, and who want their own research institutes to lead programmes. Our basic scepticism is about whether this will reduce bureaucracy or increase it. But where you stand on this question is also very much a product of how well you do out of the system now as well as your national R&D structures.
>
> (interview 1993)

National research structures continue to differ markedly, even among the largest EU member states. Both the UK and Italy lack research ministries which have the administrative power needed to harmonise national with EU strategies. Authority for R&D policy is very fragmented in Germany and it has become increasingly decentralised in France. More generally, a former chief scientist to the French government notes a trend towards:

> the organisations in charge of science policy . . . becoming bloated. An 'intermediate layer' is developing between the political level and that at which research is taking place. . . . In other words, research administration is gradually gaining on research itself.
>
> (Piganiol 1991: 29)

Rivalries between national administrations and the Commission, for whom increased R&D spending would mean increased powers, are an important factor in explaining the persistence of national R&D policy prerogatives. The Commission has neglected no argument for expanding the EU's technology policy *acquis*. It also has come under criticism for 'paying insufficient attention . . . to (R&D) work already in progress at the national level' (UK Cabinet Office 1993b: 75). For their part, national and sub-national research administrations are some of the fiercest critics of what is perceived as empire-building by the Commission. Many share a UK official's view that 'Framework gets waved around in front of people as a big EU success, but we're never sure whether this is money well-spent' (interview 1993).

As a caveat, the Maastricht Treaty's new Article 130H gives the Commission, for the first time, a treaty basis upon which to seek a true nexus of national and EU efforts. The budgetary pressures of German unification could be an important boon to this project. As never before, German officials and researchers are looking for ways of funding research programmes of national interest through EU coffers. A new text on links between the Framework programme and EUREKA, agreed in late 1992, may mark a further step towards the harmonisation of national and EU research policies. Over time, the Commission has come to view EUREKA less as an alternative to expanded EU actions in R&D and more as a collection of projects which should complement what is done under EU auspices. To date, however, the development of an EU R&D policy has had rather modest effects on national policies. European governments have shown that they are willing to pool their R&D efforts when their national goals cannot be achieved through national action. But the perceived link between national R&D prowess and national security – which has tightened since the cold war ended – often leads EU governments to act on their own unless they face compelling evidence to suggest that national action is futile. The case of R&D thus fuels Skolnikoff's (1993: 124) argument that:

> Whenever the activities of international institutions do come to pose serious challenges to governmental authority, the national base on which the international political system is organized will prove to dominate. The world remains predominantly a collection of nation-states; the undoubted increase in the roles of international organizations is a fact of life, but the authority of institutions is limited, and will remain so long into the future.

In short, European R&D policies remain more nationalised than most of us would have predicted at the dawn of the Brave New World of post-1992 Europe.

NOTES

1 I am grateful to the Secretariat-General of the European Commission for a grant which facilitated research on this project in early 1994 when I was a Visiting Research Fellow at the Centre for European Policy Studies (CEPS) in Brussels. Phil Rees of the University of York library helped me to track down key documents. Elizabeth Bomberg, Liesbet Hooghe and the editors gave valuable comments on earlier drafts. Particular thanks are due to officials in the Permanent Representations to the EU of the UK, France, Italy and Germany who kindly granted non-attributable interviews in November 1993.

2 The Framework programme groups together most EU research activities. Its individual sub-programmes, such as ESPRIT and BRITE, offer subsidies of up to 50 per cent of the total cost of R&D activities in specific areas of technology. All projects funded through the Framework programme must include at least research organisations from two different EU member states.

3 The EURATOM Treaty still provides the legal framework for the EU's very expensive and long-term R&D into nuclear fusion, which integrates almost all research done in the sector across the Union. No other sector is characterised by such a singularly unified R&D effort.

4 The pre-competitive restrictions on EU-funded R&D have become less strict over time. A recent study carried out for the UK Cabinet Office (1993b: 86) concludes that '"precompetitive" research is a label which applies only to a minority of cases'. A senior official in Ireland's public R&D agency echoes the widely held view that '(i)t is now assumed that the 4th EC Framework programme will move "nearer to the market"' (O'Doherty 1993: 149).

5 By some measures, German public R&D spending has fallen by nearly 16 per cent since 1985 (UK Cabinet Office 1993a: 60).

6 See *New Scientist*, 8 January 1993.

7 See the response of William Waldegrave, the British Science Minister, to a Parliamentary question as reprinted in *Science in Parliament*, April 1993, 50, 2: 50–1.

REFERENCES

BMFT (1991) *Report of the Federal Government on Research*, Koln: Verlag Deutscher Wirtschaftsdienst.

Cassese, S. (1993) 'Hypotheses on the Italian Administrative System', *West European Politics*, 16, July: 316–28.

Cerny, P. (1990) *The Changing Architecture of Politics: Structure, Agency and the Future of the State*, London: Sage.

Commission of the European Communities (CEC) (1992a) *Evaluation of the Second Framework Programme for Research and Technological Development*, SEC (92) 675 final, 22 August, Luxemburg: Office for Official Publications of the European Communities.

—— (1992b) *Research After Maastricht: An Assessment. A Strategy*, Luxemburg: Office for Official Publications of the European Communities.

Conrad, J. (1993) 'Reflections on Science and Technology Policy Advice to Government in Germany', *Science and Public Policy*, 20, April: 97–104.

Council and Commission of the European Communities (1992) *Treaty on European Union*, Luxemburg: Office for the Official Publications of the European Communities.

Crawford, B. (1994) 'The New Security Dilemma Under International Economic Interdependence', *Millenium*, 23,2: 85–108.

EUREKA Secretariat (1993) *EUREKA Annual Progress Report, Brussels: EUREKA Secretariat*.

Eurostat (1992) *Europe in Figures*, Luxemburg: Office for Official Publications of the European Communities, 3rd edn.

—— (1993) *Basic Statistics of the Community*, Luxemburg: Office for Official Publications of the European Communities, 30th edn.

Findlay, G. (1991) 'International Collaboration', in C.M. Canningham and P. Gummett (eds) *Science and Technology in the United Kingdom*, Essex: Longman.

Flamm, K. (1990) 'Semiconductors', in G. Hufbauer (ed.) *Europe 1992: An American Perspective*, Washington DC: Brookings Institution.

Foster, D. (1993) 'Moving the Deck Chairs', *Science in Parliament*, 50, June: 11–12.

French MRE (1992) *Projet de Loi de Finances Pour 1993: Etat de la Recherche et du Développement Technologique, Activités 1991–92 & Perspectives 1993*, Paris: Imprimerie Nationale.

Gotz, K. (1992) *Intergovernmental Relations and State Government Discretion: The Case of Science and Technology Policy in Germany*, Baden-Baden: Nomos Verlasgesellschaft.

Gummett, P. (1991) 'UK Policy: The Evolution of Science and Technology – A UK Perspective', *Science and Public Policy*, 18, February: 31–7.

HMSO (1993) *Realising Our Potential: A Strategy for Science, Engineering and Technology* (White Paper on Science and Technology), Cmmd 2250, London: HMSO.

Holdsworth, D. and Lake, G. (1988) 'Integrating Europe: The new R&D calculus', *Science and Public Policy*, 15, December: 411–25.

Howells, J. and Wood M. (1993) *The Globalisation of Production and Technology*, London: Belhaven.

Humbert, M. (ed.) (1993) *The Impact of Globalisation on Europe's Firms and Industries*, London and New York: Pinter.

Krugman, P. (1994) *Peddling Prosperity*, New York: W. W. Norton.

Laredo, P. and Callon, M. (1990) *L'Impact des Programmes Communitaires sur le Tissu Scientifique et Technique Français*, Paris: La Documentation Française.

Lie, T.C. and Santucci, G. (1993) 'Seeking Balanced Trade and Competition Conditions in the Context of Globalisation: The Case of Electronics', in M. Humbert (ed.) *The Impact of Globalisation on Europe's Firms and Industries*, London and New York: Pinter.

Mariti, P. (1993) 'Small and Medium-sized Firms in Markets with Substantial Scale and Scope Economies', in M. Humbert (ed.) *The Impact of Globalisation on Europe's Firms and Industries*, London and New York: Pinter.

Molina, A.H. (1993) 'Understanding the Emergence of a Large-scale European Initiative in Technology', *Science and Public Policy*, 21, February: 31–41.

Moore, L. (1993) 'Realising our Potential: A Lack of Real Vision', *Science in Parliament*, 50, June: 10–11.

Mowery, D. (1993) 'Does Airbus Industrie Yield Lessons for EC Collaborative Research Programmes?', in M. Humbert (ed.) *The Impact of Globalisation on Europe's Firms and Industries*, London and New York: Pinter.

Mulvey, J. (1993) 'Narrow Vision or Unfinished Business', *Science in Parliament*, 50, June: 18.

Mytelka, L.K. (1993) 'Strengthening the Relevance of Euorpean Science and Technology Programmes to Industrial Competitiveness: The Case of ESPRIT', in M. Humbert (ed.) *The Impact of Globalisation on Europe's Firms and Industries*, London and New York: Pinter.

Napolitano, G. (1988) 'European Technological Co-operation: The Italian Participation in Eureka', *Science and Public Policy*, 15 December: 376–82.

O'Doherty, D.P. (1993) 'Globalisation and the performance of Small Firms Within the Smaller European Economies', in M. Humbert (ed.) *The Impact of Globalisation on Europe's Firms and Industries*, London and New York: Pinter.

Peterson, J. (1991) 'Technology Policy in Europe: Explaining the Framework Programme and EUREKA in Theory and Practice', *Journal of Common Market Studies*, 29,3: 269–90.

—— (1993a) *High Technology and the Competition State: An Analysis of the EUREKA Initiative*, London and New York: Routledge.

—— (1993b) 'Towards a European Industrial Policy? The Case of High Definition Television', *Government and Opposition*, 24,4: 496–511.

—— (1995) 'EU Research Policy: The Politics of Expertise', in S. Mazey and C. Rhodes (eds) *The State of the European Union III*, Boulder and Essex: Lynne Rienner and Longman.

Piganiol, P. (1991) 'French S&T Policy: Laying the Foundations of French Science Policies', *Science and Public Policy*, 18, February: 23–30.

Sandholtz, W. (1992) *High-Tech Europe: The Politics of International Cooperation*, Berkeley and Oxford: University of California Press.

Sandholtz, W., Borrus, M., Zysman, J., Conca, K., Stowsky, J., Vogel, S. and Weber, S. (1992) *The Highest Stakes*, New York and Oxford: Oxford University Press.

Sharp, M. (1991) 'Europe – A Renaissance?', *Science and Public Policy*, 18, December: 393–400.

Sharp, M. and Holmes, P. (eds) (1989) *Strategies for New Technologies: Case Studies from Britain and France*, London: Philip Alan.

Sharp, M. and Pavitt, K. (1993) 'Technology Policy in the 1990s: Old Trends and New Realities', *Journal of Common Market Studies*, 21,2: 129–51.

Skoie, H. (1993) 'EC Research and Technology Policies: Some Characteristics of Developments and Future Perspectives', Oslo: Institute for Studies in Research and Higher Education, Mimeo.

Skolnikoff, E.B. (1993) 'New International Trends Affecting Science and Technology', *Science and Public Policy*, 20, April: 115–25.

Stopford, J. and Strange, S. (eds) (1992) *Rival States, Rival Firms: Competition for World Market Shares*, Cambridge: Cambridge University Press.

Stubbs, P. and Saviotti, P. (1994) 'Science and Technology Policy', in M.J. Artis and N. Lee (eds) *The Economics of the European Union*, Oxford: Oxford University Press.

UK Cabinet Office (1993a*) Annual Review of Government Funded Research and Development*, London: HMSO.
—— (1993b) *The Impact of European Community Policies for Research and Technological Development Upon Science and Technology in the United Kingdom*, July, London: HMSO.
Waldegrave, W. (1993) 'The real work begins now', *Science in Parliament* 50 (June): 6–9.
Woolcock, S. (1984) 'Information technology: the challenge to Europe', *Journal of Common Market Studies* 22,4: 315–31.
Ziegler, J.N. (1991) 'Semiconductors', *Daedalus* 120: 155–82.

13 Banking and financial services

Phil Molyneux

The legislation that forms the cornerstone of the European Union's plan for a single market in banking came into effect on 1 January 1993. The central aim of this legislation was to create the largest and most open banking market in the world with institutions competing on a so-called 'level playing field'. Minimum regulatory standards were to be implemented so as to remove the competitive advantages of domestic banks in each member state over competitors from other EU countries. This chapter provides an overview of the EU legislation relating to banking and argues that there are three main reasons why no level playing field exists in this market. First, member states have considerable freedom to act in derogation of the single market, taking advantage of the 'general good' opt-out. Second, tax obstacles in member states largely frustrate the cross-border provision of financial services, and one recent ruling of the European Court of Justice has helped keep in force these barriers. Third, there has been a wide degree of flexibility when EC law is incorporated at the national level. In addition, this chapter shows how EU banking legislation has been formulated so as to reconcile the demands of the member states, while at the same time taking account of extremely competitive forces from outside the Union.

NATIONAL BANKING PRACTICE BEFORE 1992

A broad distinction sometimes drawn between different banking systems separates bank-based systems, such as those found in Germany, France, Italy and the Netherlands, from market-based systems, such as those of the United Kingdom and the United States. In the first group, banks traditionally exhibited a stronger orientation towards the corporate sectors, whereas in the latter the open capital markets have been more important sources of corporate funding. As a result, public sector and mutual institutions have had opportunities to develop a more significant role within the so-called 'bank-orientated systems'.

Five elements characterised continental European banking compared with the British system. First, all continental banking systems hosted various special credit institutions which were typically state-owned and provided subsidised long-term funds for various sectors, notably industry, agriculture and property. Second, the role played by savings banks, co-operative banks and credit co-operative associations (together with their central institutions) was considered more important than in market-based systems. Third, European banks had a tradition of participation in the ownership and management of industrial firms. The fourth difference relates to the importance in many European countries of the local and regional organisation of banks and other financial institutions, which reflected the prevalence of small enterprises in both industry and agriculture. Finally, there was a considerable degree of similarity between continental European banking laws which had been enacted in many countries following various financial crises in the early 1930s.

What the above indicates is that continental European banking systems have a broader array of institutions performing specific types of operation. In many cases this demarcation of lines-of-business rules was governed by national regulation. For example, certain banks were only permitted to do certain types of business: fiscal advantages were granted to a certain type of institution which would make it prohibitive for others to enter the sector. In addition, continental banks were mainly governed by regulatory frameworks which were based on a relatively precise definition of the activities that the various types of banking intermediaries identified by the legislation could undertake. This tended to be based on a strict regime of prior authorisation of the structural and business decisions of banks and credit institutions.

Put simply, banking markets were quite tightly regulated. Like competed with like in highly demarcated and segmented markets. Few markets were perceived to be national. Regional and local banks had monopoly power in certain countries through branching restrictions, fiscal advantages and rigid demarcation rules relating to lines of business. The growth in the popularity of market-based *laissez-faire* economics from the early 1980s began to change bankers' and regulatory attitudes towards regulation in European banking markets. From the early 1980s there was an increasing commitment by many European governments to the deregulation of their banking systems. Deregulation in this context reflected the opening up or liberalisation of financial markets and institutions to compete more freely. For example, lines of demarcation between different types of financial institutions, such as between banks and building societies in the UK, were broken down. At the same time, regulations were needed to ensure that the deregulated firms competed in a safe and sound environment, liberalisation was accompanied by supervisory rules to protect investors and to govern business conduct. Legislation charges in banking during the 1980s were characterised by the dual regulatory forces of structural deregulation and supervisory re-regulation.

The impetus for these developments came as much from changes in the political climate as from the increased globalisation and international competition across banking markets. The 1992 single market deadline was perhaps a milestone along a regulatory path that had started a decade earlier, although it did reflect a strong commitment by European governments to deregulate.

This commitment to deregulate was heightened by the political perception that large economic gains could be generated by the removal of various barriers.

BARRIERS TO INTEGRATION IN FINANCIAL MARKETS

The single financial market implies both freedom to trade and freedom of location for firms in EU member countries. This means that regulations in one member state should not discriminate between financial products and services provided by domestic companies and those offered by undertakings based in other member states. However, in reality there have always been economic and market barriers which have had a significant impact on the integration of EU financial markets. Price Waterhouse (1988) investigated the barriers to cross-border provision of financial services in the EC prior to the implementation of the single market programme. Their findings for banking, insurance and securities business are shown in Table 13.1.

Barriers to the cross-border provision of banking services

In reviewing the legal and regulatory barriers to a non-domestic bank establishing in an EC member state, there appeared to be little overt discrimination against non-domestic entities in the Community. However, the First Banking Co-ordination Directive provided a right of entry and establishment within the EC to credit institutions which had their head office in a member state. Non-national entities had to go through the same procedure as domestic entities in order to establish a banking operation. Moreover, obtaining authorisation for other than a representative office could be time-consuming and costly in administrative terms. The Price Waterhouse (1988) report found that all banking establishments had to conform to the prescribed legal forms of the country in which business was set up. These could vary from state to state. In addition, they noted that, with the temporary exception of Spain, the entry and establishment rules for foreign banks were essentially the same as for domestic institutions. There were few problems in establishing representative offices in European countries and prior authorisation was only required in some countries, although there were licensing or prior authorisation requirements for all EC banking firms wishing to establish branches within other member states.

With the exception of the UK, all branches had to maintain their own minimum endowment capital, the definition of which would vary from state to state. This was potentially a major obstacle to trade. Some countries required 'comfort' letters. Such letters were essentially guarantees of support from the appropriate supervisory authority or parent institution, and were not generally considered to be an onerous obligation – although in Italy, a branch's operational activities were shortened if such a letter was not provided. There were no specific restrictions on the employment of foreign or EC nationals or

Table 13.1 Barriers to integration in financial markets

Barriers to establishment in banking
1 Restrictions on the legal form banks may adopt
2 Limitations on the number of branches that may be established
3 Restrictions in the takeover of domestic banks
4 Restrictions of equity or other control of domestic banks

Barriers to operating conditions in banking
1 The need to maintain separate capital funds
2 Differences in the definition of 'own capital' funds
3 The need to maintain certain capital asset ratios

Barriers to competing for business in banking
1 Limitations on services offered
2 Restrictions on local retail banking
3 Restrictions on acquisition of securities and other assets

Barriers to establishment in insurance
1 Lack of harmonisation of licensing procedures
2 Lack of harmonisation in the constitution of technical reserves

Barriers to operating conditions and competing for business in insurance
1 Direct insurance: restrictions on the placement of contracts with non-established insurers
2 Co-insurance: establishment of a permanent presence imposed on lead insurers
3 Custom and practice in government procurement policies
4 Lack of harmonisation in the supervision of insurance concerns
5 Reinsurance: compulsory or voluntary cessation of a percentage of contracts to a central pool or prescribed establishment
6 Lack of harmonisation in the fiscal treatment of insurance contracts and premiums

Barriers to establishment in securities
1 Membership of some stock exchanges limited to national citizens
2 Constraints on the establishment of offices to solicit and carry out business in secondary markets
3 Restrictions on the takeover of or equity participation in domestic institutions
4 Limitations on the establishment of securities firms in a universal banking system

Barriers to operating conditions in securities
1 Exchange controls and other equivalent measures which prevent or limit the purchase of foreign securities
2 Conflicting national prudential requirements for investors' protection
3 Discretionary taxes on the purchase of foreign securities

Barriers to competing for business in securities
1 Limited access to primary markets in terms of lead management of domestic issues
2 Restricted access to secondary markets because of national stockbroker monopolies on some stock exchanges
3 Restrictions on dealing with the investing public

Source: Price Waterhouse 1988

special discriminatory rules in terms of professional qualifications or degrees of competence and management experience.

Once certain conditions were met in relation to minimum capital requirements and the competence of personnel, there were no other obstacles to establishing subsidiaries in countries other than Spain and Italy. However, in Italy, France and Spain, there were restrictions on foreign acquisitions or participations in indigenous banks, and in all EC states some prior authorisation was required form the appropriate supervisory authority. With the exception of Spain and Italy, there were few significant, openly discriminatory rules governing the extent or range of services that could be provided. It appeared to be the custom, however, that domestic banks lead-managed domestic bond issues in most of these countries.

Overall, it appeared that the barriers to trade in banking services lay not so much in overt, discriminatory rules and regulation, but rather in national practices that applied equally to both domestic and foreign-controlled banks. Differences in licensing, minimum capital requirements and other territorial restrictions simply made some member states less attractive than others for foreign banks.

Barriers to the cross-border provision of securities services

The Price Waterhouse (1988) study also identified the barriers to establishment and operation by foreign entities in securities markets within the EC. Since banks tend to dominate these markets, especially in the universal banking countries, the obstacles to establishment described also applied in this sector. The principal obstacle to establishing a presence in a foreign securities market appeared to be regulations banning foreigners from being licensed as brokers. The importance of exchange membership has been reassessed, however, in recent years, with widespread reform of continental capital markets – except in Italy. Difficulties had been encountered by non-banking firms which wished to establish themselves in a universal banking environment – as exists, for instance, in Germany or Belgium – where a full banking licence would not be granted to an institution that did not offer a full range of banking services. Some states were changing, however and had begun to offer licences for trading in securities only. There were restrictions on the establishment of offices either to solicit secondary market business from individual or institutional investors, or to disseminate information about possible investments. Moreover, barriers were placed in the way of dealing directly with the public executing such orders. Discriminatory restriction on the lead management of domestic issues existed in some states.

In addition to exchange controls, there were other measures which, while not directly prohibiting operations in foreign securities, were designed to prevent or limit their purchase. In Spain, for instance, banks, insurance companies and collective investment companies were limited in the amount of securities that might be held in their portfolios. A small number of member states imposed discriminatory taxes on the purchases of foreign securities. While these taxes did not in most cases discriminate against foreign entities, the increased cost of undertaking business could act as a disincentive for trading securities in a particular market. National prudential requirements were also deemed to be a problem in relation to collective investment. Hence in Germany, many foreign applicants reported difficulty in meeting local requirements. This was not regarded as discriminatory, but the lack of harmonisation of rules on collective investments could make some European markets less attractive than others.

Barriers to the cross-border provision of insurance services

In the area of insurance, like the banking sector, there appeared to be little evidence of open discrimination and established foreign and domestic insurers were treated similarly. Lack of harmonisation of national laws and regulations seemed to present the major barrier to free trade, since it tended to make some member states less financially attractive than others in terms of open competition. In particular, the lack of harmonisation in the financial treatment of insurance contracts and premiums appeared problematic. In addition, the European Court of Justice had expressed concern about the discrimination exercised by some member states against non-established direct and co-insurers.

OVERVIEW OF EC/EU LEGISLATION

The internal market programme for banking services

The above discussion presented a broad overview of the obstacles to the cross-border provision of financial services in the EC in the mid-1980s. This section will discuss the Community legislation that has eliminated or diminished some of these barriers with the aim of creating a single market in banking.

The First Banking Co-ordination Directive

The creation of an integrated European financial market was one of the main objectives of the Treaty of Rome. Article 67 of the EEC Treaty called for the abolition of the restriction on the movement of capital, as well as the abolition of discrimination on the grounds of the investor's place of residence. However, despite the fact that the financial services industry is of substantial importance to the EU economy, accounting for 3 per cent of the total employment and for 6.7 per cent of its total GDP (Cecchini 1988) in 1985, the establishment of a unified European financial market was delayed for almost thirty years.

Before the 1985 White Paper (CEC 1985), progress towards the integration of financial markets was very limited. The Freedom of Establishment Directive (73/183/EEC) permitted equal treatment of home country financial firms and subsidiaries of firms from other member states on the part of national authorities. Moreover, subsidiaries of firms set up in member states were to be considered EC undertakings in all respects. The First Banking Co-ordination Directive was adopted by the Council in 1977 (77/80/EEC). The Directive established the ground rules for dealing with bank authorisation and supervision. It detailed the minimum legal requirements banks had to meet in order to be authorised in other member states. They should have adequate capital – the amount was not specified in the Directive – and be managed by at least two people of good repute and experience. If the bank met these requirements, the basic right to set up branches in other European Union member states was established.

However, branches also needed to be established in accordance with host country regulations. Dixon (1991) argued that the First Banking Co-ordination Directive was an important first step, but that the basic right of establishment did not create a free internal market. Vesala (1993) observed that host country requirements for branch establishment after 1977 still created extra costs and time delays for banks from other EC states when they opened branches in other member states, and thus sustained legal barriers to the free provision of banking services. These costs were burdensome if an institution operated in a number of European Union countries. For example, in all countries except the UK, foreign branches had to satisfy domestic capital requirements and be supported by endowment capital rather than by the capital of the main institution. The home country's solvency requirements applied to foreign branches, and varied markedly between the member states. Moreover, the number of branches that a foreign bank could open was often limited. For instance, in Spain, a foreign bank could open a maximum of three branches (see Bisigano 1992, Canals 1993). Furthermore, Baltensperger and Dermine (1990) noted that cross-border trade in banking services was substantially limited by restrictions on capital flows.

While laying down ground rules, the First Bank Co-ordination Directive left much detail open to interpretation, and a more precise Directive was required to free up the cross-border provision of banking services. Before the launch of the 1992 initiative, there was one other EC Directive which concerned banking business. This was the 1983 Directive on Consolidated Supervision, which dealt with the supervision of consolidated accounts and the harmonisation of rules relating to annual accounts of banks. The Directive extended the supervision of individual banks to banking groups, covering their domestic and foreign affiliates and their accumulated overall credit risk (CEC 1989a: 27). However, this was restricted to principals, leaving the member states free to decide whether this extended system of banking supervision should also encompass minority holdings in banks and holdings in credit institutions of a special nature, such as mortgage banks.

The 1985 White Paper

By far the most important impetus towards the reduction of barriers to the cross-border provision of banking services was provided by the 1985 Commission White Paper on the Completion of the Internal Market, drawn up by Lord Cockfield at the request of the Council of Ministers. The White Paper contained a list of measures that had to be adopted before 1992 so that people, goods, capital and services could circulate freely in the European Union. It attempted to identify the measures to be taken to remove all physical, technical and tax barriers among the member states by the end of 1992, complete with a detailed timetable for adopting them. It also put forward over 300 legislative proposals required for their removal (CEC 1985). Moreover, the White Paper described what actions remained to be taken in the area of capital movements and financial services in order to bring about a single market. It called for new and stricter criteria for the application of the EC Treaty's safeguard clauses, as well as closer monitoring of exchange controls. The main proposals were classified under three main headings: the removal of physical barriers; the removal of technical barriers, and the removal of fiscal barriers (CEC 1985, 1987: 18).

In terms of financial services, such as the free movement of financial products, the Commission planned a new policy. The exchange of financial products such as insurance policies, home-ownership savings contracts and consumer credit was to be organised according to three important principles: the minimum co-ordination of individual national rules, mutual recognition and home country control. The Commission's approach was to produce legislation which guaranteed minimum standards in the areas of financial stability and prudential practice of financial institutions (Palmer 1989: 21–37). In addition, the White Paper stated that it would create a Community-wide market for investment, making finance available to business and industry from anywhere in the European Community. The objective was to provide greater competition on the basis of minimum guarantees of protection, with the prospect of making it possible for individuals or industry to seek finance and financial services freely from any country within the Community.

The 1985 White Paper provided the impetus for considerable legislative activity. Even though Pelkmans (1992) has recently suggested that the original White Paper was not a good guide, since many of the original proposals have been significantly altered and more ambitious follow-up proposals made, it still provided the main thrust towards new EC legislation which has brought about a single market. It also lay at the core of the project to give a new impetus to European integration.

The Second Banking Co-ordination Directive

The Second Banking Co-ordination Directive (89/646/EEC) was the cornerstone of the Commission programme for a single market in banking. It was issued on 13 January 1988, approved by the EC Council of Ministers on 18 December 1989 and came into effect on 1 January 1993 (Council 1989a). By far the most important aspect of the Second Banking Directive was the provision of a 'single passport' for banks and other financial firms to operate throughout the Union. This single passport allowed any banks which were authorised to act as such in a member state to set up branches or to supply cross-border services in other EU countries, without having to obtain further authorisation from the host country. (The services which banks could provide are listed in the appendix to the Second Banking Directive, which is reproduced in Table 13.2). It confirms that the EC has adopted the universal banking model. Llewelyn (1992) showed that the list was very broad, covering the realities of the financial markets, and bringing about the gradual breakdown of the traditional demarcation lines between commercial and investment banking. He also noted that, most significantly, the list included all forms of securities transactions. It was anticipated that this would have a significant impact on those member states, such as in Italy, Spain, Greece, and Portugal, where various types of commercial banking and securities business have traditionally been separate.

Second, the Directive aimed to remove barriers to banking throughout the European Community by deregulating the requirement for branches to maintain a minimum level of endowment capital. This requirement was a major obstacle to the free establishment of branches in various EC countries (Price Waterhouse 1988: 76).

Table 13.2 List of services that credit institutions are allowed to offer under the Second Banking Directive

---

1 Deposit-taking and other forms of borrowing
2 Lending
3 Financial leasing
4 Money transmission services
5 Issuing and administering means of payment (credit cards, travellers' cheques and bankers' drafts)
6 Guarantees and commitments
7 Trading for own account or for account of customers in:
   a. money market instruments
   b. foreign exchanges
   c. financial futures and options
   d. exchange and interests rate instruments
   e. securities
8 Participation in share issues and the provision of services related to such issues
9 Money broking
10 Portfolio management and advice
11 Safekeeping of securities
12 Credit reference services
13 Safe custody services

Source: Council 1989a: 13

Third, in order to harmonise the financial system and increase competition, the Directive set out conditions for the free provision of banking services by adopting the White Paper's guidelines on mutual and home country control. According to Article 19 of the Directive, a bank wishing to establish a branch and sell services within the Union only needs to obtain permission from the regulatory authorities of its home country if it wishes to establish in another member country. Branches no longer needed to hold endowment capital for business authorised within the European Union (Article 6 of Directive 89/646/EEC). Home country control implies that the banking authority of the EU member state that has granted the banking licence to a certain institution also supervises its activities in the EU, wherever the institution operates. It thus has responsibility for supervising the financial soundness of a bank, paying particular regard to its solvency, applying and monitoring harmonisation regulations, and ensuring that effective administrative, accounting and internal control mechanisms are in place.

Overall, the Second Banking Directive provides for:

1 The harmonisation of minimum capital standards for the authorisation and continuation of banking business.
2 Supervisory control of major shareholders' and banks' participation in the non-banking sector.
3 Proper accounting and control mechanisms.
4 Standards of own funds, solvency ratios and deposit protection legislation.

Finally, the Directive allows for reciprocal access to the single market for banks from non-EU countries. Subsidiaries of non-EU country banks set up in the EU are considered to be European Union undertakings, and therefore benefit from the Directive's provision for freedom of establishment and cross-border activities. other important supporting directives include the following:

- the Own-Funds Directive, 89/299/EEC;[1]
- the Solvency Ratio Directive, 89/647/EEC;[2]
- the Money Laundering Directive, 91/308/EEC;[3] and
- the Large Exposures Directive, 92/121/EEC.

The single European market programme for securities and insurance services

Securities legislation

A single European financial market without restrictions requires a single securities market where investors may issue and trade securities within the EU freely and without hindrance. Since 1979 the Commission has issued a series of important Directives in order to achieve the operation of a single securities market. The first step was the adoption on 5 March 1979 of a Directive (79/279/EEC) co-ordinating the conditions for the admission of securities to official stock exchange listings. The Directive established the conditions that must be met by issuers of securities, including the minimum issue price, the company's period of existence, free negotiability, sufficient distribution and the provision of appropriate information for investors. On 17 March 1980 the Council adopted another Directive (80/390/EEC), which co-ordinates the requirements for the drawing up, scrutiny and distribution of the listing particulars to be published for the admission of securities to official stock exchange listings (CEC 1989a).

The third step, in 1982, was the Council Resolution on the Directive (82/121/EEC) on information to be published on a regular basis by companies whose shares were admitted to official stock exchanges. According to this Directive, companies listed on a stock exchange must publish half-yearly reports on their activities, and profits and losses. By far the most important instrument, however, was the Directive on the free marketing of units issued by investment funds (undertakings for collective investment in transferable securities), adopted by the Council in November 1985 (see Vesala 1993: Section 1.2.4). This Directive introduced for the first time in the securities sector the 'new approach' (CEC 1989a: 40) called for in the 1985 White Paper. It incorporated the principles of mutual recognition and home country control with respect to the structure of investment funds and their investment policy. Furthermore, the Council issued a Directive of 22 June 1987 (87/345/EEC) amending Directive 80/390/EEC co-ordinating the requirements for the drawing up, scrutiny and distribution of the listing particulars to be published for the admission of securities to official stock exchanges. The objective of the Directive was to ensure that listing particulars compiled in accordance with earlier Directives and approved in one member state were automatically recognised on the stock exchanges of other EC members.

In this Directive, an investment firm was described as 'any natural or legal person' whose business was related to one or more listed activities. These listed activities included market-making, brokerage, underwriting, portfolio management and providing investment advice in connection with a range of financial instruments: transferable securities, money market instruments (including certificates of deposits and Eurocommercial paper), financial futures and options, and exchange and interest rate instruments.

The Council also took two steps towards ensuring greater transparency. The first was taken in December 1988, when it agreed a Directive on the information to be published when a major holding in a listed company is acquired or disposed of (Council 1988). The aim of this instrument was to ensure that investors and the public are informed of major shareholdings, changes in holdings above or below a particular threshold, and changes in voting rights for listed companies. The requirement comes into effect once a holding reaches 10 per cent, 20 per cent, one-third, 50 per cent and two-thirds respectively. The member states may apply a single threshold in place of the 20 per cent and one-third thresholds, and 75 per cent in place of the two-thirds threshold (CEC 1989a: 41). The second step took the form of the Directive adopted by the Council on 17 April 1989 (89/298/EEC), governing requirements for the drawing up, scrutiny and distribution of the prospectus to be published when transferable securities were marketed to the public. This Directive was an important supplement to the 1982 and 1987 Directives on transparency and investor protection in the securities markets, described above.

These instruments aimed to give investment companies the opportunity to provide cross-border services on the same basis that the Second Banking Directive allowed banks to operate in different EU countries. Barriers to the cross-border provision of investment services have not been fully removed by the above Directives, however, and the EU aims to introduce two significant pieces of legislation – the Investment Services Directive and its attendant Capital Adequacy Directive – before 1996. This will create a single investment licence for EU investment firms and will, it is hoped, do for the investment industry what the Second Banking Directive has achieved in the EU's banking sector.

A note on the liberalisation of insurance services

The European Community has also attempted to ensure the freedom to provide services in insurance. Increasing regulation of the sector during the 1960s and 1970s had made it more difficult for insurance companies to operate outside the countries in which they were headquartered. However, there has been a significant delay in harmonising EU insurance legislation because the member states have widely differing arrangements for insurance operations, supervision and consumer protection rules. In this sector, the liberalisation really began with a judgment of the European Court of Justice on 4 December 1986 (CEC 1989a: 33), which brought a new momentum to efforts to achieve a free European insurance market. In response to the Commission's legal action against four member states (Denmark, France, Germany and Ireland), the judges stated that the restrictions placed by these member states on the authorisation of insurance companies from other EC countries were in part illegal and in part unjustified (CEC 1989a: 35). This stimulated the way for further progress towards a deregulated insurance market.

The Council of Ministers adopted, in June 1988, the Second Council Directive (88/357/EEC) on the co-ordination of laws, regulations and administrative provisions relating to direct insurance other than life insurance (Council 1992a). This Directive introduced a single licensing system under which an insurance company with its head office in a member state could establish branches across Community borders without being subject to further authorisation procedures in those countries. Non-life insurance policy holders would have access to the whole range of products on offer in the Community. According to the Directive (Article 57), the member states had to adopt the laws, regulations and administrative provisions necessary for their compliance with this Directive before 1 January 1994 and bring them into force no later than 1 July 1994. The Directive also provided for the co-ordination of financial rules, covering the categories, diversification and localisation of assets used to cover technical provisions, required as a basis for the introduction of the single licensing system. Provisions also relate to the law applicable to insurance contracts (CEC 1992).

THE SINGLE MARKET IN FINANCIAL SERVICES, NATIONAL MARKETS AND THE MEMBER STATES

The single market programme has had the greatest impact in those countries where the banking systems were traditionally heavily regulated. Of the larger European banking markets, Italy has witnessed the most substantial changes as a result of the EU's programme. The implementation of the Second Banking Directive, for example, introduced the universal banking model to the Italian system. Banks can now offer a full range of financial services to their customers, whereas previously certain types of banks were only permitted to operate in specific areas. A more limited effect has been experienced in Germany, which has operated universal banking practice for much of the postwar period, and the UK, where the 'big bang' reforms of 1986 allowed banks to undertake a broader array of securities business and where the 1986 Building Societies Act deregulated the building society sector. Domestic structural reform resulting from EU legislation has probably been most apparent in Italy, Spain, Portugal and Greece.

Concomitant with these developments has been the introduction of financial incentives in various countries to encourage state-owned banks to convert into privately owned joint-stock corporations. Recent examples of banks converting include the Italian banks Credito Italiano in December 1993 and Banca Commerciale Italiana in March 1994. Some governments went further and aimed to provide tax incentives to encourage de-mutualisations, bank mergers and various types of financial restructurings in the banking sectors. The explanation for these developments was partly the parlous state of public finances, as well as the desire to create domestic banks big enough to compete in the European market-place. This, in fact, was the main reason why the Spanish authorities encouraged Spanish banks to merge in the late 1980s and early 1990s.

The bulk of this restructuring took place prior to the watershed date of the single market programme. The 1993 deadline has now passed, various directives have come into force and banks and financial institutions have begun to reassess their position under the new regime. However, a number of factors, including the availability of an 'opt-out' option to member states, remaining tax obstacles and the flexibility with which governments can incorporate EU law into national legislation, threaten to hinder the realisation of a genuinely single market.

The 'general good' opt-out

There is considerable freedom for national governments to act in derogation of the single market by making use of the 'general good' opt-out allowed to member states. Historically, the European Court of Justice has resolved conflicts between Community rules and national law intended to protect consumers on the basis of EEC Treaty provisions which make exceptions to the principle of free movement of goods for reasons of public morality, public policy, public security or protection of health. In cases regarding the freedom to provide services, the Court has used the related concept of the 'general good'. The European Court's rulings in such cases have been studied in detail by Katz (1992), who shows that host state 'general good' exceptions to the freedom to provide services have been justified when they are:

- not related to areas of law already harmonised by the EU;
- not duplicative of laws already applied by home states;
- applicable without discrimination to all individuals and undertakings in the host country;
- necessary to protect the interest at stake and proportional to the protection of that interest.

In the service cases considered above, Katz noted that:

> The Court has also demonstrated willingness to distinguish between classes of consumers with respect to the degree of protection required, e.g. individual buyers of insurance policies as opposed to corporate purchasers of co-insurance. And the Court has recognised certain industries (insurance) or certain selling situations . . . as 'particularly sensitive' in nature.
>
> (Katz 1992: 5)

Katz concludes that there is a 'strong likelihood' that many local regulations protecting consumers of banking services may qualify, through the 'general good' opt-out, for derogation from the Second Banking Directive. This may also be the case for the Investment Services Directive which came into force in January 1996.

Clearly:

> the Court will have to balance carefully the competing claims of consumer protection and financial market integration. An underlying consumer interest in the benefits of competition, such as broader choice among services and credit institutions, could hasten the day when the Community seeks to harmonise regulation regarding consumer protection in the area of banking services particularly if the Court gives member states the leeway to impose local law which the Second Directive suggests they should have.
>
> (Katz 1992: 7)

This means that EU member states can opt-out of EU legislation and assert national law by appealing to the 'general good'. For example, the 'general good' exemption can be applied if it is non-discriminatory; that is, in the case of banking matters, so long as it applies to domestic as well as foreign banks.

At first this may appear to be impartial, but a host state could ban products offered only by foreign banks, as long as all banks were subject to the same ruling and as long as the 'general good' argument convinced the European Court of Justice. The wide variety of consumer protection issues relating to banking and financial service products in general could lead to repeated EU Court approval of exemptions undermining the objective of harmonisation, especially at the retail financial services level. Other anecdotal evidence suggests that member states will, or at least could, exploit the 'general good' provisions to protect local investment firms from foreign competition; for example, now the Investment Services Directive (business rules relating to recognised exchanges) has come into force in January 1996.

Excessive use of the 'general good' provision for overtly projectionist purposes is, however, unlikely because the European Court of Justice has to balance interests of the 'general good' and the goals of the single market programme. Freedom to provide cross-border financial services is by far the most important underlying principle guiding decisions of the Court, whereas the 'general good' provisions are regarded as the exceptions. A much larger stumbling-block to the provision of cross-border financial services, however, lies in different tax treatments of financial products.

Tax obstacles

Member states can use their taxation systems to promote national goals. There are two main types of tax obstacles which have traditionally stood in the way of the cross-border provision of financial services and which are unaffected by the EU single market Directives. The first consists of tax provisions which directly affect 'foreign' EU financial firms providing cross-border services in other member states. An obvious example is the withholding tax. Withholding tax applied to interest paid to the domestic lender will be fully set off against the corporation tax paid by the domestic lender on its profit margin (any excess withholding tax refunded). In the case of the foreign lender, withholding tax is a final, non-refundable tax. The second category concerns tax measures which do not specifically apply to foreign EU financial firms but do make it more costly for domestic customers to do business with foreign EU firms. Dassesse (1993) cites a number of examples: the non-availability of tax relief or interest subsidy on mortgage capital on interest repayments, if the lender is based outside the national jurisdiction, makes it more expensive for foreign firms to lend for house purchase in the EU if loans originate abroad. In addition, provisions whereby interest paid by local corporate borrowers to foreign banks will not be treated as tax-deductible expenses if it exceeds a certain ceiling increase relative costs to the foreign firm when no such ceiling is applicable when the interest is paid to a local branch.

Dassesse (1993) notes that the non-deductibility for income tax – or corporation tax – purposes of life insurance or group insurance contribution if paid to a firm established outside the member state of the individual or company concerned also increases costs to the foreign firm. A similar example relates to circumstances where personal pension plans benefit from tax rebates on condition that the plans are invested, at least for a minimum proportion, in local bonds and shares. This would exclude, for example, shares in mutual funds licensed in other member states under the 1985 UCITS Directive.

The above examples, which are by no means exhaustive, illustrate the tax disadvantages that EU financial firms may come up against in undertaking business across borders. This situation is unlikely to change dramatically in the future, given that member states jealously guard their prerogatives with respect to taxation policy, and any attempts to achieve wider co-ordination of EU tax laws would be highly problematic. The European Court of Justice appears to be sensitive to this and has generally been unwilling to find, for example, that it contravenes EU law for a tax system to discriminate against financial products supplied by foreign firms. However, two recent rulings have clouded the picture regarding its stance on national autonomy in taxation matters.

The first was the European Court of Justice Ruling on Bachmann v. Belgian Tax Authorities, delivered in January 1992.[4] Mr Bachmann was a German national who moved to Belgium and was refused tax relief in respect of premiums he paid to his German life insurance company. Belgian tax provisions refuse deductibility for tax purposes of life insurance and groups insurance premiums paid to a foreign insurer operating in Belgium on a cross-border basis, while allowing the deductibility of such premiums if paid to a Belgian insurer. Bachmann argued that the Belgian tax provision constituted an indirect restraint on the cross-border provision of services in Belgium, a restriction on the free movement of workers in the EC and a restriction on the free movement of capital and current payments in the Community. The Court of Justice ruled that, while the tax provisions did restrict the cross-border provision of insurance services and the free movement of workers, in the absence to date of Community-wide tax harmonisation, 'these restrictions were none the less justified by the need to preserve the "cohesion" of the local tax system' (Dassesse 1993: 14). In addition, the Court held that the Belgian tax provisions did not restrict the free market of capital and current payments in the Community. The above decision clearly sets a precedent for other member states to justify national tax provisions on the grounds of 'cohesion' of the local tax system, and thus appears to provide member states with greater autonomy in national taxation matters.

The second important tax ruling was the European Court of Justice judgment in the Commerzbank v. UK Inland Revenue case, delivered in July 1993.[5] This case involved a claim by the UK branch of a German bank, Commerzbank, for around £5 million of 'repayment supplement' (a form of interest) in relation to overpaid corporation tax which it had recovered in 1990 following earlier High Court proceedings. The UK tax authorities prohibited Commerzbank from reclaiming repayment supplement in respect of the overpaid tax because it was not resident in the UK for UK tax purposes. In its judgment, the European Court of Justice held that provision of UK tax legislation limiting the right to repayment supplement to UK resident companies was in breach of the right of freedom of establishment as set out by Article 52 of the Treaty of Rome (as applied to companies under Article 58). This decision, unlike the Bachmann v. Belgian Tax Authorities ruling, represents an important step forward in ruling out discrimination against non-residents in tax matters within the EU, and would appear to limit the discretion of member states in tax matters. Instances of discrimination which are particularly relevant in relation to UK branches of foreign banks include the denial of foreign tax credits, the inability to offset losses against the UK source dividends in respect of which advance corporation tax has been paid and to claim a refund of the underlying tax credits, and the devaluation of the ability to transfer losses to or from UK resident group companies. Clearly, the decision has important implications for tax policy in the EU although moves towards standardisation on income and withholding tax treatment across the Community are still a long way off and unlikely in the near future.

Discrepancies in the implementation of EU law

The potential for differences in the national implementation of EU directives is considerable and this may allow state authorities a certain degree of latitude. Italy is often thought of as the country that has been the slowest and least responsive to the implementation of EU directives in the financial services sector, a factor which is perhaps not surprising given the under-developed and state-dominated nature of its market-place (*Euromoney* 1993).

EU Directives tend to be deliberately vague so as to preserve some national discretion. A good example of the role of national discretion within the EU legislative framework relates to the existence of SIMs (Societa di Internediazione Mobiliare) in Italy. All investment business undertaken in Italy has to be conducted through a locally incorporated subsidiary known as SIM. This is clearly a breach of the provision for freedom of establishment and free provision of services set out in the Treaty of Rome. The rules relating to SIMs were introduced when drafting of the EU Investment Services Directive began. The UK government registered a formal complaint in September 1991 but the legal conflict between the EU and the Italian government is still before the Court. The speed with which this issue is resolved may be a good indicator of the EU's commitment to ensure the full and precise incorporation of EU Directives (and all their provisions) into national legislation. Other major exceptions can be found where national regulations conflict with EU rules. For example, primary dealers in government bond markets are important for monetary policy purposes, yet it is widely accepted that these institutions should fall outside the ambition of EU-wide regulations on national interest on 'general good' grounds.

Furthermore, the practical difficulties associated with the implementation of EU law into national legislation should not be underestimated:

> According to one source involved in the transposition into UK law of the bank accounts directive, the text was so opaque that it was sometimes difficult to find an interpretation that made any sense. This source says: 'There was a good deal of tension between the departmental lawyers who were looking at the words and the civil servants who wanted to achieve a practicable solution. Luckily, as well as being badly drafted it had been badly translated, so we were able to exploit discrepancies between the different language texts.'
>
> (*Euromoney* 1993: 53)

Despite these difficulties, however, the EU legislative structure does appear to encourage agreement on general concepts, but permits member states to implement Directives in a way which is adaptable to local markets. In such a system, national differences are likely to persist.

EU ACTION AND INTERNATIONAL PRESSURES FOR CHANGE

EU financial sector legislation has been driven by two main forces: first, by internal forces aimed at creating a single market with minimum standards within the EU; and second, by external commercial and regulatory forces promoting the liberalisation of the trade in financial services. The main external commercial pressure relates to the free flow of international capital. Capital can locate virtually instantaneously across the globe, according to the relevant risk-return factor. Clearly, if wholesale capital can flow freely across borders, then this will force national governments and trading blocs to establish financial sector regulations that do not deter or harm such flows, especially in the long run. As the revolution in information technology advances, it seems possible that wholesale capital funds will increasingly move between international financial centres, constantly eroding differences in national financial sector regulation.

EU action is also influenced by the Bank for International Settlements (BIS) based in Basle. This organisation establishes world-wide standards for capital and other regulatory standards for international banks. These recommendations are not legally enforceable, but none the less are implemented by international banks, because failure to implement is a sign of a weak or badly run institution. In fact, the BIS recommendations for banks' capital requirements have been closely followed by the EU's Solvency Ratio and Own Funds Directives, which become legally enforceable once transposed into national legislation. In general, in technical matters relating to the supervision of banks, the EU tends to follow developments at the BIS. This is not surprising as EU central bank governors are all represented at the BIS and have an input in recommendation setting, along (primarily) with representatives from Japan and the United States.

Clearly, external forces and developments may have a stronger impact on the banking and financial services sector in the EU than in other industries. In this case, it is probably more like high-tech industries with international competitive and standard-setting forces being as important, if not more so, than internal EU policy developments. EU banking legislation therefore has to be formulated so as to reconcile national differences within the EU while also being shaped by extremely competitive forces from outside the Union. The brief discussion in this section is intended to indicate that the EU's policy in the financial sector is influenced by international forces which reduce the EU's power in setting the regulatory agenda.

CONCLUSION

The freedom to provide financial services across borders within the EU should have markedly improved from 1 January 1993, but there are still three serious impediments towards the creation of a single market. First, member states have considerable freedom to act in derogation of the single market in the light of the 'general good' opt-out. Second, tax obstacles in the member states largely frustrate the cross-border provision of financial services and recent rulings by the EU Court of Justice appear to provide contradictory signals as to what long-term approach the Community will take towards tax harmonisation. Finally, there is a considerable degree of flexibility when EU instruments are incorporated at the national level. All these factors point towards a reasonable degree of state autonomy in setting and guiding the legislative framework for financial service firms within the EU at the national level. In addition, developments within member countries' financial systems are continually being moulded by strong international competitive forces which suggest a further lack of EU control in setting the legislative agenda.

NOTES

1 Council 1989b.
2 Council 1989c.
3 Council 1991
4 Bachmann v. Belgian Tax Authorities, Case 209/90, 28.1.92.
5 R. v. IRC ex parte Commerzbank AG, Case 330/91, 13.7.93.

REFERENCES

Baltensperger, E. and Dermine, J. (1990) 'European Banking: Prudential and Regulatory Issues', in J. Dermine (ed.) *European Banking in the 1990s*, Oxford: Blackwell.
Bisigano, J. (1992) 'Banking in the European Community: Structure Competition' and 'Public Policy', in G. Kaufman (ed.) *Banking Structures in Major Countries*, London: Kluwer Academic.

Canals, J. (1993) *Competitive Strategies in European Banking*, Oxford: Clarendon Press.

Cecchini, P. (1988) *The European Challenge in 1992: The Benefits of a Single Market*, Aldershot: Gower.

Commission of the European Communities (CEC) (1985) *Completing the Internal Market*, COM (85) 310, Brussels: Commission of the European Communities.

—— (1987) 'Europe Without Frontiers: Completing the Internal Market', *European Documentation*, Luxemburg: OOPEC.

—— (1989a) 'The European Financial Common Market', *European Documentation*, 4/1989, Luxemburg: OOPEC.

—— (1989b) 'Proposal for a Council Directive on Monitoring and Controlling the Large Exposures of Credit Institutions', OJ C 175, 11 July, Brussels: Commission.

—— (1992) *Bulletin of the European Communities*, 6.

Council (1989a) 'Second Banking Coordination Directive', 89/646/EEC, OJ L 386, Luxemburg: OOPEC, 30.11.89, 13.

—— (1989b) 'Directive on the Own Funds of Credit Institutions', 89/299/EEC, OJ L 124,16, Luxemburg: OOPEC.

—— (1989c) 'Directive on a Solvency Ratio for Credit Institutions', 89/647/EEC, OJ L 124, 16, Luxemburg: OOPEC.

—— (1991) 'Directive on Prevention of the use of the Financial System for the Purpose of Money Laundering', OJ L 166, 28/6/91, Luxemburg: OOPEC.

—— (1992a) 'Directive on the Supervision of Credit Institutions on a Consolidated Basis', OJ L 280, Luxemburg: OOPEC.

—— (1992b) 'Second Council Directive on the Co-ordination of Laws, Regulations and Administrative Provisions Relating to Direct Insurance other than Life Insurance', 88/357/EEC, OJ L 228, 11.8.92, 1, Luxemburg: OOPEC.

—— (1993) 'Directive on Capital Adequacy of Investment Firms and Credit Institutions', 93/6/EEC, OJ L141, Luxemburg: OOPEC.

Dassesse, M. (1993) 'Tax Obstacles to the Free Provision of Financial Services: The New Fronter?', *Butterworths Journal of International Banking and Financial Law*, 12–16 January.

Dixon, R. (1991) *Banking in Europe – The Single Market*, London: Routledge.

Euromoney (1993) 'EU Finance Rules Face Obstacles', May: 50–5.

Financial Industry Monitor (1993) 'New Proposals on Listing Particulars', February: 82.

Gardener, E.P.M. (1992) 'Capital Adequacy after 1992: The Banking Challenge', *Institute of European Finance Research Paper*, 92/11, Bangor: IEF.

Katz, S.E. (1992) 'The Second Banking Directive and the General Good Clause: A Major Exception to the Freedom to Provide Services?', Centre for European Policy Studies Research Report, 9, September: 1–58.

Llewellyn, D.T. (1992) 'Banking and Financial Services', in D. Swann (ed.) *The Single European Market and Beyond*, London: Routledge.

Palmer J. (1989) *1992 and Beyond*, Luxemburg: OOPEC.

Pelkmans, J. (1992) 'The Pan European Flux: Understanding a Continental Transformation', SIAA Lecture, Series No. 10, Singapore.

Price Waterhouse (1988) *The Cost of Non-Europe in Financial Services Research on the Cost of Non-Europe Basic Findings*, V, 19, Brussels: Commission of the European Communities.

Vesala, J. (1993) *Retail Banking in European Financial Integration*, Helsinki: Bank of Finland.

14 States, industrial policies and the European Union

Anand Menon and Jack Hayward

The impact of the European Union on industrial policy and policy making in France, Germany, the UK and Italy has been the focus of this book. Using the conceptual tool of the autonomy of the state, it has aimed to ascertain precisely to what degree the major West European states find their policy preferences constrained by the European Union. This conclusion will attempt to draw out from the preceding chapters an overall account of this impact. After outlining the various actions of the Community in the industrial sphere and illustrating the way in which this has made an impact on national policy, the factors that account for the very differentiated and often rather limited impact that EU action has had will be identified. It will then be suggested that other pressures on national models of industrial management have sometimes been more responsible for the developments that have taken place than Community initiatives. In conclusion, these findings will be drawn together and their implications for the study of the impact of EU action examined.

THE EU AND NATIONAL INDUSTRIAL POLICY

Once it had become clear to even the most ardent French advocates of a national champions policy (first under Gaullist and then Socialist auspices) that the European market was being successfully invaded by Japanese and American competitors but that it was not possible to secure intergovernmental agreement upon an attempt to project such an industrial policy on to the European level, new solutions had to be sought. Consistent with the notion prevalent in much of the literature focusing on a 'relaunch' of European integration in 1985, the sectoral chapters have pointed to an increased activism on the part of the EC since the mid-1980s. In areas of both traditional EC intervention, such as steel (Mény and Wright 1986) and sectors where, owing either to a lack of formal competence (aerospace) or a sustained reluctance to employ those powers available to it under the treaties (air transport) it had been inert, the Commission reacted to the more propitious environment for supranational integration that accompanied the single market initiative by stepping up its actions in the industrial sphere. Ambitious new programmes in telecommunications and broadcasting were mirrored by an increase in the funding accorded to R&D under the Framework programme as well as by the formulation of intergovernmental schemes such as ESPRIT, RACE and EUREKA. Hancher points out that, in administrative terms, despite apparent efforts to decentralise regulatory, implementation and enforcement mechanisms, such recent trends as can be discerned seem to point to an ever greater centralisation of authority at the Community level.

The major thrust of Commission policy during the later 1980s was towards a liberalisation of the European market-place. Certainly, liberalisation is not the whole story: increasing numbers of initiatives in the environmental sphere, along with a markedly anti-liberal quota policy on broadcasting, illustrated some of the inconsistencies which were to help limit the impact of EC policy (see below). Yet in both its approach to industrial policy in general (CEC 1990) and in the Commission's dealings with individual sectors, the theme of liberalisation has recurred continually. Such liberalising aspirations were most evident in the sphere of competition policy, strikingly illustrated by the de Havilland decision (see Jones, Chapter 6, this volume). Nor were sectors traditionally characterised by the existence of state-controlled monopolies exempted from the liberalising impulse of the Commission. Community involvement in telecommunications policy, as well as in the water and energy sectors, was premised on a desire for market liberalisation, incorporating independent supervision rather than self-regulation (water), and the opening up of protected national markets to competition. Increasingly, commercialisation was an important motivation behind Commission proposals on broadcasting, while the opening up of the European financial services markets provided the rationale for the various banking directives.

Yet while presenting a fairly uniform picture of European Community initiatives, this book has presented a far more complex and differentiated view of the impact that the Community has had on the industrial policies of the member states. There have been occasions when Community policy has directly impeded states in their quest to translate their preferences into policy. The ability of the state to support chosen firms or industries by means of state aids was called into question, as illustrated by the embarrassment suffered by the British government over its attempts to entice British Aerospace to purchase the Rover Group (Graham and Prosser 1991: 126–8). State-supported initiatives aimed at achieving global competitiveness, such as the proposed take over of de Havilland, also found their paths blocked by supranational competition provisions. Such was the impact of the Commission's interventions to guarantee fair competition in the European market-place that the very rationale for public ownership of industrial enterprise has been cast into doubt (Dumez and Jeunemaitre 1994: 86–8).

Less spectacular but no less important was the *indirect* influence wielded by the Community. In the first place, this exhibited itself in the way Community initiatives not directly concerning the industrial sphere inhibited certain national industrial activities. The convergence criteria contained within the Maastricht Treaty, in particular, constrained (as had fixed parities within the

ERM in the context of financial deregulation) the ability of the member states to fund industrial projects by means of deficit budgeting or increasing indebtedness. Once again, this had the effect of calling into question the rationale for the maintenance of industrial sectors in public ownership (Dumez and Jeunemaitre 1994: 87–8; *Financial Times*, 1995a). Similarly, Community initiatives concerned primarily with the provision of socio-economic collective goods, such as environmental and social protection, rather than the liberalisation of the exchange of private goods and services (Moravcsik 1993: 488–94) also exercised an impact on industrial policy, whether through the introduction of environmental regulation (in the case of water), or the market-distorting effects of unequal social provision.[1]

In the second place, the impact of the Community was indirect in that national governments found themselves constrained by the behaviour of private actors which had altered as a result of Community initiatives. Particularly striking was the role played by business throughout the inception of the Single Market programme; influential business leaders, wooed by the 'marriage brokering' role of Commissioner Davignon, exerted pressure on their national leaders to move in the direction of market deregulation on a European scale (Sandholtz and Zysman 1989). Nor did their influence end there. One of the major explanations for the perceived success of the single market project lay in the way that business expectations were altered, leading to a wave of intra-European merger and acquisition activity. In the period between 1983 and 1989, the share of mergers between national firms fell sharply from 65.2 per cent to 47.4 per cent, while those between EC firms increased from 18.7 per cent to 40 per cent, the remainder being international mergers (Cox and Watson 1995: 324). This in turn created a momentum behind the single market initiative, which increased pressure for enhanced competition legislation at the European level.

EC action has increased the difficulties encountered by states in formulating policies acceptable to domestic lobbies. Sometimes, this has been through the formation of alliances between the Commission and domestic actors, such as that which came into being between the Commission and French private commercial broadcasters, leading the French government to back down from its desire to increase national quotas on French television programmes from 40–50 per cent (although it succeeded in excluding the audio-visual sector from the 1994 GATT Agreement despite intense pressure from the US government). In other instances, EC intervention has altered the nature of existing policy networks and their influence over policy making. EC involvement on the question of water privatisation undermined the routine nature of British water policy making and hence challenged the dominance of the traditional water policy community. In still other cases, domestic constraints have been intensified by Community policies. Thus the ability of the Belgian government successfully to promote the interests of Flemish television producers was undermined by the support of French-language Belgian producers for the quotas demanded by Paris. In still other cases, EC intervention has led to

the creation of wholly new domestic actors keen to impose their own preferences on the state. The experience of water privatisation in the UK represents
just such an example, Commission insistence on independent regulation leading to the creation of a dense, complicated network of regulatory authorities
entrusted with oversight functions over the water industry. Thus the EC
reshaped the domestic political landscape, not only altering the behaviour of
existing actors, but also promoting the development of wholly new ones.

The ability of the member states to define national policy options alone has
also been potentially undermined by the progressive reorientation of some
actors towards Brussels, as Community action becomes an increasingly
important element of legislation in their sectors. As illustrated in several of
the case studies – notably on aerospace and broadcasting – important private
actors are increasingly coming to relocate some of their lobbying activities to
Brussels, thus enhancing the ability of the Commission (heavily reliant on
input from specialist groups) to formulate legislation. A related trend has
been the transnationalisation of some interest representations; as these
increasingly push for European solutions to what they perceive as European-
level problems, the scope for governments to act individually is further
restricted.

At first glance, there seem to be other indicators of a significant Community impact. Have not European level R&D schemes proliferated? Has not
the insistence of the Commission on liberalisation coincided with a steady
shift in this direction on the part of the member states, depriving them of a
traditional policy instrument in the shape of national champion firms which
could be used to support employment, budgetary or regional policy objectives? Here we must emphasise the importance of detailed research to clarify a
confusing and often opaque reality. As Peterson points out, it is all too easy
to see Europeanisation where none in fact exists – the strictly intergovernmental nature of EUREKA makes of it an alternative rather than an illustration of such communitarianisation. Thatcher emphasises the fact that,
although we may perceive a convergence between EC aims and national
actions, detailed attention to the chronology of events points clearly to the fact
that the latter preceded the former. Furthermore, while the relationship
between firms and governments has been affected by EC provisions concerning
state aids as well as by the budgetary strictures governing currency co-
operation, a whole host of other factors, notably the changing nature of
international economic interaction (see below), have been at least equally
influential in determining the shifting nature of these relationships.

Indeed, many of the preceding chapters emphasise the limits of EC influence. Agreement was not reached on a steel restructuring plan; telecommunications policies shifted in spite of rather than because of the Community;
R&D activity remains predominantly national. Even where far-reaching
policy was formulated at the European level, it was not always effective. The
quotas on broadcasting programme content have proved unenforceable; a
single market does not exist in financial services. Despite the relocation of

some interest groups to Brussels, these interests continue to put most of their effort into purely national lobbying as a means of both influencing national decisions and as a conduit into EC discussions (Grant 1993).

Even where the Community has exerted an impact, it is clear that this has been highly variable. The UK, for the moment, finds itself particularly vulnerable to the effects of EC action on water policy. Meanwhile, the UK and Holland have pressed for firmer Community action in opening up European air transport markets. While Paris enjoyed some success in persuading the Commission to adopt quotas for European programme content, it has not proved able to foster Community support for a programme of selecting and supporting 'Euro-champions'. How, then, can one explain the limited and patchy impact of Community action?

EXPLAINING THE IMPACT OF THE EU

The European Union and industrial policy

Several factors help to explain this uneven and, for proponents of a greater Europeanisation of policy, often depressing picture. The initial cluster are related to the functioning of the Community system. In the first place, a crucial issue is that of the mode of decision making (itself a function of the Treaty base) employed within the Community for specific decisions. Clearly, in sectors such as aerospace which are deliberately omitted from the purview of the treaties, the member states retain considerable autonomy (Muller 1995: 159–61). Even in sectors covered by the treaties, with the notable exception of areas such as competition policy, where the Commission enjoys substantial autonomy, the Community decision-making system is characterised by the ubiquity of the member states. The pervasive influence of the member states during policy formulation is evident even within the Commission itself, both within the *cabinets* of the individual Commissioners, characterised by one observer as 'mini-Councils within the Commission', and within the services of the Commission, where nationals, especially of the southern states, maintain strong links with their national administrations (Peterson 1995a: 74–5).

Obviously, the influence of the member states is even more pronounced within the Council. They can often frustrate attempts to create European-level policy, as evidenced during the struggles over the Commission's attempts to formulate a Community energy policy (McGowan 1995: 145–53). In a similar vein, attempts to reach agreement on a meaningful and effective Community R&D policy have been hampered by the tensions between the need, on the one hand, to secure unanimous approval of the Framework programmes (necessitating concessions towards smaller member states) and, on the other, to convince the larger states of the efficacy of Community programmes. Although many firms and some governments increasingly see the need for European-level co-ordination and co-operation in R&D activities, the fact that Community policies are, of necessity, targeted as much with equity of distribution as effectiveness in mind makes the larger states reluctant to work through Community channels. Hence the preference many of the larger member states show for EUREKA. Importantly, member state influence within the Community system is not confined to initiation and formulation stages of policy making. The comitology system, especially when management or regulatory committees are used to decide on matters of implementation, also provides them with considerable leverage.

Constraints on the policy-making effectiveness of the Commission stem not only from widespread member state influence, but also from its lack of many of the resources available to central policy-making institutions in federal systems. As Scharpf (1994: 221–2) points out, the EU lacks three of the crucial attributes which confer a relatively high degree of policy-making authority on the Federal German state: relatively homogeneous political culture and public opinion; political parties operational at both levels of governance; and, finally, a high degree of economic and cultural homogeneity. In the absence of these resources, the capacity of the Commission for autonomous action is severely circumscribed.

Even where the Commission has the ability to formulate policy in a specific area, various constraints conspire to render this a less than straightforward task. Ambiguities surrounding the nature of (and indeed desire for) a Community-level industrial policy mean that it is often unclear what Treaty stipulations actually mean. Hancher points out the inconsistency that marks the Community's approach to industrial affairs. The existence of different notions as to the path the EC should follow over industrial policy are formalised within the contradictory stipulations concerning the market and industrial policy contained not only within the treaty on European Union, but also at the heart of other landmark documents dealing with industrial policy such as the Cecchini Report. Such ambiguity results partly from the fact that EU policy is the consequence of hard-fought compromises in intergovernmental negotiations which reflect varied national conceptions of the role of, and indeed need for, industrial policy (Hayward 1995a: 8). Whatever the sources of ambiguity, however, their ultimate effect is to render the task of the Commission in implementing policy more arduous and complex.

Equally important in terms of undermining overall coherence are the internal divisions which exist within the Commission itself. The Commission is in fact severely hampered by a lack of internal consistency. The various Directorates-General not only enjoy considerable autonomy, but they have also developed their own distinctive administrative cultures and traditions, which are reflected in the different ways they go about the task of formulating policy (Cram 1994, Donnelly 1993). Parallel in many ways to the manner in which national ministries find themselves in competition over the definition of national public policy, the Commission can be bitterly divided between its various Directorates-General. Intra-Community divisions were highlighted by the reaction of the German Industrial Affairs Commissioner to the de Havilland decision, castigating the 'competition ayatollahs' for their failure to think in terms of global rather than European markets (cited in Dinan 1994: 380). Political infighting produced the opposite outcome when the Commission authorised the Mannesmann steel tubes merger, 'despite clear evidence of a resulting duopoly which would damage competition' (Wilks and McGowan 1995: 59).

Divisions within the Commission engender further confusion and ambiguity when vague Treaty stipulations are operationalised. Nor, indeed, are such tensions normally reserved for the classic struggle between DG IV and DG III (internal market questions and industrial affairs). As policy sectors cross the division between industrial and other policies – be they regional, environmental, social or cultural – other interested bureaucratic organisations join in the struggle, witness the tensions between DG X (culture) and DG III over broadcasting policy. Although – as Jones points out – attempts are being made to mitigate some of the worst conflicts that arise by making provision for prior consultation between interested Directorates-General in competition cases, the patchiness and inconsistency of EC action are still evident, as evinced by the shift in Commission competition strategy after the de Havilland decision. The Commission operates more like a confederation of functional *divisions* engaged in piecemeal intervention than an integrated entity with more than a rhetorical common purpose.

Less often mentioned, though often no less important, are the *national* cleavages within the Commission. On matters of high political salience, Commissioners rarely, if ever, vote against the position of their nation state. An illustrative example, rich in irony, was that of the ailing textile company, Boussac, which was required to repay a large proportion of the aid it had received from the French government. In the collegiate vote, Delors (who as Finance Minister had given the aid in the first place) and Claude Cheysson both abstained (Buchan and Colchester 1990: 43, 150). In this sense, the Commission's internal divisions assimilate it to a *transnational* rather than *supranational* actor.

The ability of the Commission effectively to formulate a coherent industrial strategy is also constrained by exogenous pressures. Reliance on outside experts is not merely a feature of an organisation which is chronically understaffed and often, especially in sectors characterised by high levels of technical complexity such as research and development policy (Peterson 1995b: 21–22), heavily reliant upon outside experts. It is also a deliberate policy, aimed at securing consensus, and therefore legitimacy, for initiatives. Despite such reliance, some commentators have maintained that the Commission makes an ideal and highly credible regulator precisely because it is less likely to be captured by an individual firm or industry, and hence is more inclined to be tough and enforce sanctions than are national authorities (Majone 1994: 88–92, 94).

Several case studies contained in this volume, however, show otherwise. Consultation can easily lead to capture.[2] The European advertising industry exercised a tremendous influence over the 1984 'Television Without Frontiers' Green Paper – to the point of having advertising defined as a 'service'. Sectoral divisions, moreover, are once again supplemented by national rivalries. Masi indicates that the Italian steel sector found its position prejudiced by the dominance of French and German influence within DGIV, and the consequent adoption at Community level of plans based on profitability rather than efficiency criteria, involving the cutting of Italian productive capacity. Suspicion of capture by national or sectoral interests has been further compounded, as Hancher suggests, by the lack of transparency characterising the Commission's functioning as a regulator.

The increased vulnerability of the Commission to such tactics is inextricably connected with the growing activism of the Community in the 1980s. As in the case of the nation state itself, the Commission has discovered that

> increasing intervention makes [it] more clearly an arena of social conflict and makes its constituent parts more attractive for take-over. In other words, the contradictions of civil society become more embedded in [it] as [it] more deeply penetrates civil society, potentially undermining both its coherence as a corporate actor and its autonomy.
>
> (Rueschemeyer and Evans 1985: 69)

Once again, such pressures limit the capacity of the Commission to provide a firm and consistent policy lead on industrial questions.

A final factor affecting the ability of the Commission to provide such a lead, and perhaps the most difficult to tie down analytically, concerns its political will. The apparent inability of the Commission consistently to pursue coherent objectives does not result solely from disputes within the organisation concerning the nature of such objectives or the impact of exogenous pressures upon it. It also results from the fact that the Commission is not simply a functional, technocratic organisation, but also an implicit but enormously significant political institution. Sensitivity to the prevailing political climate means that the Commission has been very flexible in the application of, for instance, competition laws. Hence the spectacular de Havilland decision proved the exception rather than the rule (Ross 1995: 176–80), with Community competition authorities proving less willing to implement the provisions of Community competition law over, for instance, the most recent tranche of state aid provided for Air France.

If the conditions of the later 1980s were propitious for the flexing of the Commission's muscles, the shift in political mood concerning integration which characterised the early 1990s was markedly less so. Hence, despite the very limited scope of Community merger and acquisition regulations, which are restricted to firms with a world-wide turnover of 5 billion ECUs and a European Community turnover of 250 million ECUs, the Commission decided in the summer of 1993, when a review of these levels had been foreseen, to maintain them for the immediate future (Wilks and McGowan 1995: 56). Moreover, treaty innovations such as the principle of subsidiarity, however ambivalent its actual implications concerning the centralisation of power at the supranational level, have proved powerful impediments on the willingness of the Commission to display the assertiveness which characterised its interventions on questions of industrial policy only a few years ago.

National variations

The differentiation of the impact exerted by the Community has not stemmed solely from divisions within and constraints operating upon the Commission. Such differentiation has operated along two axes – national and sectoral.

At the national level, the same divisions between member states that have impeded the effective formulation of a coherent Community strategy for industrial policy help account for the fact that the impact exerted by the Community was not equal across all states. EC action takes place in a physical landscape of fifteen member states characterised by widely different histories, traditions, cultures, constitutional arrangements and administrative systems. As alluded to earlier, the forms of economic management utilised vary considerably between these states. In the face of the move towards increasing liberalisation, national policy preferences were affected by EC action to different degrees, because the prevailing industrial policy mix varied greatly between countries. States in favour of a more *dirigiste* approach to industrial affairs, such as France and Italy, have increasingly found their ambitions to foster the growth of either national or European 'champions' frustrated by the emphasis on competition adopted by Community institutions (Hayward 1995a: 7–8). More liberal states such as the UK, Germany and the Netherlands found policy options at the European level generally consistent with prevailing national policy preferences. However, even in the latter countries, discrimination in favour of national firms could be detected, such as the contrast between German rhetoric concerning the role of the market in energy provision and its protectionist practices.

A striking feature that has emerged from this study is the position of the UK in relation to EC action. Of all the EC member states, the UK is the one which has pursued policies that have anticipated Commission proposals for EC action. In the spheres of telecommunications, of broadcasting policy, of air transport, of energy and of banking, the Thatcher government acted ahead of Brussels in liberalising and privatising the major companies which set the trend that was followed, with varying degrees of enthusiasm, by most of the other member states, as well as by the Commission itself, creating a convergence between national and EC policies. Despite the prevalent form of political discourse concerning the impact of the Community on British life, the UK has in fact often adopted positions more extreme than that of the EC – witness London's hostility to the new-found permissiveness of the Commission concerning successive state aid provisions in the air transport sector.

Apart from prevailing policy options, it should also be noted that the ability of the Community to impact significantly on national policy is affected by domestic institutional arrangements. France's predisposition to promote state-centred *grands projets* has adapted with reluctance to policies guided by a market rather than by an administrative logic. By contrast, the weakness of the DTI relative to the Treasury within British administration explains in part why, even when a minister such as Michael Heseltine would have wished for a more active EC-orientated role, there has been little to show in practice, and firms have been left to rely upon a reticent financial sector. In Italy, administrative chaos rendered the EC a rational and tempting alternative formulator of a coherent R&D policy. The intricate German model, with high Länder participation, restricted the degree to which Europeanisation of policy was possible. Hence the fact that broadcasting policy remained almost exclusively the concern of the Länder meant that Germany was unable to accept EC competence over this sector.

The encroaching constraints upon state autonomy exercised by a succession of cumulative, piecemeal EC interventions, as well as the less manageable enveloping pressures of economic globalisation, have not encountered an inert response from national governments. Themselves under powerful political pressures exerted by the expectations of their electorates and domestic lobbies, they have sought to reassert their capacity to protect and promote their national interests. Each has responded to the challenge in ways and with objectives that are partly common, as similar threats necessitate convergent ripostes. They are also contrasted, dictated by their historically differentiated values, institutional structures and behavioural propensities, resulting in varying industrial policy ambitions and capacity to achieve them. Let us consider briefly the way in which the four major European states, France, Germany, Italy and the UK, have sought to assert their own national policy in an inhospitable international environment.[3]

With its long-standing Colbertist commitment to a state-administered policy of industrial patriotism, which short-lived episodes of liberalisation have so far never succeeded in eliminating, we would expect France to provide the most stubborn resistance in defence of an ambitious industrial policy. It had the most effective public organisation for this purpose but proved ill-adapted to the new economic context with which it was confronted. When global production and marketing strategies were necessary to compete profitably, it has proved necessary to modify France's *dirigiste* emphasis upon public subsidies and public ownership which slowed down the decline of lame duck industries and made the transition less harsh, protected high-tech French firms from foreign predators and promoted national champions to win competitive battles in international markets. The high levels of unemployment it has tolerated reflect in part a belated acceptance that many of its firms were overmanned, so that all it can do nationally is resort to a series of improvisatory palliatives. Its privatisation programme has been devised to ensure maximum protection from foreign takeovers through the establishment of interlocking directorates of carefully selected stable consortia of shareholding firms. Although *grands projets* are no longer launched, partially successful efforts have been made to Europeanise past successes in aerospace or high-speed trains, to ensure that the old ambitions can be sustained in the new context, although biotechnology has proved a failure. French governments have alternated between preserving their own state-centred style of intervention, reluctantly accepting doses of Anglo-American liberalism and experimenting (disastrously in the case of Crédit Lyonnais) with German-style links between banks and firms.

Germany, Europe's industrial success story of the post-war period, has had to acknowledge that the politically regulated part of its social market economy must adapt to the new EC and international contexts. Whereas the economically successful manufacturing firms, notably in the chemical, engineering, electronic and automobile industries, could be left to modernise and diversify to meet the demands of foreign competition by a process of semi-corporatist self-regulation, the non-competitive sectors – declining coal and steel and infrastructural enterprises in the energy, transport, postal and telecommunications sectors – have had to face a cautious and consensual process of deregulation, privatisation and Europeanisation (Esser 1995). Unification has led to a massive extension of the social market economy's commitment to support weak sectors and regions by subsidies with the aim of re-industrialising East Germany. Under the guise of liberalising it, what has occurred is its incorporation into West German social partnership practices thanks to an enormous input of public money, with a consequent increase in the public debt. However, these practices are in the course of adaptation to the new economic environment, so that it would not be prudent to assert more than that they will remain distinctive by comparison with the Anglo-American model.

Italy had too weak a state to adopt the traditional French mode and simultaneously too concentrated and too diffuse and fragmented an industrial sector (which apart from IRI was separated from the state-owned banks) to accommodate neo-corporatism of the German type. It relied on a small number of public sector enterprises – especially IRI and ENI – and family firms – notably Fiat, Pirelli and Olivetti – with the Bank of Italy helping to make up for the relative weakness of the Finance Ministry. Italy's attempts to adapt to the globalised market economy have proved ineffective. A succession of failed takeovers of French, Belgian and German firms has meant that the restructuring of Italian industry 'has been essentially devoted to reinforcing Italian medium-sized enterprises on the domestic market, not strengthening national enterprises on the international markets' (Bianchi 1995: 105, cf. 106–7). Massive recourse to state subsidies, notably in the direction of the *Mezzogiorno* and to support ailing industries such as steel, led to an unbearable level of public debt as well as conflict with the EC Commission. Belated recourse to privatisation and the reduction of subsidies and public debt nevertheless do not suggest that Italian industrial policy by default, which relies primarily on small and medium firms operating in the black economy to provide its dynamism, will become closely aligned with either the EC or other national industrial policies. So Italy represents more an introvert than an autonomous state in the sense that it cannot so much pursue an independent policy as allow external events to take their course while seeking to avoid suffering the domestic consequences.

The UK, by tradition a free-trading country which found a policy of *laissez-faire* more congenial than did those in France who had championed the policy without succeeding in having it adopted as public policy, has embraced globalisation with the greatest enthusiasm and pursued privatisation with a resolution amounting to dogmatism. Ironically, this required a particularly assertive industrial policy identified with the governments of Mrs Thatcher. Under the guise of a rhetorical nationalism, the UK has become the haven for inward foreign investment – first mainly American, then increasingly Japanese – as a manufacturing base from which to gain access to the internal EC market, of which it has been an unstinting protagonist. British Conservative governments have championed an ultra-liberalism, in which all barriers to internationalisation should be removed, so that major British firms lose their national identity and British governments abstain from providing subsidies that infringe the canons of open competition. This amounts to a wholehearted renunciation of both protective and promotional functions in the service of the nation's interests, which was such a striking feature of the French conception of industrial policy and from which they have partially retreated with reluctance. This contrast is reflected in the behaviour within the EC of the two states, the French consistently pressing for 'Community preference', the British routinely advocating minimal restrictions upon competition (Hayward and Leruez 1990: 64–95).

While any explanation of the nature of EC impact on the member states needs to be sensitive to national differences and to varied national responses to the pressures impinging on industrial policy, it also needs to be alive to the fact that these are not constant across time. During the 1980s and early 1990s, the German model of high technology research and development was generally acknowledged to be the most successful. Yet specific national shocks and pressures have profoundly affected the impact EC initiatives are likely to have. Hence one possible repercussion of German unification, given the new constraints on German public spending that have resulted from the need to devote immense resources to modernising the infrastructure and ensuring the viability of such East German firms that could be rescued by the Treuhand, is to increase interest in Community-level high technology research and development programmes to compensate for decreasing levels of national support for such programmes. As large companies have increasingly started to turn their attention towards Brussels, its impact on national R&D policy is liable to increase.

Another variable that ought to be considered is that of the awareness of national actors of the implications of Community-level activities. Several of the case studies presented in this volume have illustrated that member states were, on occasion, ill-prepared to deal with the effects created by

Community-level actions. The British government did not, initially, anticipate legal problems at the European level in connection with its plans for water privatisation. A palpable sense of both outrage and surprise characterised French reactions to the de Havilland decision. Such national unpreparedness, while doubtless enhancing the ability of the Community to exercise a sizeable impact on national policies, will doubtless decrease as the member states become more accustomed to and prepared for the kind of Community-level initiatives and legal stipulations that characterise European-level industrial policy.

Sectoral differentiation

It should be evident that sectoral differences are as marked as national differentiation, industrial imperatives at least as important as public policies. The impact of the EC is explicable partly in terms of the nature of the industrial sectors with which it dealt as well as those it professed to ignore. Several elements have been shown to determine the nature of sectoral specificity and the way in which it works. In the first place, perceptions of the success or otherwise of national policy condition the attitude of member states to the influence of the Community. This works in two ways: perceptions that national policy is working well (German R&D) conspire to produce negative attitudes towards greater EC competence, and vice versa (Italian R&D) where EC action is interventionist. Where, however, EC action is working in favour of liberalisation and opening markets, the opposite occurs: EC intrusion is opposed by governments in sectors where national industry is felt to be weak (German arms manufacturing, French airlines) and encouraged as consistent with national preferences if national industries are competitive (British telecommunications and airlines).

A second element of sectoral differentiation concerns the nature of decision making characterising different spheres. This is a question first of the forms of domestic policy making characteristic of various sectors. Owing particularly to its connection with military procurement and public ownership, aerospace has traditionally been an area characterised by the existence of tightly-knit policy communities at the national level which conspire to limit supranational influence. Thus the very successful Airbus consortium has operated outside the EC framework, while being consistent with the need to move from national to Euro-champion firms in pursuit of market rather than military priorities (Muller 1995: 166–8). The domestic pressure facing French governments (often in conjunction with an ideological attachment to a 'national champions' philosophy) in air transport have traditionally made it hostile to EC initiatives aimed at liberalising the sector. In newer sectors such as environmental policy, where such entrenched interests may not exist, the Community has been able to foster the development of pressure groups which, in concert with the Commission, can help to reduce national autonomy, with a decisive role being played by the European Court of Justice.

Decision-making structures, of course, are seldom purely national. Several of the policy sectors investigated in this book are marked by the existence of alternative international regimes, often comprising a far wider membership than the EC, and characterised by intergovernmental forms of policy making. In the cases of both aerospace and broadcasting, the GATT regime has impinged on the ability of the EC to assume responsibility for policy. This has, of course, also increasingly been the case in the agricultural sector. An additional actor in the case of broadcasting was the Council of Europe, which reacted aggressively against Commission attempts to exercise a degree of control over policy formulation. As far as banking is concerned, the Bank of International Settlements remains a pivotal actor. Clearly, sectors characterised by the existence of powerful international regimes are less liable to be profoundly affected by EC action, although the Commission has increasingly emerged as a negotiator on behalf of member states, which exposes conflicts between national governments as a common position is sought.

Further, the technological characteristics of sectors profoundly affect their amenability to communitarianisation. Industries that were natural monopolies, such as telecommunications and electricity supply, have increasingly come to be challenged by technological developments rendering cross-border provision feasible. EC attempts to overcome resistance to imports of electricity from Belgium and France, who had a surplus power capacity (partly resolved by intergovernmental agreement, notably between France and Germany, or by the EC in the case of Spanish charges for transmitting French sales to Portugal) through the development of an Internal Energy Market have been compromised, but the Commission is continuing to promote increased competition and Europeanisation (McGowan 1995: 144–53).

In other cases, new issue areas, such as concerns about environmental quality, not only render some sectors like water prone to new forms of pressure, but also alter their political salience (a process which the Commission can and often does, as in the case of British water policy, deliberately foster). Environmental policy has also represented a conduit for Commission involvement in policy areas previously closed to it: increasing Community activism in the sphere of energy policy has been substantially linked to the increasing prominence of environmental issues on the political agenda. Such sectoral interaction brings the divisions of the Commission into potential and often actual collision, reinforcing the need for greater authority to ensure overall co-ordination and cohesion.

This brings us to the issue of the 'strategic' nature of sectors. As was noted earlier, the lack of provision for EC competence over aerospace has constrained its impact on policy. This stemmed from a perception that aerospace constituted a sector of vital national interest, over which member states were determined to retain national control. As Peterson points out, however, strategic sectors are not defined in perpetuity. As conditions change, so the sectors considered as strategic also shift. For example, the end of the cold war made the production of military aircraft and missiles less of a strategic activity than finding markets for civil aircraft and space rockets. The reasons for which steel is viewed as crucial by certain member states in the 1990s (often connected with socio-economic goals, such as preserving employment in declining regions) have little in common with those that made steel such a central industrial sector when the ECSC came into being in the 1950s (Mény and Wright 1986).

ALTERNATIVE PRESSURES ON NATIONAL POLICY

Shifting national and sectoral conditions, which play an important role in determining the extent of Community influence, are themselves often shaped by pressures and constraints independent of the Community system. Indeed, a consistent theme running through many of the chapters in this volume has been that it is often these alternative pressures, rather than Community action, which are responsible for developments in national policy. In several cases, reductions in the autonomy of the state result from a combination of these different pressures.

The first group of pressures on state autonomy that can be identified are those emanating from *within* the state. Financial pressures represent one such influence on policy. Thus within the context of a need to control inflation to sustain or retrieve international competitiveness, a general factor favouring privatisation was the reluctance to increase public borrowing, and a desire to use the receipts from the sale of public assets to reduce public debt. In other cases, policy change was not imposed upon a recalcitrant state, but rather embraced when the ministers in charge of public policy were replaced after a general election. Hence we can explain the Balladur government's shift in favour of at least a limited privatisation of France Télécom in 1994. State autonomy has been more restricted when powerful societal pressures have been brought to bear on governments. British water privatisation came about as the result of pressure exerted by powerful domestic interests within the water industry for freedom from the financial constraints imposed by the state.

Such domestic pressures have even proved capable of resisting policy developments desired by both national governments and the EC. The ITC, as Fraser illustrates, played an important role in hampering the entrance of private operators into ITV. The policy communities largely responsible for formulating national aerospace policy have jealously protected their privileged position against external interference. Thus the role of EC action must be assessed in tandem with that of domestic forces acting on the state. In cases such as the single market initiative, where the EC was allied with powerful domestic forces, its ability to exercise an impact on national industrial policy is clearly substantial.

The other variety of pressures on the autonomy of the state are those, numerous and often crucial, that emanate from outside its borders. As mentioned in the Introduction, a powerful international constraint is exerted by the shifting nature of global economic interaction. Expansions in foreign trade, and the ever-increasing economic linkages that tie states together have, according to most scholars, seriously undermined the ability of the state, acting without favourable international conditions or support from powerful foreign actors, to turn its preferences into policy. The most often cited example is probably Mitterrand's notorious U-turn on macro-economic policy in 1983, although this volume has illustrated other examples of international economic demands imposing policy shifts on nation states. As in the case of the indirect impact of the Community, such pressures often worked via the medium of business actors realising the need for different industrial strategies. Joint ventures and mergers with foreign firms would encourage or necessitate ceasing to act as agents of a particular state, with the result that governments have lost the capacity to use firms as instruments of their policy. Faced with the need to maintain international competitiveness, firms were often required to raise large sums on international capital markets, and hence pressured governments to adopt policies of privatisation. Both Deutsche Telekom and France Télécom increasingly came to realise the need to obtain greater commercial freedom in order to compete more effectively. Their inclination to work together, particularly to meet the challenge from British Telecom, both reflected the urge to adapt to the new EC rules while seeking to retain their traditional hold on their home markets. In a world where business activity is increasingly globalised, governments enjoy less ability to impose unwelcome policies on firms, which can become important actors in their own right.

International competition implies a need to respond rapidly to developments around the globe. Policy experiments in one country can often lead to emulation in others. Hence it has been argued that, while acknowledging that a revolution has occurred in European financial services, it should also be borne in mind that this 'remains a side-show', as the engines of financial change have been to a large extent non-European. An important element in the shifting British regulatory framework for financial services was based on 'copying' the American model (Moran 1994: 160, 169). In turn, the UK relayed this American influence within the EC, imparting to a defeatist adaptation the appearance of economic necessity. Furthermore, whatever its precise cause, the phenomenal expansion of private capital and its tremendously enhanced mobility exercised another market constraint on the autonomy of the state.

International economic pressures imply not only vulnerability to the changing nature of the global economic system but also, given the increasing linkages between developed states, enhanced national vulnerability to pressure from foreign actors. The American threat to exclude Philips from the American HDTV project if the Dutch voted for the 'Television Without Frontiers' Directive is one example. The American refusal to allow French and German telecommunications giants to purchase stakes in Sprint, the long-distance operator, unless their markets were liberalised and more open for competition, was another. Such pressures also, given their global nature, pose problems for proponents of a well-developed interventionist European industrial strategy. The 'shrinking economic, social and political distances that have transnationalised global affairs' (Rosenau 1989: 34) open the way for truly internationalised business collaboration, collaboration which, for many firms in many sectors, has taken a global rather than European form (see Jones, Chapter 6, this volume, on the increasingly internationalised nature of aerospace ventures). Given the increasingly blurred national roots of firms, and the ease of capital transfers and relocation, globalisation thus places a further constraint on state ability to turn preferences into policy, if these policies run counter to what international money markets demand.

Related to the rise in international interdependence is the role played by rapidly accelerating technological developments, to whose consequences states find it difficult to respond expeditiously and at their own volition. Shifting technology has had a profound impact at both sectoral and national levels. First, it has changed the nature of policy sectors, reducing the salience of some (steel and textiles), and increasing that of others (electronics and food processing). It has also rendered industries that were previously, almost by definition, national monopolies (electricity and telecommunications) both exposed to and capable of successfully competing in a more open economy. Governments have to accept that they operate in a world of penetrable markets, although they seek to favour, where they can, those industries whose products have export potential. Second, it has enhanced international interdependence through the development of, for instance, the capacity to transfer vast amounts of capital almost instantaneously around the globe. This has periodically placed governments at the mercy of forces that are beyond their control, even when they have co-operated to counteract speculative market movements.

Changing technology profoundly alters the nature of the constraints acting on the state, not only directly but also through the impact it has on domestic interests. The availability of new broadcasting technologies in the 1980s led to the prominence of new, commercially orientated actors, who lobbied in favour of increasing commercialisation, in contrast to the cosy corporatist arrangements characterising terrestrial television. Pressure for privatisation from Deutsche Telekom was the result of a realisation that new technologies allowed foreign firms, especially BT, to encroach on its national market, requiring the dynamic conservative response of changing sufficiently to circumscribe the impact of change.

While the impact of international interdependence and technological change has been both extensive and profound, it should not be forgotten that they are by no means the only form of international pressure affecting states in this policy area. More traditional military–diplomatic international factors also have a bearing on the nature of industrial policies. In particular, the end of the cold war has exercised a pervasive influence on both national and sectoral elements of industrial policy. Clearly, the unification of Germany had profound effects for the political economy of that country, not least the budgetary problems attendant on the issue of the deliberate deindustrialisation of uncompetitive firms located in the five new Länder. The investment opportunities in low-cost Central Europe, moreover, increased the incentive for EU firms to engage in industrial delocalisation. More generally, the disappearance of the massive, clearly defined Eastern threat had implications for the definition of strategic sectors. In a world where the utility of military force has been called into question, and interstate competition increasingly takes more economic forms, the importance of economically vital sectors such as R&D has been increased, while sectors previously defined as strategic because of their military value now have a lower priority. As Jones points out, this explains recent German hesitations about the European fighter aircraft. However, the need to seek a competitively optimum size through international consortia will not decrease in the coming years.

STATE AUTONOMY AND INDUSTRIAL POLICY

What emerges from the preceding analysis is a complex interrelationship between the various pressures at work on the contemporary west European state. In terms of the specific focus of this volume – the impact of Community action on national autonomy – it would appear that Community influence has been relatively minor. Certainly, the ability of the Community to impose policy solutions on member states has been limited and will continue to be so at least until the end of the millennium.

Some scholars have pointed to the importance of the role of the EC in reshaping the relationships that exist between states and firms, emphasising in this regard Community initiatives on competition, in promoting transnational business co-operation and in altering traditional domestic policy networks (Wright 1995: 342–3). Yet while enjoying a high profile, competition rulings such as those over de Havilland, Rover or Perrier have proved the exception rather than the rule. Air France has continued to receive substantial subsidies from the French state; anti-competitive practices continue to dominate aerospace procurement decisions; the achievement of a free market in energy provision has proved elusive; and the Commission has proved reluctant to use its powers to deal with anti-competitive practices, notably in the case of Eurosport. Similarly, while the Commission has, on occasion, enjoyed success in marrying the needs of national businesses in a transnational alliance (the Big '12 Roundtable' provides the clearest example), such inter-firm co-operation was more often brought about as a result of international pressures such as globalisation; the limits to a Europeanisation of national industrial enterprises are revealed by the extent of global collaboration which now occurs. Finally, there are also limits to the extent to which Community action has brought about a fundamental restructuring of domestic policy networks. Tightly-knit policy communities continue to characterise the aerospace sector. Even those firms which have chosen to expend some of their lobbying efforts in Brussels continue to attempt to exert influence over their national governments and often see the national route as the most effective one by which to influence EC policy. The combined efforts of the Commission and the Thatcher government to promote a greater commercialisation of broadcasting has failed fundamentally to undermine the cosy position of the BBC. Where restructuring has occurred, it has often come about as the result of domestic as much as European pressures.

In seeking to account for the nature of the impact of the EC, we have illustrated the need for attention to be paid to two sets of factors, first, the specific characteristics of the national systems and the sectors in question. Different states are affected in different ways by Community initiatives, with some finding long-established modes of government–industry relations challenged by supranational initiatives, while others anticipate Community action. Similarly, while Hoffmann's (1966) analysis of the strong state capable of adaptation in the face of supranational pressure might be appropriate for analysing some states – notably France – it seems rather less apposite in the case of Italy. In sectoral terms, we pointed to a number of factors – industrial performance, modes of decision making, technological characteristics and environmental and strategic concerns – which condition the amenability of a sector to Community influence.

Second, the variety of pressures acting on the state need to be considered. These can be divided into three categories. First, consideration must be accorded to the nature and workings of the Community system itself. In contrast to the overly simplistic formulations of traditional integration theories, which see supranational institutions as exerting a clear and consistent pressure on the member states, the ambivalent role of Community institutions helps explain the somewhat patchy nature of the impact exerted by the Community. Internal divisions, the impact of external actors, along with restraint exercised as a result of political sensitivity, all conspire to render the Commission incapable of providing the clear and consistent leadership that the neo-functionalists expected from it. A far more nuanced and sophisticated view of the nature of and pressures impinging on this complex actor which combines technocratic and highly politicised roles is necessary. Similarly, the European Court of Justice may sometimes act as a brake on, rather than a stimulus to, the integration process, as it has in approving derogations from the supposed single financial market on the basis of the 'general good' opt-out.

The second set of pressures on the state that we have identified are internal. Changes in government, ideological preferences, financial constraints, policy performance, administrative structures, as well as pressure from societal interests all play a part in accounting for the nature of national policy. Ideological, societal and financial pressures all conspired to render privatisation an attractive option. Any theoretical framework which purports to explain the interaction between EC initiatives and national policy must of necessity be sensitive to such factors. It must also be responsive to the fact that they do not remain constant and that, indeed, one of the crucial aspects of the impact of the EC is the way in which it alters the nature of domestic polities, leading to the creation of new actors in some instances and redirecting the lobbying efforts of existing actors in others. In this sense, the 'two-level' game (Putnam 1988) played by member states at home and within the forum of the EC is also a two-way process, with Community-level initiatives impinging on the nature of the domestic game – its players and its rules – as much as these latter can impact on Community-level decision making.

Finally, international pressures have also been vitally important in affecting the nature of policy and policy making in the four larger member states. Indeed, many of the case studies have pointed to the fact that policy developments are inexplicable without reference to international pressures on national policy makers (cf. also Hurrell and Menon 1996). Some observers have even pointed to a correlation between increasing external constraints on the state and an expansion of the scope of state activities domestically (Rosenau 1989: 34–5). Nor can the shifting priority accorded to various policy sectors be comprehended without reference to the changing exigencies of the international system.

An understanding of these myriad pressures on the state is essential because it is often only through comprehending their interaction that explanations of the impact of the EU can be arrived at. An intimate knowledge of domestic and international circumstances allows us, in the first place, to distinguish instances of Community action affecting domestic policy from those where a mere conjuncture of events disguises the real sources of national policy change. Further, the Commission has often proved most effective when working in tandem with other forces. Technological and market changes can sometimes function as 'icebreakers' (Müller 1994: 37), enabling the Commission to intervene in areas of previously purely national competence such as broadcasting (though conversely these very factors rather than the resultant Community initiatives may account for national-level policy adaptation). The Commission may, in some instances, deliberately and explicitly seek to harness other forms of pressure on the state for its own ends. Thus Commissioner Karel Van Miert, in a bid to reinforce his attempts to bring about a liberalisation of European telecommunications markets, explicitly referred to the possibility of American regulators blocking the proposed alliance between France Télécom, Deutsche Telekom and the American operator Sprint if the German telecommunications market were not liberalised (*Financial Times* 1995b). Similarly, the Commission has been quick to ally itself with domestic interest groups, governments firms or public opinion should their interests converge.

The interrelationship between domestic and international pressures on national policy points to the fact that the European Community can at times play a role in enhancing the autonomy of the state (Milward 1992). Faced with an increasingly competitive international market-place and a growing inability of national firms to compete effectively, French governments used the EC as a means of furthering national goals by fostering the development of 'Euro-champions'. This also explains the stubborn resistance in France to action that did not simply extend French priorities in to the European arena. Hence intergovernmental co-operation has tended to take priority over EC action, as in the case of France's Europeanised space programme, Arianespace. In the face of a need to enhance international competitiveness, governments can also use the EC as a means of overcoming domestic opposition to policy adaptation. Constraints can often act as resources, hence the use of EC strictures as a scapegoat enables governments to achieve desired policy objectives without incurring domestic costs. This can be seen in the case of the Italian steel industry and the way in which recent French governments have reacted to EC liberalisation proposals for air transport. Similarly, certain member states – notably France – have sought to use the bargaining influence of the EC in international negotiations to overcome global trends towards liberalisation, or pressure from competitors such as the USA.

The complex interrelationship between the pressures at work on the state gives the lie (as do Richardson and George, chapters 2 and 3 this volume) to unilateral approaches which stress the predominance of purely domestic factors over international ones, or vice versa. The 'intellectual apartheid' (Bulmer 1995: 355) that has characterised approaches principally inspired by international relations and political science is a recipe for distorted explanations of a highly intricate subject. While some scholars have attempted, in recent years, to integrate international and domestic factors into a single theoretical framework (cf. Moravcsik 1993), none has yet attempted to combine these with the requisite sensitivity to Community-level pressures, nor with the need to appreciate differences between states and between sectors. Moreover, interdisciplinary awareness must be reconciled with empirical knowledge. The sheer complexity of the relationship between the EC and its member states cautions us against attempts to engage in empirically unfounded generalisation, despite the tendency on the part of some to do this.[4] We have pointed to several factors which can aid in providing an explanation of the nature of this impact. These vary in importance over time and between the various member states we have considered. In order to further our conceptual understanding of the impact exerted by the Community on its member states, there is a need for theoretical approaches to be rooted in extensive empirical research.

Only through the combination of detailed empirical and conceptual analysis can the nature and effects of the complex phenomena of integration in Europe be understood. It is a grasp of the iterative process, involving the interaction over time of sub-national, national, EC and international actors, operating within one or more of these policy arenas, that is the prerequisite to an understanding of the outcomes of the intentions of industrial policy makers. In such a context, the state cannot be said either to have or not have autonomy in some absolute sense. It has it in a relative sense, varying with the country and sector, and in a dynamic way that exposes judgements based upon the experience even of the recent past, to rapid refutation. It is in such a turbulent and unpredictable environment that both governments and those who seek to explain their policy predicaments and choices have to strive to locate a firm footing from which to operate. The conceptual tool of state autonomy has therefore to be used circumspectly and deftly if it is to serve the purpose of ascertaining the extent and intensity of the constraints exercised by the enveloping European Union.

NOTES

1 The relationship between the provision of socio-economic goods provision and industrial policy is a two-way one. As Masi points out (this volume), industrial policy, especially when concerned with cutting excess capacity in a declining sector such as steel, also exercises a tremendous influence on socio-economic conditions.
2 For an account of perhaps the most well-known example of consultation and subsequent interest group capture, see Avery (1977).
3 For a broader comparison that is not confined to these four countries, see Hayward (1995b: 351–61, 368–70).
4 Witness, for instance, this frank admission from two respected academics: 'We write as students of world politics based in North America, whose primary research interests have not been in the subject of European integration. As a result, our grasp of the detailed institutional history of the European Community is not as firm as that of other authors in the chapters here. If our contribution has value, it lies in our sweeping, "bird's-eye" view of the contemporary political system of Europe, and in our attempt to explore how theories and concepts of political integration, developed much earlier but then largely discarded, could help us understand the contemporary dynamics of European integration' (Keohane and Hoffmann 1990:276).

REFERENCES

Avery, jun. F. (1977) *Agropolitics in the European Community: Interest Groups and the Common Agricultural Policy*, New York: Praeger.
Bianchi, P. (1995) 'Italy: The Crisis of an Introvert State', in J. Hayward (ed.) *Industrial Enterprise and European Integration: From National to International Champions in Western Europe*, Oxford: Oxford University Press.
Buchan, D. and Colchester, N. (1990) *Europe Relaunched: Truths and Illusions on the way to 1992*, London: Random Century.
Bulmer , S.J. (1995) 'The Governance of the European Union: A New Institutionalist Approach', *Journal of Public Policy*, 13(4): 351–80.
Commission of the European Communities (CEC) (1990) *Industrial Policy in an Open and Competitive Environment: Guidelines for a Community Approach*, COM (90) 556 (final), Luxemburg: Office for Official Publications of the European Communities.
Cox, A. and Watson, G. (1995) 'The European Community and the Restructuring of Europe's National Champions', in J. Hayward (ed.) *Industrial Enterprise and European Integration: From National to International Champions in Western Europe*, Oxford: Oxford University Press.
Cram, L. (1994) 'The European Commission as a Multi-organisation: Social Policy and IT Policy in the EU', *Journal of European Public Policy*, 1(2): 195–217.
Dinan, D. (1994) *Ever Closer Union? An Introduction to the European Community*, London: Macmillan.

Donnelly, M. (1993) 'The Structure of the European Commission and the Policy Formation Process', in S. Mazey and J.J. Richardson (eds) *Lobbying in the European Community*, Oxford: Oxford University Press.

Dumez, H. and Jeunemaitre, A. (1994) 'Privatisation in France 1983–1993', in V. Wright (ed.) *Privatisation in Western Europe: Pressures, Problems and Paradoxes*, London: Pinter.

Esser, J. (1995) Germany: 'Challenges to the Old Policy Style', in J. Hayward (ed.) *Industrial Enterprise and European Integration: From National to International Champions in Western Europe*, Oxford: Oxford University Press.

Financial Times (1995a) 'Assets Sale – Starting Soon', 28 March.

Financial Times (1995b) 'Telecoms Link Under Attack from Van Miert', 14 June.

Graham, C. and Prosser, T. (1991) *Privatising Public Enterprises: Constitutions, the State, and Regulation in Comparative Perspective*, Oxford, Oxford University Press.

Grant, W. (1993) 'Pressure Groups and the European Community: An Overview', in S. Mazey and J. Richardson (eds) *Lobbying in the European Community*, Oxford, Oxford University Press.

Hayward, J. (1995a) 'Introduction: Europe's Endangered Industrial Champions', in J. Hayward (ed.) *Industrial Enterprise and European Integration: From National to International Champions in Western Europe*, Oxford: Oxford University Press.

Hayward, J. (1995b) 'International Industrial Champions', in J. Hayward and E.C. Page (eds) *Governing the New Europe*, Oxford: Polity Press.

Hayward, J. and Leruez, J. (1990) 'Nationalism and the Economy', in F. de la Serre, J. Leruez, and H. Wallace (eds) *French and British Foreign Policies in Transition: The Challenge of Adjustment*, Oxford, Berg.

Hix, S. (1994) 'Approaches to the Study of the EC: The Challenge to Comparative Politics', *West European Politics*, 17(1): 1–30.

Hoffmann, S. (1966) 'Obstinate or Obsolete? The Fate of the Nation State and the Case of Western Europe', *Daedalus*, 95: 862–915.

Hurrell, A. and Menon, A. (1996) 'Politics Like Any Other? Comparative Politics, International Relations and the Study of the EC', *West European Politics*, April.

Keohane, R.O. and Hoffmann, S. (1990) 'Conclusions: Community Politics and Institutional Change', in W. Wallace (ed.) *The Dynamics of European Integration*, London: Pinter.

McGowan, F. (1995) 'The European Electricity Industry and EC Regulatory Reform', in J. Hayward (ed.) *Industrial Enterprise and European Integration: From National to International Champions in Western Europe*, Oxford: Oxford UniversityPress.

Majone, G. (1994) 'The Rise of the Regulatory State in Europe', *West European Politics* 17(3): 77–101.

Mény, Y. and Wright, V. (eds) (1986) *The Politics of Steel: Western Europe and the Steel Industry in the Crisis Years (1974–1984)*, Berlin, de Gruyter.

Milward, A. (1992) *The European Rescue of the Nation State*, London: Routledge.

Moran, M. (1994) 'The State and the Financial Services Revolution: A Comparative Analysis', *West European Politics* 17(3): 158–77.

Moravcsik, A. (1993) 'Preferences and Power in the European Community: A Liberal Intergovernmentalist Approach', *Journal of Common Market Studies*, 31(4): 473–523.

Muller, P. (1995) 'Aerospace Companies and the State in Europe', in J. Hayward (ed.) *Industrial Enterprise and European Integration: From National to International Champions in Western Europe*, Oxford: Oxford University Press.

Müller, W. (1994) 'Political Traditions and the Role of the State', *West European Politics*, 17(3): 32–51.

Peterson, J. (1995a) 'Decision-making in the European Union: Towards a Framework for Analysis', *Journal of European Public Policy*, 2(1): 69–93.

Peterson, J. (1995b) 'EU Research Policy: The Politics of Expertise', in C. Rhodes and

S. Mazey (eds) *The State of the European Union*, (Volume 3), Boulder: Lynne Rienner.

Putnam, R.D. (1988) 'Diplomacy and Domestic Politics', *International Organisation*, 42: 427–61.

Rosenau, J.N. (1989) 'The State in an Era of Cascading Politics: Wavering Concept, Widening Competence, Withering Colossus, or Weathering Change?', in J.A. Caporaso *The Elusive State: International and Comparative Perspectives*, London: Sage.

Ross, G. (1995) *Jacques Delors and European Integration*, Oxford: Policy Press.

Rueschemeyer, D. and Evans, P.B.(1985) 'The State and Economic Transformation: Towards an Analysis of the Conditions Underlying Effective Intervention', in P. B. Evans, D. Rueschemeyer and T. Skocpol (eds) *Bringing the State Back In*, Cambridge: Cambridge University Press.

Sandholtz, W. and Zysman, J. (1989) '1992: Recasting the European Bargain', *World Politics*, 42: 95–128.

Scharpf, F.W. (1994) 'Community and Autonomy: Multi–level Policy–making in the European Union', *Journal of European Public Policy*, 1(2): 219–42.

Wilks, S. and McGowan, L. (1995) 'Discretion in European Merger Control: The German Regime in Context', *Journal of European Public Policy*, 2(1): 41–67.

Wright, V. (1995) 'Conclusions: The State and Major Enterprises in Western Europe: Enduring Complexities', in J. Hayward (ed.) *Industrial Enterprise and European Integration: From National to International Champions in Western Europe*, Oxford: Oxford University Press.

Index